Multidisciplinary Perspectives on Agentic AI in Educational Systems

Munir Ahmad
https://orcid.org/0000-0003-4836-6151
Survey of Pakistan, Pakistan

IGI Global
Scientific Publishing
Publishing Tomorrow's Research Today

Vice President of Editorial	Melissa Wagner
Director of Acquisitions	Mikaela Felty
Director of Book Development	Jocelynn Hessler
Production Manager	Mike Brehm
Cover Design	Jose Rosado

Published in the United States of America by
IGI Global Scientific Publishing
701 East Chocolate Avenue
Hershey, PA, 17033, USA
Tel: 717-533-8845 | Fax: 717-533-7115
Website: https://www.igi-global.com E-mail: cust@igi-global.com

Library of Congress Cataloging-in-Publication Data

LCCN: 2025035297 (CIP Data Pending)
ISBN13: 979-8-3373-4621-2
Isbn13Softcover: 979-8-3373-4622-9
EISBN13: 979-8-3373-4623-6

British Cataloguing in Publication Data
A Cataloguing in Publication record for this book is available from the British Library.

Table of Contents

Detailed Table of Contents

This chapter explores the conceptual and technological foundations of agentic AI—a transformative paradigm redefining autonomy in learning environments. Moving beyond automation, agentic AI emphasizes co-agency between humans and intelligent systems, enabling learners to set goals, reflect, and collaborate dynamically. The chapter grounds its discussion in constructivist and socio-cognitive theories, examines the architectures that enable perception, reasoning, and decision autonomy, and illustrates applications across educational settings. It further analyzes ethical and pedagogical implications, highlighting transparency, fairness, and teacher redefinition. Concluding with emerging trends—multimodal agency, lifelong learning agents, and affective co-learning—it envisions symbiotic, self-evolving educational ecosystems.

This chapter examines the critical role of structured, ethical, and inclusive governance frameworks in deploying AI in education. It emphasizes that effective integration requires transparency, accountability, and active stakeholder participation across institutional, national, and global levels. The study highlights the necessity of multi-sector collaboration among governments, educators, technology developers, and communities to co-create policies and monitor AI applications. Proactive governance,

Agentic AI is reshaping inclusive education by enabling adaptive, personalized, and equitable learning experiences. These intelligent systems act as co-teachers, dynamically responding to individual learner needs, providing real-time feedback, and supporting differentiated instruction. Innovations such as adaptive curricula, AI-mediated collaborative platforms, and context-aware assistive technologies enhance accessibility for learners with diverse abilities. Effective implementation requires policies addressing equity and privacy, curriculum integration, and teacher training to leverage AI ethically. When thoughtfully applied, agentic AI fosters engagement, bridges learning gaps, and promotes an inclusive educational landscape.

This study examines AI tutor and mentor development and deployment to facilitate pre-service teachers' (PSTs) professional development and learning. It employs a mixed-methods triangulated approach, which combines quantitative survey responses, placement information, and qualitative insight from PSTs and their mentoring teachers. Pre-placement AI literacy training and subsequent teaching placements provided the background for data collection, with post-placement surveys and semi-structured interviews provoking reflective narratives. Remora optimization was applied to feature selection, and two-stacked ResNet was applied to predict PST performance and provide personalized advice. The results indicate that AI tutors not only support self-regulated learning but also maximize mentor feedback and render generative AI tools useful to enact.

This study aims to explore Moroccan EFL students' perceptions of using Grammarly as an AWCF tool, drawing on Davis's (1989) TAM, which focuses on perceived usefulness, perceived ease of use, attitude toward use, and behavioral intention. Using a mixed-methods research design, the study targeted 34 EFL students (18 female and 16 male, aged 20–43) from Semester 1 at the English Department of Hassan I University in Morocco. The respondents were selected using convenience sampling. Based on data collected from a Likert-scale questionnaire and some open-ended questions, findings indicate that students have positive attitudes toward Grammarly's AWCF. The AI tool is deemed useful and easy to use. Additionally, it can enhance students' writing skills, boost their confidence, and increase their motivation, making their writing experience agreeable. Despite the participants' willingness to continue using Grammarly in the future for their writing tasks, they highlighted several limitations of the tool in terms of feedback accuracy, style, tone, contextual appropriateness and overreliance.

This chapter examines the integration of agentic AI in schools, highlighting its transformative potential for personalized learning, teacher support, and administrative efficiency. It explores the conceptual foundations, systemic infrastructure, and collaborative ecosystem design necessary for effective AI deployment. Key considerations include data management, interoperability, ethical standards, and governance frameworks. The chapter emphasizes scalable, sustainable, and adaptive AI ecosystems that foster collaboration among students, teachers, administrators, and

AI agents, reshaping educational practices and preparing schools for the challenges of the 21st century.

As agentic artificial intelligence (AI) systems become increasingly embedded in educational technologies—ranging from adaptive learning platforms to predictive assessment tools—they introduce not only new pedagogical possibilities but also profound regulatory challenges. This chapter critically examines the urgent need for robust governance frameworks tailored to the distinctive features of agentic AI: autonomy, context sensitivity, and real-time decision-making. Moving beyond general data protection laws and ethical codes, it proposes a multi-layered regulatory model that addresses legal accountability, data governance, bias mitigation, and systemic equity. Informed conceptual analysis, international case sharing, and comparative policy lessons help the chapter identify the ways that, poorly regulated, agentic AI can worsen educational inequality, inhibit the agency of learners, and damage institutional trust. It proposes practical guidelines on risk-based supervision, audit of algorithms, involving of stakeholders and harmonization on a global basis.

This chapter reviews the changing role of teachers in K-12 and college lecture rooms as ChatGPT, intelligent tutoring systems and adaptive learning systems become trendier. It also points out the advantages of Artificial Intelligence (AI), i.e., the relief of teachers, individualization of the lesson and valuable data about business. The topics of interest are the willingness to teach, qualified tuition programs, and the effects that it may have on relationships between students and their teachers and AI-based teaching methods. These insights are collected with the help of research techniques that range between surveys, focus groups, literature reviews, and case studies. This review points to the significance of listening to the voices of teachers, acknowledging their concerns, and giving them the resources, training, and guidance on successful integration of AI. It also calls to the ethical design and deployment of AI, with the emphasis on fairness, openness and accountability.

"Tutoring and Mentoring in the Age of AI: An Academic Perspective" is a part that talks about how AI is changing standard educational support systems by changing the roles of tutoring and mentoring". As AI-powered intelligent teaching systems (ITS) and virtual teachers become more popular, they offer personalized, flexible learning experiences that are tuned to each student's needs. Looking at AI's capability to actively help students, provide real-time feedback, and keep track of their academic progress, this chapter shows how these technologies support and improve the work of human teachers in promoting student success. It also talks about the problems with integrating AI tools, social issues, and how the relationship between AI tools and teachers is changing to facilitate effective academic mentoring. This chapter uses current events and real-life examples to give a fair academic view on using AI as a teaching aid, focusing on how it can help students learn on their own, stay motivated, and have equal access to good coaching and mentoring systems.

In today's fast-changing educational and career environment, many students face confusion and lack proper, personalized guidance when making important professional choices. Traditional career counseling methods, although beneficial, often fall short due to limited accessibility, inherent bias, and scalability challenges. As industries evolve, a growing need has emerged for intelligent, adaptive systems capable of providing accurate, individualized career paths. An AI-powered career guidance system addresses these issues by combining artificial intelligence, machine learning, and data analytics to deliver personalized recommendations aligned with a student's academic background, skills, interests, and aspirations. The guiding concept behind such systems is to bridge the gap between students and quality career advice through smart, technology-driven solutions that adapt over time

Preface

INTRODUCTION

The rapid emergence of Agentic Artificial Intelligence—AI systems capable of autonomous decision-making, adaptive behavior, and context-sensitive action—signals a profound shift in how we conceptualize teaching, learning, and the broader educational enterprise. As these systems move from theoretical possibility to practical implementation, educators, policymakers, technologists, and researchers face an urgent need for shared frameworks, common language, and critical interdisciplinary dialogue. *Multidisciplinary Perspectives on Agentic AI in Educational Systems* was conceived with this need in mind.

This edited volume brings together leading voices from computer science, education, cognitive psychology, ethics, and policy to illuminate the transformative potential of Agentic AI across learning environments. The chapters unpack the theoretical foundations of agentive systems, survey key technological innovations, and examine pedagogical implications for instruction, assessment, and learner support. At the same time, they confront the ethical and societal challenges that accompany these technologies—bias and inequity, privacy and data governance, questions of agency and accountability, and the risks of over-reliance on automated decision-making. Together, these contributions offer a comprehensive, critically informed framework for understanding how Agentic AI may both enhance and unsettle existing educational ecosystems.

A central aim of this book is to advance interdisciplinary collaboration across fields that too often operate in isolation. AI researchers and engineers bring technical insight but may lack grounding in the realities of classroom practice. Educators and learning scientists contribute deep pedagogical experience yet may be distanced from the rapidly evolving AI landscape. Policymakers and ethicists play essential roles in governance but require meaningful engagement with both technological and educational domains. By placing these perspectives in conversation, this volume highlights unresolved tensions, identifies gaps in current scholarship—particularly around ethical design, scalability, and real-world deployment—and points toward research agendas that are both rigorous and socially responsive.

This publication is intended for a broad and diverse readership. Researchers and academics in education, learning sciences, and human-computer interaction will find analyses that push theoretical boundaries and challenge prevailing assumptions. Educators and instructional designers across K–12, higher education, and corporate training will gain practical insights into how agentive technologies can support, extend, or complicate pedagogical practice. AI developers and data scientists working in EdTech or adaptive learning systems will encounter perspectives that enrich the design of impactful and responsible tools. Ultimately, the volume seeks to serve as a foundational reference for anyone navigating the complexities of Agentic AI integration in educational institutions.

As editor, I am grateful to the contributors whose expertise, creativity, and critical engagement have shaped this collection. Their work reflects both optimism and caution—an acknowledgment that Agentic AI holds extraordinary promise, but that its benefits will be realized only through careful, collaborative stewardship. My hope is that this book not only informs but also inspires: prompting new research, deepening cross-sector partnerships, and guiding the thoughtful development of educational systems that are equitable, human-centered, and resilient in the age of intelligent agents.

ORGANIZATION OF THE BOOK

Chapter 1: Foundations of Agentic AI — Redefining Autonomy in Learning Environments

The opening chapter establishes the conceptual and technological groundwork for understanding Agentic AI and its emerging role in education. The authors trace the evolution from traditional automation to systems capable of co-agency—where learners and intelligent agents jointly shape goals, reflective processes, and collaborative knowledge building. Anchored in constructivist and socio-cognitive theories, the chapter offers a clear exposition of the architectures that support perception, reasoning, and autonomous decision-making. It situates these technologies within diverse educational settings and carefully weighs their pedagogical and ethical implications, including transparency, fairness, and shifting expectations of teachers. By identifying trends such as multimodal agency, lifelong learning agents, and affective co-learning, the chapter frames Agentic AI as a catalyst for increasingly symbiotic and self-evolving learning ecosystems.

Chapter 2: Policy, Equity, and Governance — Shaping the Future of Agentic AI in Education

Chapter 2 foregrounds the indispensable role of governance in shaping ethically grounded and equitable AI integration. The authors argue that effective implementation requires coherent, transparent, and accountable policies across institutional, national, and international contexts. Emphasizing inclusive, multi-sector collaboration, the chapter underscores the need for shared responsibility among governments, educators, technologists, and communities in designing and monitoring AI-enabled systems. Through its focus on foresight, risk assessment, and adaptive policymaking, this chapter provides a roadmap for ensuring that Agentic AI tools support learning outcomes responsibly and sustainably while protecting equity and public trust.

Chapter 3: Interdisciplinary Insights — Cognitive Science, Sociology, and AI in Learning Systems

Taking a multi-lens approach, Chapter 3 examines the cognitive, social, and institutional dynamics reshaped by the integration of Agentic AI. It emphasizes that AI should augment learners' cognitive autonomy, supporting metacognition rather than supplanting it. Sociologically, the chapter argues that equitable AI systems must honor learners' diverse contexts and experiences. Institutionally, it highlights the continued importance of educators' judgment and ethical stewardship. The authors call for co-evolutionary frameworks in which AI and human actors adapt together, supported by participatory design principles, strong ethical guidelines, and agile institutional structures capable of fostering resilient and inclusive learning environments.

Chapter 4: Pedagogical Transformations — Agentic AI as a Co-Teacher and Learning Partner

Chapter 4 explores how pedagogical practice is changing as Agentic AI systems increasingly operate as co-teachers and collaborative learning partners. These systems deliver dynamic adaptation, timely feedback, and innovative instructional strategies that promote personalization, collaboration, and engagement. The chapter traces how teacher roles and curriculum design evolve alongside these tools and stresses the foundational importance of ethical frameworks, sustained professional development, and equitable technology access. Ultimately, it positions Agentic AI as a pathway to more learner-centered, responsive, and sustainable educational models that amplify both human and technological strengths.

Chapter 5: Agentic AI for Inclusive Education — Opportunities for Accessibility and Differentiation

Focusing on inclusivity, Chapter 5 demonstrates how Agentic AI can broaden access to learning by providing adaptive, equitable, and deeply personalized experiences. Intelligent systems act as co-teachers that respond to individual needs, offer real-time adjustments, and support differentiated instruction at scale. The chapter showcases innovations such as context-aware assistive tools, adaptive curricula, and AI-facilitated collaborative environments that enhance accessibility for learners with diverse abilities. It also highlights the importance of robust equity-focused policies, teacher preparation, and privacy protections. When thoughtfully implemented, these tools can bridge learning gaps and contribute to a more inclusive educational ecosystem.

Chapter 6: AI Tutors for Enhancing Generative AI Literacy in Education

This chapter presents a rigorous mixed-methods study examining how AI tutors can strengthen generative AI literacy among pre-service teachers (PSTs). Combining survey data, placement records, and reflective qualitative insights, the authors illustrate how pre-placement AI literacy training and field experiences shape PST learning trajectories. Advanced modeling—including Remora optimization and two-stacked ResNet architectures—demonstrates the potential of AI tutors to predict performance, personalize guidance, and reinforce mentor feedback. The chapter shows that such systems not only enhance self-regulated learning but also increase PSTs' capacity to responsibly and effectively integrate generative AI tools into their teaching practice.

Chapter 7: Exploring Moroccan EFL Students' Attitudes Toward AWCF — A TAM-Based Case Study

Chapter 7 offers an empirical investigation of Moroccan EFL students' perceptions of using Grammarly as an Automated Writing Corrective Feedback (AWCF) tool, framed through the Technology Acceptance Model (TAM). Based on mixed-methods data from undergraduate learners, the study reveals generally positive attitudes: students find the tool useful, easy to use, motivating, and supportive of confidence and writing skill development. Yet the chapter balances this enthusiasm with critical reflections on the tool's limitations—particularly around feedback accuracy, stylistic nuance, contextual appropriateness, and the risk of overreliance. These insights contribute to a nuanced understanding of AI-mediated writing support in language learning contexts.

Chapter 8: Systemic Integration — Infrastructure and Ecosystem Design for Agentic AI in Schools

Chapter 8 shifts the focus to the systemic foundations required for sustainable AI adoption in schools. It investigates the infrastructural, conceptual, and collaborative elements necessary to build robust agentic AI ecosystems. Key issues include data governance, interoperability, privacy safeguards, and coherent ethical standards. The chapter highlights the importance of scalable and adaptive systems that facilitate collaboration among students, teachers, administrators, and AI agents. By outlining design principles for coherent schoolwide ecosystems, it provides practical guidance for institutions seeking to navigate the complexities of 21st-century AI-enabled education.

Chapter 9: Regulatory Frameworks for Agentic AI in Education

This chapter delves into the pressing regulatory challenges posed by increasingly autonomous AI systems in education. It argues that existing data protection laws and general ethical codes fall short in addressing issues such as real-time decision-making, context-aware adaptation, and systemic equity risks. Through comparative policy analysis and case examples, the authors propose a multi-layered regulatory structure encompassing legal accountability, algorithmic audits, bias mitigation, and risk-based oversight. The chapter warns that poorly regulated Agentic AI could exacerbate inequality and undermine learner agency, and it offers concrete strategies—including stakeholder involvement and global harmonization—to strengthen governance and institutional trust.

Chapter 10: Teacher–AI — A Collaborative Approach to Transforming Education

Chapter 10 examines the shifting landscape of teaching as AI systems—from ChatGPT to intelligent tutoring systems—become increasingly integrated into K–12 and higher education. Drawing on surveys, focus groups, case studies, and literature review, the authors explore teachers' evolving roles, apprehensions, and aspirations in this new environment. The chapter highlights the benefits of AI in reducing workload, enabling individualized instruction, and generating meaningful learning data, while also addressing the profound relational, ethical, and pedagogical questions raised by AI-mediated interaction. It concludes with a call for robust teacher support, ethical design, and responsible implementation grounded in fairness, transparency, and accountability.

Chapter 11: Tutoring and Mentoring in the Age of AI — An Academic Perspective

This chapter provides an academic examination of how AI is reshaping traditional tutoring and mentoring systems. It highlights the capacity of AI-driven tutoring platforms and virtual mentors to provide flexible, personalized learning pathways, real-time feedback, and continuous monitoring of student progress. While acknowledging the potential of these tools to enhance human tutoring, the chapter also confronts challenges around social dynamics, ethical considerations, and the evolving relationship between AI agents and educators. Drawing on contemporary examples, the authors offer a balanced perspective on how AI can support learner autonomy, motivation, and equitable access to academic support.

Chapter 12: AI-Powered Career Guidance Systems for Students

Chapter 12 focuses on the growing need for adaptive, data-driven career guidance solutions in an increasingly complex educational and workforce landscape. The chapter outlines how AI-powered systems integrate machine learning, analytics, and personalized profiles to offer tailored career recommendations aligned with students' skills, interests, and aspirations. It highlights the limitations of traditional counseling—such as accessibility and scalability—and illustrates how intelligent systems can help bridge these gaps. By addressing bias, personalization, and long-term adaptability, the chapter presents AI-driven guidance as an essential tool for preparing students to navigate dynamic and uncertain career pathways.

Chapter 13: Enhancing Learning Efficiency Using AI-Driven Adaptive Agents

The final chapter examines Adaptive Learning Agents (ALAs) and their potential to deliver highly personalized, data-rich learning experiences in higher education. Leveraging student placement data, reflective journals, and mentor input, ALAs dynamically adjust instruction to meet learners' evolving needs. Advanced modeling techniques—including Seagull Optimization for feature selection and Bi-Stacked ResNet architectures for performance prediction—enable precise personalization and real-time feedback. The chapter illustrates how ALAs enhance skill acquisition, motivation, and collaborative learning while supporting sustainable and scalable educational innovation. It closes by emphasizing the importance of aligning these emerging technologies with broader goals of ethical, effective, and future-oriented education.

CONCLUSION

Taken together, the chapters in this volume illuminate the profound ways Agentic AI is reshaping the educational landscape—technologically, pedagogically, ethically, and institutionally. What emerges across these contributions is a shared recognition that the rise of agentive systems represents not merely an extension of existing educational technologies, but a fundamental reconfiguration of how learning is supported, enacted, and governed. The authors remind us that while these systems hold extraordinary promise—greater personalization, enhanced accessibility, richer data insights, and new forms of collaboration—they also bring significant responsibilities. Ensuring transparency, safeguarding equity, and preserving human agency must remain central commitments as we navigate this evolving terrain.

This book reflects the belief that meaningful progress will come only through sustained interdisciplinary collaboration. No single field—whether computer science, education, cognitive psychology, ethics, or policy—can fully anticipate or address the complex implications of Agentic AI in isolation. The chapters collectively model the type of dialogue required: rigorous yet imaginative, critical yet constructively oriented, attentive to both immediate realities and long-term possibilities. They point to a future in which AI does not displace educators or learners, but instead works alongside them as a partner in cultivating thoughtful, adaptive, and inclusive educational systems.

As editor, I am hopeful that this volume serves not only as a reference but also as a catalyst. I invite readers to approach these ideas with curiosity and critical reflection, to challenge assumptions, and to contribute to the ongoing work of shaping AI in education with wisdom and foresight. Agentic AI presents us with an unprecedented opportunity to reinvent learning ecosystems in ways that are more responsive, equitable, and human-centered. It is my sincere aspiration that the insights gathered here help guide that endeavor—ensuring that the future of AI in education is one we design intentionally, collaboratively, and ethically.

Chapter 1
Foundations of Agentic AI Redefining Autonomy in Learning Environments

Samariddin Makhmudov
https://orcid.org/0009-0008-2046-8889
Termez University of Economics and Service, Uzbekistan

Maida Maqsood
College of International Studies, Shenzhen University, China

Umidjon Musaev
Mamun University, Uzbekistan

Mangubek Urazmetov
https://orcid.org/0009-0004-2155-7809
Urgench State University, Uzbekistan

Aiman Shahzadi
https://orcid.org/0009-0001-1098-8169
Virtual University, Pakistan

ABSTRACT

This chapter explores the conceptual and technological foundations of agentic AI—a transformative paradigm redefining autonomy in learning environments. Moving beyond automation, agentic AI emphasizes co-agency between humans and intelligent systems, enabling learners to set goals, reflect, and collaborate dynamically. The chapter grounds its discussion in constructivist and socio-cognitive theories, examines the architectures that enable perception, reasoning, and decision autonomy, and illustrates applications across educational settings. It further analyzes

DOI: 10.4018/979-8-3373-4621-2.ch001

ethical and pedagogical implications, highlighting transparency, fairness, and teacher redefinition. Concluding with emerging trends—multimodal agency, lifelong learning agents, and affective co-learning—it envisions symbiotic, self-evolving educational ecosystems.

INTRODUCTION

Artificial intelligence has long been recognized for its potential to automate repetitive tasks, personalize content delivery, and improve administrative efficiency in educational environments. However, with the evolution of AI technologies, the focus is shifting from simple automation to true agency in both machines and learners. Traditional educational AI systems, such as adaptive tutors and recommendation engines, are largely reactive: they adapt to user input or performance but remain subject to predefined rules and limited contextual knowledge. Conversely, agent AI introduces a paradigm shift by equipping systems with the ability to achieve goals, reason about the learning context, and make proactive decisions consistent with pedagogical intent. Rather than acting as static assistants, AI agents act as autonomous learning partners, capable of negotiating goals, facilitating reflection, and aligning learning paths with students.

This shift has profound pedagogical implications. The shift toward AI agents aligns with contemporary educational philosophies, such as constructivism, self-regulated learning, and humanistic education, which emphasize learner autonomy, self-determination, and empowerment. By enabling students to create their own learning paths through intelligent systems, AI agents foster deep engagement, cognitive development, and a sense of ownership over the learning process. At the same time, they encourage teachers to rethink their role, shifting from content transmitters to facilitators of an AI-powered, optimized learning ecosystem.

This chapter explores the theoretical, technical, and ethical foundations of agentic AI and its transformative potential to redefine autonomy in learning environments. It begins with the theoretical foundations of agentic systems in learning and cognitive sciences, then examines their technical architecture and functional components. The following sections describe concrete educational applications and case studies, followed by a critical discussion of the pedagogical and ethical implications. The chapter concludes with a forward-looking perspective on the future of agentic AI and its role in building intelligent, self-developing educational ecosystems.

THEORETICAL FOUNDATIONS OF AGENTIC AI

In an attempt to anchor the concept of agentic artificial intelligence (AI) in the educational context, three major theoretical strands—constructivism, self-determination theory (SDT), and the social-cognitive perspective—provide rich conceptual foundations. Together, they help explain how human learners exercise their agency, how this agency can be supported and enhanced by intelligent systems, and how a new mode of human-AI co-agency might emerge. Below, I elaborate on each of these strands and then show how they lead to a model of human-AI co-agency, in which learners and intelligent systems share control, goals, and reflection.

Constructivism and Learner Agency

Constructivist learning theory emphasizes that learners actively construct knowledge rather than passively acquire it. Researchers such as Jean Piaget and Leo Vygotsky developed cognition as a process of interaction with the environment and with meaning-making partners—and conceptually placed agency at the heart of effective learning. This idea has also been applied to fields of artificial intelligence, for example, one position paper argues that applying Piaget's theory to AI research can help model how systems can "learn to learn" rather than follow predetermined rules (Guerin, 2008).In an educational context, constructivism means that learners should have meaningful opportunities to make decisions, explore, reflect, and revise their thinking in self-constructed ways. When this is translated to agentic AI systems, AI does not simply present content or formulate the next question: it is designed to engage the learner in understanding not only what they are learning, but also how and why. In other words, the system should offer opportunities for choice, structured reflection, and meaningful challenges. From a systems perspective, researchers advocate for an architecture of "human-agent AI co-developed learning systems" that fosters this type of dynamic, interactive, and learner-centered engagement (Williams, 2025). Thus, constructivism provides the fundamental empirical and conceptual basis for treating learners as active agents and, by extension, for designing AI systems that respect, enhance, and share agency rather than control or respond to it.

Self-Determination Theory (SDT)

While constructivism focuses on the cognitive and agency aspects of learning, the motivational and affective dimensions are well represented by self-determination theory (SDT). According to SDT, humans have three fundamental psychological needs: autonomy, competence, and group belonging. Satisfying these needs promotes increased intrinsic motivation, enhanced psychological development, and self-commitment. When learners feel autonomous (i.e., they have choice and will), competent (they believe they can succeed), and associated (they feel connected and supported), they are more likely to engage in agentic and self-regulated learning.

Recent research suggests that when AI systems appear to compromise these needs—for example, by being overly proactive and taking control of decision-making—they can reduce learners' sense of competence or autonomy. For example, studies on human-AI collaboration indicate that, according to SDT (Diebel et al., 2025). AI's "active assistance" can reduce satisfaction with human competence. Transposing this principle to agentic AI in learning environments involves designing systems that promote learner autonomy (by providing relevant choices and control), competence (by gradually challenging learners and providing support only when necessary), and relatedness (through feedback, social presence, or peer-to-AI scaffolding). In short, agentic systems must be motivating, not merely pragmatic.

Socio-Cognitive Perspectives

Beyond individual cognition and motivation lies the dimension of social cognition: how learners, peers, tools, and environments interact in dynamically mediated social systems. In this literature, the concept of agency is generally defined as an actor's ability to intentionally engage in actions, plan them, monitor them, and adjust them to achieve goals. Recent work extends this concept to AI systems: how can AI act as an agent? How is agency distributed? How do human and machine agents determine their roles and goals? For example, a recent paper describes the characteristics of agency in dialogue—intention, motivation, self-efficacy, and self-regulation—by drawing on social-cognitive theory and applying them to large language models (Sharma et al., 2023). Other studies on human-AI co-agency emphasize that AI should not only follow human signals, but can also adapt to each other, control negotiations, and even suggest new paths (Katsenou et al., 2025).

In a learning environment, this suggests a transition from AI as a passive (instrumental) tool to AI as a teammate or assistant, capable of participating in the learning process with the learner rather than itself. This implies a shared context (the AI understands the learner's goals and strategies), shared control (the learner and the system jointly negotiate the next steps), and shared reflection (the system signals metacognitive activity, and these phenomena, together, influence the next cycle). Thus, the human-AI system becomes a system of co-agency, where both parties act, reflect, and adapt.

Towards Agentic AI for Learning

Combining these elements, the theoretical foundations of agentic AI in learning environments can be described as follows:

i. Learners are active creators of knowledge (constructivism), and their agency is essential for deep engagement.
ii. Their motivation and willingness to exercise their agency depend on the satisfaction of autonomy, competence, and relatedness (SDT).
iii. In sociocognitive terms, a learner's agency emerges from their interactions with their peers, devices, and environment, and increasingly with intelligent systems that may possess or share their agency.
iv. Therefore, an agentic AI system must be designed not only to adapt or assist, but also to share its agency, enabling learners to make relevant choices, reflect on them, collaborate or negotiate with the system, and jointly adopt a learning path.
v. The system must address not only what to learn, but also how, why, and when to learn, cognitive regulation, goal setting, monitoring, and reflection.
vi. This requires attention to interface design, role definition, transparency, trust, and power dynamics, as the transfer of agency from a solitary human to a collaborative human-AI system has profound pedagogical and ethical implications.

In summary, the notion of agency shifts from a characteristic of the solitary learner to a relational construct within the human-AI ecosystem. Agentic AI becomes the means by which learner autonomy is enhanced and enriched, rather than replaced. The theoretical foundations laid here provide a solid foundation for the design, implementation, and critical evaluation of such systems in learning environments.

TECHNOLOGICAL ARCHITECTURE AND ENABLING COMPONENTS

In designing an agentic AI system for learning environments, it is essential to understand both how such systems function and what technological components enable their operation. In this section, we detail the core architecture — perception, reasoning, goal formation, decision autonomy, feedback adaptation — then examine how emerging technologies (LLMs, knowledge graphs, reinforcement learning) integrate into these architectures. Finally, we discuss design frameworks (such as self-regulated learning models and explainable AI) and the ethical/safety layers required for aligned autonomy.

Core Components

An agentic learning system is composed of a series of interconnected modules that together enable intelligent, self-regulating, and adaptive behavior. The first of these, perception, involves the system's ability to sense, collect, and interpret data from multiple sources—such as learner interactions, performance analytics, environmental conditions, and contextual metadata. As highlighted in (Projectpro, 2025). This typically begins with an "Input Layer that aggregates heterogeneous data streams including user inputs, sensor data, and external systems like APIs." Through this, the agent builds a multidimensional understanding of the learner's cognitive and affective state.

Once perception establishes the contextual foundation, reasoning becomes central. This module allows the agent to interpret the perceived information and determine what it means for subsequent learning actions. Reasoning combines symbolic approaches, such as logic-based planning and inference, with data-driven methods, including large language models (LLMs) capable of chain-of-thought or tree-of-thought reasoning (AKKA, 2025). In educational contexts, this reasoning engine enables the agent to identify misconceptions, predict learner needs, and construct plausible next steps or scaffolds that align with instructional goals.

A defining feature of agentic AI is goal formation—its capacity to create, negotiate, or refine objectives rather than merely respond to preset conditions. In a learning environment, this involves co-defining learning outcomes with the student, breaking them into sub-goals, and dynamically updating them as learning progresses. This stands in contrast to adaptive AI systems, which typically react to learner performance but do not autonomously propose new or strategic goals. Goal formation thus reflects the agent's ability to operationalize intentionality and support personalized trajectories that evolve with the learner's understanding.

Building on goal formation, decision autonomy empowers the system to take initiative within defined boundaries. Agentic AI does not passively await user commands but can proactively suggest, initiate, or adjust actions that serve agreed learning goals—such as recommending new tasks, adjusting difficulty levels, prompting reflection, or offering strategic hints. This autonomy transforms the learner-AI relationship from tool use to partnership, where the system becomes a collaborator that acts purposefully while maintaining human oversight. Decision autonomy is typically moderated by ethical and pedagogical parameters to ensure alignment with learner agency and educational integrity.

Finally, feedback and adaptation form the learning system's self-regulating loop. After each decision or intervention, the system evaluates outcomes—did engagement improve, did mastery increase, or were misconceptions reduced? and adjusts its models or strategies accordingly. As described in the (Thomas, 2024). This module functions through continuous cycles of "data collection, model training, and knowledge update." This iterative refinement is what allows agentic AI to remain responsive, personalized, and context-aware over time.

When combined, these five components such as perception, reasoning, goal formation, decision autonomy, and feedback adaptation, constitute the agentic loop:

perceive → reason and set goals → decide and act → gather feedback → adapt and improve

In a learning context, this loop translates to the system observing learner behavior, autonomously suggesting or adjusting pathways, monitoring performance, and continuously refining its support strategies. This cyclical intelligence is what differentiates agentic AI from both static and reactive systems, enabling the creation of adaptive, reflective, and human-aligned learning ecosystems.

Integration of LLMs, Reinforcement Learning, and Knowledge Graphs

Modern agentic learning systems increasingly draw upon a triad of synergistic technologies, Large Language Models (LLMs), Reinforcement Learning (RL), and Knowledge Graphs (KGs), to enable dynamic, adaptive, and explainable educational experiences. Each contributes distinct yet complementary capabilities: LLMs provide linguistic and cognitive fluency; RL brings interactive optimization through feedback loops; and KGs ensure structured, interpretable knowledge grounding. Together, these components form the backbone of next-generation intelligent learning ecosystems capable of reasoning, reflection, and continual improvement.

Large Language Models (LLMs)

LLMs such as GPT, Claude, and Gemini form the dialogic foundation of agentic systems. Their capacity to understand, generate, and refine human-like discourse allows them to act as autonomous tutors, co-learners, or metacognitive companions. They support scaffolding by dynamically adjusting explanations, posing reflective prompts, and encouraging self-assessment. In agentic architectures, LLMs serve as reasoning engines, often connected to external tools or APIs for contextual augmentation (Emergentmind, 2025).

Emerging frameworks, such as Agentic Reasoning, emphasize "external tool integration," wherein LLM reasoning steps are interleaved with tool-use tokens that trigger specific functions like database queries, simulations, or knowledge retrieval. This enables the AI to move beyond static language interaction toward goal-directed reasoning, supporting learners through adaptive dialogue and problem-solving across diverse educational contexts.

Reinforcement Learning (RL)

Reinforcement Learning introduces an essential dimension of adaptivity and improvement over time. Through continuous interaction with the learner and the environment, RL agents refine their instructional strategies, intervention timing, and decision-making policies. In educational applications, RL can govern when and how the system should provide feedback, pose challenges, or modulate difficulty levels. For example, the KG-R1 framework demonstrates how RL can optimize retrieval-augmented generation in knowledge-graph environments, balancing exploration and exploitation to achieve better contextual reasoning (Song et al., 2025). Applied to learning systems, this allows agentic AI to model personalized scaffolding trajectories—identifying which strategies yield better cognitive engagement or learning outcomes. Over time, the system evolves its teaching policy based on empirical reinforcement signals such as learner accuracy, engagement duration, or emotional cues, thus emulating aspects of human pedagogical intuition.

Knowledge Graphs (KGs)

Knowledge Graphs provide the semantic backbone of agentic systems by encoding relationships among entities, concepts, and events in a structured, machine-readable form. In learning environments, KGs can represent learner profiles, domain ontologies, instructional resources, and learning trajectories.

By serving as long-term, verifiable memory stores, KGs ensure the explainability and consistency of AI reasoning processes—addressing one of the core ethical and operational challenges in educational AI. As observed in recent literature, "Knowledge Graphs are rapidly transitioning from static data representations to become dynamic, actionable foundations for the next generation of agentic AI systems" (Luo et al., 2025). In a practical architecture such as Graph-RAG (Graph-based Retrieval-Augmented Generation), the LLM queries the knowledge graph to retrieve relevant contextual information, ensuring that generated responses are both factual and context-aware. The graph evolves continuously as the learner progresses, recording competencies, misconceptions, and learning interactions.

Toward a Unified Architecture

When integrated, LLMs, RL, and KGs form a cohesive ecosystem of reasoning, adaptation, and memory. The LLM interprets learner inputs and generates pedagogical responses; the RL module optimizes these responses over time through performance feedback; and the KG anchors all reasoning in verified knowledge and learner history. In this multi-turn reinforcement loop, the system learns not only the subject matter but also how best to teach it—progressing toward autonomous, reflective pedagogy. For example, an agentic tutor might retrieve relevant concepts from the KG, engage the learner in Socratic dialogue through the LLM, and then use RL-based feedback to adjust its instructional approach in subsequent interactions.

Implications for Learning Environments

The convergence of these technologies marks a pivotal step toward symbiotic human–AI co-learning systems. LLMs humanize the interface; RL personalizes the experience; and KGs stabilize and contextualize knowledge exchange. Together, they enable educational agents that are transparent, self-improving, and pedagogically aware—a cornerstone for the emerging paradigm of agentic intelligence in education.

Frameworks for Designing Agentic AI in Learning Environments

Designing agentic AI systems for education requires a synthesis of educational theory, AI systems architecture, and human-centered design. To ensure that such systems enhance rather than replace human learning agency, developers must draw from conceptual frameworks that integrate cognitive science, pedagogy, explainability, and ethical design principles. Three complementary approaches, Self-Regulated Learning (SRL) frameworks, Explainable AI (XAI) mechanisms, and Human-in-the-Loop (HITL) or Co-Agency models, offer essential guidance for the construction of agentic learning architectures.

Self-Regulated Learning (SRL) Models

Self-Regulated Learning (SRL) frameworks emphasize learners' ability to set goals, monitor progress, apply strategies, and reflect on outcomes. These processes are inherently agentic and align directly with the architecture of autonomous learning systems. In an SRL-aligned agentic AI, the system does not simply deliver content—it scaffolds the learner's metacognitive development by prompting goal formation, offering feedback loops, and supporting adaptive strategy refinement.

For example, during the forethought phase, the agentic AI can assist in defining learning goals based on prior performance or preferences. In the performance phase, it can provide feedback and suggest strategy adjustments through real-time analytics. Finally, in the reflection phase, it can engage the learner in dialogic evaluation—asking reflective prompts or generating progress summaries. By aligning the agentic AI's goal formation, decision autonomy, and feedback adaptation modules with SRL cycles, the system becomes a dynamic coach that cultivates self-directed learning and resilience.

Explainable AI (XAI) Mechanisms

For agentic AI to be trusted in educational contexts, it must communicate why it acts the way it does. Explainable AI (XAI) mechanisms are therefore essential, ensuring that learners and educators can understand, question, and learn from the system's reasoning. In such designs, Knowledge Graph-based reasoning plays a central role.

Because every knowledge node and decision link is explicitly represented, the system's logic becomes traceable and interpretable. As described in recent literature, "Since all knowledge and reasoning steps are represented in the graph, the system inherently logs its 'chain of thought' in a traceable form." This graph-based explainability provides transparency without overwhelming the user—enabling the system to justify a recommendation (e.g., why a learner was advised to review a specific topic) or clarify the reasoning path ("Node A → Node B → Decision C"). Moreover, embedding XAI in agentic learning systems reinforces accountability and pedagogical alignment, allowing educators to audit the system's suggestions and ensuring that the AI's reasoning remains pedagogically sound and ethically transparent.

Human-in-the-Loop and Co-Agency Frameworks

Agentic AI must operate in partnership with human actors, teachers, mentors, and learners, rather than replacing them. The Human-in-the-Loop (HITL) and Co-Agency paradigms emphasize this balance, ensuring that autonomy is shared and negotiated rather than unilaterally automated.

In these frameworks, human oversight is embedded through interfaces for supervision, reflection, and co-decision making. Educators may approve or modify system recommendations, while learners can negotiate goals or reject system-suggested pathways. Some emerging architectures even feature modular agents assigned specific roles (e.g., "Goal Setter," "Feedback Coach," "Ethics Monitor") under human supervision. This structure ensures that the AI's autonomy remains bounded by human values, educational context, and learner well-being (Krishna et al., 2025). Such co-agency models foster mutual learning: the AI adapts to human feedback, while humans develop greater awareness of their learning processes through interaction with the agentic system.

Ethical and Safety Layers for Aligned Autonomy

As agentic AI systems gain decision-making autonomy in educational environments, they must be designed within a robust ethical and safety framework that ensures their actions remain pedagogically aligned, transparent, and human-centered. Aligned autonomy refers to the balance between system independence and adherence to ethical, social, and educational values. This requires embedding multi-layered safeguards across the system architecture, from algorithmic constraints to human oversight mechanisms, so that autonomy serves learning, not merely automation.

Autonomy Constraints and Guardrails

Agentic AI systems must operate within well-defined boundaries that align with curricular goals, pedagogical ethics, and institutional regulations. Without such guardrails, autonomous decisions risk deviating from intended learning objectives. A core mechanism for implementing these constraints is through knowledge graph–based validation or ontology encoding, which formally specifies permissible actions and task domains. For instance, an agent should not assign learning tasks beyond the learner's course scope or modify assessment criteria autonomously. Research in "graph-based orchestration" architectures highlights how human-in-the-loop workflows and graph constraints can maintain alignment between AI autonomy and educational intent. These boundaries ensure that even as the agent exhibits initiative, its decisions remain pedagogically legitimate and ethically safe.

Transparency and Auditability

Transparency is central to trust in educational AI. Every reasoning step, recommendation, and system decision must be traceable. Embedding audit trails within the agent's memory layer, particularly via a knowledge graph structure, enables provenance tracking of actions and rationale. This means that both learners and educators can review how and why the system arrived at certain conclusions, fostering accountability. In institutional contexts, such traceability also supports compliance with educational standards, regulatory audits, and data ethics guidelines. Transparent architectures transform opaque AI behavior into interpretable, reviewable decision processes that enhance stakeholder confidence.

Bias Mitigation and Fairness

Bias in agentic learning systems can manifest through unbalanced recommendations, unequal feedback, or skewed assessments based on demographic or behavioral patterns. To mitigate this, fairness-aware algorithms must be integrated at both the data and decision layers. Monitoring modules can continuously assess outcome parity across diverse learner groups, while fairness constraints can be embedded in the reinforcement learning policy governing adaptive interventions. Bias mitigation is not only an ethical requirement but also a pedagogical one—ensuring that personalization does not inadvertently reinforce inequity. In this sense, fairness contributes directly to the legitimacy and inclusivity of agentic learning systems.

Learner Trust, Privacy, and Data Security

Agentic AI relies heavily on data-rich perception and memory modules, which capture sensitive learner information such as performance metrics, behavioral logs, and potentially emotional cues. Protecting this data is paramount. Systems must adhere to privacy-by-design principles, including informed consent, minimal data retention, encryption, and secure storage. Transparent communication about data use—why it is collected, how it benefits the learner, and who has access—strengthens learner trust. Furthermore, governance frameworks such as GDPR and emerging educational data ethics standards provide benchmarks for responsible data handling in AI-mediated learning environments.

Balancing Adaptation and Over-Dependence

A paradox of agentic AI is that, if too effective or autonomous, it may reduce rather than enhance learner agency. Over-reliance on AI-generated guidance can lead to passivity, diminishing self-regulation skills. To counter this, design architectures must include reflective scaffolds—mechanisms that encourage learners to question, evaluate, and sometimes override system suggestions. This not only preserves human decision-making but also cultivates meta-cognitive awareness. In practice, adaptive autonomy can be implemented through graduated control, where system assistance decreases as learner competence increases, promoting long-term self-efficacy.

Safe Intervention and Human Oversight

Agentic AI must also recognize its limitations and escalate issues when necessary. A dedicated monitoring module can track system confidence levels, learner frustration, or prolonged stagnation, triggering human educator intervention when thresholds are crossed. Such escalation ensures that the AI never acts beyond its competence or ethical boundary. Human oversight thus becomes an integral safety valve, preserving educational integrity and providing emotional and contextual sensitivity that AI cannot fully replicate.

AGENTIC AI IN LEARNING ENVIRONMENTS

In this section, we move from theory to practice, exploring how agentic-AI systems are being applied in real educational contexts to reshape how learners engage, reflect, and collaborate. The goal is to highlight how the core ideas of autonomy, co-agency, and dynamic scaffolding manifest in concrete applications across K-12, higher education, and professional learning.

Personalized Learning Pathways and Autonomous Tutoring Agents

One of the primary applications of agentic AI is in the creation of truly personalized learning trajectories and autonomous tutoring agents. Unlike traditional adaptive systems that respond primarily to learner performance, agentic systems anticipate learner needs, negotiate goals with learners, and dynamically adjust the pathway. For example, a review article describes how agentic AI "continuously assess[s] and respond[s] to learner performance, preferences, and engagement in real-time" to deliver personalized education (Babar, 2025). In practice, an AI-powered tutoring agent might begin with a diagnostic of prior knowledge, jointly define learning goals with the student (e.g., "I want to be able to apply X concept in Y context"), and then autonomously suggest tasks (exercises, simulations), monitor progress, intervene when needed (suggest extra scaffolding or alternative approaches), and reflect on the path with the learner. This dynamic loop, goal negotiation, action, monitoring, adaptation, is foundational to agentic systems. As one article observes, agentic AI systems in education are now able to "anticipate needs and take proactive measures" (for example, alerting a teacher of declining engagement or recommending resources before the student asks) (Akhil, 2025). In K-12 settings, this may look like a virtual tutor that adapts in real time to a child's attention span and emotional state; in higher education, it may involve scaffolding complex tasks or research projects tailored to student interest and readiness. The key shift is from "system adapts to you" to "system collaborates with you in shaping your learning path".

AI Companions Fostering Metacognitive Reflection

Beyond task assignment and feedback, agentic learning systems increasingly serve as companions that prompt metacognitive reflection—helping learners think about how they are learning, what strategies they are using, and when to revise their approach. One recent survey of agentic AI in education points out that such systems "offer personalized feedback with multiple explanations of complex concepts and encourage learners to engage in metacognitive reflection" (Brohi et al., 2025). For instance, rather than simply telling a student their answer is incorrect, the agent may ask: "What strategy did you use here? What alternative could you try? Would you like to revisit your approach?" Through that dialogic scaffolding, the learner becomes more self-aware and more self-regulated. In professional learning ecosystems, such companion agents might serve as persistent mentors, retaining memory of a learner's past performance, preferences, goals, and challenges—and reminding the learner to reflect on progress, reconsider strategies, and set new goals. This marks a shift from AI as a one-time tool to AI as a learning partner with a longitudinal view of the learner's agency.

Collaborative Learning Agents

Agentic AI is also making inroads into collaborative and simulation-based learning environments: not just one-on-one tutoring, but multi-learner, multi-agent, simulation-rich ecosystems. For example, a recent paper on "Collaborative Learning in Agentic Systems" introduces mechanisms by which multiple agentic systems can work together, share knowledge, and support collective learning dynamics, emphasizing open-ended, evolving learning tasks rather than fixed assignments (Nath et al., 2025). In a virtual classroom, an agent might monitor group interactions, suggest optimal groupings based on complementary skills, mediate peer scaffolding, and prompt shared reflection (e.g., "You and your peer solved the problem in different ways—what can you learn from each other?"). In simulation contexts—such as medical education—a multi-agent frameworks may simulate patients, doctors, and other roles, enabling learners to navigate complex team-based scenarios (Wei et al., 2024). These collaborative agentic systems help replicate real-world complexity, foster teamwork and co-agency (learner-agent, peer-agent, agent-agent) and can scale interactive experiences that would otherwise be too resource-heavy.

K-12, Higher Education and Professional Learning

K-12: In younger learning environments, agentic AI supports differentiated instruction, scaffolds executive functioning (e.g., planning, monitoring progress), and enhances engagement through gamified, responsive agents. For instance, tools using agentic AI provide immediate feedback, adapt pacing, and detect engagement drops (Akhil, 2025). Higher Education: In universities and colleges, agentic AI systems are used for generating lecture materials aligned to course objectives, providing individualized practice, assisting with research projects, and supporting student self-regulation (Yuhan, 2025). For example, systems may dynamically generate assignments, monitor student work, provide feedback, and identify learners at risk of dropping out—then intervening with scaffolding or peer-group formation.

Professional Learning & Lifelong Education

In corporate or adult learning settings, agentic AI serves as autonomous mentors, career-long companions, and collaborators. These systems maintain learner profiles, track skill progression over time, suggest next steps, facilitate simulations relevant to industry contexts, and enable collaborations across dispersed teams. In sum, the versatility of agentic AI spans a spectrum of learners and contexts—offering adaptability, scalability, and deeper engagement. The applications and case scenarios above illustrate how agentic AI is redefining autonomy in learning environments—not merely automating tasks, but enabling shared agency, reflection, co-planning, and collaboration. From personalized tutoring to metacognitive companions, from collaborative virtual simulations to long-term professional learning partnerships, these systems embody the shift from assistance to participation: learners are no longer passive recipients of AI-driven adaptation, but active co-constructors of their learning journey with intelligent systems. In the next section, we turn to the pedagogical and ethical implications of this shift—including how roles of educators and learners evolve, and what new safeguards are necessary.

PEDAGOGICAL AND ETHICAL IMPLICATIONS

The advent of agentic AI in learning environments brings about profound shifts in pedagogical practice and surfaces critical ethical questions. As systems move from being assistive tools to partners in learning, the roles of educators and learners evolve, raising tensions between autonomy and accountability, promising personalization but risking bias or over-dependence. Below, we critically examine four inter-linked dimensions: the changing teacher/learner roles; balancing autonomy, accountability and transparency; bias, dependence and value-alignment challenges; and ethical frameworks for agency and responsible learning design.

Shifts in Teacher and Learner Roles

In traditional educational models, teachers predominantly act as knowledge transmitters and organizers of learning, while learners follow set paths. With agentic AI, these roles are being redefined. Research shows that integration of AI significantly alters the teacher's role, transforming it from instructor to facilitator, mentor or co-designer of learning experiences. For example, a study of higher-education teachers found that AI integration "significantly enhances student agency… [but] largely affects teachers' roles in promoting student agency" (Creely & Carabott, 2025). Moreover, a recent qualitative study on K-12 teachers in AI-enabled contexts found that many educators grapple with shifting authority, evolving professional identity and tensions between technology and pedagogy (Tripathi et al., 2025).

From the learner's side, agency increases when intelligent systems support goal-setting, reflection and decision-making. But this means learners must step into more active roles—self-regulating, making meaningful choices, reflecting on their strategies—which not all may be prepared for. The shift from passive recipient to co-creator implies new pedagogical architectures, new scaffolding of metacognitive skills, and a rethink of assessment and accountability structures. Teachers become designers of agentic systems, mediators of human–AI collaboration, and orchestrators of learning ecosystems rather than sole content experts (Manzoor et al., 2025).

Balancing Autonomy, Accountability and Transparency

One of the central tensions in agentic AI systems is: how to promote learner autonomy while ensuring accountability and transparency? Autonomy means giving learners meaningful choices, agency over their learning process, and the capacity to reflect and adjust. However, with increased AI assistance comes the risk of over-dependence, diminished self-regulation, or misguided decision-making if the AI is opaque. Ethical literature emphasizes that AI systems in education must remain transparent and explainable, so that learners and educators understand why particular decisions or recommendations are made (Zhang, 2025).

Moreover, when agentic AI systems intervene (e.g., recommending next steps, scaffolding tasks, assessing performance), questions arise: Who is accountable when the recommendation fails or leads the learner astray? As one paper on AI in assessment argues: "When an AI grading system unfairly penalizes a student, determining accountability can be challenging" (Patki et al., 2023). Therefore, in designing agentic systems, it is crucial to embed mechanisms for transparency (explainable AI), traceability (audit logs of decision-paths), learner/educator acceptability (understanding and consenting to interventions), and human oversight. Only then can autonomy be balanced with accountability and trust.

Addressing Bias, Over-dependence, and Value Alignment Challenges

Agentic AI promises personalization and responsiveness, but also carries risks of bias, reinforcing inequalities, and diminishing genuine learner agency. Algorithms are not neutral: they encode values, assumptions and historical biases present in training data and system design. Studies highlight that AI in education can "replicate or even amplify existing biases" if not carefully designed (Danisa, 2025).

Over-dependence is another risk: learners might defer too much control to the AI partner, reducing their own cognitive effort, critical thinking or metacognitive engagement. A scoping review found that while generative AI may enhance learner agency, it "also risks exacerbating educational inequalities and diminishing learner autonomy in certain contexts" (Roe & Perkins, 2024). Value-alignment becomes essential when AI systems share agency: What values do they promote? Whose goals are privileged? Are all learners afforded equal opportunity? Designing systems aligned to inclusive, equitable, culturally-responsive values is a non-trivial challenge. Ethical design must anticipate and mitigate the risk that agentic AI shapes learners into certain patterns of behavior or thinking rather than supporting their independent formation of strategy, reflection and identity.

Ethical Frameworks for Agency and Responsible Learning Design

Given these pedagogical shifts and ethical hazards, robust frameworks are needed to guide the design, deployment and governance of agentic AI in learning environments. Several key principles emerge:

i. Ensuring that AI augments, not replaces, human educators and learners; preserving human dignity, critical thinking and relational dimensions of learning.
ii. Systems must make their reasoning visible to stakeholders, support reflection on how decisions are made, and allow challenge or override.
iii. Mitigate algorithmic bias, ensure inclusive access, monitor outcomes for disparate impacts, and avoid reinforcing structural inequalities.
iv. Design for shared agency, learners and educators retain meaningful control, choice, reflection and decision-making capacity; the AI partner supports rather than controls.
v. Clear governance structures for monitoring system behavior, data use, decision trails, and recourse in case of harm or unintended outcomes.

Ethical literacy and professional development: Educators and learners need competence in interpreting AI behavior, recognizing ethical risks, and contributing to the design and governance of AI-enhanced environments. A study emphasizes that professional learning is crucial for teachers to address the ethical challenges of AI in education. In practice, operationalizing such frameworks means embedding ethical reflection in system design (e.g., prompts that ask learners "why did you choose this route?", providing options rather than pre-set pathways), designing audit-capable architectures (logging learner-agent interaction, reason-paths), establishing institutional policies on AI use, ensuring oversight committees (including educators, learners, technologists) and continuous evaluation of impact on equity and agency.

The transformative potential of agentic AI in education is matched by its disruptive and ethically complex nature. On the pedagogical front, roles of teachers and learners shift to collaborative, co-constructive paradigms; learners gain agency but also must negotiate new responsibilities. Ethically, the design and deployment of such systems must balance autonomy with accountability, personalize without biasing, enable rather than enable dependency, and align technology with educational values of equity, choice, reflection and human development. Ethical frameworks anchored in human-centered design, transparency, fairness, agency and accountability provide the essential scaffolding for responsible implementation. As we move toward agentic learning ecosystems, educators, designers, policymakers and learners must remain reflexive, critical and collaborative to ensure that autonomy is truly empowered, not merely transferred to machines. Table 1 synthesizes major ethical and pedagogical implications emerging from the integration of agentic AI in education. It highlights not only the potential risks but also actionable design and governance strategies for maintaining transparency, equity, and shared human–machine agency in learning environments.

Table 1. Ethical and pedagogical implications of agentic AI in learning environments

Dimension	Key Ethical / Pedagogical Risks	Implications for Teaching and Learning	Responsible Design and Mitigation Strategies
Learner Autonomy	Over-dependence on AI guidance; erosion of self-regulation	Learners may rely excessively on automated feedback, reducing critical reflection	Embed *reflective prompts* and *choice mechanisms*; design for *co-agency* rather than automation
Teacher Role Transformation	Diminished pedagogical authority; uncertainty over professional identity	Teachers risk being seen as supervisors rather than mentors	Provide *AI literacy* and *co-design training* for teachers; highlight their role as *learning orchestrators*
Transparency and Explainability	Black-box AI decisions hinder trust and understanding	Learners/teachers cannot interpret AI reasoning or feedback	Integrate *Explainable AI (XAI)* interfaces; use *traceable decision logs*
Bias and Fairness	Algorithmic bias perpetuates inequality	Disadvantaged learners receive poorer recommendations	Conduct *bias audits*; use *diverse training datasets*; ensure *equitable personalization*
Value Alignment	Misaligned learning goals; reinforcement of unintended behaviors	AI optimizes performance metrics rather than holistic learning	Encode *human-centered values*; involve educators in *value calibration*

continued on following page

Table 1. Continued

Dimension	Key Ethical / Pedagogical Risks	Implications for Teaching and Learning	Responsible Design and Mitigation Strategies
Accountability	Ambiguous responsibility when AI errors occur	Ethical and legal confusion in assessment or feedback	Define *human-in-the-loop governance* and *institutional oversight policies*
Ethical Literacy	Teachers and learners lack the capacity to critique AI outputs	Unquestioned acceptance of AI recommendations	Embed *AI ethics modules* in curricula; foster *critical digital literacy*

FUTURE DIRECTIONS AND CONCLUSION

As we look ahead, the evolution of agentic AI in learning environments promises to unfold along several transformative vectors—each carrying significant potential to reshape how learners, educators, and institutions engage with knowledge, agency, and autonomy.

One of the most compelling developments is the emergence of multimodal agency. Future agentic systems will not only reason over text but will integrate vision, speech, sensor data, gesture and even physiological signals to sense the learning context holistically—thus enabling richer feedback, more immersive interaction, and deeper personalization. Alongside this, the notion of lifelong learning agents is gaining ground: persistent AI companions that evolve with the learner across contexts, transitions, careers and domains, maintaining memory of prior goals, strategies, successes and setbacks. And perhaps most philosophically, we are approaching affective co-learning systems: agents capable of recognizing, interpreting and responding to learners' emotional and metacognitive states, thereby engaging not just with what is being learned, but how and why, encouraging reflection, resilience and self-regulation.

Policy and Governance Considerations

With these advancements come weighty implications for policy, governance and institutional design. As agentic learning ecosystems scale, issues of data privacy, learner autonomy, bias mitigation, accountability and access become central. Researchers emphasize the need for frameworks that ensure these systems are transparent, auditable and equitable. Educational institutions and policymakers must consider not just what technologies to adopt, but how they align with core pedagogical values: learner agency, inclusivity, human-AI collaboration, and ethical design. Structural readiness (infrastructure, educator training, regulatory regimes) will determine whether agentic AI enhances or undermines educational equity and quality.

In conclusion, the promise of agentic AI in education is not simply about more automation or smarter tutors—it is about reshaping the learning ecosystem to be more dynamic, relational and emergent. Learners are no longer passive recipients but co-creators; educators become orchestrators of human–AI symbiosis; systems evolve rather than simply respond. In this vision, educational environments themselves become self-evolving ecosystems, where agentic AI, human learners and institutions engage in continuous cycles of goal-setting, action, reflection and adaptation. If designed thoughtfully, these systems can augment autonomy, deepen human–machine co-agency, and support lifelong growth. Yet this future also demands vigilance: we must ensure that autonomy is empowered and not outsourced; that algorithmic power is not concentrated; and that the human dimension of learning remains central. The next chapter in educational transformation may well be written not by tools alone, but by the partnerships between humans and agentic systems working together toward curiosity, understanding and purpose.

REFERENCES

Akhil, B. (2025). *Agentic AI in Education: Revolutionizing Learning*. https://www.meratutor.ai/lms/blog/agentic-ai-in-education/

AKKA. (2025). *Agentic AI architecture 101: An enterprise guide*. https://akka.io/blog/agentic-ai-architecture?

Babar, P. A. (2025). Agentic AI for Personalized Education and Adaptive Learning Environments. *International Journal of Computing and Engineering*, *7*(12), 1–10. DOI: 10.47941/ijce.2973

Brohi, S., Mastoi, Q. U. A., Jhanjhi, N. Z., & Pillai, T. R. (2025). A Research Landscape of Agentic AI and Large Language Models: Applications, Challenges and Future Directions. *Algorithms 2025, Vol. 18, Page 499, 18*(8), 499. DOI: 10.3390/a18080499

Creely, E., & Carabott, K. (2025). Teaching and learning with AI: An Integrated AI-Oriented Pedagogical Model. *Australian Educational Researcher*, *52*(6), 1–22. DOI: 10.1007/s13384-025-00913-6

Danisa, A. (2025). *The Ethics of Using AI in Education*. https://www.brainzmagazine.com/post/the-ethics-of-using-ai-in-education?

Diebel, C., Goutier, M., Adam, M., & Benlian, A. (2025). When AI-Based Agents Are Proactive: Implications for Competence and System Satisfaction in Human–AI Collaboration. *Business & Information Systems Engineering*, •••, 1–20. DOI: 10.1007/s12599-024-00918-y

Emergentmind. (2025). *Agentic LLMs Overview*. https://www.emergentmind.com/topics/agentic-llms

Guerin, F. (2008). Constructivism in AI: Prospects, progress and challenges. *AISB 2008 Convention: Communication, Interaction and Social Intelligence - Proceedings of the AISB 2008 Symposium on Computing and Philosophy*.

Katsenou, R., Kotsidis, K., Papadopoulou, A., Anastasiadis, P., & Deliyannis, I. (2025). Beyond Assistance: Embracing AI as a Collaborative Co-Agent in Education. *Education Sciences 2025, Vol. 15, Page 1006, 15*(8), 1006. DOI: 10.3390/educsci15081006

Krishna, A., Shinde, A., Ardham, S., & Malhotra, C. (2025). *A Collaborative Multi-Agent LLM Approach for Knowledge Graph Curation and Query from Multi-Modal Data Sources*. DOI: 10.36227/techrxiv.173886317.71891930/v1

Luo, H. E. H., Chen, G., Lin, Q., Guo, Y., Xu, F., Kuang, Z., Song, M., Wu, X., Zhu, Y., & Tuan, L. A. (2025). *Graph-R1: Towards Agentic GraphRAG Framework via End-to-end Reinforcement Learning*. https://arxiv.org/pdf/2507.21892

Manzoor, A., Hameed, A., & Sultan, F. (2025). AI as a Teaching Partner: Redefining Educator Roles in the Digital Age. `, *3*(02), 2262–2276. https://assajournal.com/index.php/36/article/view/544

Nath, S., Peridis, C., Benjamin, E., Liu, X., Kolouri, S., Kinnell, P., Li, Z., Liu, C., Dora, S., & Soltoggio, A. (2025). *Policy Search, Retrieval, and Composition via Task Similarity in Collaborative Agentic Systems*. https://arxiv.org/pdf/2506.05577

Patki, M., Sanadi, S., Jadhav, S., Musale, A., & Kadam, K. (2023). Ethical Implications of Utilizing Artificial Intelligence in Education for Assessment. *International Conference on Computers in Education, 2*, 600–608. DOI: 10.58459/icce.2023.1439

Projectpro. (2025). *AI Agent Architectures: Modular, Multi-Agent, and Evolving*. https://www.projectpro.io/article/ai-agent-architectures/1135?

Roe, J., & Perkins, M. (2024). *Generative AI and Agency in Education: A Critical Scoping Review and Thematic Analysis*. https://arxiv.org/pdf/2411.00631

Sharma, A., Rao, S., Brockett, C., Malhotra, A., Jojic, N., & Dolan, B. (2023). *Investigating Agency of LLMs in Human-AI Collaboration Tasks*. https://www.microsoft.com/en-us/research/publication/investigating-agency-of-llms-in-human-ai-collaboration-tasks/

Song, J., Wang, S., Shun, J., & Zhu, Y. (2025). *Efficient and Transferable Agentic Knowledge Graph RAG via Reinforcement Learning*. https://arxiv.org/pdf/2509.26383

Thomas, S. (2024). Agentic AI: The Power of Genai and LLMs in Autonomous Systems. *International Journal of Core Engineering & Management*, *12*(7).

Tripathi, T., Sharma, S. R., Singh, V., Bhargava, P., & Raj, C. (2025). Teaching and learning with AI: A qualitative study on K-12 teachers' use and engagement with artificial intelligence. *Frontiers in Education*, *10*, 1651217. DOI: 10.3389/feduc.2025.1651217

Wei, H., Qiu, J., Yu, H., & Yuan, W. (2024). MEDCO: Medical Education Copilots Based on A Multi-Agent Framework. *Lecture Notes in Computer Science, 15630 LNCS*, 119–135. DOI: 10.1007/978-3-031-91813-1_8

Williams, P. (2025). *Human-AI Learning: Architecture of a Human-agenticAI Learning System*. DOI: 10.20944/preprints202508.1351.v1

Yuhan, G. (2025). *Agentic AI in Higher Education.* https://ascode.osu.edu/news/agentic-ai-higher-education?

Zhang, J. (2025). Ethics of Artificial Intelligence in Education: Balancing Automation and Human-Centered Learning. *Applied Mathematics and Nonlinear Sciences*, *10*(1), 20250843. Advance online publication. DOI: 10.2478/amns-2025-0843

Chapter 2

Policy, Equity, and Governance Shaping the Future of Agentic AI in Education

Jan Vrba
https://orcid.org/0000-0002-8404-5091
Akademia Jagiellonska w Toruniu, Czech Republic

Syed Ali Reza
https://orcid.org/0009-0001-8967-1972
University of the Potomac, USA

Munir Ahmad
https://orcid.org/0000-0003-4836-6151
Survey of Pakistan, Pakistan

Khabibullo Rajabov
Tashkent State Transport University, Uzbekistan

Boljon Sapaeva
Mamun University, Uzbekistan

ABSTRACT

This chapter examines the critical role of structured, ethical, and inclusive governance frameworks in deploying AI in education. It emphasizes that effective integration requires transparency, accountability, and active stakeholder participation across institutional, national, and global levels. The study highlights the necessity of multi-sector collaboration among governments, educators, technology developers, and

DOI: 10.4018/979-8-3373-4621-2.ch002

communities to co-create policies and monitor AI applications. Proactive governance, incorporating foresight, risk assessment, and adaptive policy mechanisms, is essential to ensure AI tools enhance learning outcomes ethically, equitably, and sustainably.

INTRODUCTION

Agentic AI refers to artificial intelligence systems that possess a degree of autonomy, decision-making capability, and goal-oriented behavior, enabling them to take actions proactively rather than merely responding to predefined commands. In the educational context, agentic AI can function as intelligent tutors, adaptive learning companions, automated curriculum designers, and even classroom management assistants, continuously adjusting learning pathways to suit each student's needs, context, and progress. Unlike traditional AI tools that are reactive and narrowly task-focused, agentic AI has the capacity to independently select strategies, anticipate learner needs, and engage in dynamic problem-solving, making it a potentially transformative force in education.

However, with this transformation comes a set of complex challenges that go beyond technical implementation. The very autonomy that makes agentic AI powerful also raises critical questions about control, accountability, and the societal values embedded within its design and operation. Policy plays a crucial role in setting the boundaries for responsible innovation, ensuring compliance with legal standards, and protecting educational integrity. Equity considerations are equally central—without deliberate safeguards, agentic AI risks amplifying existing inequalities, such as disparities in access to technology, digital literacy, and culturally relevant content. Governance, spanning both institutional and cross-sectoral mechanisms, is essential to ensure transparency, safeguard against misuse, and align AI systems with human-centered educational goals (Artsn & Bozkurt, 2025; Raheem & Hossain, 2025).

This chapter explores how policy, equity, and governance intersect to shape the future of agentic AI in education. It examines the current policy landscape, the risks and opportunities for equitable implementation, and the governance frameworks required to ensure ethical, inclusive, and sustainable adoption. By weaving together global trends, case examples, and forward-looking recommendations, the chapter aims to provide educators, policymakers, and technology leaders with a roadmap for harnessing agentic AI's potential while safeguarding against its unintended consequences. Ultimately, it argues that the future of AI in education will be determined not only by technological capabilities but by the human decisions that guide, regulate, and ethically embed those capabilities in learning environments.

POLICY LANDSCAPE FOR AGENTIC AI IN EDUCATION

Around the world, three layers shape how agentic AI enters classrooms: (1) horizontal AI frameworks, (2) data-protection and children's rights regimes, and (3) sector guidance for education. In the EU, the AI Act classifies education-related AI that decides admissions, evaluates learning outcomes, places learners, or proctors exams as "high-risk", triggering obligations for risk management, data governance, transparency, human oversight, and post-market monitoring. Article 6 ties these obligations to Annex III's education use-cases, with a narrow derogation where risk is demonstrably insignificant (FLI, 2025; Wilmerhale, 2024). In the United States, there is no omnibus AI law yet, but baseline protections come from FERPA (student records) and COPPA (online services for under-13s); a 2023 Executive Order (14110) directs federal agencies to advance safe, secure AI, including in education (Federal Register, 2023; FTC, 1998). The UK supplements UK-GDPR with the Children's Code (Age-Appropriate Design Code), setting 15 design standards for services likely to be accessed by children, widely relevant to edtech (ICO, 2024). China's 2023 Interim Measures for Generative AI impose provider duties on safety, data quality, transparency, and content governance for public gen-AI services that may be embedded in learning tools (China Aerospace Studies Institute, 2023). Singapore pairs voluntary testing and assurance via AI Verify with a 2024 Model AI Governance Framework for GenAI that schools and vendors can adapt for procurement and auditing (Infocomm Media Development Authority, 2024). Multilaterally, OECD AI Principles and UNESCO's Guidance for Generative AI in Education and Research provide widely referenced norms for human-centered, rights-respecting educational AI (OECD, 2024; UNESCO, 2023).

Gaps, Ambiguities, and Conflicting Regulations

Several cross-cutting frictions persist in the evolving policy landscape for agentic AI in education, each of which complicates the path toward coherent, enforceable, and equitable governance. One persistent challenge relates to scope and thresholds. In the European Union, for example, the AI Act's classification of certain educational applications as "high-risk" under Annex III has triggered ongoing debates among policymakers, legal practitioners, and edtech deployers. The key question is at what point a classroom tool that merely "steers" learning—such as an adaptive tutor recommending the next lesson—crosses into the territory of "evaluation" or "placement" with legal consequences. This distinction is not always clear-cut in practice, and proving eligibility for the Article 6 low-risk derogation requires careful evidence gathering and documentation. Disputes over scope not only create uncertainty for vendors and institutions but also risk inconsistent enforcement across EU member states (FLI, 2025; Williom Fry, 2024; Wilmerhale, 2024).

A second point of tension arises from the overlap between AI-specific obligations and pre-existing privacy and data-protection regimes. In most jurisdictions, student-facing AI systems are subject to dual layers of regulation: one focused on AI system safety, risk management, logging, human oversight, and transparency; the other centered on lawful data processing, data minimization, and age-appropriate consent or verification. In the United States, for instance, the Family Educational Rights and Privacy Act (FERPA) and the Children's Online Privacy Protection Act (COPPA) already constrain how student data can be collected and shared. In the United Kingdom, the General Data Protection Regulation (UK-GDPR) is reinforced by the Children's Code, which demands high privacy-by-default and age-appropriate design. In Brazil, the Lei Geral de Proteção de Dados (LGPD) similarly sets explicit safeguards for children's data. Yet these overlapping regimes are implemented with varying scope, terminology, and enforcement vigor, forcing deployers to reconcile potentially conflicting compliance requirements across jurisdictions—often without clear guidance on precedence (DLA Piper, 2024; FTC, 1998).

A third friction concerns limits on edtech commercialization. In the U.S., recent COPPA enforcement actions and proposed rule changes have sought to curtail behavioral advertising and tighten constraints on the reuse of student data for non-core educational purposes. While such measures aim to safeguard learners' privacy and prevent exploitative practices, they also limit revenue models that many smaller edtech providers rely on. Schools and districts are thus left with a narrower range of vendors, and in the absence of practical procurement guidelines, they may struggle to evaluate whether remaining options meet both pedagogical needs and evolving legal requirements (Perkins Coie, 2023; White Board Advisors, 2024).

The fourth area of ambiguity lies in assurance and audits. Many regulatory frameworks, particularly the EU AI Act, call for conformity assessment, third-party audits, and transparency obligations. However, education-specific standards for these processes are still underdeveloped. General AI assurance frameworks rarely address the unique risks of bias in educational contexts, such as discrimination against regional dialects in automated grading systems or inaccessibility for learners with disabilities. Even in countries with emerging voluntary testing ecosystems, such as Singapore's AI Verify initiative, there is still a shortage of benchmark datasets, audit protocols, and impact assessment templates tailored to the educational sector (Andreea et al., 2025; Madelaine, 2025).

Finally, policy velocity presents a temporal challenge. Privacy laws, such as COPPA or GDPR, are already enforceable and carry significant penalties for noncompliance. By contrast, some AI Act obligations in the EU will be phased in over several years. This staggered implementation creates timing gaps that force schools and vendors to make difficult sequencing decisions about what to prioritize first. In some cases, institutions may overcomply early in certain AI domains to reduce future retrofit costs; in others, they may delay AI-specific safeguards until the legal deadlines approach, creating uneven readiness across the sector (Madelaine, 2025).

Given the complexity and interdependence of these issues, a comparative table mapping each friction point against representative jurisdictions, relevant laws, enforcement timelines, and sector-specific guidance could serve as a valuable reference. This table would allow readers to quickly visualize how similar challenges manifest differently across regions and where harmonization efforts might be most impactful. It would also make explicit where guidance gaps persist—particularly in procurement, sector-specific audits, and jurisdictional scope definitions. The table provides an overview of cross-cutting regulatory frictions in agentic AI for education.

Table 1. Cross-cutting regulatory frictions in agentic AI for education

Friction Point	Description	Representative Jurisdictions	Relevant Laws / Instruments	Enforcement Timeline	Sector-Specific Guidance
Scope & Thresholds	Unclear boundaries between "learning support" vs. "evaluation/placement" triggering high-risk AI obligations.	EU	AI Act – Annex III (education uses), Article 6 low-risk derogation	Staged rollout: 2024–2026	Pending EC guidance notes on Annex III interpretation
Overlap: AI vs. Privacy Law	AI-specific duties (risk mgmt., oversight) overlap with privacy rules (lawful basis, minimization, age verification).	US, UK, Brazil	FERPA, COPPA (US); UK-GDPR + Children's Code; LGPD (Brazil)	Active	Student Privacy Compass (US), ICO Age-Appropriate Design Code (UK)
Edtech Commercialization Limits	Restrictions on behavioral advertising and secondary data use narrow vendor business models.	US	COPPA enforcement + proposed updates	Active; proposals in comment phase	FTC edtech compliance guidance
Assurance & Audits	General AI audit requirements lack education-specific benchmarks (e.g., bias in grading, accessibility).	EU, Singapore	AI Act (EU); AI Verify (Singapore)	EU phased; AI Verify voluntary	AI Verify methodology; no education-tailored audit protocols yet
Policy Velocity	Privacy protections enforceable now, AI rules phased in later—creates sequencing dilemmas.	EU, US, UK	GDPR/ UK-GDPR, COPPA, AI Act	Privacy laws active; AI Act phased 2024–2026	Varies; early compliance encouraged by some ministries

EQUITY CONSIDERATIONS IN AI-DRIVEN LEARNING ENVIRONMENTS

Risks of Bias, Exclusion, and Inequitable Access

Bias in agentic AI emerges when the systems are trained on datasets that fail to adequately represent the diversity of the learner population (Hughes et al., 2025). This can occur when the training data underrepresents certain demographic groups, overlooks linguistic and cultural variations, or embeds historical inequities from past educational practices. The effects of such bias can be subtle yet harmful—grading algorithms might penalize students for using regional dialects, adaptive learning platforms might incorrectly lower the difficulty level for learners from certain backgrounds, and recommendation systems could disproportionately direct female students away from STEM-related subjects. These biases undermine fairness and, if left unchecked, risk perpetuating cycles of educational inequality and limiting opportunities for already marginalized groups.

Exclusion occurs when AI systems are not designed to accommodate the full range of learner needs and contexts. For instance, students with disabilities may find that educational platforms lack compatibility with assistive technologies such as screen readers or alternative input devices. Language minorities may be disadvantaged when interfaces, instructions, or content are offered only in dominant languages, preventing them from fully engaging with the material. Cultural exclusion also arises when AI-generated resources reflect only a narrow set of pedagogical norms, historical narratives, or societal values, leaving students from different cultural backgrounds feeling disconnected from the learning process.

Inequitable access is often the cumulative outcome of bias and exclusion, and it can occur even in schools that appear technologically advanced. While students may have physical access to devices and AI-powered platforms, the content or system functionality may not be relevant, appropriate, or tailored to their specific needs. In these cases, access becomes superficial—students can log in and use the tools, but the benefits are unevenly distributed. This form of inequity can be particularly insidious, as it hides behind the appearance of inclusivity while continuing to disadvantage certain learners in practice.

Taken together, bias, exclusion, and inequitable access form an interconnected web of challenges that can quietly erode the promise of agentic AI in education. Even when these issues arise from different sources—such as skewed datasets, inaccessible design, or culturally narrow content—their impact often converges in a single outcome: certain learners are left behind. These systemic patterns set the stage for a broader and more persistent barrier to educational equity—the digital divide—where disparities in infrastructure, connectivity, and technological literacy amplify the very inequities AI was meant to address.

Digital Divide

The digital divide represents the gap between those who have reliable access to digital technologies and those who do not, a disparity that extends far beyond mere device ownership (Bentley et al., 2024; Božić, 2023). In the context of agentic AI in education, this divide can manifest in three critical dimensions: infrastructure, skills, and meaningful usage.

Infrastructure disparities refer to the unequal distribution of the physical and technological resources needed to access AI-powered learning environments. This includes stable internet connectivity, up-to-date hardware, adequate power supply, and access to secure learning platforms. In rural and low-income communities, internet service may be unreliable or prohibitively expensive, and devices may be outdated or shared among multiple family members, limiting consistent engagement with AI-based learning tools. Without addressing these foundational infrastructure issues, even the most advanced educational AI systems cannot deliver equitable benefits.

Skills gaps highlight the differences in digital literacy and competency between individuals who are adept at navigating technology and those who are not. These disparities affect not only students but also educators and parents, who may struggle to set up, manage, or troubleshoot AI-based learning applications. Limited skills in navigating digital platforms, interpreting AI-generated feedback, or integrating AI recommendations into learning activities can severely restrict the potential of AI tools, leaving some learners unable to fully participate in modern education.

Meaningful usage disparities occur when individuals technically have access to AI-driven learning systems but lack access to content and features that are relevant, inclusive, and pedagogically effective for their specific needs. This includes the absence of culturally responsive materials, a lack of linguistic diversity, and failure to adapt to local educational contexts. Even with strong infrastructure and basic digital skills, AI-powered education may fail to deliver value if it does not align with learners' lived realities. This gap risks creating a scenario where access is superficial technology is present, but its transformative potential remains untapped. Table 2 presents a summary of three dimensions of the digital divide in agentic AI-enhanced education.

Table 2. Dimensions of the digital divide in agentic AI-enhanced education

Dimension	Examples	Impact on Learners
Infrastructure	Unstable internet in rural schools; outdated computers; limited access to secure platforms	Limits ability to use AI tools consistently; interrupts learning flow; reduces exposure to AI-driven resources
Skills	Low digital literacy among students, teachers, or parents; lack of AI tool training	Underutilization of available technology; dependence on traditional methods; slower adaptation to AI-based learning
Meaningful Usage	AI tools available only in dominant languages; culturally irrelevant content; rigid pedagogy	Learners disengage; cultural alienation; reduced learning gains despite access to technology

These socio-economic divides not only limit the reach of AI-powered learning but also risk reinforcing pre-existing inequalities, creating a feedback loop in which disadvantaged groups are further marginalized in the knowledge economy.

Strategies to Ensure Inclusivity and Cultural Responsiveness

Mitigating inequities in AI-driven education requires a proactive, layered approach (Umoke et al., n.d.; Wang, 2025). On the design side, developers must embed fairness-aware machine learning techniques to reduce algorithmic bias and continuously audit their systems against diverse, representative datasets. Co-designing tools with educators and learners from varied socio-economic, linguistic, and cultural backgrounds ensures that the technology reflects a broad spectrum of needs and perspectives. Accessibility compliance—such as adherence to the Web Content Accessibility Guidelines (WCAG)—should be mandatory, ensuring that AI tools are functional for students with disabilities from the outset rather than as an afterthought.

Cultural responsiveness is equally important. AI platforms should integrate localized content, pedagogical norms, and examples that resonate with learners' lived experiences. Multilingual interfaces, inclusive imagery, and culturally relevant narratives can enhance engagement and promote a sense of belonging. On the policy side, governments can bridge infrastructure gaps by subsidizing devices, expanding broadband access in rural areas, and incentivizing the development of open-source AI tools tailored for public education systems. Public–private partnerships can pool resources and expertise to deliver context-sensitive solutions at scale.

Finally, monitoring and accountability mechanisms are critical. Educational institutions should conduct equity impact assessments for AI tools before adoption, evaluating not only technical performance but also differential impacts across demographic groups. Continuous feedback loops—where students, parents, and teachers can report inequities—allow for timely intervention. Equity in AI-driven education is not a static achievement but an ongoing process requiring vigilance, adaptability, and collective responsibility. Figure 1 presents the idea of how equitable AI in education works.

Figure 1. Conceptual overview of equitable AI in education

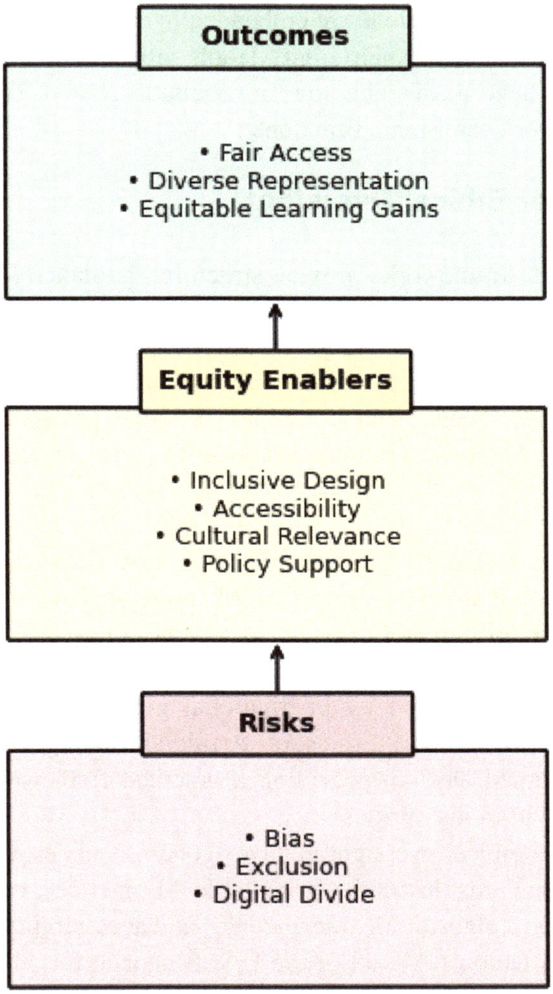

GOVERNANCE MODELS FOR RESPONSIBLE AI INTEGRATION

Ensuring the responsible integration of AI in education requires governance models that balance innovation with safeguards. These models must operate across multiple levels—school, institutional, national, and global—to ensure that ethical, cultural, and social considerations are embedded in every stage of AI deployment. Strong governance frameworks help align AI tools with human values, mitigate risks, and ensure that the benefits of technology are equitably shared. Table 3 summarizes the governance layers, their main functions.

Frameworks for Ethical Oversight

Ethical oversight frameworks provide structured guidance for the responsible development, deployment, and monitoring of AI in educational contexts. They ensure that AI tools and systems are aligned with pedagogical goals, protect learners' rights, and operate transparently and fairly. These frameworks serve as a foundation for institutions, governments, and international bodies to implement checks and balances that prevent misuse or unintended negative consequences of AI in learning environments.

- At the institutional level, schools and universities can form dedicated AI ethics committees that review proposed AI tools, approve their use, and continuously monitor outcomes. These committees ensure that AI implementations support educational objectives and uphold ethical standards. Internal policies can be informed by international guidance, such as UNESCO's Recommendation on the Ethics of Artificial Intelligence or the IEEE's Ethically Aligned Design, providing a practical framework for day-to-day governance within institutions.
- National-level ethical oversight involves governments establishing legal and regulatory standards that define acceptable AI practices, particularly regarding data privacy, algorithmic transparency, and accessibility. Regulations like the European Union's AI Act or the U.S. Blueprint for an AI Bill of Rights set expectations for developers and institutions while safeguarding citizens' rights. Effective national frameworks consider local cultural, social, and economic contexts, ensuring that AI technologies are both compliant and relevant to the needs of learners in each country.
- Global ethical oversight emphasizes international cooperation to harmonize AI standards and promote shared best practices. Platforms such as the OECD AI Principles, UNESCO's ethical AI guidelines, and the Global Partnership on AI facilitate cross-border knowledge sharing and standard-setting. These

global frameworks help align national strategies, reduce regulatory inconsistencies, and provide a consistent approach to protecting learners' rights, fostering responsible AI adoption across diverse educational contexts.

Stakeholder Roles

A robust governance ecosystem depends on the active participation of all stakeholders:

- Governments play a central role in establishing the legal, financial, and regulatory framework for AI governance in education. They provide the necessary infrastructure for oversight, ensure that AI deployments comply with ethical, safety, and equity standards, and can encourage responsible innovation through funding, grants, or public-private partnerships. By setting clear policies and accountability mechanisms, governments create an environment where AI can be deployed safely and effectively in learning contexts.
- Schools and educators act as the frontline implementers of AI technologies in classrooms. They evaluate AI tools to ensure alignment with pedagogical objectives, monitor their impact on student learning outcomes, and identify potential problems such as algorithmic bias or excessive reliance on automation. Educators' practical insights and continuous feedback are critical for ensuring that AI supports, rather than undermines, teaching and learning processes.
- Technology companies are responsible for designing and developing AI systems that are transparent, explainable, and capable of mitigating bias. To create tools that meet real classroom needs, companies should engage in co-design processes with educators and other stakeholders. By prioritizing ethical design, accountability, and practical applicability, technology providers help ensure that AI tools enhance learning experiences while maintaining trust and fairness.
- Communities and parents provide essential perspectives on the cultural appropriateness, inclusivity, and broader social impact of AI in education. They can act as external monitors, ensuring that AI systems respect student privacy, dignity, and well-being. Their engagement helps bridge the gap between policy and practice, reinforcing a governance model that is accountable to the learners and communities it serves.

The effective governance of AI in education emerges from the dynamic interaction among these stakeholders. Rather than a top-down imposition, governance becomes a shared process where governments, educators, technology companies, and communities collectively shape ethical, safe, and equitable AI practices. Mutual accountability ensures that decisions reflect diverse perspectives and respond to the practical realities of educational environments.

Transparency, Accountability, and Participatory Governance Mechanisms

Transparent and participatory governance mechanisms build trust in AI systems by making their operations visible and understandable to all stakeholders.

- Transparency in AI governance ensures that decision-making processes, underlying data sources, and system limitations are clearly documented and accessible to all stakeholders. By providing dashboards, audit reports, or explainable AI interfaces, institutions make the operation of AI systems understandable to teachers, students, parents, and policymakers. Transparent practices foster trust, allowing stakeholders to see how decisions are made and identify potential biases or errors.
- Accountability establishes clear mechanisms for addressing errors, harm, or unintended consequences caused by AI systems. This includes defining liability frameworks, conducting independent audits, and performing regular impact assessments. By setting explicit channels for redress, stakeholders are assured that AI systems are not operating without oversight and that responsible parties can be held answerable for their decisions.
- Participation involves actively including teachers, students, parents, and community representatives in the design, deployment, and governance of AI tools. Mechanisms such as participatory workshops, citizen juries, and public consultations ensure that diverse perspectives shape policy and technological choices. Engaging stakeholders in this way enhances the legitimacy, relevance, and fairness of AI systems in educational contexts.

Effective AI governance is dynamic, evolving alongside technological advancements, societal expectations, and educational needs. By embedding transparency, accountability, and participation into governance models, educational institutions can ensure that AI supports outcomes that are fair, inclusive, and aligned with human values. Continuous adaptation helps maintain trust and responsiveness as AI tools become more sophisticated.

Table 3. Comparative summary of governance layers for responsible AI in education

Governance Layer	Main Functions	Example Mechanisms
Institutional	• Align AI tools with curriculum and pedagogy • Monitor ethical compliance at the school/ university level • Address local safeguarding concerns	• Academic ethics committees • Institutional AI review boards • Teacher-led evaluation panels
National	• Set AI usage standards for education • Regulate data protection and student rights • Fund equitable access initiatives	• Ministry of Education AI policies • National EdTech accreditation programs • Legislative data privacy frameworks
Global	• Provide universal ethical principles • Promote cross-border interoperability • Encourage inclusive and culturally sensitive AI use	• UNESCO AI in Education Guidelines • OECD AI Principles • IEEE Ethically Aligned Design standards

FUTURE DIRECTIONS

The rapid pace of AI innovation in education necessitates policy frameworks that are both coherent and adaptive. Coherence requires that policies at institutional, national, and international levels are aligned, reducing conflicts or gaps that could undermine governance. Adaptive policies, on the other hand, are flexible enough to accommodate emerging AI technologies, evolving educational practices, and shifting societal expectations. Policymakers should adopt iterative regulatory processes that include regular review cycles, stakeholder feedback mechanisms, and scenario-based planning to anticipate potential risks. Integration of best practices from global AI governance initiatives, such as UNESCO's Recommendation on the Ethics of Artificial Intelligence or the OECD AI Principles, can guide while allowing for contextual adaptation to local cultural, socio-economic, and educational realities. Such frameworks should also define clear responsibilities for governments, educators, technology providers, and communities, fostering a shared approach to oversight and accountability.

Promoting AI innovation in education while safeguarding learners' rights requires governance models that balance opportunity with risk mitigation. One approach is a risk-tiered model, where AI systems are categorized based on potential impact on learners and society. Low-risk tools, such as adaptive learning apps with limited data collection, may be fast-tracked for deployment, whereas high-risk systems, such as predictive analytics affecting student progression, undergo rigorous review and ethical assessment. Sandboxes or controlled experimental environments can enable institutions to pilot innovative AI solutions under supervision, facilitating learning and iteration without exposing students to untested risks. Embedding privacy-by-design, bias mitigation, and explainability principles in AI development ensures that technological innovation does not compromise ethical standards. Additionally, multi-stakeholder advisory boards comprising educators, policymakers, ethicists, and technologists can provide ongoing guidance, balancing the pursuit of educational innovation with the protection of rights, equity, and trust.

The long-term vision for AI in education should prioritize equity, inclusivity, and ethical governance. AI systems should be designed to reduce disparities rather than reinforce them, offering personalized support that accounts for diverse learning needs, socio-economic backgrounds, and cultural contexts. Ethical governance requires transparency in decision-making, accountability for errors or harms, and meaningful participation of all stakeholders—students, teachers, parents, and communities—in shaping AI policies and practices. By combining adaptive policy frameworks with innovation-risk balancing models, educational institutions can create an ecosystem where AI tools empower learners, enhance pedagogical outcomes, and foster lifelong learning while upholding human-centered values. This vision positions AI not merely as a technological adjunct but as a catalyst for inclusive, fair, and high-quality education globally.

CONCLUSION

This study highlights the critical importance of structured, ethical, and inclusive governance frameworks in the deployment of AI in education. Key insights underscore that effective AI integration requires transparency, accountability, and stakeholder participation at every level—from institutional committees to national policies and global guidelines. The research also emphasizes that AI's potential to enhance learning outcomes and equity can only be realized if governance mechanisms proactively address risks such as bias, exclusion, and data privacy concerns.

A central theme emerging from this analysis is the need for collaboration across sectors. Governments, educational institutions, technology developers, and communities must work together to co-create policies, monitor AI applications, and ensure that innovations align with pedagogical goals and societal values. Such multi-stakeholder engagement fosters mutual accountability, strengthens trust, and enables AI systems to serve as tools for inclusive and effective education rather than sources of unintended harm.

Finally, the study calls for proactive governance approaches that anticipate challenges before they arise. Reactive measures, implemented only after errors or harms occur, are insufficient in the context of rapidly evolving AI technologies.

By embedding foresight, risk assessment, and adaptive policy mechanisms into AI governance, stakeholders can ensure that AI-enabled educational tools remain ethical, equitable, and aligned with human-centered values. Ultimately, this proactive, collaborative, and ethically guided approach provides a roadmap for leveraging AI to transform education responsibly and sustainably.

REFERENCES

Andreea, S., Vasileios, R., & Katerina, D. (2025). *Conformity Assessments under the EU AI Act: A step-by step guide.*

Artsn, M., & Bozkurt, A. (2025). Charting new horizons: What agentic artificial intelligence (AI) promises in the educational landscape. *EDULEARN25 Proceedings*, 2019–2023.

Bentley, S. V, Naughtin, C. K., Mcgrath, M. J., Irons, J. L., Patrick, ·, & Cooper, S. (2024). The digital divide in action: how experiences of digital technology shape future relationships with artificial intelligence. *AI and Ethics 2024 4:4, 4*(4), 901–915. DOI: 10.1007/s43681-024-00452-3

Božić, V. (2023). Artifical Intelligence as the Reason and the Solution of Digital Divide. *Language Education and Technology, 3*(2), 96–109. https://langedutech.com/letjournal/index.php/let/article/view/53

China Aerospace Studies Institute. (2023). *Interim Measures for the Management of Generative Artificial Intelligence Services.* https://www.cac.gov.cn/2023-07/13/c_1690898327029107.htm

Federal Register. (2023). *Safe, Secure, and Trustworthy Development and Use of Artificial Intelligence.* https://www.federalregister.gov/documents/2023/11/01/2023-24283/safe-secure-and-trustworthy-development-and-use-of-artificial-intelligence

FLI. (2025). *Annex III: High-Risk AI Systems Referred to in Article 6(2) | EU Artificial Intelligence Act.* https://artificialintelligenceact.eu/annex/3

FTC. (1998). *Children's Online Privacy Protection Rule ("COPPA").* https://www.ftc.gov/legal-library/browse/rules/childrens-online-privacy-protection-rule-coppa

Hughes, L., Dwivedi, Y. K., Malik, T., Shawosh, M., Albashrawi, M. A., Jeon, I., Dutot, V., Appanderanda, M., Crick, T., De', R., Fenwick, M., Gunaratnege, S. M., Jurcys, P., Kar, A. K., Kshetri, N., Li, K., Mutasa, S., Samothrakis, S., Wade, M., & Walton, P. (2025). AI Agents and Agentic Systems: A Multi-Expert Analysis. *Journal of Computer Information Systems, 65*(4), 489–517. DOI: 10.1080/08874417.2025.2483832

ICO. (2024). *Introduction to the Children's code.* https://ico.org.uk/for-organisations/uk-gdpr-guidance-and-resources/childrens-information/childrens-code-guidance-and-resources/introduction-to-the-childrens-code/

Infocomm Media Development Authority. (2024). *Model Al Governance Framework for Generative Al Fostering a Trusted Ecosystem.* https://aiverifyfoundation.sg/wp-content/uploads/2024/05/Model-AI-Governance-Framework-for-Generative-AI-May-2024-1-1.pdf

Madelaine, H. (2025). *The European Commission opens public consultation on high-risk AI systems.* https://www.insideglobaltech.com/2025/06/24/the-european-commission-opens-public-consultation-on-high-risk-ai-systems/

OECD. (2024). *AI Principles Overview.* https://oecd.ai/en/ai-principles

Perkins Coie. (2023). *FTC's COPPA Enforcement Action Provides Lessons for Edtech Providers.* https://perkinscoie.com/insights/update/ftcs-coppa-enforcement-action-provides-lessons-edtech-providers

Piper, D. L. A. (2024). *Data protection laws in Brazil - Data Protection Laws of the World.* https://www.dlapiperdataprotection.com/index.html

Raheem, T., & Hossain, G. (2025). Agentic AI Systems: Opportunities, Challenges, and Trustworthiness. *2025 IEEE International Conference on Electro Information Technology (EIT)*, 618–624. DOI: 10.1109/eIT64391.2025.11103638

Umoke, C. C., Nwangbo, S. O., & Onwe, O. A. (n.d.). *AI-Driven Educational Policy Design: Enhancing Equity and Access through Intelligent Data Analytics. International Journal of Computer Science and Mathematical Theory.* IJCSMT International Journal of Computer Science and Mathematical Theory., DOI: 10.56201/ijcsmt.v11.no3.2025.pg1.19

UNESCO. (2023). *Guidance for generative AI in education and research.* https://www.unesco.org/en/open-access/cc-sa

Wang, V. (2025). Ethics and Equity in AI-Driven Education. In *AI Integration Into Andragogical Education* (pp. 231–254). IGI Global Scientific Publishing. DOI: 10.4018/979-8-3373-0502-8.ch010

White Board Advisors. (2024). *Proposed Changes to Federal Privacy Rules May Impact Edtech.* https://whiteboardadvisors.com/proposed-changes-to-federal-privacy-rules-coppa-edtech-impact/

Williom Fry. (2024). *Is your Annex III AI System High-Risk? Definitely Maybe.* https://www.williamfry.com/knowledge/is-your-annex-iii-ai-system-high-risk-definitely-maybe

Wilmerhale. (2024). *What Are High-Risk AI Systems Within the Meaning of the EU's AI Act, and What Requirements Apply to Them?* https://www.wilmerhale.com/en/insights/blogs/wilmerhale-privacy-and-cybersecurity-law/20240717-what-are-highrisk-ai-systems-within-the-meaning-of-the-eus-ai-act-and-what-requirements-apply-to-them

Chapter 3
Interdisciplinary Insights: Cognitive Science, Sociology, and AI in Learning Systems

Irim Shehzadi
https://orcid.org/0009-0004-3121-1369
PMAS Arid Agricultural University, Pakistan

Jan Vrba
https://orcid.org/0000-0002-8404-5091
Akademia Jagiellonska w Toruniu, Czech Republic

Sunehra Khan Sajin
https://orcid.org/0009-0008-2409-7632
University of Dhaka, Bangladesh

Sultanov Sirojbek Xabibullayevich
Tashkent State Transport University, Uzbekistan

ABSTRACT

This chapter explores the transformative impact of agentic AI in education through cognitive, social, and institutional lenses. It argues that AI should augment rather than replace human learning, ensuring cognitive autonomy and metacognitive control. Socially, AI must promote equity by respecting diverse learner contexts. Institutionally, AI should enhance—rather than displace—the educator's role, embedding ethical oversight and human judgment. The chapter calls for co-evolutionary frameworks that position AI as a dynamic partner in education and outlines the need for ethical policies, participatory design, and adaptive institutions to create inclusive, resilient learning environments.

DOI: 10.4018/979-8-3373-4621-2.ch003

INTRODUCTION

An increase in agentic AI-artificial intelligence systems that can make autonomous choices and behave flexibly is a revelational event in terms of the structure and delivery of learning environments. In contrast to sedentary tools or fixed training platforms, agentie AI solutions like the intelligent tutor, conversational agent or recommender engine work more or less proactively. Not only do these systems aid learners, but they also monitor, analyze and take action on human behavior to determine learning processes, sometimes without the explicit human supervision. Since AI and, more broadly, machine learning are taking over the functions previously taken by teachers, peers, and coaches, it is necessary to comprehend not only the manner of operations of these systems, but the ways in which they interactively partake in shaping cognitive and social dimensions of human learning.

Understanding the entire picture of human-AI communication requires a holistic viewing framework of cognitive science, sociology and computer science (S. Shkurko, 2025; Walter, 2024). Cognitive science is useful to understand the functioning of learners, their attentional allocation, and the need to sustain the motivation towards the AI-enabled feedback. Sociology provides ways of learning more about the contextual backgrounds and influences of these interactions, in terms of wider social norms, identity formations, and institutional forms. Computer science brings the technical foundations of how AI agents are modeled, trained, and deployed- along with the implicitly provided assumptions, affordances and limitations that these systems entail. A silo approach is leading to neglect of important dynamics; it will only be through multidisciplinary synthesis that the dynamics of feedback cycles and emergent properties that characterize human-AI learning ecosystems can be explored.

The chapter aims to answer some of these cross-cutting questions where these disciplines intersect: what happens to learning when mediated through agentic AI? What is the cognitive and motivational effects of the interactions that learners have with autonomous systems? What is the impact of social identities and cultural norms on such interactions? And what kind of changes should educational institutions undergo to integrate AI, properly and safely, into their systems and operations? To provide answers to these questions, it is organized into four main sections. It considers first the cognitive basis of human-AI learning such as load, memory and motivation. Second, it examines the social processes of human-AI interaction, specifically identity, trust and coagency. Third, it discusses the manner in which institutions are transforming as a result of AI meshing in pedagogy, assessment, and policy. It lastly synthesizes these views to suggest ways of designing equitable, adaptive AI-infused learning systems. With this structure, this chapter seeks to provide a minced, interdisciplinary idea of how the agentic AI has not only been supplementary, but is also transfiguring the way we learn and teach.

COGNITIVE FOUNDATIONS

The implementation of agentic AI in the process of learning has created a drastic alteration in the way of engaging and managing the cognitive process of attention, memory, and motivation. AI systems may dynamically engage the learners unlike the static learning materials, which make adjustments according to the needs of the learners and personal guidance. Such abilities can maximize cognitive loads, maintain concentration and augment memory consolidation. Nonetheless, there also exist crucial issues based on dependency, cognitive offloading, and lack of metacognition involvement that need to be analyzed critically through the prism of cognitive psychology.

Cognitive Load Modulation

Modulation of cognitive load, which is based on Cognitive Load Theory (CLT) proposed by Sweller (1988), is one of the major ways that agentic AI is affecting the learning process. CLT assumes that the capacity of human working memory is limited, and the learning may take place ineffectively at the time when this capacity is overfilled because of bad instructional design or complexity of material to be learned. Cognitive load is essentially divided into three dimensions; intrinsic load (the inherent difficulty of the content), extraneous load (the inefficiencies of the delivery of the content), and germane load (the mental effort applied toward processing). Systems of agentic AI such as intelligent tutoring systems (ITS), adaptive learning platforms, and virtual instructors, which are powered by AI, are capable of controlling and optimizing these types of loads in real-time through interaction with learning users.

An example is that intelligent tutoring systems such as MATHia developed by Carnegie Learning contains a machine learning algorithm to automatically identify that a student is not managing a particular concept and scaffold accordingly. Should a student pick an answer too often, or be slow to come up with the answer, the AI can simplify the explanation or deconstruct a problem down to easier steps or even visually point out important details. This assists in reducing extraneous load by separation of irrelevant or unnecessary data and assists germane load by focusing the attention of the learner towards valuable processes presented in the solving of a problem (Van Merriënboer & Sweller, 2005). Likewise, Knewton manufactures an individualized learning tool called Alta, which stores information based on the interactions of students and generates individualized learning paths in order to teach each student to maximize the concepts that he/she has shown to have trouble with therefore ensuring the instruction will be suitable to the existing mental grasp of the student.

Adaptive pacing is another potent tool through which agentic AI can control the cognitive load. In a regular classroom, or fixed e-learning setting, most students are expected to learn at the same pace, despite their individual backgrounds and individual learning pace. Against cognitive overload, agentic AI systems can sense indications: i.e., repeated wrong answers or lowered frequency of interaction rate and slow down accordingly. To pick an example, an AI-supported language learning application, such as Duolingo, reduces the decrease of a deluge of new words whenever there is less accuracy in the response of learners, thus avoiding its overwhelming and supplying more opportunity to entrench the novice vocabulary into long-term memory.

In addition to the segmentation of the content and its pacing, artificial intelligence may be used to facilitate multimodal content adaptation in environmental cognition to accommodate other cognitive types. Eye-tracking, facial expression or how a person talks can be analyzed to give hints on whether the learner is getting lost or bored and take actions by shoving off the wordy text to pictorial diagrams or analogies or providing audio descriptions. This responsiveness does not only contend with extraneous load but also makes the learner more involved and makes it easier to assimilate new information with already existing knowledge schemas and hence boosts germane load.

Also, agentic AI has the capacity to strengthen metacognitive plans that facilitate cognitive efficiency. Such systems as Metacog and the ASSISTments give feedback not only about correctness but also about a solution strategy, asking learners to think about their thought process and change their strategies. Such AI systems allow self-regulated learning, which is essential to effectively deal with intrinsic and germane load, by helping learners understand how their minds work.

Attention and Memory

Focusing and remembering are core mental processes during the learning process, and neither one takes place without significant emotional and motivational involvement of the learner. The agentic AI systems, including watching, interpreting, and acting on the emotional and behavioral cues, provide new opportunities to assist in the adjustment of attention and optimize encoding in the memory. By observing the behavior of the learner in real-time e.g. which buttons are pushed the most, how long a pause is taken, which navigational decisions are made, etc. such systems are able to detect indicators of loss of interest or cognitive overload. More sophisticated systems can include eye-tracking, analyses of facial expressions or even physiologically based measures (e.g., heart rate variability) to measure the degree of concentration, expression of fatigue, or even frustration. When these states are identified, it becomes possible to introduce interventions like motivational messages, instructions rephrasing, or dynamic difficulty changes interventions-another sort of adaptive feedback that can reengage one and contribute to a meaningful process of learning.

Such interventions are informed by the principles of affective computing that is the branch of computer science linked to psychology, and it entails the detection and reaction to human feelings within the context of computerized systems (Cambria, 2016). To illustrate, in case a learner continually fails at a problem, AI tutor, such as AutoTutor, can deduce possible frustration and act through empathetic feedback, encouraging messages, or hints without relaying the answer (DMello & Graesser, 2012). On the one hand, this approach decreases counterproductive emotions that may interfere with attention and, on the other hand, keeps a learner within his/her zone of proximal development (L. S. Vygotsky, 2020) which is that zone of learning where a learner is challenged adequately but not too much to the point that his/her progress can no longer be facilitated. Controlling the emotional-climate of the learning experience, AI systems ensure the right level of arousal, which acts as key to encoding of the newly acquired data into long-term memory (Tyng et al., 2017).

Besides, cognitive involvement onto personalized mechanisms reinforces further the personal involvement. The agentic AI systems are frequently informed by the reinforcement learning models which adapt the timing of feedback, its type, and frequency of the feedback going by an individual learner profile. As an example, ALEKS (Assessment and Learning in Knowledge Spaces) models learning using data and decides when a student should be able to review, proceed, or re-learn. In active reinforcement, ALEKS not only maintains interest since the sequence of the instructions is based on the level of knowledge the learner has already reached, but also facilitates spaced repetition, another strategy that improves memory, hence enhancing the long-term retention (Kang, 2016). Such systems are successful in lessening the processes of making cognitive decisions of what the learners want to learn next. In so doing, they are able to save their attentional resources and concentrate more on the current content.

Moreover, when the context of learning involves the emotional engagement and relevance, the attention and memorization processes are strengthened, which can be achieved through the means in part of agentic AI. As an example, affective conversations (e.g., the celebration of a learner achievement or concern in case of failure by an AI companion) may foster the feeling of social presence even in online settings. This connection has been observed to increase attention attainability as well as student perseverance (Kim & Biocca, 1997). Such emotional intelligence cannot be described as unrealistic as well because systems, such as Replika and Woebot, albeit aiming to assist people with mental health complications, show that, even when it comes to mental health treatment, the power of the human connection can be achieved through the means of emotionally charged personalized communication with AI agents.

Cognitive Risks

Although agentic AI systems promise to provide exceptional value in learning support, new risks on cognitive grounds are introduced once the learners have started to outsource crucial cognitive functions to machines. Among them, there is the issue of cognitive offloading, or the process of delegating a task that could otherwise be performed internally with the help of external computing systems. This can be seen in an educational setting where some learners rely too much on AI in order to memorize facts, learn a procedure, or to help them solve a problem as opposed to learning directly. Such delegation has the potential of boosting efficiency in the short run, particularly in routine or repetitive jobs but it can also be done at the expense of deep learning and skill building.

Indicatively, a student who uses math solving AI tools such as Photomath or Wolfram Alpha can get step-by-step answers even though they do not appreciate the reasoning behind the mathematics puzzle. May though these tools are helpful with verifications and aids, when it comes to the normal habits of dependence, the useditting may inculcate to the learner to ignore the mental energy and the learning and retention may be superficial. This may dysfunctionally affect metacognitive regulation, namely, the skill to personally evaluate knowledge, and recognize gaps in knowledge, and in order to handle this, adjustment strategies (Flavell, 1979). By not having to grapple with error identification, reflections on errors, or when to ask assistance any longer, students may never acquire the skills that are required in independent learning and resiliency in academia.

The second danger is the loss of critical thinking and problem-solving skills, including situations when the learners use responses by the AI without analyzing them. AI tutors and chatbots tend to be confident and fluent in their answers thereby resulting in over-trusting the machine even in cases where the system is not correct or in context at the right time. It is especially risky in critical or formative learning contexts, like medical training, legal study, or scientific research, where the unexamined trust of machine-produced outputs may perpetuate a misconception or other unethical decision-making. A study by Thomas Metzinger, (2019) cautions that once learners lack knowledge on rightful adoption of AI literacy and ability to critically evaluate, they stand a higher chance of uncritically following recommendations, dimming their judgment and autonomy.

In addition, the danger of excessive dependence increases among the learners with a lack of confidence, previous knowledge, or opportunities of alternative support. When this happens, potentially the AI systems end up being default epistemic authorities because one only believes in them due to their perceived lack of alternatives rather than a result of their transparency or explanations. Such a dynamic can disproportionately impact the marginalized in certain settings or learners in under-resourced environments, furthering the historically inequitable state of education. Unless well-scaffolded, systems enabled by AI have the potential to unwittingly increase dependence, instead of empowerment or agency.

In this regard, to overcome these risks, it would be important to build AI systems with the innate capacity to support metacognition and critical reflection. As an example, intelligent tutors may occasionally require a learner to justify his or her answers before being told the answer, or provide a what-if situation to encourage more critical thinking. Learning tools such as Cognitive Tutor and ASSISTments have started to include such functions in which they are prompted to describe their strategies or to provide feedback upon errors (Heffernan & Heffernan, 2014). Moreover, educational curriculum should introduce AI literacy as a basic skill which would not only provide students with information about operating AI tools, but also on how to challenge them or conflict them with other information and how these facts can be verified and to what extent automation should be applied as compared to direct intervention.

SOCIAL DYNAMICS AND IDENTITY

Nevertheless, even though the brain processes are at the core of the learning process of an individual, the social context of the interaction between humans and an AI is just as important as brain processes in educational experiences. When learners interact with AI systems, they are not interacting in a vacuum, they arrive with sociocultural expectations, identity postures and assumptions of roles that come to play within the practice of perceiving and or communicating with AI tutors, coaches and peers agents. Being in the core of social psychology and cultural circumstances, these are the factors that mediate trust, engagement and the perception of artificial intelligence as a viable learning partner. The trend towards agentic AI as an ability to take actions, modify its actions and behave in a perceived intentional manner is problematic to traditional hierarchies and norms within an educational context.

Socio-Cultural Norms

Socio-cultural norms are critical as they determine the learning process among learners, their anticipations, behaviors, and perceptions concerning AI in the learning space. Such norms determine what should be appropriate, credible, and trustworthy in a definite cultural/social group and, therefore, have a direct effect on the relationship between learners and AI tutors, coaches, or assistants. According to high power-distance cultures (typical of most Asia and the Middle East), educational authority is traditionally viewed as the preserve of wise human teachers in the form of instruction, in addition, moral teachings and emotional guidance. Under this situation, learners might feel that AI lacks the needed authority, empathy or cultural knowledge to be able to assist in meaningful instruction, which can adversely affect their engagement or trust in assisted learning environments that involve AI.

In contrast, AI can be perceived as an inseparable component of the learning environment on a greater scale in the societies where technological integration is advanced, including Scandinavian countries or South Korea. The commonly observed aspect is that in such settings the AI agents are not considered as a substitute to the teaching staff but as players or digital companions through which people learn. This represents a more culturally embedded ease of automation and machine-driven decision-making that may lead to further untroubled integration of AI into training and informal education context (Selwyn, 2019).

Besides a cultural context, individual identifications also filter the actions of the learners and AI. Age is especially suspect: digital natives (those that have developed in a world surrounded by technology) tend to be more comfortable communicating with AI and, in some cases, anthropomorphize said systems or treat it as an equal.

It also affects AI interactions because of gender and language background. To illustrate, it has been found that female students as well as linguistically diverse ones might feel less comfortable or trust AI systems that are not inclined to support conveying the principle of inclusive design or represent the style of communication with them (Buolamwini, 2018). Prejudges baked into the AI systems e.g. insensitivity towards non native accents or different skin color in a speech recognition tools, can generate alienation and suspiciousness, and amplify the sense of marginality in least represented communities.

A good example is chatbots AI in higher learning. Though some of the students might find it good that they get quick and consistent support through AI, other students, especially first-generation students or those belonging to underrepresented groups of people, might not want their support to come in the field of AI, but rather touched by people. This highlights the value of being culturally responsive in designing AI to consider not just the functional requirements of learners but also consider their socio-emotional and identity-related experiences.

Trust, Accountability, and Perceived Agency

Effective and ethical collaboration between human and AI in education is characterized by trust, accountability and perceived agency. There are no automatic privileges given to AI systems; therefore, trust has to be earned toward consistent, transparent and culturally sensitive interactions. The more learners think the system is really transparent, statistics are honest and it shows awareness of their own needs and situations, the more likely, they will actively interact with AI. This trust can also improve motivation, build autonomy and develop more profound learning. Nevertheless, the very concept of trust in AI is weak and prone to degradation caused by their faults, bias, or adversarial examples.

As an example, say an AI tutor is always prompting feedback that comes across as peripheral to whatever a learner might be working on. One who makes this claim of irrelevance and misalignment will eventually lose trust in the answers given by the system. According to research conducted by Holmes et al. (2019), students were less inclined to reading or executing AI-generated suggestions of writing when feedback was ambiguous or did not correlate with earlier entries. In these cases, the learners might lose interest in the lesson and thus refuse to use the technology or might end up over-relying on its use due to confusion and this is counterproductive to learning.

Agency, as it is perceived also makes a difference. By having a feeling that they control the learning process and can make an informed choice connected with the use of the AI tool, learners are more likely to feel the ownership and responsibility concerning their results. On the other extreme, AI systems can be presented in a manner in which learners perceive the systems to be empowered when they work in opaque ways or where learning takes place in a one-sided manner. Such disproportion may result in the excessive trust in AI suggestions or, conversely, the denial of AI input as a whole. Both consequences interfere with the synergetic possibility of human and machine.

These dynamics also get difficult due to the problem of accountability. In more established learning establishments, the lines of accountability are more succinct-teachers lead the process of an instruction, students learn and the given institution has the supervisor role. In artificial intelligence (AI) facilitated environments these lines are blurred. When a student completes a bad grade on a paper that the AI taught him how to do, whose fault is it? The student that has got the wrong idea of what the AI suggests? The AI itself? Which teacher incorporated the tool? Or the architects that did not foresee the abuse at all? Such a vagueness is highly problematic from both ethical and practical considerations. Once responsibility is not clearly assigned, one will feel hard to correct the mistakes, enhance the system workability or safeguard the learners against injuries (Williamson & Eynon, 2020).

These issues are why critical AI literacy is such an important topic to develop: an understanding not only of how AI systems are constructed, but also of their weaknesses and consequences in societal and technological terms. The point is that, by teaching learners how to question, analyze and reason about the AI-generated content, teachers will enable them to become thoughtful users instead of obedient recipients of the machine output. To illustrate, it is possible to train students to triangulate the AI feedback with their human guidance or any other trusted resource in the attempt to reinforce both critical thinking and trust in the system.

Co-Agency Concept

The idea of co-agency or collective involvement of not only humans but also AI systems in the achievement of a common purpose provides an interesting viewpoint in the study of the process of redefining roles in AI-mediated learning. Historically, educational agency was quite asymmetrical: teachers, with authority and teaching purpose, positioned themselves as able to instruct; students positioned themselves as able to be instructed or to reject or interpret. In an AI-augmented space, however, this order is broken. Smart systems have now become prompters, providers of feedback, scaffold decisions, and learning pathways in real time hence, making them active participants in the learning process instead of being mere tools.

This change to distributed agency produces opportunities and tensions. On the one side, the independence of AI systems in terms of personalization and responsiveness can make learners feel empowered. The student who had problems in math, as an example, can be helped by an AI tutor that would comprehend trends in misunderstanding and create personalized scaffolding, thereby building confidence and competence. Such blending coagency involving AI atop rather than replacing the human capacity can endorse learner self-direction and enthusiasm.

Conversely, coagency can as well reduce the feeling of control by a learner. In cases where AI systems control much of the learning process- either disregarding student decisions, enforcing linear trajectories, or overriding user input- AI systems can unintentionally destroy learner agency. Such systems may in some cases view as intrusive or even patronizing when the AI recommends against what students want to achieve, do not fit into the cultural situation they are in or are just not learning in their preferred way. The created dissonance may result in lack of engagement or blinded trust in the results promised by AI, both of which will impede the growth of critical thinking and self-managed learning.

Such dynamics bring about significant issues regarding negotiation and pliability in coagentic systems. Should students be making decisions and troubleshooting--and learning to do so--challenges AI recommendations? This would enhance so-called epistemic agency, or the process of knowledge construction in which students are the owners. However, such resistance entails that learners learn to disregard AI suggestions when and how to, which not all students may do, especially younger or less assertive students.

On the other hand, in the event that AI systems decide to resort to the selection of learners, rather than making pedagogically superior decisions on their own, would it constitute a correct decision? In that case, the system would have to prioritize both of the following: the need to respect learner agency and the need to enforce effective learning. E.g., AI writing help may be able to suggest a complex re-restructuring of a student paragraph but what happens when the student actually wants their original copy should the system support their preference to maintain motivation? Or challenge it gently to make sure that one develops skills?

To work around the challenges of this balance involves the design of the AI systems and their negotiation capabilities that should be flexible and able to alter the locus of control depending on the specific needs, capabilities, and objectives of the learner. Transparency mechanisms (e.g., "Why were these recommendations given to me?"), opt-in levels of autonomy (e.g., "guided" vs. "exploratory" modes), and meta-cognitive carefully-designed messages that motivate learners to consider their choices may be part of such systems.

INSTITUTIONAL ADAPTATION

With agentic artificial intelligence becoming part of classrooms, learning platforms, and administrative agendas, educational institutions are going through profound structural changes. The systems are not simply supplementing current practices, but transforming underlying routines, re-conceptualizing the purposes of teachers and students, and creating new logics of assessment, accountability and policy delivery. The core of this change is a feedback loop that is becoming increasingly circular and forms the basis of educational practices, and educational priorities and limitations in turn influence how AI is designed, implemented and assessed.

Instructional and Assessment Routines

Perhaps the most explicit and impactful change that AI is bringing to education regards the organization and operationalization of instructional and assessment routine. However, historically, there has been a lot of episodic and summative education assessment where an assessment was done at the conclusion of learning cycles either by a standardized test or a final project. Such assessments tend to offer limited glimpses of learner performance, at a point in time that is technically too late to point to any suitable remedial action. Nonetheless, AI technology learning environments like Knewton, Carnegie Learning, or Squirrel AI, now provide adaptable alternatives where a continuous formative assessment is built into the foundation of the instruction (Roll & Wylie, 2016). Such systems may track the interactions of the learners on a real-time basis, diagnose the misconceptions in the learner as they develop and adapt the presentation of content or provide feedback in response.

An example is that a platform teaching algebra would note that an individual using it would constantly use the distributive property incorrectly. The system can give specific exercises, visual examples, or other sets of problems to clear up the misconception at that moment instead of requiring the student to wait until a teacher identifies the error on a test or assignment. It is such a paradigm shift in terms of evaluation as a cumulative final process shifted into assessment as a diagnostic and process-based tool, a primary characteristic of the persona, AI-augmented learning environments (Luckin & Holmes, 2016).

In addition to instructional personalization, another area aided by AI-driven assessment is more proactive type of prediction. Observing changes in behavior metrics like response time, log in frequency, engagement on discussions and help seeking tendencies, platforms can predict academic risk, and can alert those who might require specialized assistance. As an illustration, Georgia State University incorporated predictive models using hundreds of variables, such as course performance and registration patterns, triggering automatic academic advising interventions to help raise graduation rates substantially (Elazab, 2024). Such APPS are a move towards pro-actively data informed decision-making where potentially impairing effects can be intervened against before performance has decreased too much.

The ways in which assessment occurs and when this happens are also changing with AI-driven systems, which makes universities and other educational institutions review their design of curricula. The long-held belief that there are certain logical steps to be completed in a chronologically defined order of learning, the concept that the subject is delivered in a lineal pattern is being abandoned over the emerging form of modular, adaptive curriculum. These are curricula that can dynamically be reconfigured depending on the progress of the learner and therefore the students have an opportunity of progressing in their areas of excellence and areas of need additional assistance to them are provided. To take one example, math educational platforms such as ASSISTments adjust the content of instruction, but also give actionable dashboards to teachers, indicating where students are struggling and what kind of pedagogical intervention to select (Heffernan & Heffernan, 2014).

This is a developing practice, where scaffolding learning pathways over time is of most importance and in need of a more flexible, granular perspective on progress. It questions institutional convention concerning fixed academic schedules, credit based on the number of hours, and standardized rates of progress, and opens the door to alternatives such as competency-based education (CBE), in which students progress when they have mastered the material, and not based on the number of time they spend in their courses.

However, these advancements do not go without worries. Matters of data privacy, algorithmic bias, overdependence on automation, and transparency are still considerable. Teachers and policymakers will have to be critical about generating insights based on AI, interpreting it, and taking action. As AI increasingly promises efficiency and personalization in its applications, many beg the question on how we can strike a balance between efficiency and efficiency-seeking with the humanistic values of education to make sure that technology plays an augmentative rather than deterministic role in teaching and learning.

Role of Educators

The introduction of AI education is not only changing the students experience; it is significantly changing the work of teachers as well. Previously taken as one who delivers the content and organizes the classroom, a teacher is now commonly becoming a facilitator or orchestrator of the AI-enhanced learning experiences. Under this different paradigm, teachers no longer just impart knowledge; rather, they interpret multifaceted data dashboards produced by the AI systems, facilitate AI feedback to students, and utilize professional judgment in the situation when the automatically coming recommendations need some contextualization (Luckin & Holmes, 2016).

As an example, in an AI-powered language learning engine, artificial intelligence tutor can immediately correct grammar, pronunciation, and vocabulary. Nevertheless, the teacher would participate in the interpretation patterns in the responses including the frequent mistakes in the students and create highly specific interventions by resolving to underlying linguistic notions of misconceptions. Additional reasons why teachers might have to intervene are the ability to recognize any emotional deregulation shown by the students which might not be properly recognized or resolved by an AI system, confirming again the human connection part that cannot be or is simply not provided by the technological means of teaching.

This changing role requires a new portfolio of skills. Instructional staff should achieve a certain degree of AI literacy: they should learn how algorithms operate and what sorts of prejudice may potentially exist in systems, and consider ethical issues emerging in AI-enhanced education. They also require data literacy so that they can responsibly interpret learner analytics and act on them in a responsible pedagogical manner. Moreover, human-centered design thinking would be vital when aligning the use of AI to fit the needs of different learners and remain empathetic and inclusive in teaching and learning (Zawacki-Richter et al., 2019).

Nonetheless, these are emerging skills, and most of the teaching staff was not trained to address them. Without institutional backing up, in terms of the targeted professional development, collaborative working spaces, and participatory forms of training, teachers can become overloaded or marginalized, due to the technologies meant to enrich their practice. To guarantee human agency as well as to make AI tools recursive feedback loop, as Holmes et al. (2019) maintain, it is critical that educators be empowered to determine how AI can and should be used in classrooms.

Recursive Feedback Loop

On a systemic level, there is a highly potent and potentially problematic recursive feedback loop created between the tools used in education and the institutional structures which they grow within as a result of the use of AI in education. Majorities of the AI systems applied in the educational sector, including predictive analytics engines, adaptive learning systems and recommendation engine, are trained on massive historical learner data. The examples of such metrics are grades given to students, their attendance patterns, behavioral records, and dismal results on standardized tests. Although this type of data is a strong basis of AI-enabled personalization and prediction, it reflects the institutionalized biases, assessment preferences, and pedagogical norms that have been built in the education systems over years of time (Prinsloo, 2020).

These AI systems that are deployed do not work in a vacuum. This is when they start to affect the systems that created training data and enforce certain concepts of what is good or successful or effective learning. As an example, an AI-driven tutoring system that has been directed to maximize test scores can place emphasis on drill and fact-recall based content in place of exploration or critical thinking activities. Its emphasis can guide the learners and instructors to surface patterns of learning and in a more restricted scope of study, pedagogy focused on what can be most measured (and countable) by the algorithm instead of most educational relevant (Selwyn, 2019).

This has been termed lock-in by some to be gradual in reducing pedagogical diversity and force underpinning compulsory, dominant or culturally insensitive knowledge. As an example, learning practices based on indigenous knowledge, oral storytelling or communal problem-solving can be hard to translate into data sets and can quickly find themselves left out of AI-supported systems. This phenomenon has a cumulative systemic impact over time, in which curricular priorities and instructional priorities are in subtle but deliberate ways altered to focus on those modes of learning that are most easily subjected to modeling and measurement, unless conscious efforts to counter the bias are undertaken during the design of the system (Benjamin, 2019).

Moreover, the use of the legacy data negatively affects the fairness and equity. When training the AI models on data that represent historical inequality, like underrepresentation of marginalized students in advanced courses or lower performance because of structural disadvantages, one can end up with a situation where the system reproduces or even increases existing inequalities by using them as guise of objectivity. Educational institutions will perpetuate past dynamics of exclusion in new digital systems unless they develop investigatory methods to audit, retrain and question the values that AI systems encode on their behalf (Hao, 2019).

Addressing these risks requires urgently new forms of reflexivity in the design and deployment of AI technologies, whereby stakeholders in AI take critical stances about the aims, premises, and ramifications of their systems. Explicit practices to document the use of the algorithms and their effect, participatory design, and impact assessment on education can help mitigate possible distortions of the educational mission by AI. The potential of AI can be supercharged to instigating the diversity and equity of learning without losing it only by building in ethical safeguards and preserving pluralistic definitions of educational success with institutions.

Equity, Systemic Bias, and Inclusion

This puts under sharp lenses the interdependent issue of equity, systemic bias and inclusion regarding AI-enhanced education. Due to the increase in the usage of AI by the education system through such procedures as adaptive learning, student risk profiling, and others, the AI system acquires and may increase the historical and structural inequality. The training data applied to learn these models are often constructed with the residue of historic inequalities of race, gender language, disability and socioeconomic status. As an example, when previously marginalized groups of students were graded on average lower in the past because of poor school funding or other systemic practices of discrimination, there is a risk that such AI systems will make misinformed inferences and label such learners as low-achievers or high-risk, whether it reflects their potential or not (Binns, 2018).

These types of biases cannot be considered only as technical failures but also representation of underlying systemic problems. AI, without critical oversight, has the potential to further the reinvention of stereotyping and further the production of exclusionary education. E.g. natural language processing (NLP) tools can fail with students who speak non-standard dialects or do not have English as first language. Some proctoring software or classroom monitoring tools are facial recognition systems, which displayed less efficacy on students with darker skin color, or those with particular features of their faces, resulting in a disproportional surveillance or punishment (Buolamwini, 2018).

Besides algorithmic bias, the vital issue is the other side of access to AI-supported educational resources inequity. Increased funding and opportunity may enable wealthier schools and cities facilities to have better infrastructure, trained employees, and the necessary resources to utilize and test new AI technology. By contrast, schools in remote areas or rural or low cash income settings, or in conflict zones, may either not share in the advantages of smarter systems or be subjected to inferior, so-called one-size-fits-all, automated technologies that will further dis-empower educators and learners. This digital divide becomes a threat to amplify any extant disparity in educational opportunity, instead of closing it.

To deal with these dangers, the educational policy should not be restricted to implementing technologies, it has to target socio-political processes that condition these processes. This includes:

- Ensuring that datasets utilized in AI models are representative, updated on a regular basis and socially aware annotated.
- The role of participatory processes to be engaged in an educator, students, parents, and marginalized communities to develop and evaluate AI tools.
- Requiring transparency and accountability concerning the decision-making process and influence of the AI systems on various groups.
- Giving targeted investments and capacity building in under-resourced schools ensuring that it is not left behind.

Above all, the implementation of AI governance in education should be based on human rights and social justice theories. This implies putting the dignity of students, their autonomy, and cultural identity above the algorithmic efficiency or cost-saving. With the rise in the power of the intelligent systems, educational institutions should uphold a strong intention of equity as both design requirement and policy requirement so that AI can benefit all learners but not a privileged few.

CONCLUSION

In the wake of agentic AI systems becoming an increasingly central aspect of education, their influence is much broader than economic improvement in the technical sense-it enters into the cognitive, social, and institutional essence of the learning process. In the preceding chapter, we have explored such effects using a multidisciplinary approach by utilizing cognitive sciences, sociology, and even computer science in trying to comprehend not just how AI contributes to learning, but also how AI is affected by, and in turn affects human systems it is located within. There is one main implication that becomes manifest by synthesizing these pieces of insights, and that is, the future of AI in education has to be ethical, inclusive, and in tandem with the cognitive and social realities of human learners.

With regard to cognition, the aim of AI ought to be to complement the human capabilities instead of superseding them, performing a delicate balancing act between assistance and autonomy. This entails the reduction of risk factors of cognitive offloading and also having learners keep metacognitive control of learning experiences. Socially, AI should be receptive and representative of the different cultural, emotional, and identity circumstances, within which learning takes place and serve as an opportunity to promote fair participation among various groups of learners. Institutionally, AI must be used to augment the role of the educator and not replace it and should be instilled with human judgment and ethical consideration at all tiers of design and implementation.

There should be a new generation of interdisciplinary frameworks, frameworks that will focus not merely on user-centered design but will embrace the notion of co-evolutionary thinking in guiding future development. These models would not only view AI more as a tool but as a companion of the learning practices which adapts to the needs of the learners but AI should also be influenced by pedagogical aims, cultural, and institutional values. Research should also change toward longitudinal research capturing the reciprocal influences of human and AI agents, and toward a participatory approach that can include educators and students in the design of AI systems as well as voices at the margins.

It is not about making AI smarter only, but it is about making our educational institutions smarter, and more humane, and just in the presence of smart technologies. This will necessitate the policies that favor transparency, accountability and ethical governance; professional pathways of development that make educators more empowered and the presence of infrastructure that support equitable access to high-level AI systems. Therefore, by engaging the sophisticatedness of the relationship between human and AI, designing innovation with ethical, cognitive, and cultural sensitivity, we will have learning environments that not only react to the current reality but are resistant to the future one.

The transformative potential of AI and adaptive institutions is that within this emerging world, institutions that can learn and reform themselves will be in the best position to realize that power. But the idea is not to automate education, but to reinvent it as a shared endeavor of human and machine action, where students are empowered, difference is welcomed and intelligence both human and artificial collaborate to make education do more.

REFERENCES

Benjamin, R. (2019). *Race after Technology: Abolitionist Tools for the New Jim Code*. Polity Press.

Binns, R. (2018). Fairness in Machine Learning: Lessons from Political Philosophy. *Proceedings of Machine Learning Research*, ●●●, 81.

Buolamwini, J. (2018). Gender Shades: Intersectional Accuracy Disparities in Commercial Gender Classification *. In *Proceedings of Machine Learning Research* (Vol. 81).

Cambria, E. (2016). Affective Computing and Sentiment Analysis. *IEEE Intelligent Systems*, *31*(2), 102–107. Advance online publication. DOI: 10.1109/MIS.2016.31

D'mello, S., & Graesser, A.DMello. (2012). AutoTutor and affective autotutor: Learning by talking with cognitively and emotionally intelligent computers that talk back. *ACM Transactions on Interactive Intelligent Systems*, *2*(4), 1–39. Advance online publication. DOI: 10.1145/2395123.2395128

Elazab, M. (2024). Artificial Intelligence and Future of Teaching and Learning. *International Journal of Internet Education*, *23*(2), 1–16. Advance online publication. DOI: 10.21608/ijie.2024.414601

Flavell, J. H. (1979). Metacognition and cognitive monitoring: A new area of cognitive-developmental inquiry. *The American Psychologist*, *34*(10), 906–911. Advance online publication. DOI: 10.1037/0003-066X.34.10.906

Hao, K. (2019). AI is sending people to jail—and getting it wrong. In *MIT Technology Review*.

Heffernan, N. T., & Heffernan, C. L. (2014). The ASSISTments ecosystem: Building a platform that brings scientists and teachers together for minimally invasive research on human learning and teaching. *International Journal of Artificial Intelligence in Education*, *24*(4), 470–497. Advance online publication. DOI: 10.1007/s40593-014-0024-x

Holmes, W., Bialik, M., & Fadel, C. (2019). *Artificial Intelligence in Education*. Promise and Implications for Teaching and Learning.

Kang, S. H. K. (2016). Spaced Repetition Promotes Efficient and Effective Learning: Policy Implications for Instruction. *Policy Insights from the Behavioral and Brain Sciences*, *3*(1), 12–19. Advance online publication. DOI: 10.1177/2372732215624708

Kim, T., & Biocca, F. (1997). Telepresence via television: Two dimensions of telepresence may have different connections to memory and persuasion. *Journal of Computer-Mediated Communication, 3*(2), 0. Advance online publication. DOI: 10.1111/j.1083-6101.1997.tb00073.x

Luckin, R., & Holmes, W. (2016). Intelligence Unleashed: An argument for AI in Education. In *UCL Knowledge Lab: London, UK.*

Thomas Metzinger. (2019). Ethics washing made in Europe. *Der Tagesspiegel, 20*(2).

Prinsloo, P. (2020). Big data in education. The digital future of learning, policy and practice. *International Studies in Sociology of Education, 29*(1–2), 183–186. Advance online publication. DOI: 10.1080/09620214.2019.1690546

Roll, I., & Wylie, R. (2016). Evolution and Revolution in Artificial Intelligence in Education. *International Journal of Artificial Intelligence in Education, 26*(2), 582–599. Advance online publication. DOI: 10.1007/s40593-016-0110-3

Selwyn, N. (2019). *Should Robots Replace Teachers? AI and the Future of Education.* John Wiley & Sons, Inc.

Shkurko, S. Y. (2025). Human-AI Interaction from an Evolutionary Neurosociological Perspective. In *Handbook of Neurosociology* (pp. 387–409). Springer.

Sweller, J. (1988). Cognitive load during problem solving: Effects on learning. *Cognitive Science, 12*(2), 257–285. Advance online publication. DOI: 10.1207/s15516709cog1202_4

Tyng, C. M., Amin, H. U., Saad, M. N. M., & Malik, A. S. (2017). The influences of emotion on learning and memory. In *Frontiers in Psychology* (Vol. 8). Issue AUG., DOI: 10.3389/fpsyg.2017.01454

Van Merriënboer, J. J. G., & Sweller, J. (2005). Cognitive load theory and complex learning: Recent developments and future directions. In *Educational Psychology Review* (Vol. 17, Issue 2). DOI: 10.1007/s10648-005-3951-0

Vygotsky, L. S. (2020). Mind in society: The development of higher psychological processes. In *Accounting in Australia*. RLE Accounting.

Walter, S. (2024). Harmonising humans and technology: Exploring the dynamics of cognitive production, artificial intelligence and social communication in cybernetic systems. *Open Research Europe, 4*(201), 201. DOI: 10.12688/openreseurope.18418.1

Williamson, B., & Eynon, R. (2020). Historical threads, missing links, and future directions in AI in education. In *Learning, Media and Technology* (Vol. 45, Issue 3). DOI: 10.1080/17439884.2020.1798995

Zawacki-Richter, O., Marín, V. I., Bond, M., & Gouverneur, F. (2019). Systematic review of research on artificial intelligence applications in higher education – where are the educators? In *International Journal of Educational Technology in Higher Education* (Vol. 16, Issue 1). DOI: 10.1186/s41239-019-0171-0

Chapter 4
Pedagogical Transformations:
Agentic AI as a Co-Teacher and Learning Partner

Nishanova Zamira Taskarayevna
National Pedagogical University of Uzbekistan, Uzbekistan

Baykunusova Gulmira Yuldibayevna
National Research University, Uzbekistan

Nilufar Niyazova
Mamun University, Uzbekistan

Irim Shehzadi
https://orcid.org/0009-0004-3121-1369
PMAS Arid Agricultural University, Pakistan

Shavkat Turayev
Mamun University, Uzbekistan

ABSTRACT

The integration of agentic AI in education is transforming pedagogy by enabling AI systems to act as co-teachers and learning partners, dynamically adapting to learner needs, providing timely feedback, and supporting innovative instructional strategies. These systems foster personalized learning, collaborative problem-solving, and enhanced engagement while reshaping teacher roles and curriculum design. Ethical frameworks, professional development, and equitable access are essential

DOI: 10.4018/979-8-3373-4621-2.ch004

for responsible implementation. Thoughtful integration of agentic AI promises learner-centered, adaptive, and sustainable educational environments that enhance both human and technological potential.

INTRODUCTION

The landscape of education is undergoing a profound transformation, driven by rapid advancements in artificial intelligence (AI) (Sajja et al., 2025; Sein Minn, 2022). Over the past decades, AI technologies have evolved from basic automation tools to sophisticated systems capable of adaptive learning, personalized feedback, and intelligent tutoring. Traditional applications of AI in education, such as automated grading, content recommendation, and virtual assistants, have primarily functioned as reactive support tools, responding to student input or teacher instructions. While these systems have enhanced efficiency and accessibility, they often lack the autonomy and contextual awareness needed to actively shape learning experiences.

In this context, agentic AI emerges as a novel paradigm, redefining the role of technology in educational environments. Unlike conventional AI, agentic AI possesses the capacity for autonomous decision-making, adaptive learning, and proactive engagement. These systems can perceive contextual information, interpret learner needs, and initiate actions aligned with pedagogical objectives, effectively functioning as both a co-teacher and a collaborative learning partner. By operating alongside human educators, agentic AI can support differentiated instruction, foster student engagement, and enhance the overall quality of learning outcomes (Artsn & Bozkurt, 2025; Dai et al., 2024; Katsenou et al., 2025; Raheem & Hossain, 2025).

Studying agentic AI as a co-teacher is significant for multiple reasons. First, it challenges traditional notions of teacher-centered instruction, highlighting the potential for AI to participate actively in instructional design and delivery. Second, it offers new avenues for personalized learning, allowing students to receive timely guidance and feedback tailored to their unique strengths and challenges. Third, examining the integration of agentic AI provides insights into the evolving dynamics of human-AI collaboration in educational settings, including the ethical, pedagogical, and practical considerations that accompany this shift.

This chapter explores the transformative potential of agentic AI in contemporary education, examining both theoretical foundations and practical applications. By understanding how AI can function as an autonomous co-teacher and learning partner, educators and researchers can envision a more interactive, adaptive, and learner-centered future for teaching and learning.

CONCEPTUAL FOUNDATIONS OF AGENTIC AI

Understanding the pedagogical potential of agentic AI begins with a clear conceptual foundation. Agentic AI represents a shift from traditional AI applications toward systems capable of autonomous, context-aware decision-making and proactive participation in learning processes. At its core, agentic AI is designed not merely to respond to instructions but to perceive, interpret, and act within dynamic educational environments, enabling it to function as a co-teacher and collaborative learning partner.

Definition and Key Characteristics

Agentic AI can be broadly defined as an advanced form of artificial intelligence designed to operate autonomously, adaptively, and proactively within educational environments. Unlike traditional AI, which primarily responds to predefined commands or provides static support, agentic AI exhibits intelligent behaviors that allow it to perceive context, interpret learner needs, and take independent actions to enhance teaching and learning outcomes. By functioning as a co-teacher and learning partner, agentic AI is capable of dynamically influencing learning processes, offering both real-time support and strategic guidance. This transformative capability positions agentic AI as a critical component of next-generation educational systems, where it not only complements human instructors but also fosters deeper engagement, personalization, and collaboration among learners.

Autonomy

Autonomy is one of the defining characteristics of agentic AI (Acharya et al., 2025). Whereas conventional AI systems rely heavily on human input to function, merely responding to user queries or executing pre-programmed tasks, agentic AI possesses the capacity to act independently based on contextual awareness. For example, in a mathematics classroom, an agentic AI system can monitor a student's progress on problem-solving exercises, recognize repeated errors, and automatically suggest alternative learning strategies or hints without waiting for teacher intervention. This level of autonomy enables AI to anticipate instructional needs, adjust the difficulty of tasks in real time, and identify opportunities for enrichment or remediation.

Autonomy also extends to classroom management and pedagogical decision-making. Agentic AI can recommend grouping strategies for collaborative activities, suggest discussion prompts tailored to students' comprehension levels, or alert teachers to emerging patterns of difficulty within the class (Hosseini & Seilani, 2025). By acting independently in these ways, agentic AI reduces cognitive and administrative burdens on educators, allowing them to focus on higher-order teaching functions such as mentoring, critical thinking facilitation, and socio-emotional support. In essence, autonomy transforms AI from a reactive tool into an intelligent collaborator capable of taking initiative in the service of pedagogical goals.

Adaptability

Adaptability is another cornerstone of agentic AI, reflecting its ability to continuously learn and refine its strategies based on interactions with both students and educators. Unlike static AI systems that operate on fixed rules or models, agentic AI evolves in response to real-time data, adjusting its recommendations, feedback, and instructional approaches to accommodate individual learning styles, proficiency levels, and classroom dynamics (Bandi et al., 2025; Murugesan, 2025; Raheem & Hossain, 2025). For instance, an agentic AI tutor in a language learning platform may detect that a learner struggles with verb conjugations but excels in vocabulary acquisition. In response, it can emphasize targeted exercises on conjugation while introducing advanced vocabulary tasks to maintain engagement and promote balanced skill development.

Beyond individual learners, adaptability also enables AI to respond to contextual changes within the educational environment. This includes variations in class size, curriculum pacing, or the integration of new content areas. By dynamically adjusting its support strategies, agentic AI ensures that instruction remains effective, personalized, and aligned with overarching learning objectives. Importantly, adaptability allows AI to refine its own decision-making models over time, learning from successes and errors, and optimizing its interventions for future interactions.

Proactive Engagement

Proactive engagement is the hallmark that distinguishes agentic AI from conventional reactive systems. Rather than waiting for learners or teachers to request assistance, agentic AI anticipates challenges, identifies gaps in understanding, and initiates interventions designed to enhance comprehension, motivation, and skill acquisition (Diebel et al., 2025; Hughes et al., 2025). For example, in an online science course, an agentic AI system might detect that a student is consistently struggling with a specific concept, such as Newtonian mechanics. The system can proactively introduce supplementary materials, interactive simulations, or problem-based scenarios to reinforce understanding before the student experiences frustration or disengagement.

Proactive engagement extends beyond academic support to fostering holistic learning experiences. Agentic AI can monitor emotional cues, participation levels, or engagement patterns, responding with encouragement, personalized prompts, or collaborative opportunities to sustain learner motivation. By taking initiative, agentic AI effectively becomes an active partner in the learning process rather than a passive tool. This proactive capacity allows AI to anticipate learning trajectories, scaffold experiences, and cultivate a sense of agency among students, thereby aligning technological capabilities with pedagogical principles of active, student-centered learning.

In combination, autonomy, adaptability, and proactive engagement define the conceptual essence of agentic AI, positioning it as a transformative force in education. By integrating these characteristics, agentic AI systems are not only capable of responding to immediate instructional needs but can also contribute to long-term learning strategies, curricular design, and personalized support, fundamentally reshaping how educators teach and students learn.

Distinctions from Conventional AI in Education

While traditional AI applications in education—such as automated grading systems, content recommendation engines, or chatbots- have enhanced operational efficiency, they largely function as reactive instruments. In contrast, agentic AI represents a paradigmatic shift in educational technology, as shown in Table 1.

Table 1. Comparison of conventional AI and agentic AI

Feature	Conventional AI	Agentic AI
Decision-making	Follows pre-defined rules or reacts to prompts	Makes autonomous, context-informed decisions
Learning approach	Limited adaptability, requires explicit human input	Continuously adapts based on learner interaction and feedback
Engagement	Passive, reactive assistance	Proactive, initiates instructional and supportive actions
Role in pedagogy	Supportive tool for teachers	Co-teacher and collaborative learning partner

This distinction highlights why agentic AI is particularly suited for complex, interactive learning environments where adaptability, personalized support, and context-awareness are critical.

Theoretical Foundations Supporting AI-Human Collaboration

The deployment of agentic AI in educational contexts is not merely a technological innovation; it is deeply grounded in established cognitive, motivational, and social learning theories. These theories provide a framework for understanding how learners acquire knowledge, develop skills, and interact with intelligent systems, while also guiding the design and integration of AI to maximize educational impact. By aligning AI functionalities with human learning principles, educators and developers can ensure that agentic AI enhances learning experiences in meaningful, pedagogically sound ways.

Cognitive Load Theory

Cognitive Load Theory (CLT) posits that learners have a limited working memory capacity, and instructional design must carefully manage this load to optimize learning (Ouwehand et al., 2025; Sweller, 2023; Sweller & Chandler, 1991). Agentic AI contributes directly to reducing extraneous cognitive load by scaffolding complex tasks, sequencing information logically, and providing timely guidance. For example, in a mathematics classroom, an agentic AI system can break down multi-step algebraic problems into smaller, digestible steps, providing hints or visual cues at each stage. This allows learners to focus on understanding underlying concepts rather than being overwhelmed by task complexity.

Moreover, agentic AI can dynamically adjust the difficulty of tasks based on real-time learner performance, ensuring that cognitive load remains within optimal levels. By monitoring patterns of errors and time-on-task metrics, AI can adaptively intervene—offering additional practice, simplified examples, or alternative explanations. This intelligent scaffolding aligns with CLT principles and enhances the efficiency and effectiveness of learning, particularly in subjects with high intrinsic complexity, such as STEM disciplines.

Constructivist Learning Theory

Constructivist learning theory emphasizes that learners actively construct knowledge through experience, reflection, and interaction (Hein, 1991). Agentic AI operationalizes these principles by creating interactive, adaptive, and experiential learning environments. For instance, in a virtual science lab, an AI system can guide students through simulations of chemical reactions, prompting them to make predictions, observe outcomes, and refine hypotheses based on feedback. This mirrors the constructivist emphasis on discovery, experimentation, and meaning-making.

In addition, Vygotsky's concept of the zone of proximal development (ZPD) is particularly relevant. Agentic AI can function as a digital scaffold, offering guidance just beyond the learner's current capability. By providing hints, modeling problem-solving strategies, and gradually reducing support as competence develops, AI promotes autonomous learning while maintaining alignment with the learner's developmental readiness. This adaptive scaffolding ensures that learners remain challenged yet supported, fostering deep engagement and conceptual understanding.

Self-Determination Theory

Self-Determination Theory (SDT) highlights the importance of intrinsic motivation, emphasizing autonomy, competence, and relatedness as key psychological needs (Deci & Ryan, 2012). Agentic AI supports each of these dimensions by personalizing learning experiences, providing timely feedback, and fostering meaningful interactions. For example, an AI-driven language learning platform can allow students to choose topics of personal interest, adjust pacing, and receive feedback tailored to their specific strengths and weaknesses, promoting a sense of autonomy and ownership over the learning process.

AI also nurtures competence by offering appropriately challenging tasks and positive reinforcement when learners demonstrate mastery. Through proactive encouragement and constructive feedback, learners gain confidence and develop a growth mindset. Finally, agentic AI can support relatedness by facilitating collaborative activities, peer-like interactions, and social engagement even in remote learning contexts, ensuring that learners feel connected to both human and AI collaborators.

Social Learning Theory

Social Learning Theory emphasizes learning through observation, imitation, and modeling. Agentic AI can replicate these mechanisms in both digital and blended learning environments (Bandura & Walters, 1977). For instance, an AI tutor in a coding platform can demonstrate problem-solving strategies, allowing learners to observe step-by-step reasoning and replicate processes in their own work. By providing guided practice, AI models desirable behaviors, strategic thinking, and problem-solving approaches.

Furthermore, agentic AI can facilitate peer-like interactions by mediating group tasks, suggesting collaborative strategies, and monitoring participation. In online discussion forums or project-based learning environments, AI can provide prompts, pose reflective questions, and simulate peer responses, effectively extending the benefits of social learning to contexts where human peers may be limited. This capability enables learners to acquire knowledge socially, develop critical thinking skills, and engage in collaborative problem-solving even in asynchronous or remote settings.

Collectively, these theoretical perspectives illustrate why agentic AI is uniquely positioned to enhance human learning. Cognitive Load Theory informs AI's scaffolding and task sequencing, constructivist principles guide adaptive and experiential learning experiences, Self-Determination Theory ensures motivational alignment, and Social Learning Theory facilitates modeling, collaboration, and peer-like engagement. By embedding these theories into its design and operation, agentic AI transcends the role of a passive educational tool, becoming an active, context-aware partner that aligns technology with human learning needs.

These foundations not only justify the pedagogical integration of AI but also provide critical guidance for developers and educators seeking to design systems that are effective, learner-centered, and ethically responsible, paving the way for sustainable, intelligent, and transformative educational practices. By grounding agentic AI in these cognitive and motivational frameworks, educators and designers can ensure that AI integration is not only technically sophisticated but also pedagogically meaningful. The system thus moves beyond simple automation to enhance human learning experiences in profound and measurable ways.

AGENTIC AI IN LEARNING ENVIRONMENTS

The integration of agentic AI in educational settings has the potential to reshape how teaching and learning occur, moving beyond traditional automation to create dynamic, interactive, and learner-centered experiences. By functioning as both a co-teacher and a collaborative learning partner, agentic AI offers practical applications that enhance instructional delivery, assessment, and student engagement in classrooms and digital platforms alike.

AI as a Co-Teacher

Agentic AI, when positioned as a co-teacher, represents a profound shift in the educational paradigm, moving beyond the traditional notion of AI as a mere assistive tool. Rather than replacing human instructors, agentic AI functions as an active collaborator, complementing educators across multiple dimensions of the teaching process (Ishaq et al., 2025; Radhika et al., 2025). Its integration enables a more responsive, adaptive, and personalized instructional environment, while simultaneously alleviating the administrative and cognitive burdens that often limit teachers' capacity for creativity and mentorship.

Instructional Support

One of the primary contributions of agentic AI as a co-teacher lies in enhancing instructional delivery and lesson planning. AI systems can analyze historical and real-time learner data to identify patterns in comprehension, engagement, and performance, allowing educators to design adaptive learning pathways. For example, in a middle school mathematics class, an agentic AI system could monitor students solving algebraic problems and dynamically provide alternative explanations or visualizations for those who struggle, while simultaneously offering enrichment activities for advanced learners.

Beyond content delivery, agentic AI supports classroom management and pacing. In blended or online learning environments, AI can monitor student participation, flag disengagement, and suggest timely interventions such as interactive polls, guided discussions, or small-group activities. In traditional classrooms, AI dashboards can provide teachers with real-time insights into student progress, allowing educators to adjust lesson pacing, reallocate instructional time, or modify activity sequences to optimize learning outcomes. By offering these forms of instructional support, agentic AI ensures that teaching is both responsive and data-informed, bridging gaps between individual learner needs and curriculum objectives.

Feedback and Assessment

Another crucial dimension of AI as a co-teacher is continuous feedback and assessment, which extends far beyond conventional grading mechanisms (Hooda et al., 2022). Agentic AI systems can monitor learner interactions at a granular level, detecting errors, misconceptions, and patterns of misunderstanding as they occur. For instance, in an online language learning platform, AI can track pronunciation errors, grammar mistakes, or sentence structure difficulties, provide instant, individualized corrective feedback while highlighting progress trends over time.

The ability to generate formative assessments in real time allows teachers to intervene promptly, addressing learning gaps before they accumulate into significant misunderstandings. AI can also suggest targeted remediation activities or differentiated exercises tailored to each student's skill level, ensuring that learners remain challenged yet supported. Furthermore, AI-driven assessment tools reduce the manual workload of teachers, freeing them to focus on higher-order instructional tasks such as interpreting student progress in context, mentoring learners, and providing socio-emotional support.

Differentiated Instruction

Agentic AI excels in differentiated instruction, a pedagogical approach that adapts teaching methods, materials, and pacing to accommodate the diverse needs of learners. By continuously analyzing student performance, engagement metrics, and learning preferences, AI can propose personalized learning paths that align with individual strengths and weaknesses. For example, in a high school science class, an AI system might detect that one student learns best through visual simulations, while another benefits from textual explanations and guided exercises. The system can then deliver content in multiple formats, adjusting the level of complexity and the sequence of activities accordingly.

Differentiated instruction through AI is particularly valuable in large classrooms or online courses with hundreds of learners, where teachers may struggle to provide individualized attention. By handling routine, data-intensive tasks such as grading quizzes, tracking engagement, and monitoring progress, AI frees educators to concentrate on higher-order pedagogical responsibilities, including facilitating discussions, mentoring students, and encouraging critical thinking. This collaboration ensures that each student receives personalized attention without overburdening the teacher, thereby enhancing both learning quality and instructional efficiency.

Empowering Educators and Enhancing Pedagogy

By sharing teaching responsibilities, agentic AI fundamentally redefines the teacher's role. Rather than being consumed by administrative duties or repetitive tasks, educators can focus on fostering creativity, curiosity, and critical thinking. AI acts as a cognitive partner, offering insights, recommendations, and actionable data, which allow teachers to make informed pedagogical decisions. Moreover, the co-teaching model promotes reflective practice: educators can analyze AI-generated data to evaluate the effectiveness of instructional strategies, refine lesson designs, and identify opportunities for professional growth.

In essence, agentic AI as a co-teacher is not a replacement for human expertise but an amplifier of pedagogical potential. It transforms instruction into a more adaptive, data-informed, and learner-centered process, enabling teachers to devote greater attention to mentorship, socio-emotional support, and the cultivation of critical thinking skills. By integrating AI in this collaborative role, educational systems can achieve more personalized, engaging, and effective learning experiences for every student.

AI as a Learning Partner

Beyond its role as a co-teacher, agentic AI also functions as a learning partner, actively engaging students in personalized, interactive, and collaborative experiences (He et al., 2021; Maiti & Goel, 2025). In this capacity, AI shifts from assisting teachers to directly supporting learners, fostering autonomy, critical thinking, and sustained engagement. By leveraging real-time data and intelligent algorithms, agentic AI can create learning environments that respond dynamically to individual needs while encouraging participation, exploration, and collaboration.

Personalized Learning

Personalization is a defining feature of AI as a learning partner. Agentic AI continuously analyzes a learner's behavior, performance, interaction patterns, and preferences to tailor content, tasks, and assessments. For example, in an online coding platform, AI can identify a student who consistently struggles with loops and recursion. The system might then recommend targeted exercises, interactive tutorials, or step-by-step walkthroughs specifically designed to address these challenges. Conversely, if a learner demonstrates proficiency in functions and arrays, the AI may suggest advanced problem sets to deepen their understanding and maintain engagement.

Personalized learning with agentic AI also extends to adaptive pacing and differentiated instruction. AI can adjust the difficulty and sequence of content based on ongoing performance, ensuring that learners are neither bored by tasks that are too easy nor overwhelmed by tasks that are too complex. This continuous, individualized adaptation not only improves knowledge retention but also increases motivation, as students experience a sense of progress and mastery tailored to their unique learning trajectories.

Scaffolding and Guidance

Agentic AI excels in providing scaffolding and just-in-time guidance, which supports learners in navigating complex problem-solving tasks without diminishing cognitive challenge. For instance, in a physics simulation, AI can prompt a student to consider specific variables, suggest alternative approaches to an experiment, or highlight conceptual connections, allowing the student to progress independently while receiving subtle guidance. Unlike traditional tutoring systems that provide solutions directly, agentic AI strategically scaffolds learning, encouraging reflection and reasoning while maintaining an appropriate level of difficulty.

This type of guidance promotes independent thinking and metacognition, as learners are encouraged to evaluate their decisions, reflect on outcomes, and self-regulate their learning strategies. The AI can also track progress over time, identifying areas where the student consistently struggles and offering targeted prompts or additional practice, ensuring a sustained and structured learning process. By balancing support with challenge, AI as a learning partner fosters resilience, problem-solving skills, and a deeper understanding of the subject matter.

Collaborative Problem-Solving

Another critical dimension of agentic AI as a learning partner is facilitating collaborative problem-solving. AI can actively orchestrate group activities by assigning roles, monitoring participation, suggesting strategies, and mediating interactions. For example, in a virtual classroom, AI might group students with complementary skill sets, guide them through a project workflow, and provide feedback on collaboration quality. By monitoring dynamics such as participation frequency, idea contribution, and conflict resolution, AI ensures that teamwork is effective, equitable, and educationally meaningful.

On digital platforms, agentic AI can simulate peer interactions, particularly in remote or hybrid learning contexts where human collaboration may be limited. AI agents can prompt discussion, pose reflective questions, model problem-solving strategies, or even simulate debates, enabling students to experience cooperative learning even without constant human presence. This enhances not only cognitive development but also social and communication skills, reinforcing the principles of collaborative learning and social constructivism.

Empowering Learners and Transforming Educational Experiences

By serving as a learning partner, agentic AI transforms education into a participatory and learner-centered process. Students gain immediate, individualized support while developing autonomy, critical thinking, and problem-solving abilities. The AI's adaptive guidance and collaborative facilitation foster an environment where learners are encouraged to take ownership of their educational journey, experiment with new ideas, and engage meaningfully with peers and content alike.

Moreover, the presence of AI as a learning partner can enhance motivation and engagement by providing dynamic feedback, gamified challenges, and personalized learning paths. Students experience learning as an interactive and responsive process, rather than a static or passive one, which increases persistence and deepens conceptual understanding. Through these mechanisms, agentic AI supports a holistic approach to education, blending cognitive, emotional, and social dimensions to cultivate independent, reflective, and collaborative learners.

Case Studies and Examples of Integration

The practical integration of agentic AI across diverse educational contexts demonstrates its adaptability, scalability, and pedagogical potential. These case studies highlight how AI can function as both a co-teacher and a learning partner, offering personalized support, enhancing engagement, and enabling educators to focus on higher-order instructional tasks. By examining implementations across K-12, higher education, and online learning platforms, we can observe the transformative impact of agentic AI on modern pedagogy.

K-12 Classrooms

In K-12 settings, agentic AI systems are increasingly being employed to provide personalized instruction and real-time feedback (Diliberti et al., n.d.). A notable example is Carnegie Learning's MATHia, an AI-driven tutoring platform integrated alongside classroom teaching. MATHia continuously monitors student interactions, tracks errors, and identifies areas of difficulty, delivering targeted practice exercises and hints in real time. This allows students to progress at their own pace while receiving immediate feedback, reinforcing conceptual understanding and skill acquisition.

Beyond content delivery, AI in K-12 classrooms can support differentiated learning and classroom management. For instance, AI dashboards allow teachers to identify students who require additional support or enrichment, enabling them to group students strategically, adjust lesson pacing, and provide tailored interventions. In subjects such as mathematics and science, where conceptual understanding often varies widely among students, AI systems provide an adaptive scaffold, allowing teachers to focus on facilitating critical thinking, problem-solving discussions, and socio-emotional development.

Higher Education

Agentic AI has also found a prominent role in higher education, particularly in large-scale online or hybrid courses. A well-documented case is Georgia Tech's "Jill Watson," an AI teaching assistant developed using IBM Watson technology. Jill Watson was deployed in online courses to answer routine student questions, provide clarification on assignments, and facilitate discussion forums. Remarkably, students often did not realize they were interacting with an AI, which demonstrates the system's ability to emulate peer-like responsiveness and maintain high levels of engagement.

In addition to answering queries, AI teaching assistants in higher education can provide automated feedback on written assignments, detect misconceptions in discussion posts, and identify patterns in student performance. This enhances scalability, allowing instructors to manage large cohorts without compromising the quality of support. Furthermore, AI systems can analyze learning analytics to inform curriculum adjustments, highlight at-risk students, and optimize instructional strategies based on evidence rather than intuition alone. Such capabilities exemplify the synergy between human educators and agentic AI, where each complements the strengths of the other.

Online Learning Platforms

Massive Open Online Courses (MOOCs) and other digital learning platforms have also leveraged agentic AI to deliver personalized, adaptive learning experiences on a scale. Platforms like Khan Academy and Coursera have implemented AI-driven recommendation engines that analyze learner data—including engagement patterns, quiz performance, and content preferences—to suggest tailored exercises, remedial resources, or advanced challenges.

For example, on Coursera, AI systems can recommend specific modules to students struggling with particular concepts while simultaneously promoting enrichment materials for advanced learners. In addition, AI facilitates learning analytics at scale, tracking student progression, completion rates, and engagement metrics across entire courses. This data enables instructors to intervene proactively, design more effective learning pathways, and maintain learner motivation in massive, often asynchronous, educational environments.

Implications Across Educational Levels

These examples collectively demonstrate that agentic AI is not limited to any single educational level or modality. In K-12 classrooms, it supports personalized practice and differentiated instruction; in higher education, it enhances scalability and provides intelligent instructional support; and in online learning platforms, it enables adaptive learning at scale, leveraging data to inform pedagogy.

The overarching lesson is that agentic AI can be effectively embedded in diverse contexts, offering scalable, context-sensitive, and learner-centered support. By complementing human expertise, facilitating individualized learning, and enabling proactive interventions, AI empowers educators to focus on higher-order teaching and fosters deeper, more engaging learning experiences. As such, these case studies illustrate the practical feasibility, pedagogical value, and transformative potential of agentic AI in shaping the future of education.

PEDAGOGICAL TRANSFORMATIONS ENABLED BY AGENTIC AI

The integration of agentic AI in educational environments is not merely a technological enhancement; it fundamentally reshapes teaching and learning practices. By functioning as both a co-teacher and a learning partner, agentic AI introduces transformative changes in teacher roles, student engagement, and assessment methodologies, promoting a more interactive, learner-centered educational experience.

Shifts in Teacher Roles

The introduction of agentic AI into educational environments redefines the traditional responsibilities of teachers, transitioning their roles from authoritative knowledge deliverers to facilitators, mentors, and strategic designers of learning experiences. This shift allows educators to focus on higher-order cognitive and creative tasks while AI manages routine, data-intensive functions.

In the facilitator role, teachers guide discussions, encourage inquiry, and foster critical thinking, relying on AI to handle repetitive or administrative instructional tasks. For example, in a blended learning mathematics classroom, AI can continuously monitor student problem-solving attempts, detect misconceptions, and suggest individualized interventions. This allows teachers to focus on facilitating inquiry-based learning, posing thought-provoking questions, and guiding students through conceptual explorations rather than spending time on basic practice exercises. By supporting differentiated instruction at scale, AI enables teachers to ensure that each student receives the appropriate level of challenge and guidance.

As mentors, educators leverage AI-generated insights to provide holistic support that integrates cognitive and socio-emotional development. AI systems can track performance data, engagement levels, and even affective states, helping teachers identify students' strengths, learning preferences, and areas for growth. For instance, in a language arts class, an AI system may flag a student's difficulty with writing coherence, prompting the teacher to offer tailored guidance, peer collaboration opportunities, or supplementary resources. This data-informed mentorship allows teachers to nurture both intellectual growth and emotional well-being, fostering a more personalized and supportive learning environment.

In the strategist role, teachers assume responsibility for curriculum design, instructional planning, and data-informed decision-making. Agentic AI provides actionable insights into learning patterns, engagement metrics, and skill acquisition, enabling educators to optimize lesson sequencing, resource allocation, and pedagogical approaches. For example, AI analytics may reveal that students struggle with a particular concept in physics across multiple sections, prompting the teacher to redesign instructional strategies, integrate alternative resources, or adjust collaborative activities. This strategic approach empowers teachers to innovate and refine teaching practices continuously, using AI as a cognitive and analytical partner rather than a mere tool.

Overall, these role shifts empower educators to operate at higher cognitive and creative levels, focusing on mentorship, inquiry facilitation, and pedagogical innovation while AI manages adaptive, data-driven instructional support.

Changes in Student Engagement and Autonomy

Agentic AI also transforms student engagement and fosters learner autonomy by creating adaptive, responsive, and interactive learning environments. By providing personalized guidance and scaffolding, AI shifts students from passive recipients of information to active, self-directed learners.

AI-driven learning systems encourage students to take initiative by offering interactive problem-solving tasks, adaptive challenges, and real-time feedback. For instance, in a digital chemistry lab, an AI system may propose experimental scenarios that require students to hypothesize, test, and analyze outcomes. Such activities promote curiosity, critical thinking, and active engagement, allowing students to participate meaningfully in constructing knowledge rather than passively receiving information.

Agentic AI enhances learners' control over pacing, content selection, and learning strategies. By providing timely guidance without overtly directing decision-making, AI scaffolds learning in ways that encourage self-regulation and independent problem-solving. For example, in an online mathematics platform, students may choose which topics to tackle first, while AI monitors performance and provides adaptive hints to prevent stagnation. This process cultivates confidence, strategic thinking, and the ability to plan and manage one's own learning, essential skills for lifelong education.

Personalized feedback, gamified learning elements, and adaptive learning paths provided by AI increase intrinsic motivation and sustain engagement. For example, AI can introduce badges, progress indicators, or challenges aligned with learners' performance, fostering a sense of achievement and progression. Additionally, AI can vary tasks and problem types to maintain interest, ensuring that even complex or traditionally challenging subjects remain engaging.

By combining active participation, autonomy, and motivation, agentic AI creates a learning culture where students assume responsibility for their educational journey while benefiting from intelligent, context-aware support.

New Forms of Assessment, Feedback, and Collaborative Learning

Agentic AI introduces innovative approaches to assessment and collaboration, moving beyond traditional exams and static feedback to dynamic, continuous, and socially interactive practices.

AI enables ongoing evaluation of student learning, tracking comprehension, progress, and misconceptions in real time. For example, in a computer science course, an AI system can analyze coding attempts, detect recurring errors, and generate reports on student proficiency. Continuous assessment allows educators to intervene promptly, tailor instruction to evolving learner needs, and reduce the reliance on high-stakes exams.

Feedback provided by agentic AI is personalized, context-sensitive, and actionable. By analyzing learner responses, engagement patterns, and performance data, AI generates hints, alternative strategies, or targeted exercises to enhance understanding. For instance, in a foreign language course, AI can detect specific vocabulary gaps and provide personalized exercises, pronunciation tips, and contextual examples to accelerate skill acquisition.

AI also enhances group learning and peer interactions. In digital classrooms, AI can assign roles, monitor contributions, suggest collaborative strategies, and simulate peer dialogue. For example, during a project-based activity in an online environmental science course, AI can guide students through brainstorming, research, and presentation stages, ensuring equitable participation and effective teamwork. AI-driven facilitation promotes cooperation, negotiation, and social learning, extending opportunities for collaboration beyond physical classroom boundaries.

These pedagogical transformations demonstrate that agentic AI is not a passive addition to education but an active catalyst for reimagining teaching, learning, and assessment. By enabling adaptive instruction, personalized feedback, collaborative engagement, and continuous evaluation, AI fosters environments where both teachers and students can thrive. The integration of AI supports innovative, learner-centered practices that promote engagement, autonomy, and skill development while enhancing instructional effectiveness.

CHALLENGES AND ETHICAL CONSIDERATIONS

While agentic AI offers transformative potential for education, its integration is accompanied by a complex set of challenges and ethical considerations. These challenges span technical, pedagogical, and societal dimensions, necessitating careful planning, governance, and reflective practice to ensure AI-enhanced learning remains equitable, trustworthy, and effective.

Bias, Privacy, and Accountability

Agentic AI systems are susceptible to bias arising from training datasets, algorithmic design, and operational contexts. These biases can inadvertently reinforce stereotypes, marginalize certain groups, or produce skewed assessments. For example, an AI tutoring system trained primarily on data from high-performing students may offer recommendations that favor certain learning strategies, disadvantaging students with alternative learning styles. Similarly, AI-generated assessments may unintentionally reward specific cultural knowledge or linguistic patterns, disadvantaging students from diverse backgrounds. Addressing bias requires ongoing auditing, inclusive data collection, and algorithmic transparency to ensure equitable learning outcomes.

Effective agentic AI relies on extensive data collection, including student performance metrics, behavioral patterns, and even socio-emotional indicators such as engagement levels or stress signals. This highly sensitive information raises significant privacy concerns. Protecting student data requires comprehensive governance frameworks that specify data collection practices, storage protocols, access controls, and retention policies. Secure encryption, anonymization, and compliance with legal standards such as GDPR or FERPA are essential to safeguard learner privacy. Transparency in how data is used—ensuring that students and parents understand what is collected, why, and how it informs instruction—is also critical for trust and acceptance.

Agentic AI introduces challenges in assigning responsibility when outcomes are unexpected or harmful. For instance, AI-driven interventions might produce inaccurate feedback, reinforce misconceptions, or bias grading. Establishing clear accountability mechanisms is essential to delineating the roles and responsibilities of educators, AI developers, and institutions. Policies should define how AI errors are identified, reported, and corrected, as well as the extent to which teachers can override AI recommendations. Accountability frameworks ensure that AI supports pedagogical goals ethically and responsibly, rather than operating as a black-box system without oversight.

Teacher-Student-AI Dynamics and Trust

Integrating AI into classrooms transforms interpersonal and instructional dynamics, requiring careful attention to trust among all participants.

Educators must trust that AI systems provide accurate, reliable, and contextually appropriate guidance. Lack of transparency in AI decision-making can erode this trust, causing teachers to either underutilize the system or rely excessively without critical oversight. For example, if an AI recommendation for grouping students contradicts a teacher's understanding of classroom dynamics, skepticism may reduce engagement with the technology. Building trust requires explainable AI models, clear documentation of AI logic, and opportunities for teachers to validate or adjust AI outputs.

Learners must perceive AI as supportive, fair, and unbiased. If students feel overly monitored, misjudged, or constrained by AI interventions, engagement and motivation may decline. For example, in an adaptive learning system that tracks responses in real time, students may feel pressured or anxious if feedback is perceived as punitive rather than constructive. Designing AI interactions that are transparent, encouraging, and responsive to individual needs is critical to maintaining positive student experiences and fostering intrinsic motivation.

Effective integration of AI requires a careful balance between human and machine roles. AI should augment rather than replace human judgment, allowing educators to maintain mentorship, socio-emotional support, and ethical oversight. Thoughtful instructional workflow design ensures that AI complements teachers' expertise, enhances peer collaboration, and preserves the human-centered nature of learning. For example, AI may provide personalized hints in problem-solving activities, while teachers focus on guiding reflection, discussion, and synthesis.

Equity, Access, and Inclusivity

While agentic AI has the potential to democratize education, uneven access and design limitations can exacerbate existing inequities.

Students in under-resourced schools or regions may lack access to devices, stable internet, or technical support, preventing them from benefiting fully from AI-enhanced learning. Bridging this gap requires investments in infrastructure, low-cost device programs, and offline-compatible AI solutions.

AI systems trained on narrow datasets may fail to accommodate diverse languages, cultural norms, or educational practices. For example, language learning AI optimized for English-speaking contexts may not provide accurate feedback for speakers of other languages, or may misinterpret culturally specific expressions.

Inclusive AI design requires culturally responsive datasets, multi-lingual capabilities, and awareness of local educational contexts.

Developers and educators must ensure that AI supports learners with disabilities, varied learning abilities, and diverse socio-cultural backgrounds. Features such as text-to-speech, visual aids, adjustable difficulty levels, and customizable interfaces can help accommodate diverse needs. Avoiding one-size-fits-all designs is crucial to prevent systemic disadvantages for any group of learners.

Addressing these challenges necessitates an ethical, human-centered approach to agentic AI integration. Policymakers, educators, and developers must collaborate to establish guidelines for fairness, transparency, and accountability, while also promoting equitable access, inclusive pedagogy, and adaptive support mechanisms. By proactively mitigating risks, AI can enhance education while respecting learners' rights, diversity, and socio-emotional well-being.

CONCLUSION

The integration of agentic AI in education marks a pivotal shift in pedagogy, offering unprecedented opportunities to enhance teaching effectiveness, personalize learning, and foster meaningful collaboration between humans and intelligent systems. As co-teachers and learning partners, agentic AI systems can dynamically adapt to learner needs, provide timely feedback, and support innovative instructional strategies, ultimately transforming traditional educational paradigms.

Potential developments in agentic AI are pointing toward increasingly sophisticated co-teaching models, where AI not only assists with routine tasks but also actively participates in curriculum design, scaffolding, and collaborative learning. Future AI systems may leverage advanced analytics, natural language understanding, and multimodal interactions to provide richer, context-aware support, enabling educators to deliver highly personalized and engaging learning experiences at scale.

The adoption of agentic AI also carries policy, curriculum, and professional development implications. Policymakers must establish ethical frameworks, data governance standards, and equitable access policies to ensure AI benefits all learners. Curricula may need redesigning to integrate AI-enabled learning activities, with an emphasis on problem-solving, collaboration, and digital literacy. Simultaneously, teacher professional development programs should focus on AI literacy, co-teaching strategies, and the effective use of AI-generated insights, preparing educators to leverage AI as a pedagogical ally.

Finally, the vision for AI-enhanced education emphasizes sustainability, ethics, and learner-centered design. Agentic AI should complement human instruction, empower learners, and uphold inclusive practices while respecting privacy, mitigating bias, and fostering trust. By aligning technological innovation with pedagogical values, education systems can create environments where human-AI collaboration enriches learning outcomes and nurtures adaptive, autonomous, and motivated learners.

REFERENCES

Acharya, D. B., Kuppan, K., & Divya, B. (2025). Agentic AI: Autonomous Intelligence for Complex Goals - A Comprehensive Survey. *IEEE Access : Practical Innovations, Open Solutions, 13*, 18912–18936. DOI: 10.1109/ACCESS.2025.3532853

Artsn, M., & Bozkurt, A. (2025). Charting new horizons: What agentic artificial intelligence (AI) promises in the educational landscape. *EDULEARN25 Proceedings*, 2019–2023.

Bandi, A., Kongari, B., Naguru, R., Pasnoor, S., & Vilipala, S. V. (2025). The Rise of Agentic AI: A Review of Definitions, Frameworks, Architectures, Applications, Evaluation Metrics, and Challenges. *Future Internet 2025, Vol. 17, Page 404, 17*(9), 404. DOI: 10.3390/fi17090404

Bandura, A., & Walters, R. H. (1977). *Social learning theory* (Vol. 1). Prentice hall Englewood Cliffs, NJ.

Dai, L., Jiang, Y.-H., Chen, Y., Guo, Z., Liu, T.-Y., & Shao, X. (2024). Agent4EDU: Advancing AI for Education with Agentic Workflows. *Proceedings of the 2024 3rd International Conference on Artificial Intelligence and Education*, 180–185. DOI: 10.1145/3722237.3722268

Deci, E. L., & Ryan, R. M. (2012). Self-determination theory. *Handbook of Theories of Social Psychology, 1*(20), 416–436.

Diebel, C., Goutier, M., Adam, M., & Benlian, A. (2025). When AI-Based Agents Are Proactive: Implications for Competence and System Satisfaction in Human–AI Collaboration. *Business & Information Systems Engineering*, •••, 1–20. DOI: 10.1007/s12599-024-00918-y

Diliberti, M. K., Schwartz, H. L., Doan, S. Y., Shapiro, A., Rainey, L. R., & Lake, R. J. (n.d.). *Using Artificial Intelligence Tools in K-12 Classrooms*. Retrieved October 16, 2025, from www.getbento.info/about

He, Z., Huang, C., He, T., & Bo, K. (2021). Applying an Intelligent Learning Partner in Teacher Education for Improving CT-Related TPACK. *Lecture Notes in Computer Science (Including Subseries Lecture Notes in Artificial Intelligence and Lecture Notes in Bioinformatics), 12830 LNCS*, 152–163. DOI: 10.1007/978-3-030-80504-3_13

Hein, G. E. (1991). Constructivist learning theory. *Institute for Inquiry, 14*.

Hooda, M., Rana, C., Dahiya, O., Rizwan, A., & Hossain, M. S. (2022). Artificial Intelligence for Assessment and Feedback to Enhance Student Success in Higher Education. *Mathematical Problems in Engineering, 2022*, 1–19. Advance online publication. DOI: 10.1155/2022/5215722

Hosseini, S., & Seilani, H. (2025). The role of agentic AI in shaping a smart future: A systematic review. *Array (New York, N.Y.), 26*, 100399. DOI: 10.1016/j.array.2025.100399

Hughes, L., Dwivedi, Y. K., Li, K., Appanderanda, M., Al-Bashrawi, M. A., & Chae, I. (2025). AI Agents and Agentic Systems: Redefining Global it Management. *Journal of Global Information Technology Management, 28*(3), 175–185. DOI: 10.1080/1097198X.2025.2524286

Ishaq, S. M., Bangulzai, A. R., & Asif, M. (2025). Artificial Intelligence as a Co-Teacher: Enhancing Educator Efficiency through Intelligent Systems. *The Critical Review of Social Sciences Studies, 3*(3), 1324–1342. DOI: 10.59075/gy5b5f42

Katsenou, R., Kotsidis, K., Papadopoulou, A., Anastasiadis, P., & Deliyannis, I. (2025). Beyond Assistance: Embracing AI as a Collaborative Co-Agent in Education. *Education Sciences, 15*(8), 1006. DOI: 10.3390/educsci15081006

Maiti, P., & Goel, A. (2025). Can an AI Partner Empower Learners to Ask Critical Questions? *International Conference on Intelligent User Interfaces, Proceedings IUI*, 314–324. DOI: 10.1145/3708359.3712134

Minn, S. (2022). AI-assisted knowledge assessment techniques for adaptive learning environments. *Computers and Education: Artificial Intelligence, 3*, 100050. Advance online publication. DOI: 10.1016/j.caeai.2022.100050

Murugesan, S. (2025). The Rise of Agentic AI: Implications, Concerns, and the Path Forward. *IEEE Intelligent Systems, 40*(2), 8–14. DOI: 10.1109/MIS.2025.3544940

Ouwehand, K., Lespiau, F., Tricot, A., & Paas, F. (2025). Cognitive Load Theory: Emerging Trends and Innovations. *Education Sciences 2025, Vol. 15, Page 458, 15*(4), 458. DOI: 10.3390/educsci15040458

Radhika, K., Sai Vamsee, B., Sushruth Samson Kumar, K., & Rayalu, G. V. R. (2025). The Co-teacher—A Tool for Learning Using ChatGPT. *Cognitive Science and Technology, 2025*, 325–339. DOI: 10.1007/978-981-97-9266-5_33

Raheem, T., & Hossain, G. (2025). Agentic AI Systems: Opportunities, Challenges, and Trustworthiness. *2025 IEEE International Conference on Electro Information Technology (EIT)*, 618–624. DOI: 10.1109/eIT64391.2025.11103638

Sajja, R., Sermet, Y., & Demir, I. (2025). End-to-End Deployment of the Educational AI Hub for Personalized Learning and Engagement: A Case Study on Environmental Science Education. *IEEE Access : Practical Innovations, Open Solutions, 13*, 55169–55186. DOI: 10.1109/ACCESS.2025.3554222

Sweller, J. (2023). The Development of Cognitive Load Theory: Replication Crises and Incorporation of Other Theories Can Lead to Theory Expansion. *Educational Psychology Review, 35*(4), 1–20. DOI: 10.1007/s10648-023-09817-2

Sweller, J., & Chandler, P. (1991). Evidence for Cognitive Load Theory. *Cognition and Instruction, 8*(4), 351–362. Advance online publication. DOI: 10.1207/s1532690xci0804_5

Chapter 5
Agentic AI for Inclusive Education Opportunities for Accessibility and Differentiation

Abdullaeva Dilbar Ubaydullaevna
National Pedagogical University of Uzbekistan, Uzbekistan

Umida Sadikova
Mamun University, Uzbekistan

Erkin Iskandarov
Urgench State University, Uzbekistan

Aiman Shahzadi
https://orcid.org/0009-0001-1098-8169
Virtual University, Uzbekistan

Zebo Saidjanova
Mamun University, Uzbekistan

ABSTRACT

Agentic AI is reshaping inclusive education by enabling adaptive, personalized, and equitable learning experiences. These intelligent systems act as co-teachers, dynamically responding to individual learner needs, providing real-time feedback, and supporting differentiated instruction. Innovations such as adaptive curricula, AI-mediated collaborative platforms, and context-aware assistive technologies enhance accessibility for learners with diverse abilities. Effective implementation requires

DOI: 10.4018/979-8-3373-4621-2.ch005

policies addressing equity and privacy, curriculum integration, and teacher training to leverage AI ethically. When thoughtfully applied, agentic AI fosters engagement, bridges learning gaps, and promotes an inclusive educational landscape.

INTRODUCTION

Inclusive education has become a cornerstone of equitable learning, emphasizing that all learners, regardless of ability, background, or socio-economic status, should have access to high-quality educational opportunities. Globally, inclusive education initiatives aim to reduce barriers to learning, promote diversity, and foster environments where every student can participate fully and achieve their potential. The United Nations' Sustainable Development Goal 4 (SDG 4) highlights the imperative of ensuring inclusive and equitable quality education, reflecting a growing recognition that education systems must adapt to the varied needs of learners rather than expecting learners to conform to a fixed instructional model.

Despite this growing emphasis, traditional classrooms often struggle to provide differentiated instruction and equitable access. Learners with disabilities, language differences, or diverse learning preferences may encounter barriers that limit their engagement, comprehension, and academic progress. Teachers face challenges in addressing these differences effectively due to constraints in time, resources, and instructional support. Consequently, many learners are at risk of being underserved, leading to gaps in achievement, motivation, and long-term educational outcomes.

Recent advancements in artificial intelligence (AI) offer promising avenues to overcome these challenges, with agentic AI emerging as a particularly transformative approach. Unlike conventional AI systems, which primarily respond to explicit instructions or perform repetitive tasks, agentic AI possesses autonomy, contextual awareness, and proactive decision-making capabilities. In educational settings, these systems can perceive learners' needs, adapt instructional strategies in real time, and provide personalized feedback and learning pathways. By acting as intelligent co-teachers or learning partners, agentic AI has the potential to enhance accessibility, facilitate differentiation, and create learning environments that respond dynamically to individual student requirements.

This chapter explores the role of agentic AI in promoting inclusive education, with a focus on accessibility and differentiated instruction. It examines the mechanisms through which agentic AI can support diverse learners, highlight practical applications and case studies, and addresses the ethical, pedagogical, and operational considerations involved in its implementation. By the end of the chapter, readers will gain a comprehensive understanding of how agentic AI can reshape educational practices, empowering educators to deliver more equitable, adaptive, and effective learning experiences for all students.

UNDERSTANDING AGENTIC AI IN EDUCATION

The integration of artificial intelligence in education has opened new possibilities for personalized, adaptive, and inclusive learning experiences. Among the diverse types of AI, agentic AI stands out for its ability to act autonomously, make context-aware decisions, and engage proactively with learners. Understanding its definition, characteristics, and role in educational environments is critical to appreciating its potential in transforming inclusive education.

Definition and Key Characteristics

Agentic AI refers to a class of intelligent systems designed to operate with a high degree of autonomy, enabling them to perceive, interpret, reason, and act within dynamic environments without requiring constant human intervention. Unlike traditional AI systems, which typically follow pre-defined rules or respond passively to user commands, agentic AI possesses the ability to initiate actions based on environmental cues, learner behaviors, and contextual information. This capability allows agentic AI to go beyond reactive task execution, functioning instead as a proactive, adaptive, and context-sensitive partner in educational settings (Kostopoulos et al., 2025; Ouhnine, 2026). Agentic AI is not simply a tool for performing automated tasks; it is an intelligent system capable of understanding complex learning environments, identifying learner needs, and dynamically adjusting its behavior to optimize educational outcomes (Holmes et al., 2019).

The key characteristics of agentic AI can be categorized into autonomy, contextual awareness, and proactive decision-making, each contributing uniquely to its educational impact:

Autonomy

Agentic AI can independently make decisions within the scope of its programmed objectives, adjusting its actions in response to changes in the learning environment. This autonomy allows the system to perform continuous monitoring and intervention without requiring direct teacher input at every step. For instance, an agentic AI tutoring system can determine which instructional activity a student should engage in next, adapting the difficulty level or content type based on ongoing performance data (Zawacki-Richter et al., 2019). Autonomy also enables AI systems to operate in distributed or blended learning environments, supporting multiple learners simultaneously while maintaining individualized attention.

Contextual Awareness

Beyond executing tasks, agentic AI can perceive and interpret contextual information. This includes monitoring learner performance, engagement levels, learning preferences, and even emotional or motivational states where applicable. By understanding the situational context, agentic AI can make informed decisions about when and how to intervene (Liu, 2025). For example, if a student appears disengaged during a lesson, the AI may introduce an interactive simulation or multimedia content aligned with the learner's interests to re-engage them. Contextual awareness also allows agentic AI to recognize patterns of misconceptions across multiple learners, enabling targeted remediation or group-level interventions that support broader classroom learning objectives (Baker et al., 2016).

Proactive Decision-Making

Unlike conventional AI that merely reacts to user inputs, agentic AI anticipates learner needs and potential challenges, initiating interventions before problems become critical. This proactive capability ensures that learners receive timely support and guidance, enhancing the effectiveness of instruction (Champaneria, 2025). For example, the system might identify a student struggling with fractions and automatically provide additional practice exercises or alternative explanations before the learner experiences significant difficulty. Proactive decision-making also extends to facilitating collaborative learning, suggesting peer partners or group activities that maximize engagement and mutual learning opportunities (Kostopoulos et al., 2025).

Together, these characteristics empower agentic AI to function as an intelligent co-teacher and learning partner, offering personalized guidance, adaptive feedback, and context-sensitive support tailored to individual learner profiles. In classrooms, agentic AI enhances instructional effectiveness by complementing the educator's expertise, enabling differentiated learning pathways, and ensuring that diverse learner needs are met efficiently. Its combination of autonomy, contextual awareness, and proactive engagement positions agentic AI as a transformative force in education, capable of reshaping traditional pedagogical practices while fostering inclusive and adaptive learning environments (Elazab, 2024; Luckin et al., 2018).

Distinction from Conventional AI

The fundamental distinction between agentic AI and conventional AI lies in reactivity versus proactivity, a difference that profoundly shapes their application in educational settings. Conventional AI systems, such as automated grading software, rule-based tutoring programs, or basic recommendation engines, primarily operate by executing pre-defined instructions or responding to explicit inputs. These systems perform repetitive or routine tasks efficiently, but their actions are largely reactive: they wait for user input or specific triggers before providing output. For example, an automated grading tool might score a multiple-choice exam based solely on fixed answer keys, providing feedback that is uniform for all students regardless of individual learning needs. While effective for standardized tasks, conventional AI lacks the capacity to interpret nuanced learner behavior, anticipate challenges, or adapt dynamically to diverse educational contexts (Mallik & Gangopadhyay, 2023).

In contrast, agentic AI operates with a higher degree of autonomy and intelligence, enabling it to function as a proactive participant in the learning process. It continuously monitors learner performance, engagement, and preferences, analyzing patterns in real time to identify gaps or misconceptions. Unlike conventional AI that provides static responses, agentic AI can tailor interventions for individual learners, such as recommending targeted exercises for students struggling with specific concepts, offering scaffolded explanations, or adjusting the difficulty level of tasks based on progress. This capability allows agentic AI to anticipate learner needs and implement strategies before challenges escalate, thereby fostering more effective and personalized learning experiences (Kamalov et al., 2025; Yan, 2025).

Another important distinction lies in contextual adaptability. Conventional AI typically lacks the capacity to understand the broader learning environment, such as group dynamics, classroom interactions, or learner emotional states. Agentic AI, on the other hand, incorporates context-aware algorithms that interpret situational cues and adjust instructional strategies accordingly. For instance, in a mixed-ability classroom, agentic AI can suggest peer pairing arrangements, collaborative projects, or differentiated assignments, ensuring that every student participates meaningfully and benefits from social learning opportunities (Bozkurt, 2025; Ng et al., 2025). This dynamic responsiveness is particularly valuable in in inclusive classrooms, where learner needs are highly diverse and constantly evolving.

Moreover, agentic AI contributes to continuous learning and improvement, both for the system itself and for educators. By analyzing patterns across multiple learners and learning sessions, agentic AI can refine its recommendations, improve predictive accuracy, and provide teachers with actionable insights on student progress. Conventional AI, by contrast, is generally limited to fixed rules and predefined outputs, offering minimal insight into broader trends or long-term learning trajectories (Diebel et al., 2025).

While conventional AI remains valuable for automating routine educational tasks, agentic AI transcends these limitations by combining proactive engagement, contextual awareness, and adaptive intervention. This enables it to function as a collaborative co-teacher, supporting differentiated instruction, anticipating learner needs, and fostering inclusivity. By moving from reactivity to proactivity, agentic AI fundamentally reshapes the classroom, offering a more personalized, equitable, and effective learning environment compared to traditional AI approaches.

AI Role in Learning Environments

In educational settings, agentic AI serves as a multifaceted enabler, reshaping traditional pedagogical practices, enhancing learner engagement, and promoting inclusivity. Unlike conventional instructional tools, agentic AI integrates autonomous decision-making, contextual awareness, and proactive intervention to create adaptive learning environments that respond dynamically to the needs of individual learners and groups. Its contributions are evident across several critical dimensions of teaching and learning, including personalized instruction, engagement, differentiation, and accessibility.

Personalized Learning

One of the most significant impacts of agentic AI is its ability to provide truly personalized learning experiences. By continuously analyzing student performance, engagement metrics, learning preferences, and prior knowledge, agentic AI can tailor instructional content, sequencing, and pacing to individual learner needs. For example, if a student demonstrates difficulty with a particular concept, the AI can provide alternative explanations, interactive simulations, or additional practice exercises specifically aligned with their learning style. Conversely, for advanced learners, the system can accelerate content delivery, introduce enrichment materials, or suggest independent exploration activities. This level of personalization ensures that learners progress at a pace suited to their capabilities while maintaining high levels of motivation and achievement. Over time, personalized learning pathways created by agentic AI not only improve academic outcomes but also foster self-directed learning and autonomy among students (Kamalov et al., 2025; Yan, 2025).

Enhanced Engagement

Agentic AI also contributes significantly to learner engagement by introducing interactive, adaptive, and context-sensitive interventions. It can detect waning attention, boredom, or frustration through behavioral or performance cues and respond with engaging strategies. These might include gamified exercises, adaptive quizzes, scenario-based learning activities, or multimedia resources aligned with student interests. For instance, in a history lesson, an AI system could transform static content into an interactive timeline or role-playing simulation that captivates learners and encourages active participation. By responding dynamically to engagement levels, agentic AI promotes curiosity, persistence, and a sense of ownership over the learning process, which are critical components of inclusive and effective education (Bozkurt, 2025; Mallik & Gangopadhyay, 2023).

Facilitating Differentiation

Differentiated instruction is essential in diverse classrooms where students possess varying abilities, learning speeds, and preferences. Agentic AI supports teachers in implementing differentiation more efficiently and accurately. It can analyze data on individual student performance and identify areas of strength or difficulty, allowing educators to provide targeted support without slowing the overall class pace. For example, an AI system might recommend small-group activities for learners requiring remediation, individualized enrichment projects for high-achieving students, or customized feedback for each learner's submissions. By enabling data-driven differentiation, agentic AI reduces the cognitive load on teachers, allowing them to focus on higher-order instructional strategies while ensuring that each student receives the support, they need to thrive (Yan, 2025).

Supporting Accessibility

Beyond personalization and engagement, agentic AI enhances educational accessibility, ensuring that learners with disabilities or special needs can participate fully in classroom activities. AI-driven assistive features such as text-to-speech, speech-to-text, sign language interpretation, captioning, and visual content customization allow students with visual, auditory, or cognitive impairments to access learning materials effectively. For example, a student with hearing impairment can follow real-time captions or AI-mediated sign language translations, while a learner with dyslexia can receive simplified text presentations and adaptive reading exercises. These accessibility enhancements foster an inclusive environment where all students, regardless of their abilities, have equitable opportunities to learn and succeed (Ng et al., 2025).

By combining autonomy, contextual awareness, and proactive engagement, agentic AI transforms traditional learning environments into dynamic, responsive, and co-constructed spaces. Educators are empowered to address the unique needs of each learner, while students experience instruction that adapts to their pace, style, and capabilities. The result is a more inclusive classroom culture that promotes equity, reduces learning gaps, and supports high-quality education for all. In essence, agentic AI acts not merely as a tool but as a collaborative partner, enhancing both the teaching process and the learning experience, and paving the way for educational environments that are more adaptive, engaging, and accessible than ever before.

ACCESSIBILITY ENHANCEMENT THROUGH AGENTIC AI

Inclusive education requires that all learners, regardless of physical, sensory, or cognitive abilities, can fully participate in learning experiences. Traditional educational approaches often struggle to meet the diverse needs of students with disabilities due to standardized content, limited teacher resources, and the absence of real-time adaptive support. Agentic AI provides transformative solutions, offering proactive, context-aware, and personalized support that goes beyond conventional accommodations. By integrating autonomy, contextual understanding, and adaptive interventions, agentic AI enhances accessibility across multiple domains, ensuring equitable learning opportunities for all students.

Support for Learners with Disabilities

Agentic AI significantly improves access for learners with visual, auditory, and cognitive impairments by providing adaptive, responsive, and personalized assistive technologies.

Visual Impairments

For students with low vision or blindness, agentic AI leverages technologies such as screen readers, tactile feedback devices, and context-aware audio descriptions. These systems can interpret images, diagrams, and interactive content, translating them into accessible formats. Unlike static assistive tools, agentic AI monitors learner interactions in real time, dynamically adjusting content presentation and complexity to optimize comprehension and engagement (Kooli & Chakraoui, 2025). For example, a visually impaired learner navigating an online science module may receive auditory explanations synchronized with tactile graphics or haptic feedback, allowing them to fully grasp spatial and graphical information.

Auditory Impairments

Learners with hearing difficulties benefit from AI-powered sign language interpreters, automated captioning, and speech-to-text tools. Agentic AI enhances these tools by integrating contextual awareness—understanding lesson flow, learner attention, and previous comprehension—allowing explanations and visual cues to be tailored for optimal understanding. In classroom settings, real-time AI translation of lectures into sign language or captions ensures that deaf or hard-of-hearing students remain fully engaged, participate actively in discussions, and can interact seamlessly with peers and teachers.

Cognitive and Learning Disabilities

Students with dyslexia, ADHD, or other cognitive challenges face difficulties in processing complex or voluminous information. Agentic AI addresses these needs by breaking content into manageable segments, providing multimodal explanations (text, audio, visuals), and offering personalized scaffolding strategies (Ayeni et al., 2024). For instance, a learner struggling with reading comprehension may receive stepwise guidance, interactive exercises, and memory aids that reinforce understanding without overwhelming them. The AI can adapt instructional approaches dynamically, offering repetition, simplification, or enrichment based on ongoing learner performance.

Through these assistive technologies, agentic AI transforms accessibility from a reactive accommodation to a proactive, integrated support system, continuously monitoring, adapting, and optimizing instruction for learners with disabilities.

Personalized Learning Pathways

Beyond addressing specific disabilities, agentic AI facilitates personalized learning pathways for all students, accommodating differences in prior knowledge, learning styles, and pacing.

Adaptive Content Delivery

Agentic AI continuously analyzes learner performance and engagement, dynamically adjusting the difficulty, sequence, and format of instructional materials. For example, a student struggling with algebra may be provided with interactive visual aids, guided problem-solving exercises, and contextual hints, while a more advanced learner progresses to complex applications or enrichment tasks. This ensures each learner remains challenged yet supported, promoting mastery and confidence (Panjwani-Charania & Zhai, 2024).

Flexible Learning Modalities

By offering content across multiple modalities—including text, audio, video, interactive simulations, and gamified exercises—agentic AI caters to individual preferences and enhances comprehension. Students can engage with material in the form that suits them best, making learning more accessible and engaging, particularly for those with varied cognitive or sensory needs.

Continuous Feedback and Support

Immediate, context-sensitive feedback allows learners to understand mistakes, reinforce concepts, and track progress. For example, a student practicing a science experiment virtually may receive real-time prompts correcting errors, clarifying misconceptions, or suggesting alternative approaches. This continuous guidance maintains motivation, reduces frustration, and promotes self-regulated learning (Perry et al., 2024).

Personalized learning pathways created by agentic AI ensure that students are neither left behind nor disengaged, fostering equitable outcomes and supporting inclusive classroom dynamics.

DIFFERENTIATION AND PERSONALIZED LEARNING

Differentiated instruction and personalized learning are critical components of inclusive education, enabling each learner to engage with content in ways that match their abilities, interests, and pace. Agentic AI offers innovative solutions to implement these strategies effectively, providing educators with tools to monitor, adapt, and optimize learning for diverse student populations.

Adaptive Assessment and Feedback

One of the most powerful contributions of agentic AI to inclusive and personalized learning is its ability to facilitate continuous, adaptive, and real-time assessment. Traditional assessment methods, such as periodic tests or static quizzes, often fail to capture the ongoing learning progress of students and may not provide timely, individualized guidance. Agentic AI addresses these limitations by integrating performance tracking, personalized feedback, and adaptive formative assessments into everyday learning, enabling educators to respond proactively and students to receive support tailored to their unique needs (Halkiopoulos & Gkintoni, 2024).

Real-Time Performance Tracking

Agentic AI continuously monitors student interactions, engagement patterns, and performance across a variety of tasks, exercises, and learning activities. By analyzing this data, AI systems can identify trends, strengths, and areas requiring intervention. For example, a student who consistently struggles with word problems in mathematics may be flagged for targeted support, while another who demonstrates advanced problem-solving skills may be offered enrichment tasks. Real-time tracking allows teachers to detect learning gaps before they widen, reducing the likelihood of students falling behind and enabling timely, evidence-based interventions. Additionally, aggregated performance data across the classroom provides valuable insights into group-level trends, helping educators adjust instructional strategies and address common misconceptions (Ihichr et al., n.d.).

Personalized Feedback

Beyond tracking performance, agentic AI delivers instant, context-sensitive feedback that is tailored to the needs of each learner. Unlike conventional feedback mechanisms, which are often generic, delayed, or one-size-fits-all, AI-driven feedback can address the specific errors, misconceptions, or learning challenges that a student encounters (Yaseen et al., 2025). For instance, a student struggling with algebraic equations may receive step-by-step guidance, hints highlighting critical problem-solving strategies, or supplementary practice exercises targeting the exact skill deficit. Feedback can also be adaptive in modality: visual learners may receive annotated diagrams, while auditory learners receive spoken explanations. This personalization not only strengthens understanding but also fosters learner confidence, motivation, and self-efficacy by reinforcing progress and providing targeted support exactly when it is needed.

Formative Assessment Support

Agentic AI excels at designing dynamic, adaptive formative assessments that continuously evaluate and challenge learners in ways aligned with their current abilities. These assessments automatically adjust in difficulty based on learner responses, ensuring that tasks remain appropriately challenging without being discouraging.

For example, if a student demonstrates proficiency in basic geometry, the AI can introduce more complex problems involving proofs or real-world applications, while struggling students receive scaffolded questions that reinforce foundational concepts. By integrating assessment into everyday learning activities, agentic AI transforms evaluation from a static checkpoint into an ongoing, interactive learning process, promoting deeper understanding and continuous growth.

Furthermore, adaptive assessment combined with AI-driven feedback supports differentiated instruction at scale. Teachers can leverage insights generated by the AI to personalize lesson plans, group students effectively, and allocate instructional time more efficiently (Yao & González-Vélez, 2025). Students, in turn, benefit from a learning environment where feedback is immediate, actionable, and aligned with their individual needs, reducing frustration, promoting engagement, and fostering self-directed learning. Agentic AI transforms assessment and feedback from a reactive, summative process into a proactive, continuous, and learner-centered system, ensuring that each student receives the support necessary to succeed while allowing educators to make informed, data-driven instructional decisions. By integrating real-time monitoring, personalized feedback, and adaptive formative assessment, agentic AI enhances learning outcomes, maintains motivation, and fosters a culture of equity and inclusivity in the classroom.

Curriculum Differentiation

Curriculum differentiation is a cornerstone of inclusive education, allowing educators to address the diverse needs, abilities, and learning styles of students. In traditional classrooms, differentiation often requires substantial time and effort from teachers, making it challenging to meet the individual needs of each learner, particularly in large or heterogeneous classes. Agentic AI offers a transformative solution by enabling dynamic, data-driven customization of instructional content, sequencing, and delivery. Through its autonomous and context-aware capabilities, agentic AI allows educators to provide personalized learning experiences efficiently and effectively, ensuring that all students have equitable opportunities to achieve mastery and remain engaged.

Individualized Learning Paths

Agentic AI can design and manage custom learning trajectories for each student, taking into account their prior knowledge, skill levels, learning pace, and interests. For instance, in a mathematics classroom, one learner may require additional practice on fractions, while another is ready to explore advanced algebraic concepts (du Plooy et al., 2024). The AI system can sequence lessons accordingly, introducing prerequisite concepts for one student while offering enrichment activities for another. Beyond academic content, AI can integrate learner interests—such as science, sports, or art—into assignments and examples, fostering motivation and relevance. Over time, these individualized pathways evolve as the system continuously monitors performance, engagement, and comprehension, ensuring that learning remains appropriately challenging and personalized.

Content Customization

Agentic AI facilitates multimodal content adaptation, ensuring that learning materials are accessible, engaging, and suited to varying cognitive levels and learning styles. Text-based content can be supplemented with audio explanations, interactive simulations, visual diagrams, and gamified exercises. For example, a student struggling with reading comprehension can receive simplified text, text-to-speech narration, and visual annotations, while a more advanced student engages with complex case studies or problem-solving simulations. By tailoring content to both ability and modality, agentic AI allows learners to engage with material in ways that maximize understanding, retention, and active participation. This capability is particularly valuable for students with learning differences, language barriers, or cognitive challenges.

Scalable Differentiation

One of the most significant advantages of agentic AI is its ability to scale differentiation across entire classrooms, including large and diverse student populations (Mahmoud & Sørensen, 2024). Teachers can provide individualized instruction without being overwhelmed by the logistical demands of personalizing content manually. For example, in a classroom of 40 students, agentic AI can simultaneously deliver multiple lesson pathways, assign tasks suited to varying abilities, and monitor progress in real time, freeing teachers to focus on facilitation, guidance, and mentoring. This scalability ensures that differentiation is not limited by class size or resource constraints, making inclusive and equitable education feasible across a wide range of learning environments.

By integrating individualized learning paths, adaptive content customization, and scalable delivery, agentic AI ensures that every learner receives instruction tailored to their specific needs. This approach promotes deeper understanding, strengthens engagement, and supports mastery of content, while reducing disparities between high-achieving and struggling students. Ultimately, curriculum differentiation powered by agentic AI transforms classrooms into responsive, adaptive learning ecosystems, where instruction is continuously optimized to meet the evolving needs of all students.

Collaboration and Peer Learning Support

While agentic AI is widely recognized for supporting individualized learning, its potential to enhance collaborative and peer-based learning is equally significant. Social interaction and cooperative learning are essential components of inclusive education, as they foster not only cognitive development but also interpersonal skills, empathy, and social inclusion. Agentic AI facilitates these processes by actively mediating group activities, promoting equitable participation, and providing real-time scaffolding for communication and problem-solving, ensuring that collaborative learning is effective, structured, and inclusive.

Group Formation and Matching

Agentic AI can intelligently form learning groups by analyzing student data, including prior performance, complementary skill sets, learning styles, and individual interests. For instance, in a science project, the AI may pair students who excel in experimentation with those skilled in data analysis or presentation, creating synergistic teams that maximize collective strengths. Beyond academic compatibility, AI can also consider social-emotional factors, ensuring that quieter or marginalized students are included in groups where they can contribute meaningfully. This targeted group formation reduces the likelihood of social exclusion, enhances peer learning opportunities, and supports the development of collaborative problem-solving skills.

Facilitation of Collaborative Tasks

Once groups are formed, agentic AI can guide collaborative activities by providing clear instructions, defining roles, and monitoring interactions in real time. For example, in a group discussion or project-based learning activity, the AI can track contributions from each student, provide prompts or reminders to less active participants, and highlight progress toward shared objectives. By offering these interventions dynamically, agentic AI ensures equitable participation and prevents dominant learners from overshadowing others, creating a balanced environment where all students engage meaningfully. Additionally, AI can provide adaptive challenges to groups, adjusting the complexity of tasks according to collective performance, thereby maintaining motivation and promoting deeper learning.

Support for Peer Feedback

Agentic AI also strengthens the quality and effectiveness of peer assessment and collaborative discussions. Many students struggle to give constructive feedback or critically evaluate peer contributions, particularly in large or diverse classrooms. AI systems can scaffold this process by providing structured prompts, guiding students on how to articulate suggestions, asking probing questions, and evaluating work against clear criteria. For instance, during a writing workshop, the AI may suggest questions like, "How could your peer clarify this argument?" or "Can you provide an example to support this point?" This structured approach fosters critical thinking, reflective learning, and communication skills while ensuring that peer feedback remains constructive, inclusive, and supportive.

By mediating collaborative learning in this way, agentic AI extends personalization beyond individual instruction to group dynamics and social learning. It not only ensures that all students have opportunities to contribute and learn from peers but also fosters the development of essential interpersonal skills, teamwork, and social inclusion. In classrooms where learners have diverse abilities, learning styles, and backgrounds, AI-supported collaboration reduces barriers to participation, encourages mutual support, and enhances the overall learning experience. Agentic AI transforms peer learning from a loosely structured activity into a strategically guided, inclusive, and adaptive process, where cognitive, social, and emotional growth occur simultaneously. By combining intelligent group formation, facilitation of collaborative tasks, and structured support for peer feedback, agentic AI creates learning environments that are not only personalized but also socially equitable, inclusive, and conducive to holistic development.

CHALLENGES AND ETHICAL CONSIDERATIONS

While agentic AI offers substantial potential to enhance accessibility and differentiation in education, its implementation also raises several challenges and ethical considerations. Addressing these concerns is critical to ensure that AI integration promotes equity, preserves human agency, and supports the broader goals of inclusive education.

Data Privacy, Algorithmic Bias, and Equity Issues

The effectiveness of agentic AI in education relies heavily on the collection, analysis, and interpretation of learner data. While this data-driven approach enables highly personalized instruction and adaptive support, it also raises critical ethical and practical considerations related to privacy, fairness, and equity. Ensuring that these systems are deployed responsibly requires a comprehensive understanding of potential risks and proactive strategies to mitigate them.

Data Privacy

Agentic AI systems continuously collect and process sensitive information, including academic performance, learning behaviors, engagement patterns, and sometimes demographic or personal data. Protecting this information is paramount to safeguarding students' rights and maintaining trust in AI-enabled learning environments. Schools and developers must adhere to legal and regulatory frameworks such as GDPR, FERPA, or national privacy laws, implementing best practices for secure storage, encryption, and controlled access. Data should be anonymized wherever possible, and its use must be strictly limited to educational purposes. For example, analytics on student engagement should inform personalized lesson adjustments but should never be repurposed for marketing or non-educational profiling. Transparent communication with students, parents, and educators about what data is collected, how it is used, and who has access is essential for ethical implementation and community trust.

Algorithmic Bias

AI models are only as impartial as the data on which they are trained. If training datasets are incomplete, unrepresentative, or reflect societal biases, agentic AI can inadvertently perpetuate or amplify inequities. For instance, learners from underrepresented socio-economic backgrounds or with non-standard learning profiles may receive fewer effective recommendations or adaptive support, limiting their opportunities for success. Addressing algorithmic bias requires continuous monitoring, bias detection protocols, and iterative model refinement. Developers should incorporate diverse and representative datasets, test AI outputs across demographic and ability groups, and establish feedback mechanisms for educators to flag problematic recommendations. By proactively managing bias, AI can provide equitable support that benefits all learners rather than reinforcing existing disparities.

Equity Considerations

Beyond model fairness, access to agentic AI technologies can create or exacerbate educational inequities. Resource-rich schools may more easily implement AI-enabled platforms due to better infrastructure, funding, and trained personnel, while under-resourced schools may struggle to benefit from these innovations. To address this, policymakers and educational leaders must develop equitable deployment strategies, including funding initiatives, access to appropriate hardware, reliable internet connectivity, and teacher professional development. For example, rural schools or low-income districts may require government support or public-private partnerships to implement agentic AI effectively. Ensuring equity also involves providing inclusive training for teachers, so they can utilize AI tools confidently to support all learners, not just those in well-resourced environments.

In sum, while agentic AI offers unprecedented opportunities for personalized and inclusive education, its deployment carries significant ethical and equity responsibilities. Protecting student data, mitigating algorithmic bias, and ensuring equitable access are critical to preventing harm, fostering trust, and maximizing the positive impact of AI. Educational leaders, developers, and policymakers must work collaboratively to establish guidelines, mechanisms, and ethical practices that balance innovation with fairness, privacy, and social responsibility. By addressing these challenges proactively, agentic AI can be leveraged to enhance learning outcomes while promoting equity and inclusivity across diverse educational contexts.

Teacher Roles and Potential Over-Reliance on AI

Agentic AI holds the potential to transform teaching and learning by serving as a co-teacher, learning assistant, and facilitator of personalized instruction. However, it is essential to recognize that AI is a complementary tool, not a replacement for human educators. The effectiveness of agentic AI in inclusive and differentiated education depends on teachers' ability to integrate AI insights thoughtfully while maintaining their central role in fostering learning, motivation, and social-emotional development.

Evolving Teacher Roles

The integration of agentic AI requires teachers to adopt new and evolving roles. Educators shift from being primary content deliverers to facilitators, mentors, and decision-makers, interpreting AI-generated data and insights to guide instructional choices. For example, an AI system may highlight a group of students struggling with a particular concept, but it is the teacher who determines whether to provide targeted interventions, modify lesson pacing, or design supplementary activities. Professional development and continuous training are crucial to equip teachers with the skills to understand AI outputs, translate them into actionable pedagogical strategies, and effectively mediate student learning. Moreover, teachers play a key role in contextualizing AI recommendations—considering social-emotional needs, classroom dynamics, and cultural factors that AI alone may not fully capture. By embracing these roles, teachers can enhance their instructional impact, foster critical thinking, and maintain personal connections with students, even in AI-augmented classrooms.

Risk of Over-Reliance

While agentic AI offers real-time assessment, adaptive content delivery, and personalized feedback, over-reliance on AI poses potential risks. Excessive dependence on automated recommendations may inadvertently diminish teacher judgment, creativity, and responsiveness. For instance, if a teacher relies solely on AI-generated lesson plans or feedback, they may miss opportunities to address nuanced learning needs, adapt to emergent classroom situations, or incorporate innovative teaching strategies. Furthermore, students may perceive learning as overly mechanical or impersonal if human engagement is minimized, potentially affecting motivation, trust, and relational development. To mitigate these risks, educators must strike a careful balance between leveraging AI for efficiency and maintaining human oversight, interpretive expertise, and direct interaction with learners.

Maintaining this balance also involves critical reflection and ethical considerations. Teachers must evaluate AI recommendations for potential biases, relevance, and applicability, ensuring that all students benefit equitably. For example, if AI suggests grouping students based on prior performance, teachers may need to adjust groups to prevent reinforcing achievement gaps or inadvertently isolating certain learners. By exercising professional judgment, teachers ensure that AI complements rather than constrain instructional decision-making. Agentic AI can enhance teacher effectiveness, reduce administrative burden, and support personalized learning, but it cannot replace the human qualities essential to education—empathy, creativity, intuition, and relational guidance. Teachers remain central to shaping learning environments, mediating AI outputs, and fostering inclusion. When implemented thoughtfully, the partnership between AI and educators can amplify learning outcomes while preserving the critical human dimension of teaching, ensuring that technology serves as a supportive ally rather than a substitute.

Ensuring Inclusivity Without Compromising Human Agency

Inclusive education emphasizes not only access to learning but also the empowerment of students and educators to participate meaningfully in the educational process. While agentic AI offers unprecedented opportunities for personalization, accessibility, and differentiation, its integration must be carefully managed to preserve human agency, ensuring that technology serves as a supportive tool rather than a prescriptive authority.

Maintaining Student Autonomy

One of the central challenges in AI-enhanced learning is striking a balance between guidance and independence. AI systems can provide recommendations, adaptive content, and targeted interventions, but these should support rather than dictate learner choices. Prescriptive AI that rigidly directs learning paths risks undermining student autonomy, motivation, and self-regulation. For example, while an AI might suggest a set of exercises for a student struggling with fractions, learners should have the freedom to choose alternative practice problems, explore supplementary resources, or adjust pacing according to their preferences. By enabling students to exercise decision-making, AI supports the development of self-directed learning skills, fostering agency, critical thinking, and ownership of the learning process.

Ethical Decision-Making

Developers and educators share responsibility for ensuring that AI interventions adhere to ethical standards and respect cultural and individual differences. Inclusive AI design must consider diverse learner backgrounds, values, and preferences to prevent intrusive, biased, or culturally insensitive practices. For instance, AI recommendations should avoid stereotyping students based on prior performance, socio-economic background, or language proficiency. Furthermore, ethical considerations extend to transparency: learners and teachers should understand how AI generates recommendations, what data it relies upon, and what potential limitations exist. Clear communication and informed consent help safeguard learner rights, promote trust, and enhance the legitimacy of AI-supported interventions.

Collaborative Human-AI Interaction

Effective inclusive learning environments emerge when AI functions as a collaborative partner, complementing rather than supplanting teacher judgment. Teachers remain central in interpreting AI outputs, contextualizing suggestions, and fostering meaningful engagement between students and technology. For example, during a group project, agentic AI can recommend optimal peer groupings or scaffold collaborative tasks, but teachers guide interactions, mediate conflicts, and ensure that social-emotional needs are addressed. By emphasizing collaboration, AI becomes a co-facilitator, augmenting human capacity to support inclusion while preserving the relational, interpretive, and ethical dimensions of teaching.

Additionally, maintaining human agency requires continuous monitoring and reflection. Educators must evaluate AI interventions for unintended consequences, such as over-reliance on automated guidance or inadvertent reinforcement of inequities. Incorporating student feedback into AI-mediated learning experiences ensures that learners remain active participants, shaping how technology supports their education. For example, learners could indicate preferences for different learning modalities, pacing, or task difficulty, allowing AI to adjust recommendations dynamically without removing choice or oversight. By proactively addressing these challenges, education systems can maximize the benefits of agentic AI while safeguarding equity, privacy, and human agency. Thoughtful integration ensures that AI empowers learners, enhances teacher effectiveness, and supports inclusive practices without compromising autonomy, creativity, or relational engagement. When inclusivity and human agency are prioritized, AI becomes a transformative ally—enabling personalized, accessible, and equitable learning experiences while maintaining the essential human dimensions of education.

CONCLUSION

The integration of agentic AI in education represents a transformative opportunity to advance inclusivity, accessibility, and personalized learning. As intelligent co-teachers and learning partners, agentic AI systems offer the ability to dynamically adapt to individual learner needs, provide real-time feedback, and facilitate differentiated instruction at scale. Emerging innovations—including adaptive curricula, AI-mediated collaborative learning platforms, and context-aware assistive technologies—hold significant promise for creating educational environments that are both equitable and responsive to the diverse abilities and preferences of students.

To realize this potential, several strategic recommendations are essential. Policymakers should develop guidelines that ensure equitable access to AI-driven educational tools while safeguarding data privacy and minimizing algorithmic bias. Curriculum designers must consider integrating AI-supported personalization into instructional planning, enabling flexible learning pathways that accommodate varying learner profiles. Teacher training programs should emphasize the complementary role of AI, equipping educators with the skills to interpret AI insights, implement adaptive strategies, and maintain active engagement with students. Collectively, these measures can foster a balanced and ethical integration of agentic AI within educational systems.

In summary, agentic AI offers unprecedented opportunities to transform accessibility and differentiation in inclusive education. By enabling personalized learning pathways, supporting learners with disabilities, and facilitating collaborative engagement, agentic AI can help bridge gaps in traditional instructional models. When implemented thoughtfully and ethically, these systems empower educators, enhance student outcomes, and contribute to a more inclusive and equitable educational landscape, paving the way for a future in which all learners can thrive.

REFERENCES

Ayeni, A. O., Ovbiye, R. E., Onayemi, A. S., & Ojedele, K. E. (2024). Corresponding author: Ayobami O Ayeni AI-driven adaptive learning platforms: Enhancing educational outcomes for students with special needs through user-centric, tailored digital tools. *World Journal of Advanced Research and Reviews, 2024*(03), 2253–2265. DOI: 10.30574/wjarr.2024.22.3.0843

Baker, R. S., Martin, T., & Rossi, L. M. (2016). Educational Data Mining and Learning Analytics. *The Handbook of Cognition and Assessment*, 379–396. DOI: 10.1002/9781118956588.ch16

Bozkurt, A. (2025). Algorithmically manufactured minds: Generative and agentic AI in a time of post-truth, reconfiguration of student agency and death of critical pedagogy. In *Open Praxis* (Vol. 17, Issue 2, pp. 206–210). International Council for Open and Distance Education Oslo, Norway.

Champaneria, H. K. (2025). From Insight to Impact: Architecting AI-Driven Learning Ecosystems for Personalized, Predictive and Proactive Education. *Journal Of Engineering And Computer Sciences*, *4*(7), 791–801.

Diebel, C., Goutier, M., Adam, M., & Benlian, A. (2025). When AI-Based Agents Are Proactive: Implications for Competence and System Satisfaction in Human–AI Collaboration. *Business & Information Systems Engineering*, •••, 1–20. DOI: 10.1007/s12599-024-00918-y

du Plooy, E., Casteleijn, D., & Franzsen, D. (2024). Personalized adaptive learning in higher education: A scoping review of key characteristics and impact on academic performance and engagement. *Heliyon*, *10*(21), e39630. DOI: 10.1016/j.heliyon.2024.e39630 PMID: 39524879

Elazab, M. (2024). Artificial Intelligence and Future of Teaching and Learning. *International Journal of Internet Education*, *23*(2), 1–16. Advance online publication. DOI: 10.21608/ijie.2024.414601

Halkiopoulos, C., & Gkintoni, E. (2024). Leveraging AI in E-Learning: Personalized Learning and Adaptive Assessment through Cognitive Neuropsychology—A Systematic Analysis. *Electronics 2024, Vol. 13, Page 3762, 13*(18), 3762. DOI: 10.3390/electronics13183762

Holmes, W., Bialik, M., & Fadel, C. (2019). *Artificial Intelligence in Education.* Promise and Implications for Teaching and Learning.

Ihichr, A., Oustous, O., El Bouzekri, Y., Idrissi, E., & Lahcen, A. A. (n.d.). A Systematic Review on Assessment in Adaptive Learning: Theories, Algorithms and Techniques. *IJACSA) International Journal of Advanced Computer Science and Applications, 15*(7), 2024. Retrieved October 26, 2025, from www.ijacsa.thesai.org

Kamalov, F., Calonge, D. S., Smail, L., Azizov, D., Thadani, D. R., Kwong, T., & Atif, A. (2025). Evolution of ai in education: Agentic workflows. *ArXiv Preprint ArXiv:2504.20082*.

Kooli, C., & Chakraoui, R. (2025). AI-driven assistive technologies in inclusive education: Benefits, challenges, and policy recommendations. *Sustainable Futures : An Applied Journal of Technology, Environment and Society*, *10*, 101042. DOI: 10.1016/j.sftr.2025.101042

Kostopoulos, G., Gkamas, V., Rigou, M., & Kotsiantis, S. (2025). Agentic AI in Education: State of the Art and Future Directions. *IEEE Access : Practical Innovations, Open Solutions*, *13*, 177467–177491. DOI: 10.1109/ACCESS.2025.3620473

Liu, Y. (2025). Psychological Adaptation and Affective Feedback in AI-Enhanced Education: A Systematic Review. *Simen Owen Academic Proceedings Series*, *1*, 17–27.

Luckin, R., Holmes, W., Griffiths, M., & Forcier, L. B. (2018). *Artificial intelligence and the future of learning*. The Brookings Institution.

Mahmoud, C. F., & Sørensen, J. T. (2024). Artificial Intelligence in Personalized Learning with a Focus on Current Developments and Future Prospects. *Research and Advances in Education*, *3*(8), 25–31. DOI: 10.56397/RAE.2024.08.04

Mallik, S., & Gangopadhyay, A. (2023). Proactive and reactive engagement of artificial intelligence methods for education: A review. *Frontiers in Artificial Intelligence*, *6*, 1151391. DOI: 10.3389/frai.2023.1151391 PMID: 37215064

Ng, D. T. K., Chan, E. K. C., & Lo, C. K. (2025). Opportunities, challenges and school strategies for integrating generative AI in education. *Computers and Education: Artificial Intelligence*, *8*, 100373. DOI: 10.1016/j.caeai.2025.100373

Ouhnine, I. (2026). The Future of Human Autonomy: Will Agentic Artificial Intelligence Augment or Replace Human Decision-Making. In *Transparency in AI-Assisted Management Decisions* (pp. 79–108). IGI Global Scientific Publishing.

Panjwani-Charania, S., & Zhai, X. (2024). AI for Students with Learning Disabilities: A Systematic Review. *Uses of Artificial Intelligence in STEM Education*, 469–493. DOI: 10.1093/oso/9780198882077.003.0021

Perry, N., Sun, C., Munro, M., Boulton, K. A., & Guastella, A. J. (2024). AI technology to support adaptive functioning in neurodevelopmental conditions in everyday environments: A systematic review. *NPJ Digital Medicine*, *7*(1), 370. DOI: 10.1038/s41746-024-01355-7 PMID: 39702672

Yan, L. (2025). From Passive Tool to Socio-cognitive Teammate: A Conceptual Framework for Agentic AI in Human-AI Collaborative Learning. *ArXiv Preprint ArXiv:2508.14825*.

Yao, Y., & González-Vélez, H. (2025). AI-Powered System to Facilitate Personalized Adaptive Learning in Digital Transformation. *Applied Sciences 2025, Vol. 15, Page 4989, 15*(9), 4989. DOI: 10.3390/app15094989

Yaseen, H., Mohammad, A. S., Ashal, N., Abusaimeh, H., Ali, A., & Sharabati, A. A. A. (2025). The Impact of Adaptive Learning Technologies, Personalized Feedback, and Interactive AI Tools on Student Engagement: The Moderating Role of Digital Literacy. *Sustainability 2025, Vol. 17, Page 1133, 17*(3), 1133. DOI: 10.3390/su17031133

Zawacki-Richter, O., Marín, V. I., Bond, M., & Gouverneur, F. (2019). Systematic review of research on artificial intelligence applications in higher education – where are the educators? In *International Journal of Educational Technology in Higher Education* (Vol. 16, Issue 1). DOI: 10.1186/s41239-019-0171-0

Chapter 6

AI Tutors for Enhancing Generative AI Literacy in Education

Usharani Bhimavarapu
https://orcid.org/0000-0002-0246-1420
Koneru Lakshmaiah Education Foundation, India

ABSTRACT

This study examines AI tutor and mentor development and deployment to facilitate pre-service teachers' (PSTs) professional development and learning. It employs a mixed-methods triangulated approach, which combines quantitative survey responses, placement information, and qualitative insight from PSTs and their mentoring teachers. Pre-placement AI literacy training and subsequent teaching placements provided the background for data collection, with post-placement surveys and semi-structured interviews provoking reflective narratives. Remora optimization was applied to feature selection, and two-stacked ResNet was applied to predict PST performance and provide personalized advice. The results indicate that AI tutors not only support self-regulated learning but also maximize mentor feedback and render generative AI tools useful to enact.

INTRODUCTION

Use of AI mentors and AI tutors to educate is the answer to the increasing need for personalized learning. The students in a typical class do not receive individual attention as the teacher-student ratio is enormous. AI technology can recognize the performance of the students and personalize the learning process according to the necessity, thus providing individual need-based assistance. Intelligent systems

DOI: 10.4018/979-8-3373-4621-2.ch006

can alert where intelligence is required and give practice to the individual. Also, AI teachers can give immediate feedback compared to normal teaching that spans days. Immediate feedback through AI allows learners to self-tune in real-time. AI also recognizes learning trend patterns by monitoring progress continuously. Thus, students can learn subjects at their own pace. Self-study is also enabled by AI coaches. Thus, the requirement of AI tutors is established as per the requirement of increased availability along with increased efficiency in learning.

AI teachers are hired to address the problem of balance of geography and time limit of learning. Low-resource schools or remote locations' students do not have any access to quality teachers. AI-based platforms ensure round-the-clock best-class learning with zero geographical limitation. They are accessible 24/7 for working students or other-bound students for ease. This center is relatively accessible for working or other-bound students. Multilingual instruction is also offered by AI instructors, and language disability will be removed. Explanation tunability can be made possible by the software in the sense of the culture of the learner. This preparedness offers education equity. AI counseling ensures that counseling will not be interrupted without being constrained by availability of human resources. AI teachers therefore have the responsibility of enhancing access to information globally.

Learning design and learning effectively is most likely going to be the greatest task of AI teachers. Lectures have always been passive and will certainly result in learning at a surface level. AI instructors utilize active approaches such as simulation, quizzes, and game-based training. They are capable of motivating and stimulating the students. Adaptive questioning allows the system to ask questions to the students without intimidating them. AI guidance provides example-based learning from concept to application. AI institutes application and understanding of mind. AI frustrates or puts the students to sleep by providing them with study material specific to their requirements. Continuous adaptation maintains the difficulty level in its best possible state. This kind of involvement of the student maximizes intellectual capability as well as interest in learning.

Trainers of AI and advisors are providing real-time feedback identification with knowledge gap fill. Every student possesses his/her own learning rate as well as learning style, and repeated teaching of few items is not beneficial. AI monitors performance values alongside where the students always get stuck. Later on, the teacher provides customized exercises or another explanation. Independent weak points consideration blocks future AI knowledge accumulation. Aside from that, AI may detect misconceptions before internalization. The mentorship includes goal setting, time management, and learning skills training. Data-intervention intervention enables intervention in the specific and not general. Early troubles known block the ideal learning achievements. That is why the required demand is that AI tutors need to be placed in central roles to give one-to-one remediation and help.

The second central function of AI tutors is to assist teachers rather than replace them. Teachers need to spend a considerable amount of time doing an amazing amount of tasks such as planning lessons and marking. AI is able to perform the roles of monitoring, evaluation, and provision of content. That leaves space for the instructors to attend to more than fundamentals. The classroom management and student needs are also taught by mentors. AI analysis can guide learning choice and that can be utilized by educators. Interactive AI-human interfaces enable human-AI interfaces. Mechanisms for differentiated learner differentiation can also be suggested by AI. Teachers are paired with AI in a bid to deliver quality learning. In that regard, AI tutors are cooperative aides to human teachers.

AI tutors facilitate lifelong learning beyond school. Learning is in a classroom where there is no room for ongoing skill improvement. Ongoing learning occurs in AI systems through updating to adapt to learner needs. AI systems offer up-to-date content, track learning of skills, and suggest further learning paths. Career and advisory professional capability advises students. Students learn according to business requirement or leisure pastimes. Learning is facilitated at any point in life. AI stimulated curiosity-driven discovery and problem-solving. AI individualized learning over a lifetime is achieved. AI tutors create intellectual growth a lifetime process.

Most required in AI tutors is providing learning to students. The disabled students are not able to learn in the regular classrooms. AI can be applied to tailor content for visual, hearing, or cognitive disabilities. With the levels of future challenge, text-to-speech and speech-to-text, the level playing field is given for accessibility. The mentors can deliver multiple streams of learning depending on the capability of the student. It gives a level playing field to all the students. AI facilitates ongoing management and feedbacking of the neurodiverse students through interaction. System flexibility provides for incorporation of various learning profiles without stigmatization. AI equitable education facilitates empowerment and equity. AI tutors are thus a critical learning equity and access necessity. AI tutors are solid self-regulation interventions and facilitation of motivation.

Students cannot maintain focus or study routines. AI coaches monitor level of engagement and remind or nudge in this regard. Gamification, rewards, and monitoring strategies are applied in motivation elicitation. Brain overloading is achieved by AI with breaking down long content into segments. The system tracks progress while it feels a sense of accomplishment. Furthermore, user input provided improves goaling and progress tracking. AI responsibility develops self-learning habits. Motivation-learning is empowered and facts accomplishment recollection. AI tutors are thus the cornerstones of creating disciplined and regulated learners. AI teachers are the solution to student rolls swelling to an all-time high.

LITERATURE REVIEW

Large classes cannot be provided with personal attention by schools. AI technology can handle thousands of students in parallel without compromising quality. Mentorship elements can track thousands of students' performance in parallel. That scalability is cheaper than hiring more teachers. AI platforms are simply filled with new content and pedagogy methods. That ease ensures learning content stays current and encyclopedic. Mass deployment guarantees equitable allocation of learning support. Companies can invest in pedagogics and infrastructure development with AI managing limited mentoring. AI teachers are therefore the time of need for delivering learning needs of the day in the best way possible. Finally, AI teachers and mentors craft education policy from data. AI processes and aggregates learning data in real-time. Strength points and weakness points, and trends, are achieved. They are used by teachers and policymakers to guide optimal pedagogy and curriculum. Predictive analytics allow anticipatory forecasting of issues so response plans will be anticipatory. Personalized recommendation optimizes learner performance and satisfaction. AI mentoring provides learners evidence-based advice on career and learning trajectories. Real-time feedback loops maximize teaching and learning. AI-readiness causes education to accelerate in accordance with the tempo of innovation. Synergistic convergence of access, analytics, and customization makes it possible for AI teachers to redefine learning models in the future. Clever systems of such nature are therefore a requirement of learning in the future. Mudzar et al. (2022) definitely give us an entire overview of the Fourth Industrial Revolution's new skills base workforce, but theirs is very speculative in nature with far too much literature synthesis and without context-specific, practical-level data to have available to us when applying in applying skill development programs to different learning settings.

Goldin et al. (2022) provide a conceptual reference architecture of the integration of the digital technology of Education 4.0 but fail to empirically verify the architecture with big data and limit its implementation to real education environments. Cónego et al. (2021) provide Education 4.0's theoretical starting point of the learning factory but conduct the research mainly in industry and engineering disciplines and therefore limit its applicability across other studies' disciplines. Costan et al. (2021) critically examine the application of Education 4.0 across the world's developing nations but are unable to report issues without presenting real, scalable solutions and cannot be readily translated into policymaker policy. González-Pérez and Ramírez-Montoya (2022) attribute 21st-century skill infrastructure to Education 4.0 drivers but systematic review is plagued by studies with included heterogeneity that can impact homogeneity on setting and putting in place identified factors. Bonfield et al. (2020) write about design pedagogy and pedagogy of Education 4.0 but reflection is speculative and limited empirical evidence exists to support statements, hence possibly necessarily limited applied use to pedagogy. Miranda et al. (2021) utilize case studies in Engineering Education to adopt Education 4.0 but single-institution context and limited sample size results in generalizability only possible within other research environment or other field. Chiu (2021) puts constraints on chemical education pedagogy at the time of digitalization and AI but is an example of a single-course publication whose implementation in multilateral curricula cannot be confirmed. Mhlanga and Moloi (2020) offer COVID-19 impacts on South African digitalization but writers first-hand facts and rumour analysis reports which may possibly be discovered to be limited in the explanation of long-term challenges or trends. Peterson et al. (2020) tried out the other surprise shift to distance learning within a single system during the COVID-19 pandemic but with just a single environment and probably not something to be replicated on scale to cover concerns of an entire system for other learning environments. Lastly, Guo et al. (2020) study K-12 distance learning in rural China but constrained by study scope and size and by restricting the scope of its conclusion to more technologically equipped urban or other environments. Mogos et al. (2018) studies technology-enhanced learning in Industry 4.0 for engineering education but from only one context of engineering classes alone, with extrapolation restricted to other coursework.

Moraes et al. (2022) also refer to the advantages of Industry 4.0 technology and adoption of Education 4.0, but the article employs conceptual advantages with limited empirical facts, thus limited applicability. Ciolacu et al. (2018) offer an AI warning system for reporting student performance but present early experiments on the system with few stringently controlled experiments on large populations and thus limited evidence of success on diverse student populations. Chen et al. (2020) offer AI-aided methods for learning from student performance but offer proof in the form of quantitative data independent of quality issues that make contextual determinants of learning inapplicable. Tahiru (2021) is a criticism of an AI tool in education but publication-skewed and without testing the future, non-English language to add to, thereby closing the window for analysis. Miao et al. (2021) offer AI in education policy recommendations but not locally specific and lacking local exemplars and therefore limitationally implementable in some education system. Carbonell (1970) have instruction based on AI and no appropriate pioneering effort today for big schools. Psotka et al. (1988) offer intelligent tutoring system knowledge but outdated facts and outdated technologies of only marginal utility to current AI development. Piramuthu (2005) outline knowledge-based web agents and intelligent tutoring systems but no realities of deployment and integration. Mousavinasab et al. (2021) provides a systematic review of intelligent tutoring systems but heterogeneously varied test processes between studies and therefore challenging to compare between studies. Alrakhawi et al. (2023) provides an overview of the usage and effect of intelligent tutoring systems on empiric outcomes heterogeneously dispersed over circumstances and therefore beset with generalizability. Song et al. (2017) write about conversational agent learning systems, but only for short-term interaction, not for longitudinal follow-up to learning. Shute and Psotka (1994) characterize the older intelligent tutoring systems, but the study does not consider the current AI technologies and thus generalizability to present education uses is challenging. VanLehn (2011) is a comparison of human tutoring and intelligent tutoring systems with small setting and sample variability that can compromise external validity. Fernoaga et al. (2018) present a didactic tutorial from intelligent chatbots but restrict testing to single packages of software, reducing use in the long term. Hamam (2021) is a literature review of chatbots in higher education without experimental test and syntheses largely secondary evidence. Satu et al. (2015) are discussing AIML-based chat programs but not the system design in this paper but the overall pedagogical efficacy. The new AI Tutors & Mentors model is attempting to eliminate some of the shortcomings of existing models as it employs human insight to enhance state-of-the-art AI solutions to more specialized learning and competence acquisition in everyday life.

As compared to previous theory- or field-based models (Mogos et al., 2018; Moraes et al., 2022), the model used in this study comprises combining bi-stacked ResNet and Remora Optimization models with feature selection in order to attain high precision in PSTs' learning outcomes prediction for different learning environments. Generative AI provides real-time dynamic feedback on the limitation of static short-term evaluation being common with current dominant smart intelligent tutoring systems (Ciolacu et al., 2018; Chen et al., 2020). The model also covers longitudinal observation through pre- and post-placement questionnaires, reflective dairies, and semi-structured interviews in a bid to avoid the limitation of lack of existence of contextual and qualitative data like in previous studies (Tahiru, 2021; Miao et al., 2021). By combining human critique and AI-guidance critique, the system reduces the one mode generalizability and low sample verifications of literature (Psotka et al., 1988; Piramuthu, 2005). Combining the AI-guidance modules with chatbots provides everyday day-to-day conversation and customized learning paths and counter the restricted task-specificity of previous applications of chatbots (Fernoaga et al., 2018; Hamam, 2021). System flexibility to adapt is also appropriate in facilitating technology usage and interaction variability among learners (VanLehn, 2011; Song et al., 2017) and facilitating context-sensitive and scalable support. Overall, the model in this case is an evidence-based, robust model that unifies predictive analytics, AI-driven personalization, and human mentoring towards improved learning outcomes, effective acquisition of skills, and purposeful professional development directly as a reaction to earlier conceptual, geo-localized, or technologically constrained models.

MATERIALS AND METHODS

Triangulated mixed-methods design was utilized in this study integrating quantitative response of survey, placement outcomes, and qualitative response of PSTs' and mentor teachers' from semi-structured interview. Pre-placement AI literacy training for six weeks and five weeks teaching placement were given to the participants. Post-placement survey questionnaires and placement reports were collected and reflective comments were obtained through semi-structured interview in third week. Data preprocessing comprised data cleaning, encoding, and normalization to ensure reliability and consistency of the data. Feature selection was done utilizing Remora Optimization for best-fit features while keeping the emphasis on improving the performance of the model. Bi-stacked ResNet architecture was used ultimately to integrate quantitative and qualitative data for individualized AI tutoring and PST outcome predictive modeling.

Material

The study employed a mixed-methods triangulated approach of collecting rich data of the pre-service teacher (PST) experience based on quantitative feedback of survey, placement outcome, and qualitative feedback of PSTs and mentor teachers. This was followed by six weeks of pre-placement training in the form of AI literacy training, which was then followed by five weeks of placement teaching. End-of-placement report details and questionnaire comments were collected in efforts to monitor performance and experience to agreed standards. Semi-structured interviews were conducted within three weeks of placement in efforts to collect reflective data before memories had time to disappear. Its three most important survey questions were mentor support (1–5), independent learning (6–9), and generative AI use (10–20) and a 5-point Likert scale was used to collect standard measurable answers. Eight individual PSTs were interviewed from an open call for volunteers and the findings gave more qualitative data on the connection between mentor support, usability skill with AI, and PSTs' reflection. This cost-effective process supplemented data triangulation since it was supplemented by qualitative rich description and the quantitative standard test. The dataset had real-time and longitudinal data on the mentoring and AI-based learning process through pre-placement training, performance at placement, and post-placement comment. The combined dataset in general indicated to some extent the overall experience of PSTs' professional development that professional development would be better explained through mentorship and AI technology.

Preprocessing

The merged dataset was rigorously preprocessed to render it accurate, consistent, and verifiable. The questionnaires' responses were checked for completeness and missing or inconsistent values and were treated by imputation or deletion as a function of missing data proportion. The Likert items were coded to numbers statistically for ease in statistical computation while direction of scoring was treated with care. Placement report information were normalized to allow comparison with performance across different mentors and environments to compare. Qualitative interview verbatim transcript was cleaned out by deleting redundancy, filler, and non-content data without loss of meaning. Themes were coded to allow matching with mentoring support, self-regulated learning strategy, and generative use of AI items in questionnaires. Quantitative outliers and anomalies were operationalized and tested for non-measurement of true variability items and entry error. Data were preprocessed and normalized to allow merging quantitative and qualitative data into triangulated analysis. All preprocessing data were anonymously stored and encrypted to preserve participant anonymity. Preprocessing future-proofed interview and survey data for thematic and statistical analysis.

Feature Selection

Feature selection in this study was performed employing the Remora Optimization Algorithm (ROA) in extracting the important features from the obtained data. The ROA is a symbiotic metaheuristic model inspired by the behavior of the remora fish attaching itself to host animals for its advantage but not fragile with environmental changes. Levelling the use advantage of ROA, spurious or noisy, or redundant variables derived from quantitative survey responses and coded qualitative data were systematically eliminated on a continuous basis from datasets to be analyzed, enhancing follow-up dataset data quality. The algorithm produces estimates of sets of attributes from a compromise fitness function in terms of dimension reduction and prediction quality in order to extract only significant variables.

The algorithm improves computation cost and model performance through shrinking feature space without losing useful information. The process of optimisation goes through several sets of features and adjusts selection according to feedback that it has gained from the fitness assessment. Features that included mentorship, self-learning strategy, and generative application of AI were thus common, with most PST performance drivers being the focus. In addition, ROA's robustness against local optima ensures consistent selection even when the data is high-dimensional and complex. Such resultant feature subset was therefore utilized as a benchmark for further predictive modeling as well as statistical modeling. Remora Optimization application typically improved readability of data sets on average and yielded more stable and more accurate data in terms of the relationship between mentoring and AI tools to PST growth.

Bistacked Resnet

AI guide and instructor employed in this research were applied through utilizing a bi-stacked Residual Network (ResNet) structure for enhancing personal learning as well as future PST performance prediction. Bi-stacked ResNet is a combination of two residual stacks of networks, thus enabling the system to learn composite and hierarchical feature extractions from multi-dimensional data such as survey responses, placement grades, and qualitative data encoded.Subolving vanishing gradient problem is optimized in such an architecture as learning models deep has the ability to infer intricate patterns in an attempt to acquire mentorship guidance, auto-didactic rituals, and generative deployment of AI.Bi-stacked ResNet recognizes better simultaneous processing of structured and unstructured data, PST learning performance drivers, and AI tool compatibility.

Reuse and re-refining of traits towards predictability and strength model strengthening is enabled by stacked layer facilitation. Pre-placement activity type categorized labeled sets and placement reports for training and post-placement reflective feedback for testing for generalizability. Adaptive weighting is also incorporated in the model such that it can be able to assign weightage to important learning indicators with an aim to enable individual-level feedback and recommendation generation. Through this deep learning architecture, AI tutors deliver precise, contextually relevant feedback, following each of their PST's learning path. Bi-stacked ResNet then emerges as the basic computational building element of AI mentoring, integrating performance prediction and customized guidance. In general, this paper demonstrates how new neural architectures could possibly be leveraged in order to enable more effective provision of intelligent, data-aware tutoring and mentoring services.

EXPERIMENTAL FINDINGS

Experimental results supported enhanced learning performance and motivation of pre-service teachers (PSTs) through AI tutorship and mentorship. Quantitative feedback in terms of responses in reports and questionnaires showed outstanding enhancement in independent learning ability, use of mentoring guidance, and application of generative AI functionality. Remora Optimization feature selection identified the most significant variables influencing PST performance and then further described them through the bi-stacked ResNet model. Predictive modeling was too effective in PST outcome prediction, as is also the potential ability of AI tutors to personalize teaching. Semi-structured interview qualitative results also validated above findings whereby more reflection practice and adaptive learning action were noted among PSTs. Overall, recent outcomes confirm that through the integration of AI-recommended mentoring and regular counseling, student achievement as well as professional development could be greatly improved.

Table 1 shows quality of communication, timeliness of feedback, encouragement, accessibility, quality of advice. PSTs rated mentors extremely high across all areas and, for most, extremely high in timeliness of feedback and accessibility. Communication rates and instruction clarity are highly high on all the measures, which indicates assessment of ability to communicate clearly about expectations by mentors. Support Encouragement was strongly high, indicating PSTs were positively encouraged in placements by mentors. Variability in some of the ratings is an indication of variability in approach style to mentoring. Higher Accessibility scores indicated ease of access of the mentor to provide support. Support Worldwide requested individual dimensions, and they depicted PSTs were well supported in general. Low scores on some rows provide areas for improvement, i.e., balance of frequency of feedback. On a global scale, overall, Table 1 depicts the worth of support provided at the right time to maximize PST learning experience.

Table 1. Mentor support ratings

Communication Quality	Feedback Timeliness	Encouragement	Accessibility	Guidance Clarity	Overall Support
4	5	4	5	4	4
5	5	5	4	5	5
4	4	4	4	4	4
3	4	3	4	3	3
5	5	4	5	5	5
4	4	4	4	4	4
3	3	3	3	3	3
5	5	5	5	4	5
4	4	5	4	4	4
5	4	4	5	5	5

Table 2 indicates that PSTs utilized self-regulated learning (SRL) strategies, i.e., goal setting, time management, self-monitoring, use of strategy, reflection, and motivation. Ratings indicate that most PSTs utilized SRL strategies with placement effectiveness. Reflection and goal setting were consistent in all stages, demonstrating that PSTs were able to reflect and plan for learning. Use of strategy and time management were inconsistent, demonstrating uneven pace. Motivation scores also indicate that the majority of students had sound motivation. Self-monitoring was utilized by PSTs when tracking progress and adjusting strategy. Evidence captures the interactive dynamic of SRL in which facilitation to situation was provided by the mentor. Low ratings for some entries indicate areas where more guidance can be added. In general, Table 2 entries establish that SRL has strong effects in maximizing learning achievement with teacher placements.

Table 2. Self-regulated learning strategies

Goal Setting	Time Management	Self-Monitoring	Strategy Use	Reflection	Motivation
4	5	4	4	5	4
5	4	5	5	4	5
4	4	4	4	4	4
3	3	3	3	3	3
5	5	5	4	5	5
4	4	4	5	4	4
3	4	3	3	3	3
5	5	5	5	5	5
4	4	4	4	4	4
5	5	4	5	5	5

Table 3 is a compilation of PSTs' self-reported comfort level with generative AI tools like familiarity, frequency of use, task support, creativity enhancement, error minimization, and overall satisfaction. Task support and error minimization, frequency of use and familiarity were given high ratings by the PSTs. Evidence for effectiveness in doing is presented here regarding the application of AI to lesson planning and preparation of resources. Higher scores on the creativity measure pedagogical creativity facilitated by AI. Total satisfaction verifies experience-based effectiveness of AI tools. Variation on scored items measures experience and ease with technology variation. The table situates the application of AI as an aid tool in cognitive and creative learning processes. The findings are shifting towards the application of AI as an aid tool in learning. Table 3 is the picture of AI deployment to facilitate instruction design and interaction.

Table 3. Generative AI tool usage

AI Tool Familiarity	Frequency of Use	Task Assistance	Creativity Boost	Error Reduction	Overall Satisfaction
4	5	4	4	5	4
5	4	5	5	4	5
4	4	4	3	4	4
3	3	3	3	3	3
5	5	5	4	5	5
4	4	4	4	4	4
3	3	3	3	3	3
5	5	5	5	5	5
4	4	4	4	4	4
5	5	5	5	5	5

Table 4 indicates PST instructional planning, classroom management, student interaction, instruction delivery, test development, and professionalism in six dimensions. Successful performance by the majority of PSTs predominantly in professionalism and designing lessons substantiate preparedness and readiness. Readiness and preparedness were alternately moderate, i.e., difficulty in managing or communicating mixed ability students. Instructional delivery and test design reflected best instructional practices among most participants. High scores indicate AI direction and support impacted participants significantly. Low scores indicate special areas of criticism. Table identifies PST competences for placement. It unmistakably illustrates how AI use and mentorship guidance would promote effective competence in teaching.

Table 4. Placement performance metrics

Lesson Planning	Classroom Management	Student Engagement	Instruction Delivery	Assessment Design	Professionalism
4	5	4	5	4	5
5	5	5	4	5	5
4	4	4	4	4	4
3	3	3	3	3	3
5	5	5	5	5	5
4	4	4	4	4	4
3	3	3	3	3	3
5	5	4	5	5	5

continued on following page

Table 4. Continued

Lesson Planning	Classroom Management	Student Engagement	Instruction Delivery	Assessment Design	Professionalism
4	4	4	4	4	4
5	5	5	5	5	5

Table 5 tracks reflective practices such as self-reflection, peer acceptance, learning diaries, planning for construction, adjustive response, and knowledge level. Planning and enhancing were mid-level scores by PSTs that indicated PSTs were engaging in learning activities. Include peer rating because feedback was mid-level and indicated collaboration at different levels. Collaboration by most PSTs was tracked using learning journals. Adjustive strategies indicate responsiveness in teaching lessons. The extent of understanding is an indication of reflection and critical thinking by students. Poor performance in certain areas indicates that they need more guidance from a mentor. The table substantiates reflection practice and sustains AI-guidance.

Table 5. Reflective practices

Self-Reflection	Peer Feedback Integration	Learning Journals	Improvement Planning	Adaptive Strategies	Insight Depth
4	5	4	4	5	4
5	4	5	5	4	5
4	4	4	4	4	4
3	3	3	3	3	3
5	5	5	5	5	5
4	4	4	4	4	4
3	3	3	3	3	3
5	5	5	5	5	5
4	4	4	4	4	4
5	5	5	5	5	5

Table 6 indicates comparison of performance of AI tutor in personalization, accuracy of feedback, adaptive suggestions, learning assistance percentage provided, increase in engagement, and overall effect. Greater adaptive suggestion and feedback accuracy scores are evidence of on-time and explanatory AI feedback. Personalization actions attest that AI systems adapted learning pathways to significant degrees to PST individual needs. Engagement increase is evidence of the engaging nature of AI instructors. Learning rate support attests responsiveness capacity to variable learners. Distraction in some scores is evidence of divergence of PSTs' alignment from AI instruction. Collective impact defines the strength of these factors combining together. Table 6 captures human guidance support by AI teachers. From the table, one can see how AI application for adaptive learning student-focused is.

Table 6. AI tutors effectiveness

Personalization	Feedback Accuracy	Adaptive Suggestions	Learning Pace Support	Engagement Increase	Overall Impact
4	5	4	5	4	5
5	4	5	4	5	5
4	4	4	4	4	4
3	3	3	3	3	3
5	5	5	5	5	5
4	4	4	4	4	4
3	3	3	3	3	3
5	5	5	5	5	5
4	4	4	4	4	4
5	5	5	5	5	5

Table 7 shows engagement in PST under participation, initiative, cooperation, concentration, responsiveness, and interaction with AI tools. High levels of engagement were displayed by all the PSTs in teamwork and application of AI tools in most instances. Initiative and participation levels were high during teaching activities. Responsiveness and attention level was high in most instances, demonstrating responsiveness and attention during placements. Discrepancy in activity under activities is established via discrepancy in some observation. AI tool interaction judgments are an indicator of successful adoption of technology during teaching activity. The table shows the correlation of mentoring and AI utilization. Outcomes commend engagement measures as an effective measure of successful placement. In summary, Table 7 shows active PSTs' engagement during learning.

Table 7. PST engagement metrics

Participation	Initiative	Collaboration	Attention	Responsiveness	AI Tool Interaction
4	5	4	5	4	5
5	4	5	4	5	5
4	4	4	4	4	4
3	3	3	3	3	3
5	5	5	5	5	5

continued on following page

Table 7. Continued

Participation	Initiative	Collaboration	Attention	Responsiveness	AI Tool Interaction
4	4	4	4	4	4
3	3	3	3	3	3
5	5	5	5	5	5
4	4	4	4	4	4
5	5	5	5	5	5

Table 8 shows comparisons of mentor-PST interaction in approachability, responsiveness, transfer of knowledge, providing constructive feedback, trust, and consistency of direction. Rankings affirm that majority of the mentors were friendly and provided positive feedback. High responsiveness and knowledge-sharing scores mean effective communication was sustained. Trust-building activities show PSTs enhanced trusting mentors. Consistency of aid establishes reliability and constant guidance. Inconsistency on some measures suggests individual mentoring style determines quality of interaction. The table suggests greater mentor-PST interaction is responsible for learning gains. On a general level, Table 8 defines relational and communicative elements of mentorship.

Table 8. Mentor-PST interaction quality

Approachability	Responsiveness	Knowledge Sharing	Constructive Feedback	Trust Building	Support Consistency
4	5	4	5	4	5
5	4	5	4	5	5
4	4	4	4	4	4
3	3	3	3	3	3
5	5	5	5	5	5
4	4	4	4	4	4
3	3	3	3	3	3
5	5	5	5	5	5
4	4	4	4	4	4
5	5	5	5	5	5

Table 9 shows PST technology integration skills, i.e., AI literacy, computer software skills, digital tool usage, adoption of technology, technical assistance, and level of confidence. Most of the PSTs positioned themselves in high levels of AI literacy and computer software competence. Use of technology resources and web use were very heterogeneous, meaning that PSTs were familiar with several different technologies. Trouble-shooting indicator and confidence measures tell us if PSTs fix technical problems independently or not. Altogether, the table suggests technological literacy as a measure of successful exploitation of AI tutors. Under-performing sub-domains would need specific training in order to enhance the level of expertise.

Table 9. Technology integration competence

AI Literacy	Software Skills	Digital Resource Use	Technology Adaptation	Troubleshooting	Confidence Level
4	5	4	5	4	5
5	4	5	4	5	5
4	4	4	4	4	4
3	3	3	3	3	3
5	5	5	5	5	5
4	4	4	4	4	4
3	3	3	3	3	3
5	5	5	5	5	5
4	4	4	4	4	4
5	5	5	5	5	5

Table 10 is measuring the outcome of learning, i.e., retention of memory, utilization of algorithms, critical thinking, problem-solving, creative thinking, and building confidence. High scores in utilization of skills and retention signify successful on-placement learning. Scores on critical thinking and problem-solving reflect the ability of PSTs to apply what they learn. Increase in confidence and creativity reflected in the outcome through increased motivation and sensitivity. Small variation in some rows reflects varying patterns of students' developments. The table clearly demonstrates that AI mentorship enhances various areas of learning. Table 10 in general reassures us that PSTs' cognitive and affective development is enhanced by AI mentors and tutors.

Table 10. Learning outcome improvements

Knowledge Retention	Skill Application	Critical Thinking	Problem Solving	Creativity	Confidence Boost
4	5	4	5	4	5
5	4	5	4	5	5
4	4	4	4	4	4
3	3	3	3	3	3

continued on following page

Table 10. Continued

Knowledge Retention	Skill Application	Critical Thinking	Problem Solving	Creativity	Confidence Boost
5	5	5	5	5	5
4	4	4	4	4	4
3	3	3	3	3	3
5	5	5	5	5	5
4	4	4	4	4	4
5	5	5	5	5	5

CONCLUSION

The study shows that AI mentors and tutors can be of immense assistance in PST professional development in the form of timely feedback and carefully crafted comments. The study corroborates mixed analysis of placement review, reflective interviews, and survey response, as corroborated by the efficacy of utilizing captures the design and implementation of AI tutor and mentor to facilitate pre-service teachers' (PSTs) learning and development. This employs mixed-method triangulated methodology, i.e., quantitative feedback using surveys, placement records, and qualitative results from PSTs and mentoring teachers. Pre-placement training in AI literacy and subsequent follow-up teaching placements served as building blocks to collect data, whereas post-placement surveys and semi-structured interviews gathered reflective accounts. Remora optimization was used for feature selection and two-stacked ResNet to construct prediction models of PST performance and generate personalized comments. The result demonstrates that AI tutors not only complement self-regulated learning but also complement mentor feedback and make generative AI tools their value. The methodology demonstrates how adaptive, data-driven systems of mentorship can produce adaptive, customized learning processes in teacher training.

REFERENCES

Alrakhawi, H., Jamiat, N., & Abu-Naser, S. (2023). Intelligent tutoring systems in education: A systematic review of usage, tools, effects and evaluation. *Journal of Theoretical and Applied Information Technology*, *101*, 1205–1226.

Bonfield, C. A., Salter, M., Longmuir, A., Benson, M., & Adachi, C. (2020). Transformation or evolution?: Education 4.0, teaching and learning in the digital age. *Higher Education Pedagogies*, *5*(1), 223–246. DOI: 10.1080/23752696.2020.1816847

Carbonell, J. R. (1970). AI in CAI: An artificial-intelligence approach to computer-assisted instruction. *IEEE Transactions on Man-Machine Systems*, *11*(4), 190–202. DOI: 10.1109/TMMS.1970.299942

Chen, Z., Zhang, J., Jiang, X., Hu, Z., Han, X., & Xu, M., Savitha, & Vivekananda, G. N. (2020). Education 4.0 using artificial intelligence for students performance analysis. *Intelligent Automation & Soft Computing*, *23*, 124–137.

Chiu, W.-K. (2021). Pedagogy of emerging technologies in chemical education during the era of digitalization and artificial intelligence: A systematic review. *Education Sciences*, *11*(11), 709. DOI: 10.3390/educsci11110709

Ciolacu, M. I., Tehrani, A. F., Binder, L., & Svasta, P. (2018, October 25–28). Education 4.0—Artificial intelligence assisted higher education: Early recognition system with machine learning to support students' success. In *Proceedings of the IEEE 24th International Symposium for Design and Technology in Electronic Packaging (SIITME)* (pp. 23–30). Ia i, Romania. DOI: 10.1109/SIITME.2018.8599203

Cónego, L., Pinto, R., & Gonçalves, G. (2021). Education 4.0 and the smart manufacturing paradigm: A conceptual gateway for learning factories. In Camarinha-Matos, L. M., Boucher, X., & Afsarmanesh, H. (Eds.), *Smart and sustainable collaborative networks 4.0*. PRO-VE. DOI: 10.1007/978-3-030-85969-5_68

Costan, E., Gonzales, G., Gonzales, R., Enriquez, L., Costan, F., Suladay, D., Atibing, N. M., Aro, J. L., Evangelista, S. S., Maturan, F., Selerio, E.Jr, & Ocampo, L. (2021). Education 4.0 in developing economies: A systematic literature review of implementation barriers and future research agenda. *Sustainability (Basel)*, *13*(22), 12763. DOI: 10.3390/su132212763

Fernoaga, P. V., Sandu, F., Stelea, G. A., & Gavrila, C. (2018, April 19–20). Intelligent education assistant powered by chatbots. In *Proceedings of the 14th International Scientific Conference of eLearning and Software for Education (eLSE)* (pp. 376–383). Bucharest, Romania.

Goldin, T., Rauch, E., Pacher, C., & Woschank, M. (2022). Reference architecture for an integrated and synergetic use of digital tools in Education 4.0. *Procedia Computer Science*, *200*, 407–417. DOI: 10.1016/j.procs.2022.01.239

González-Pérez, L. I., & Ramírez-Montoya, M. S. (2022). Components of Education 4.0 in 21st century skills frameworks: Systematic review. *Sustainability (Basel)*, *14*(3), 1493. DOI: 10.3390/su14031493

Guo, Y. J., Chen, L., Guo, Y., & Chen, L. (2020, December 13–17). An investigation on online learning for K12 in rural areas in China during COVID-19 pandemic. In *Proceedings of the Ninth International Conference of Educational Innovation through Technology (EITT)* (pp. 13–18). Porto, Portugal. DOI: 10.1109/EITT50754.2020.00009

Hamam, D. (2021). The new teacher assistant: A review of chatbots' use in higher education. In Stephanidis, C., Antona, M., & Ntoa, S. (Eds.), *HCI International 2021—Posters. HCII 2021. Communications in Computer and Information Science* (Vol. 1421). Springer. DOI: 10.1007/978-3-030-78645-8_8

Mhlanga, D., & Moloi, T. (2020). COVID-19 and the digital transformation of education: What are we learning on 4IR in South Africa? *Education Sciences*, *10*(7), 180. DOI: 10.3390/educsci10070180

Miao, F., Holmes, W., Huang, R., & Zhang, H. (2021). *AI and education guidance for policy-makers*. UNESCO Publishing.

Miranda, J., Navarrete, C., Noguez, J., Molina-Espinosa, J. M., Ramírez-Montoya, M. S., Navarro-Tuch, S. A., Bustamante-Bello, M. R., Rosas-Fernández, J. B., & Molina, A. (2021). The core components of education 4.0 in higher education: Three case studies in engineering education. *Computers & Electrical Engineering*, *93*, 107278. DOI: 10.1016/j.compeleceng.2021.107278

Mogos, R., Bodea, C. N., Dascalu, M., Lazarou, E., Trifan, L., Safonkina, O., & Nemoianu, I. (2018). Technology enhanced learning for Industry 4.0 engineering education. *Revue Roumaine des Sciences Techniques—Électrotechnique et Énergétique*, *63*, 429–435.

Moraes, E. B., Kipper, L. M., Hackenhaar Kellermann, A. C., Austria, L., Leivas, P., Moraes, J. A. R., & Witczak, M. (2022). Integration of Industry 4.0 technologies with Education 4.0: Advantages for improvements in learning. *Interactive Technology and Smart Education*, *20*(2), 271–287. DOI: 10.1108/ITSE-11-2021-0201

Mousavinasab, E., Zarifsanaiey, N., Kalhori, S. R. N., Rakhshan, M., Keikha, L., & Saeedi, M. G. (2021). Intelligent tutoring systems: A systematic review of characteristics, applications, and evaluation methods. *Interactive Learning Environments, 29*, 142–163. DOI: 10.1080/10494820.2018.1558257

Mudzar, N. M. B. M., & Chew, K. W. (2022). Change in labour force skillset for the fourth industrial revolution: A literature review. *International Journal of Technology, 13*(5), 969–978. DOI: 10.14716/ijtech.v13i5.5875

Peterson, L., Scharber, C., Thuesen, A., & Baskin, K. (2020). A rapid response to COVID-19: One district's pivot from technology integration to distance learning. *Information and Learning Science, 121*(5/6), 461–469. DOI: 10.1108/ILS-04-2020-0131

Piramuthu, S. (2005). Knowledge-based web-enabled agents and intelligent tutoring systems. *IEEE Transactions on Education, 48*(4), 750–756. DOI: 10.1109/TE.2005.854574

Psotka, J., Massey, L. D., & Mutter, S. A. (Eds.). (1988). *Intelligent tutoring systems: Lessons learned.* Lawrence Erlbaum Associates.

Satu, M. S., Parvez, M. H., & Al-Mamun, S. (2015, November 26–27). Review of integrated applications with AIML based chatbot. In *Proceedings of the International Conference on Computer and Information Engineering (ICCIE)* (pp. 87–90). Rajshahi, Bangladesh. DOI: 10.1109/CCIE.2015.7399324

Shute, V. J., & Psotka, J. (1994). Intelligent tutoring systems: Past, present, and future. Human Resources Directorate Manpower and Personnel Research Division, 2–52.

Song, D., Oh, E. Y., & Rice, M. (2017, July 17–19). Interacting with a conversational agent system for educational purposes in online courses. In *Proceedings of the 10th International Conference on Human System Interactions (HSI)* (pp. 78–82). Ulsan, Republic of Korea. DOI: 10.1109/HSI.2017.8005002

Tahiru, F. (2021). AI in education: A systematic literature review. *Journal of Cases on Information Technology, 23*(1), 1–20. DOI: 10.4018/JCIT.2021010101

VanLehn, K. (2011). The relative effectiveness of human tutoring, intelligent tutoring systems, and other tutoring systems. *Educational Psychologist, 46*(4), 197–221. DOI: 10.1080/00461520.2011.611369

Chapter 7

Exploring Moroccan EFL Students' Attitudes Toward AWCF: A TAM-Based Case Study at Hassan I University

Morad Bakir
https://orcid.org/0009-0000-2082-7193
Ibn Tofail University, Kenitra, Morocco

Khadija Anasse
Ibn Tofail University, Kenitra, Morocco

Wadiai Boudribila
Hassan I University, Settat, Morocco

Hicham El Ghraoui
Hassan I University, Settat, Morocco

Taoufiq Zoubairi
Cadi Ayyad University, Morocco

Yassine Edder
Ibn Tofail University, Kenitra, Morocco

ABSTRACT

This study aims to explore Moroccan EFL students' perceptions of using Grammarly as an AWCF tool, drawing on Davis's (1989) TAM, which focuses on perceived usefulness, perceived ease of use, attitude toward use, and behavioral intention. Using a mixed-methods research design, the study targeted 34 EFL students (18 female and 16 male, aged 20–43) from Semester 1 at the English Department of Hassan I University in Morocco. The respondents were selected using convenience sampling. Based on data collected from a Likert-scale questionnaire and some open-ended questions, findings indicate that students have positive attitudes toward Grammarly's AWCF. The AI tool is deemed useful and easy to use. Additionally, it can enhance students' writing skills, boost their confidence, and increase their motivation, making their writing experience agreeable. Despite the participants'

DOI: 10.4018/979-8-3373-4621-2.ch007

willingness to continue using Grammarly in the future for their writing tasks, they highlighted several limitations of the tool in terms of feedback accuracy, style, tone, contextual appropriateness and overreliance.

INTRODUCTION

In today's fast and savvy era, AI-powered tools have revolutionized traditional educational practices by offering a myriad of opportunities, particularly in language learning. Among these AI tools is Grammarly, which offers Automated Written Corrective Feedback (AWCF). This latter has garnered growing attention among scholars in recent years and has been advocated for providing personalized, immediate, and data-informed feedback on learners' written work, alleviating the correction burden placed upon educators, especially with large classes where personalized feedback is often constrained by time and resources. (Ranalli, 2018).

So far, the effects of such feedback (AWCF), especially on English as a Foreign Language (EFL) students' writing, remain underexplored (Fan, 2023). This gap is particularly evident in Moroccan higher education, where the pedagogical significance of AI tools remains debatable, as their adoption is still in its nascent stages and requires further investigation (Azennoud, 2024, p. 212; Ejjami, 2024, p. 3). Therefore, the current study seeks to bridge this gap in the literature by exploring Moroccan EFL students' attitudes toward Grammarly's AWCF at the University of Hassan I, focusing on their perceptions of its usefulness, ease of use, and acceptance. Guided by Davis's (1989) Technology Acceptance Model (TAM), the study establishes a theoretical basis to understand the factors driving students to embrace or reject AWCF as a supplementary resource for writing development.

LITERATURE REVIEW

AWCF Definition

Automated Written Corrective Feedback (AWCF) is an innovative technological tool that runs on AI and, more specifically, on natural language processing (NLP) and consists of a scoring engine and a feedback engine (Grimes & Warschauer, 2010). These systems were basically conceived to assist language learners, especially novice (EFL) writers, in improving their writing performance by providing automated feedback on their written work, including grammatical errors, lack of ideas, and motivation issues (Guo et al., 2021; Ofrita et al., 2023; Y. Yang & Tian, 2024).

Among those widely-used AWCF platforms is Grammarly. This platform is touted as the most popular AWCF system in the world, with an estimated 40 million users and 50,000 organizations (Grammarly, 2025). Since its inception in 2009, students have used Grammarly to check for plagiarism, identify grammatical errors, and assist them with writing basics and mechanics. Later on, more updated features, such as AI writing assistance and AI text detection, were added to the platform to align its use with current trends in technology.

Advantages of Grammarly as an AWCF tool

To explore the potential advantages of Grammarly and its impact on writing performance, extensive academic literature substantiates its significance in educational contexts. Recent Studies by Barrot (2021), Fitria et al. (2022), Calma et al. (2022), Azennoud (2024), and El Missi et al. (2024) have yielded significant insights into the dynamics surrounding the use of AWCF tools by language learners.

Barrot's (2021) quasi-experimental study, focusing on university students in the Philippines, reveals that Grammarly's AWCF helps students in several ways. The software enables students to notice their writing mistakes, promotes their metalinguistic awareness by providing adaptive metalinguistic explanations, encourages them to assume control of their learning and make well-informed choices about their writing, and eventually, improves their writing accuracy. Furthermore, the software helps students improve their writing through self-directed learning by making them identify and correct fundamental and structural issues independently (Barrot, 2021).

In the Indonesian context, Fitria et al. (2022) conducted a mixed-method study to explore the perceptions of 35 students using Grammarly in their undergraduate thesis writing. The authors found that students generally have positive perceptions of using Grammarly. The software is deemed helpful in providing both direct and indirect corrective feedback on students' grammatical mistakes. Furthermore, its swiftness and immediacy make it time-saving, which boosts students' motivation and self-confidence, thereby enabling users to detect and rectify their mistakes independently (Fitria et al., 2022).

Furthermore, Calma et al.'s (2022) investigation into Grammarly's impact on students' writing proficiency underscores its efficacy as a pedagogical resource that can be used beyond error correction. According to the researchers, the tool can be employed to enhance students' self-evaluation skills and autonomous learning in the sense that they can use it outside the classroom as a pre-class task to evaluate their writings individually, and then during class, they can work in small groups to revise and discuss the feedback provided by the tool. Afterward, teachers can hold a whole class discussion by having students discuss how they will address their writing issues based on Grammarly's feedback (Calma et al., 2022).

In another quantitative study in the Moroccan context by Azennoud (2024), the author focused on learners' perspectives and experiences with two AWCF tools. To this end, they approached 67 Moroccan EFL university students through an online questionnaire to assess their views on the effectiveness of Grammarly and Chatgpt in improving their writing accuracy. The study results showed that incorporating AI-powered tools in writing yielded remarkable improvements in students' written work. Using such tools reduced students' grammatical and spelling mistakes, offering personalized feedback tailored to their specific needs, which resulted in boosting their motivation, engagement, and self-directed learning (Azennoud, 2024).

In the same vein, El Missi et al. (2024) conducted a mixed-method study to explore Moroccan Masters students' perceptions of the usefulness of Grammarly in their academic writing, targeting 60 students. Grounded on Davis's (1989) TAM model, findings indicate that most students find Grammarly user-friendly and helpful, especially in the revising and editing stages of the writing process, thereby significantly impacting their academic writing quality. Furthermore, the students highlight its role in enhancing their writing skills by providing error-checking capabilities that are crucial for producing high-quality assignments (El Missi et al., 2024).

In sum, the aforementioned studies collectively echo students' positive perceptions toward Grammarly use by showcasing several benefits. The AI-powered tool serves as a valuable pedagogical tool, helping students identify and correct their writing mistakes independently, provide personalized feedback, boost self-confidence and motivation, and promote autonomous learning.

Drawbacks of Grammarly in EFL Writing

Despite the evidence that Grammarly is invaluable for EFL writers, several limitations of the tool have been reported in the research literature, potentially impeding its large-scale employment as an AI tool. Such limitations include cognitive load, stylistic rigidity, contextual inaccuracy, technical constraints, and, notably, students' overreliance on the tool.

One significant concern, as reported by Cavaleri and Dianati (2016), is Grammarly's cognitive overload. According to the authors, Grammarly's feedback can sometimes be misleading and difficult to understand. Thus, students feel overwhelmed by its volume, leading to frustration and disengagement from the learning process (Llausas et al., 2024).

Moreover, the program sometimes fails to interpret complex sentences or creative writing, suggesting changes that do not align with students' tone and style. As a result, they become frustrated and fail to maintain their unique voice in their writing (El Missi et al., 2024). In line with this view, Koltovskia (2020) argues that students should not fully rely on Grammarly because it disregards writers' style and voice by imposing a generic writing style that may not accurately reflect the author's artistic taste.

Another major limitation of Grammarly, as highlighted by Fitriana and Nurazni (2022), is that it may alter sentence length and meaning. Therefore, writers are required to double-check their writing for potential contextual misunderstandings. According to El Missi et al, (2024), Grammarly tends to overlook nuances in subject-specific terminology, which makes it generate incorrect suggestions that do not accurately reflect the intended meaning or context of the writing. Therefore, there is a need for a nuanced use of the tool alongside teachers ' guidance to compensate for its contextual limitations and optimize its application along with other writing resources (Tsania & Puspitasari, n. d.) .

Furthermore, Vo and Nguyen (2021, p. 465) and O'Neill and Russel (2019) assert that Grammarly does not accurately detect all errors. The tool appears to be most appealing to students with lower proficiency (O'Neill & Russell, 2019), while more proficient students may question its feedback quality and be less inclined to incorporate it into their manuscripts (Koltovskaia, 2020).

In addition to the cognitive, stylistic, semantic, and contextual challenges posed by the adoption of Grammarly's AWCF, some persisting technical issues emerge as limitations of the program among EFL students, such as guidance on its use, the limited features of its free version, and the need for a reliable internet connection.

In terms of use, some students struggle with the platform's features, especially those who have never used the platform before. This suggests a need for physical training and additional practice using the software to enhance its deployment among EFL students (Rao, 2019) .

Additionally, Although the free version of Grammarly remains helpful, it does not include all the necessary features writers might need (El Missi et al., 2024; Fitriana & Nurazni, 2022) . While Grammarly Premium offers advanced features such as a plagiarism checker, an AI-powered writing assistant, and an AI detector (Yang, 2023), the free version only provides users with a grammar checker, a spelling checker, and a punctuation checker. Astuti and Sumarni (2023) and Maypida and Damanik (2024) attest that Grammarly's free version has limited features while its Premium version has all the essential features students need. However, this latter is too expensive and not affordable to all of them (Astuti & Sumarni, 2023; Maypida & Damanik, 2024).

As for internet connection, since Grammarly is a cloud-based program, it must connect to the central server via the internet to retrieve data. This process requires a stable and high-speed internet connection to ensure smooth delivery of direct feedback and enable users to easily upload or download input (Fitriana & Nurazni, 2022; Maypida & Damanik, 2024; Ummah & Bisriyah, 2022) .

Another significant limitation of the tool is related to overreliance on it. El Missi et al, (2024) argue that overreliance on Grammarly might hinder students writing skills development. That is, students should identify and understand their writing errors on their own in order to develop into good writers in the future. Zaragoza et al. (2024) echoed this concern, noting that the excessive use of Grammarly can compromise academic integrity as it impedes the development of original and critical thinking skills (p. 674). Zuhriah et al. (2024) further explain that "as students continuously use Grammarly, they may feel less confident in their ability to correct and revise their writing without the help of the tool, ultimately affecting their overall writing skills" (p. 98).

In brief, despite Grammarly's significant role in developing writing skills, students need to be critically aware of its limitations. In this sense, they must not entirely and blindly rely on it; otherwise, they may end up making more mistakes (Vo & Nguyen, 2021). Indeed, by recognizing Grammarly's limitations, students will able to employ the program properly, especially when it is used with other writing resources (Anastasia et al., 2024) or guided by instructors (Martínez-Carrasco & Chabert, 2023) who can provide their feedback on students 'untreatable mistakes while using Grammarly for treatable ones (Koltovskaia, 2023).

Technology Acceptance Model (TAM)

Davis's (1989) Technology Acceptance Model (TAM) is a widely renowned theoretical framework seeking to explain and evaluate individuals' acceptance and adoption of new technologies (See Figure 1). Since its inception, the Technology Acceptance Model (TAM) has witnessed substantial evolution through extensive research, refining its core principles and theoretical basis. Nevertheless, the model's two fundamental key components, as suggested by Davis (1989), remain perceived usefulness (PU) and Perceived ease of use (PEOU).

Figure 1. The technology acceptance model

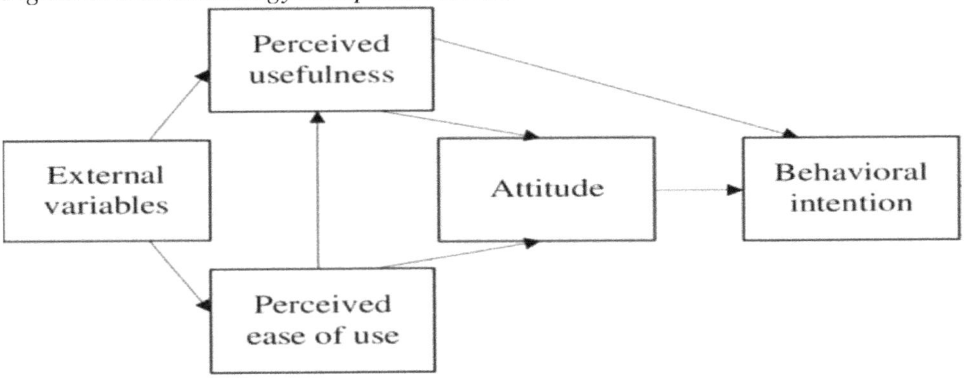

(Davis, 1989)
Note. This is a visual representation of TAM as suggested by Davis (1989)

According to Davis and Granić (2024), Perceived usefulness (PU) indicates how individuals believe that adopting a particular technology will enhance their performance. Essentially, if a user perceives that a new digital tool will help them complete tasks more efficiently, they are more likely to accept and use it, whereas Perceived Ease of Use (PEOU) refers to the extent to which users find technology easy to use. Or (2024) alleges that when users perceive technologies as user-friendly and effortless, they are more inclined to accept and adopt them (p. 560).

Prior research investigating the relationship between perceived usefulness (PU) and perceived ease of use (PEOU) of digital systems has shown that perceived usefulness predicts user acceptance more than perceived ease of use. Cheng et al. (2006), for instance, found that there is a significant positive correlation between PU and PEOU, indicating that the more individuals perceive a system as useful, the more they perceive it as easy to use, which in turn shapes their behavioural intention to adopt it (Cheng et al., 2006; Sandema-Sombe, 2019).

Objectives of the Study

The present study aims:

1. To explore How Moroccan EFL students at Hassan I University perceive the usefulness of Grammarly's automated writing corrective feedback (AWCF) in improving their writing
2. To assess students' perceptions of Grammarly ease of use as an AWCF tool within the writing context.

3. To investigate students' acceptance level of Grammarly's AWCF and identify the factors influencing their behavioural intention to use it in future.

Research Questions

1 How do Moroccan EFL students perceive the usefulness and ease of use of Grammarly's AWCF in improving their writing?
2 To what extent do Moroccan EFL students accept or reject Grammarly's AWCF as a supplementary tool for developing their writing?
3 To what extent do students' perceptions of usefulness and ease of use influence their behavioural intention to use Grammarly in the future?

Hypotheses

H1: Moroccan EFL students positively perceive Grammarly's usefulness (PU) and ease of use (PEOU) in improving their writing.
H2: Students with higher (PU) and (PEOU) will have a more positive attitude toward using Grammarly.
H3: Students with higher perceptions of Grammarly's (PU) and (EOU) will show greater intention to accept and use it as a supplementary writing tool in the future.

METHODOLOGY

Research Design

The implemented design of the current study is a mixed-method research design combining quantitative and qualitative approaches to gain a comprehensive understanding of Moroccan EFL students' perceptions toward using Grammarly as an AWCF tool based on Davis's (1989) Technology Acceptance Model, focusing on perceived usefulness, perceived ease of use, attitude toward use, and behavioural intention.

Participants

The study sample consisted of 34 students in Semester 2 (18 females, 16 males, aged 20–43) from the English Department at Hassan I University. The respondents were selected using convenience sampling. Initially, 44 students were invited to participate based on their willingness and familiarity with the research topic. However, only 34 respondents completed the questionnaire, as 10 students decided to withdraw from the study (See Figure 2 and Table 1).

Figure 2. Proportion of participants by gender

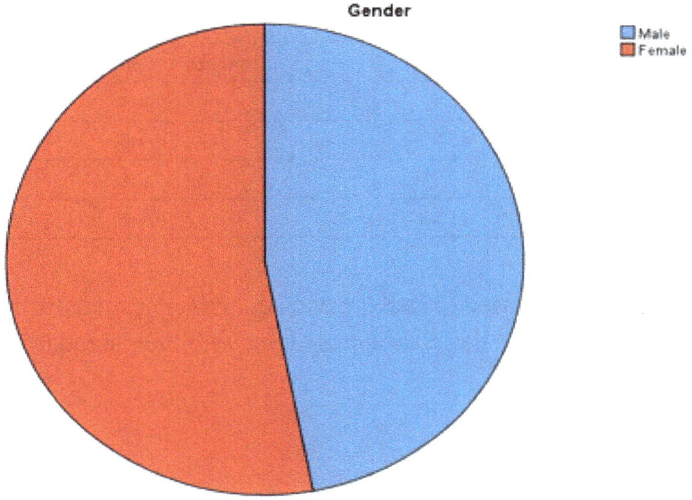

Table 1. Age of participants

Age	Percentage
18-23	**70,6%**
24-29	**20,6%**
30-35	**5,9%**
36-41	**2,9%**

Research instrument

The main research instrument used in this study is a Likert scale questionnaire designed based on Davis's (1989) Technology Acceptance Model, followed by a set of open-ended questions to collect qualitative data. The questionnaire consisted of four sections developed using Qualtrics and distributed via WhatsApp. The four sections cover participants' demographics, perceived usefulness, perceived ease of use, attitude towards use, and behavioral intention to use Grammarly. To measure internal consistency, the questionnaire underwent several modifications, including a pilot study and a Cronbach's Alpha test using SPSS. Table 2 illustrates the Cronbach's Alpha coefficient for each scale and its constructs, indicating that the data collection instruments are reliable.

Table 2. Cronbach's Alpha coefficient

Scales	**Items**	**Cronbach's Alpha coefficient**
Perceived Usefulness	5	0,814
Perceived Ease of Use	5	0,913
Attitude Towards Use	5	0,848
Behavioural Intention	5	0,915

Descriptive statistics were used to analyze data, quantifying students 'responses by calculating the means for the three variables along with their standard deviation (See Table 3).

Table 3. The means and their standard deviation

Descriptive Statistics					
	N	Minimum	Maximum	Mean	Std. Deviation
PU	34	1.40	5.00	2.3118	.81082
PEOU	34	1.00	4.80	2.1588	.71143
ATT	34	1.00	4.20	2.0118	.64937
BIU	34	1.40	5.00	2.4471	.92777
Valid N (listwise)	34				

Note. This table shows the mean scores and standard deviations for PU, PEOU, ATT, and BIU among the 34 participants

Procedure

With the collaboration of a university professor who had integrated Grammarly as part of his writing course, a group of 34 students enrolled in Semester 2 at the University of Hassan were selected to participate in the study. Prior to data collection, all the necessary permissions were obtained from the department, and participants were informed that their participation was voluntary and confidential and that they could withdraw from the study at their convenience. In the first data collection phase, a TAM-based questionnaire was administered online to students to explore their perceptions of Grammarly's Automated Writing Corrective Feedback (AWCF). Following the questionnaire, a subset of students (N= 8) was invited to participate in semi-structured interviews to gain deeper insights into their experiences and attitudes toward using Grammarly.

RESULTS AND DISCUSSION

As stated before, the main research instrument used for this study is a 5-point Likert scale questionnaire (See Figure 3) and open-ended questions to measure students' perceived usefulness, ease of use, and behavioural intention to use Grammarly and assess their overall experience with the AI tool. The quantitative data gathered from the questionnaire were coded based on established norms and subsequently entered into the Statistical Package for the Social Sciences (SPSS) for further analysis using descriptive statistics, such as Mean and Standard Deviation. Additionally, five open-ended questions were used to interview a sub-section of the participants (N= 8) to collect qualitative insights on their experience with the AI tool, including its benefits and limitations.

Figure 3. 5-point Likert scale

1 = Strongly Agree → 2 = Agree → 1 = Neutral → 1 = Disagree → 5 = Strongly Disagree

Perceived Usefulness of Grammarly

In terms of PU, the quantitative data from the Likert-scale questionnaire (See Table 4) reveal nuanced perceptions of Grammarly's usefulness among students. The results indicate that students perceive Grammarly as useful in improving their writing quality (mean = 2.41), most effective for error correction (mean = 2.03), and helps students understand grammar and structure (mean=2.29). Furthermore, its perceived usefulness impacts academic performance (mean = 2.26) and increases writing productivity among students (mean = 2.56

These findings are in line with, and support to a great extent, Barrot's study (2021), which indicated that students hold positive attitudes towards the use of Grammarly's AWCF, emphasizing its capacity to draw students' attention to their writing errors and improve writing by minimizing grammatical and structural errors.

Table 4. Statistical analysis of Grammarly perceived usefulness

Statistics						
		1.Using Grammarly improves the overall quality of my writing.	**2.Grammarly helps me correct errors I might not notice myself.**	**3.Grammarly enhances my understanding of grammar and structure.**	**4.Grammarly improves my academic performance in writing tasks.**	**5.Using Grammarly increases my productivity in writing assignments.**
N	Valid	34	34	34	34	34
	Missing	0	0	0	0	0
Mean		2,41	2,03	2,29	2,26	2,56
Std. Deviation		1,258	,937	1,001	1,109	1,021

Note. PU item statistics (N=34)

Perceived Ease of Use of Grammarly

Concerning Grammarly's perceived ease of use (PEOU) Statistics, (See Table 5), the respondents generally find the tool easy to use (mean = 2.21), straightforward (mean = 2.29), and with a clear and easy-to-operate interface (mean = 2.24). Additionally, they can easily comprehend and apply Grammarly's writing suggestions (mean = 2.00) and without technical assistance (mean = 2.06)

These results are consistent with the ones from El Missi et al.'s (2024) study where most participants reported positive perceptions concerning Grammarly's ease of use and highlighted its significant impact on their writing quality.

The aforementioned findings support H1, as respondents collectively agreed that Grammarly is useful, easy to use, and positively impacts their writing quality.

Table 5. Statistical analysis of Grammarly pereceived ease of use

Statistics						
		1.Grammarly is easy to use.	**2.Learning to use Grammarly was straightforward.**	**3.Grammarly's interface is clear and easy to navigate.**	**4.Grammarly's suggestions are easy to understand and apply.**	**5.I can use Grammarly without needing technical help.**
N	Valid	34	34	34	34	34
	Missing	0	0	0	0	0
Mean		2,21	2,29	2,24	2,00	2,06
Std. Deviation		,946	,719	,819	,778	,851

Note. PEOU item statistics (N=34)

Attitudes Towards Grammarly Use

Quantitative data on students' attitudes toward Grammarly (See Table 6) reveal strong positive attitudes (means = 2,15), particularly regarding confidence in Grammarly' s utility (mean = 1.24), engagement (mean = 2,12), enjoyment (mean = 2.44), and overall benefits for EFL students (means = 2.15–2.44)

These findings align with Fitria et al. (2022), who found that students perceive Grammarly positively due to its swift, immediate, and time-saving feedback, which positively affects students' motivation and boosts their self-confidence in their writing abilities.

Table 6. Statistical analysis of participants attitudes towards Grammarly use

Statistics						
		1.I enjoy using Grammarly for writing support.	**2.Grammarly is a beneficial tool for EFL students.**	**3.Grammarly makes writing correction more engaging.**	**4.I have a positive attitude toward using Grammarly.**	**5.I feel confident using Grammarly to improve my writing.**
N	Valid	34	34	34	34	34
	Missing	0	0	0	0	0
Mean		2,44	2,12	2,12	2,15	1,24
Std. Deviation		1,021	,808	,880	,857	,431

Note. ATT item statistics (N=34)

Behavioral Intention to Use Grammarly

With regard to Behavioral Intention to use Grammarly (See Table 7), the results show positive intention to continue using Grammarly in the future (means=2.03-2.76), with a strong agreement for recommending it to peers (mean=2.03) and regular planned use (mean=2.76). This suggests that students are generally inclined to adopt Grammarly in their writing journey in the long run.

These results corroborate from previous studies, notably by Cheng et al. (2006), where it was found that the more individuals find specific software useful, the easier it becomes for them to use it, and eventually, they will be more inclined to continue using it in the future.

Table 7. Statistical analysis of participants' behavioral intention to use Grammarly

Statistics						
		1.I intend to continue using Grammarly in the future.	**2.I plan to use Grammarly regularly in my writing.**	**3.If Grammarly is available, I will use it to correct my writing productions.**	**4.I would recommend Grammarly to other EFL students.**	**5.I am likely to rely on Grammarly for future writing tasks.**
N	Valid	34	34	34	34	34
	Missing	0	0	0	0	0
Mean		2,41	2,76	2,26	2,03	2,76
Std. Deviation		1,158	1,103	,931	1,000	1,156

Note. BIU item statistics (N=34)

PU and PEOU as Predictors to Students Attitudes Toward Grammarly (ATT)

To understand and quantify the relationship between one or more independent variables (predictors) and a dependent variable (outcome), a multiple regression analysis is necessary. To this end, and based on the good results of Cronbach's alpha, all items representing a particular scale were computed into one by calculating the means for the three variables along with their standard deviations (as shown in Table 3).

To test Hypothesis 2 (H2), which states that students with higher perceived usefulness (PU) and perceived ease of use (PEOU) will have a more positive attitude toward using Grammarly, a multiple regression analysis was conducted. The results revealed that the model was statistically significant, $F(2, 31) = 42.954$, $p < .001$, indicating that PU and PEOU together significantly predict students' attitudes (ATT) toward Grammarly. The model explained approximately 73.5% of the variance in attitude ($R^2 \approx .735$), suggesting a strong relationship between the predictors and the outcome variable (See Table 8).

Both PU ($\beta = .560$, $p < .001$) and PEOU ($\beta = .365$, $p = .009$) were significant positive predictors of attitude. Specifically, an increase in PU was associated with a 0.448 unit increase in ATT, while a one-unit increase in PEOU was linked to a 0.333 unit increase in ATT, holding other variables constant (See Table 9).

The results align with Davis's (1981) Technology Acceptance Model (TAM), confirming that tools like Grammarly are more likely to be adopted by students when they are perceived as both useful (PU) and user-friendly (PEOU). These findings, in turn, support H2, emphasizing that students who perceive Grammarly as useful and easy to use are more likely to have a favorable attitude toward its use.

Table 8. ANOVA results for regression model predicting ATT

ANOVA[a]						
Model		Sum of Squares	df	Mean Square	F	Sig.
1	Regression	10,225	2	5,113	42,954	,000[b]
	Residual	3,690	31	,119		
	Total	13,915	33			

a. Dependent Variable: ATT
b. Predictors: (Constant), PEOU, PU
Note. ANOVA: PU and PEOU significantly predict ATT (*p* < .001)").

Table 9. Regression coefficients for PU/PEOU predicting ATT

Coefficients[a]						
		Unstandardized Coefficients		Standardized Coefficients		
Model		B	Std. Error	Beta	t	Sig.
1	(Constant)	,255	,201		1,271	,213
	PU	,448	,104	,560	4,301	,000
	PEOU	,333	,119	,365	2,806	,009

a. Dependent Variable: ATT
Note. Regression Coefficients for Perceived Usefulness (PU) and Perceived Ease of Use (PEOU) Predicting Attitude Toward Grammarly (**ATT**)

PU and PEOU as Predictors to Students' Behavioral Intention to Use Grammarly (BIU)

The regression analysis in Table 10 supports H3, confirming that students with higher Perceived Usefulness (PU) and Perceived Ease of Use (PEOU) exhibit significantly greater Behavioural Intention to Use (BIU) Grammarly. The overall model is statistically significant (See Table 10) (F (2, 31) = 19.35, $p < .001$), explaining 55.5% of the variance in BIU ($R^2 = .555$). Both PU ($\beta = 0.44$, p = .014) and PEOU ($\beta = 0.37$, p = .038) are significant predictors, with PU having a slightly stronger effect. This aligns with the Technology Acceptance Model (TAM), demonstrating that students are more likely to adopt Grammarly when they find it both useful and easy to use.

The findings suggest that enhancing PU may be more impactful than improving PEOU alone, though both factors are critical for adoption. The significant F-value ($p < .001$) confirms the model's robustness, while the unstandardized coefficients (PU: $B = 0.63$; PEOU: $B = 0.595$) indicate that for every 1-unit increase in PU/PEOU, BIU increases by approximately 0.6 units (See Table 11).

Table 10. ANOVA results for regression model predicting BIU

ANOVA[a]						
Model		Sum of Squares	df	Mean Square	F	Sig.
1	Regression	24,561	2	12,281	19,350	,000[b]
	Residual	19,674	31	,635		
	Total	44,235	33			

a. Dependent Variable: BIU
b. Predictors: (Constant), PEOU, PU
Note . ANOVA: PU and PEOU significantly predict BIU (*p* < .001)").

Table 11. Regression coefficients for PU/PEOU predicting BIU

Coefficients[a]						
Model		Unstandardized Coefficients		Standardized Coefficients		
		B	Std. Error	Beta	t	Sig.
1	(Constant)	-,329	,464		-,709	,484
	PU	,630	,241	,441	2,616	,014
	PEOU	,595	,274	,366	2,169	,038

a. Dependent Variable: BIU
Note. Regression Coefficients for Perceived Usefulness (PU) and Perceived Ease of Use (PEOU) Behavioural Intention to Use Grammarly (**BIU**)

To gain deeper insights into students' perception of Grammarly in terms of its usefulness, ease of use, and intention to use it in the future, a sub-section of participants was interviewed using open-ended questions (N=8). Their answer further cast light on the benefits regarding the use of the AI-powered tool in question in their writing endeavor:

- Participant 1: " My overall experience using Grammarly has been very positive. It is easy to use and helps catch grammar mistakes, spelling errors, and suggests better word choices."
- Participant 2: " My overall experience using Grammarly has been very positive. It's a helpful tool for catching grammar, spelling, and punctuation errors that I might overlook. I especially appreciate the real-time feedback and clarity suggestions, which help improve the tone and readability of my writing."
- Participant 3: " Grammarly is user - friendly and It helps correcting the structures of my sentences making them well arranged and grammatically correct."
- Participant 4: " Grammarly helped improve my writing performance by making me more aware of common mistakes I tend to make, like wordiness or

misused commas. Over time, I started to internalize some of its feedback, which made me more confident and efficient in editing my own work."

- Participant 5: " Grammarly is easy to navigate and helped me write with fewer mistakes, choose better words, and make my sentences clearer. It made my writing more correct and easier to understand."
- Participant 6: " Grammarly helps me write more accurately and saves time during editing. So, I would continue using Grammarly."
- Participant 7: "It helps me to correctly write my tasks and learn from my mistakes, especially I notice every mistake I make it. "
- Participant 8: "Grammarly helped me write with fewer mistakes, choose better words, and make my sentences clearer. It made my writing more correct and easier to understand .So, I would definitely continue using it."

Overall, all the students acknowledge the significance of Grammarly and consider it to be a valuable tool. They also assert that they would continue using the tool in the future because it is easy to use, helps them notice grammar, punctuation, and spelling mistakes, and suggests better word choices. Furthermore, the tool provides real-time feedback, saves time during the editing stage, corrects sentence structures, and improves the readability of written work, making students confident in the editing process and, in turn, making their writing experience positive.

Challenges and Limitations of Using Grammarly

Despite the reported benefits of Grammarly use, eight respondents (N=8) highlighted some of the challenges they encountered while using the AI-powered tool. According to the interviewees, these challenges include:

- Participant 1: " I found the real-time grammar and spelling checks most helpful—they catch basic errors quickly and help me write more confidently. The clarity and tone suggestions were also useful for making my writing more professional and easier to understand. However, I sometimes found the suggestions too rigid or out of context, especially with creative writing or technical content. It was challenging when Grammarly tried to change my phrasing in ways that didn't fit my intended meaning."
- Participant 2: " The most helpful feature is grammar correction because it helps me fix mistakes quickly. The most difficult part is when Grammarly gives a suggestion that doesn't match what I mean."
- Participant 3: " My overall experience using Grammarly has been very positive. It's a helpful tool for catching grammar, spelling, and punctuation errors that I might overlook. I especially appreciate the real-time feedback and clar-

ity suggestions, which help improve the tone and readability of my writing. While it's not perfect and sometimes makes suggestions that don't fit the context, it's a great second set of eyes—especially for professional or academic writing."

- Participant 4: " Grammarly sometimes suggests wrong alternatives alternatives for some words."
- Participant 5: "I think that the grammar suggestions were most helpful; tone detection was a bit challenging. "
- Participant 6: "Although Grammarly was helpful, I wouldn't continue using it long-term because I don't want to become too reliant on it and prefer developing my own writing and editing skills and to learn more and to correct my mistakes. "
- Participant 7: "I had to look for a hotspot to connect to my Grammarly, I could not use my phone because my mobile data connection was insufficient for reliable usage and i can 't afford to have a WIFI at home."
- Participant 8: "I couldn 't use certain features because I have to upgrade to Grammarly Premuim. I think that the paid version offers more than the free one."

Based on students' responses, it can conclude that Grammarly has several limitations. Participants 1 and 5 reported that some of the suggestions provided by the tool were too rigid, particularly in creative writing or technical content. This indicates that Grammarly fails to adapt to nuanced or specialized writing styles and imposes prescriptive grammatical conventions that can override the natural flow and students' tone or intent. This aligns well with previous research by Cavaleri and Dianati (2016), El Missi et al. (2024), Koltovskia (2020), and Llausas et al. (2024) stating that Grammarly sometimes tends to provide fallible suggestions and overlooks students' tone and style, making them frustrated and unengaged.

Another significant shortcoming of the tool, as identified by Participants 2, 3, and 4, is Grammarly's contextual inaccuracy. The tool's inability to fully grasp contextual and semantic nuances in writing poses a significant challenge for students. Although the three participants framed Grammarly as efficient, they also underscored the tool's occasional mismatches, where its suggestions can lead to semantic inaccuracies (Participant 4), misalign with their intended meaning (Participant 2), or fall short of fitting the overall context of the writing (Participant 3). These findings align with a previous study by Fitriana and Nurazni (2022), which indicated that Grammarly poses significant contextual and semantic challenges for students.

Despite their positive attitude towards Grammarly, Participant 6 expressed his reluctance to adopt Grammarly in the long term. He stated that he would not continue using it in the future, fearing that he might become too reliant on it, which might impede the development of his writing skills. This implies that AI writing tools should complement, rather than circumvent, the learning process. These findings support El Missi et al. (2024) and Zaragoza et al.'s (2024) reference to Grammarly' s limitations by attesting that some students expressed concern that overreliance on such an AI tool might hinder their learning as they might become less proactive in recognizing and correcting their errors independently.

Participants 7 and 8 raised two critical but often overlooked limitations of Grammarly, which are reliable and stable internet connectivity and the constraints of the free version. Grammarly is a cloud-based writing tool that requires an active internet connection for most of its features to function properly. Additionally, its free version does not allow students to access all the other features, such as plagiarism detection and an AI detector. Students will need to upgrade their accounts to benefit from these features fully. Unfortunately, most students do not have access to the Internet at home because they cannot afford it since they come from underprivileged families. These findings correspond with earlier research by El Missi et al. (2024), Fitriana and Nurazni (2022), Sumarni (2023), and Yang (2023) that have alluded to the technical issues that are associated with Grammarly's use, especially in terms of Internet connectivity and the constraints of its free version compared to the Premium one.

CONCLUSION

The current study sought to investigate the perception of Smester 2 students at Hassan I University towards using Grammarly for error-checking in their writing class using Davis's (1989) Technology Acceptance Model. The findings revealed that the respondents generally hold a positive attitude toward Grammarly. The AI tool is deemed useful for error correction and easy to use. Additionally, it has the capacity to enhance students' writing skills, boost their confidence, and increase their motivation, making their writing experience agreeable. Although participants expressed their willingness to continue using Grammarly in the future in their writing tasks, they also highlighted several limitations that impact its effectiveness in academic and EFL writing contexts. First, the tool often provides fallible and rigid suggestions, especially in creative or technical writing, overriding students' tone and intent. Second, Grammarly misinterprets contextual and semantic nuances, and suggests corrections that might alter writers 'intended message. Third, the risk of overreliance on Grammarly emerges as potential threat that might hinder the development of students' independent writing skills. Fourth, technical constraints and accessibility issues, such as the need for reliable internet access and the lack of advanced features in the tools free hinder their effective usability among students.

LIMITATIONS OF THE STUDY

When analyzing the findings of this study, several limitations can be noted. Firstly, due to the relatively small sample size (N=34), the results may not be generalizable to all Moroccan university EFL learners. Thus, further research can be conducted with a larger and more diverse participant pool to validate these findings Moreover, there is a need for experimental research with a control group and an experimental group to draw robust conclusions and make comparisons about the efficacy of the AI-powered tool in question. Additionally, more longitudinal studies are needed to capture how variables evolve over time. Furthermore, this study also opens avenues for potential future research to explore the mediating effects of Attitude (ATT) or moderators, such as prior experience, to refine these insights.

For instance, future longitudinal studies could examine the long-term impact of attitude on students writing skills development, just as mixed-methods studies might deepen understanding of motivational and cognitive aspects. Additionally, a closer look at contextual elements like pedagogically methods or cultural dimensions could help help elucidate how these dynamics interact in EFL learning environments.

PEDAGOGICAL IMPLICATIONS

Several pedagogical implications emerge from the findings of this study for EFL instruction. Grammarly, as an AI-powered writing tool, provides learners with immediate, personalized, and formative feedback. Thanks to it, students can identify and correct errors independently, promoting their writing autonomy. Additionally, this tool stimulates students' engagement and motivation while allowing them to learn at their own pace. All these benefits align well with learner-centered approaches to learning, which prioritize learners' active participation in the learning process and shift the focus from the teacher, emphasizing students' engagement, autonomy, and personalized learning experiences. When students actively interact with AI software, they become more aware of their writing strengths and weaknesses. Thus, policymakers are called to integrate AI writing tools into educational institutions, and more specifically, into writing instruction to promote students' writing skills and proficiency. Moreover, to ensure equitable access to such AI-powered tools for all students, educational institutions must be equipped with reliable internet and updated hardware to alleviate the burden placed upon them and enable them to utilize these tools effectively in their academic endeavors.

REFERENCES

Anastasia, W., Murtisari, E., & Isharyanti, N. (2024). Less-proficient EFL students' use of Grammarly in writing : Behavior, cognition, and affect. *The JALT CALL Journal*, *20*(1), 1–25. DOI: 10.29140/jaltcall.v20n1.1089

Astuti, D., & Sumarni, S. (2023). Grammarly in students' self-directed learning for writing skills : Advantages and disadvantages. *INSANIA : Jurnal Pemikiran Alternatif Kependidikan*, *28*(1a), 36–50. DOI: 10.24090/insania.v28i1a.8899

Azennoud, A. (2024). Enhancing Writing Accuracy and Complexity through AI-Assisted Tools among Moroccan EFL University Learners. *International Journal of Linguistics and Translation Studies*, *5*(4), 211–226. DOI: 10.36892/ijlts.v5i4.529

Barrot, J. S. (2021). Using automated written corrective feedback in the writing classrooms : Effects on L2 writing accuracy. *Computer Assisted Language Learning*, *36*(4), 584–607. DOI: 10.1080/09588221.2021.1936071

Calma, A., Cotronei-Baird, V., & Chia, A. (2022). Grammarly : An instructional intervention for writing enhancement in management education. *International Journal of Management Education*, *20*(3), 100704. DOI: 10.1016/j.ijme.2022.100704

Cavaleri, M., & Dianati, S. (2016). *You want me to check your grammar again ? The usefulness of an online grammar checker as perceived by students.*

Cheng, F.-F., Wu, J., Huang, Y.-W., & Yen, D. (2006). *An Empirical Investigation of User Acceptance of Wireless Technology at Work.*

Davis, F., & Granić, A. (2024). *Revolution of TAM.*, DOI: 10.1007/978-3-030-45274-2_3

Davis, F. D. (1989). Perceived Usefulness, Perceived Ease of Use, and User Acceptance of Information Technology. *Management Information Systems Quarterly*, *13*(3), 319–340. DOI: 10.2307/249008

Ejjami, R. (2024). *Revolutionizing Moroccan Education with AI: A Path to Customized Learning.* *6*(3).

El Missi, M., Jarmouni, R., & Chibi, M. (2024). Exploring Students' Perceptions of Using Grammarly in Academic Writing : Master Students of the English Department as a Case Study. *International Journal of Innovative Research and Development.* Advance online publication. DOI: 10.24940/ijird/2024/v13/i6/JUN24003

Fan, N. (2023). Exploring the Effects of Automated Written Corrective Feedback on EFL Students' Writing Quality : A Mixed-Methods Study. *SAGE Open*, *13*(2), 21582440231181296. DOI: 10.1177/21582440231181296

Fitria, R. A., Sabarun, S., & Miftah, M. Z. (2022). STUDENTS' PERCEPTION OF THE USE OF GRAMMARLY IN UNDERGRADUATE THESIS WRITING. *PROJECT (Professional Journal of English Education)*, *5*(2), 366. DOI: 10.22460/project.v5i2.p366-371

Fitriana, K., & Nurazni, L. (2022). Exploring Students' Perception of Using Grammarly to Check Grammar in Their Writing. [Journal of English Teaching]. *JET*, *8*(1), 15–25. DOI: 10.33541/jet.v8i1.3044

Grammarly. (2025). *About Us | Grammarly*. https://www.grammarly.com/about

Grimes, D., & Warschauer, M. (2010). *Utility in a Fallible Tool : A Multi-Site Case Study of Automated Writing Evaluation.*

Guo, Q., Feng, R., & Hua, Y. (2021). How effectively can EFL students use automated written corrective feedback (AWCF) in research writing? *Computer Assisted Language Learning*, •••, 1–20. DOI: 10.1080/09588221.2021.1879161

Koltovskaia, S. (2020). Student engagement with automated written corrective feedback (AWCF) provided by Grammarly : A multiple case study. *Assessing Writing*, *44*, 100450. DOI: 10.1016/j.asw.2020.100450

Koltovskaia, S. (2023). Postsecondary L2 writing teachers' use and perceptions of Grammarly as a complement to their feedback. *ReCALL*, *35*(3), 290–304. DOI: 10.1017/S0958344022000179

Llausas, S. M., Ruiz, E., Ayucan, S. M., & Evardo, O. J.Jr. (2024). A Systematic Literature Review on the Use of Grammarly in Improving the Writing Skills of ESL/EFL Students. *International Journal of Multidisciplinary: Applied Business and Education Research*, *5*(9), 3507–3516. DOI: 10.11594/ijmaber.05.09.10

Martínez-Carrasco, R., & Chabert, A. (2023). Writing on steroids? Accuracy of automatic corrective feedback in L2 competence development. *Bellaterra Journal of Teaching & Learning Language & Literature*, *16*(3), e1142. DOI: 10.5565/rev/jtl3.1142

Maypida, A., & Damanik, E. S. D. (2024). *Exploring Grammarly's Effectiveness in EFL Writing through a Student Perception Study.*

Mendoza Zaragoza, N. E., Téllez Tula, Á., & Herrera Corona, L. (2024). Artificial Intelligence in Thesis Writing : Exploring the Role of Advanced Grammar Checkers (Grammarly). *Estudios y Perspectivas Revista Científica y Académica, 4*(2), 649-683. DOI: 10.61384/r.c.a.v4i2.248

O'Neill, R., & Russell, A. M. T. (2019). Grammarly : Help or hindrance ? Academic Learning Advisors' perceptions of an online grammar checker. *R. O.*

Ofrita, H., Darmis, A., & Rosmanizar, R. (2023). The Effect of Automated Written Corrective Feedback (AWCF) on Students' Writing at SMP 47 Pekanbaru. *Jurnal Pendidikan Tuntas, 1*(4), 352–361. DOI: 10.37985/jpt.v1i4.282

Or, C. (2024). Watch That Attitude! Examining the Role of Attitude in the Technology Acceptance Model through Meta-Analytic Structural Equation Modelling. *International Journal of Technology in Education and Science, 8*(4), 558–582. DOI: 10.46328/ijtes.575

Ranalli, J. (2018). Automated written corrective feedback : How well can students make use of it? *Computer Assisted Language Learning, 31*(7), 653–674. DOI: 10.1080/09588221.2018.1428994

Rao, M. (2019). *Usage of Grammarly – Online Grammar and Spelling Checker Tool at the Health Sciences Library, Manipal Academy of Higher Education, Manipal : A Study.*

Sandema-Sombe, C. N. (2019). *Relationship between perceived usefulness, ease of use, and acceptance of business intelligence systems.* Walden University.

Tsania, N. A., & Puspitasari, D. (n. d.). *STUDENTS' EXPERIENCES IN USING GRAMMARLY APPLICATION : A CASE STUDY.*

Ummah, L. K., & Bisriyah, M. (2022). EFL students' perception of Grammarly's feedback and how they deal with the inaccuracy. [Journal of English Educators Society]. *JEES, 7*(2). Advance online publication. DOI: 10.21070/jees.v7i2.1687

Vo, N. H. K. V., & Nguyen, Q. T. (2021). *Applying Grammarly as an Online Grammar Checker Tool to Enhance Writing Skills for English-Major Students.*

Yang, H. (2023, février 24). *Grammarly Free vs Premium : What's the Difference?* https://prowritingaid.com/grammarly-free-vs-premium

Yang, Y., & Tian, Y. (2024). Exploring the Chinese AWCF Platform's value in improving CSL learners' writing performance in a ChatGPT context. *NaN, NaN*, NaN-NaN. DOI: 10.1075/csl.24008.yan

Chapter 8
Systemic Integration Infrastructure and Ecosystem Design for Agentic AI in Schools

Karshiyeva Dilafruz Suyunovna
National Pedagogical University of Uzbekistan, Uzbekistan

Nilufar Niyazova
Mamun University, Uzbekistan

Latofat Salayeva
Urgench State University, Uzbekistan

Munir Ahmad
https://orcid.org/0000-0003-4836-6151
Survey of Pakistan, Pakistan

Sardor Sharifzoda
Mamun University, Uzbekistan

ABSTRACT

This chapter examines the integration of agentic AI in schools, highlighting its transformative potential for personalized learning, teacher support, and administrative efficiency. It explores the conceptual foundations, systemic infrastructure, and collaborative ecosystem design necessary for effective AI deployment. Key considerations include data management, interoperability, ethical standards, and governance frameworks. The chapter emphasizes scalable, sustainable, and adaptive

DOI: 10.4018/979-8-3373-4621-2.ch008

AI ecosystems that foster collaboration among students, teachers, administrators, and AI agents, reshaping educational practices and preparing schools for the challenges of the 21st century.

INTRODUCTION

The rapid evolution of artificial intelligence (AI) is reshaping educational landscapes worldwide. Among emerging AI paradigms, agentic AI, intelligent systems capable of autonomous decision-making, adaptive problem-solving, and proactive interaction, offers transformative potential for schools. Unlike traditional AI tools that function as passive assistants, agentic AI can actively support students' learning journeys, provide real-time pedagogical feedback, and facilitate adaptive curriculum pathways, effectively becoming a collaborative educational partner. This shift marks a critical juncture in reimagining how teaching and learning processes are designed and delivered.

Despite its promise, the integration of agentic AI in schools presents complex challenges. Technical barriers such as interoperability with existing digital infrastructures, data privacy concerns, and maintenance of AI systems can limit effective deployment. Equally significant are social and organizational challenges, including teacher preparedness, acceptance of AI-mediated pedagogy, and the alignment of AI actions with curriculum goals and ethical standards. Conversely, the opportunities are substantial: agentic AI can enable personalized learning experiences, enhance administrative efficiency, promote equity in educational access, and foster the development of 21st-century skills through interactive and responsive learning environments.

To realize these opportunities, a systemic approach to integration and ecosystem design is essential. Systemic integration emphasizes the alignment of technological, organizational, and pedagogical components within schools, ensuring AI tools function cohesively with human stakeholders and existing learning infrastructures. Ecosystem design extends this approach by conceptualizing schools as dynamic, interconnected networks of agents—including students, teachers, administrators, and AI systems—that co-create learning experiences, share resources, and adapt collaboratively to changing educational demands. Together, these approaches provide a holistic framework to guide the strategic deployment of agentic AI, balancing innovation with sustainability, usability, and ethical considerations (Berisha Qehaja, 2025; Daher, 2025; Kayal, 2024; Kotsis, n.d.).

This chapter addresses several key objectives. First, it seeks to analyze the infrastructural and organizational requirements necessary for effective AI integration in schools. Second, it explores strategies for designing ecosystems that facilitate meaningful collaboration between human and AI agents. Third, it examines the potential impacts of agentic AI on teaching, learning, and school governance, highlighting both opportunities and constraints. Finally, the chapter aims to provide actionable insights and design principles to inform policymakers, school leaders, and technology developers in creating sustainable, ethically aligned, and pedagogically effective AI-driven educational environments.

CONCEPTUAL FOUNDATIONS AND THEORETICAL FRAMEWORK

The integration of agentic AI in schools requires a solid understanding of both its conceptual underpinnings and the theoretical frameworks that support its effective deployment. This section explores the definition and characteristics of agentic AI, examines relevant educational theories that align with AI agency, and presents frameworks for systemic integration and ecosystem design in educational contexts.

Definition of Agentic AI and Its Role in Learning Environments

Agentic AI refers to intelligent systems capable of autonomous decision-making, adaptive learning, and proactive engagement in dynamic environments (Acharya et al., 2025). Unlike conventional AI, which primarily executes pre-defined instructions or responds to explicit queries, agentic AI actively perceives contextual information, interprets user needs, and initiates actions aligned with specific learning objectives. In educational contexts, this autonomy allows AI to function as an active participant rather than a passive assistant, bridging the gap between automated support and intelligent, context-aware facilitation. Agentic AI can dynamically adjust its behavior based on classroom interactions, student engagement, and institutional goals, enabling a flexible and responsive learning environment. This autonomy also supports teachers by anticipating student needs, identifying emerging learning patterns, and recommending instructional adjustments, effectively acting as a collaborative partner in pedagogy.

Personalization is one of the most significant contributions of agentic AI in education (Ashwani, 2025; Xiao & He, 2025). By continuously analyzing student performance data, learning behaviors, and engagement metrics, AI systems can adapt content, instructional pacing, and assessment strategies to each learner's profile. This enables differentiated instruction tailored to individual strengths, weaknesses, and learning preferences, enhancing motivation and mastery of content. Beyond static personalization, agentic AI can also anticipate future learning needs, suggest remedial or enrichment activities, and dynamically adjust learning paths in real time. This level of personalization supports equitable access to education, helping learners progress at their own pace while maximizing engagement and minimizing frustration. Over time, personalized AI interventions can improve retention, foster intrinsic motivation, and contribute to long-term academic success.

Agentic AI actively mediates collaborative learning by organizing group activities, monitoring interactions, and providing scaffolds to support equitable participation (Edwards et al., 2025; Wang et al., 2025). It can suggest discussion prompts, propose collaborative strategies, and track group dynamics to ensure that all students are contributing meaningfully. By fostering cooperative problem-solving, peer-to-peer learning, and knowledge sharing, AI enhances the social and cognitive dimensions of learning. Additionally, agentic AI can adapt collaborative tasks based on group performance, individual engagement, and learning objectives, ensuring that projects remain productive and aligned with educational goals. This creates opportunities for students to develop critical thinking, teamwork, and communication skills within a supportive and structured framework.

Agentic AI provides real-time formative assessment and feedback, continuously monitoring student understanding and engagement (Hughes et al., 2025). By identifying misconceptions, learning gaps, and performance trends, AI can deliver immediate, actionable guidance to students while providing teachers with detailed analytics to inform instructional adjustments. At the administrative level, AI generates insights from complex datasets, aiding decisions about resource allocation, curriculum adjustments, and overall school performance. This dual-level impact—supporting both learners and institutional management—ensures that educational decisions are data-driven, evidence-based, and pedagogically sound, fostering efficiency and effectiveness across the school ecosystem.

The transformative potential of agentic AI extends beyond individual instruction (Liu et al., 2025). By integrating with school-wide systems, AI can optimize resource allocation, scheduling, infrastructure management, and curriculum design. Its capacity to analyze trends across classes, grades, and student populations enables administrators to make strategic decisions that enhance institutional efficiency and learning outcomes. Agentic AI acts as a bridge between micro-level classroom interventions and macro-level institutional planning, creating a coherent, interconnected educational ecosystem. Through continuous adaptation, real-time analytics, and alignment with school goals, agentic AI contributes to dynamic, responsive, and innovative educational environments that benefit students, educators, and administrators alike.

Educational Theories Supporting AI Agency

Constructivist theories emphasize that learners actively construct knowledge through interaction with their environment rather than passively receiving information (Hein, 1991). Agentic AI aligns with this paradigm by providing adaptive challenges, scaffolding tasks, and supporting exploratory problem-solving. For example, AI can present context-specific prompts, modify task difficulty based on student responses, and simulate authentic real-world scenarios that demand critical thinking. By enabling learners to interact dynamically with content and peers, AI facilitates deep understanding, conceptual connections, and long-term knowledge retention, reinforcing the principles of constructivist learning environments.

Personalized learning theory underscores the need to tailor instruction to individual learners' interests, abilities, and learning styles (Kaswan et al., 2024). Agentic AI operationalizes this by analyzing data to identify gaps, predict challenges, and recommend targeted interventions. It can adjust learning paths, recommend supplementary materials, and modify instructional pacing, ensuring instruction is responsive and relevant. By providing students with autonomy and choice, AI promotes motivation and engagement, supporting differentiated instruction and creating a learning environment where diverse learners can thrive. Personalized AI interventions also foster self-directed learning, enabling students to take ownership of their educational journey.

Social learning theory highlights learning through observation, collaboration, and social interaction (Bandura & Walters, 1977). Agentic AI can function as a facilitator of social learning, mediating group discussions, guiding peer interactions, and modeling effective problem-solving approaches. By monitoring group dynamics and providing feedback on collaborative performance, AI ensures equitable participation and encourages cooperative learning. These interactions help students develop communication skills, team-based problem-solving abilities, and shared knowledge construction, enhancing both cognitive and social dimensions of learning. AI-mediated social learning also allows for real-time interventions to address conflicts, imbalances in participation, or knowledge gaps within groups.

Cognitive load theory addresses the limitations of working memory and the need to manage instructional complexity (Ouwehand et al., 2025; Sweller & Chandler, 1991). Agentic AI contributes by structuring content, sequencing tasks, and adjusting instructional demands to match each student's cognitive capacity. It can present information in digestible chunks, offer just-in-time hints, and scaffold complex tasks to prevent overload. By dynamically modulating difficulty and pacing, AI enhances learning efficiency, comprehension, and retention, ensuring that learners are challenged appropriately without experiencing cognitive strain. This enables optimized instructional design, particularly for complex subjects or learners with varying proficiency levels.

Integrating these educational theories ensures that agentic AI is pedagogically grounded. Rather than merely automating tasks, AI facilitates active, collaborative, and personalized learning, supporting students' cognitive, social, and emotional development. By aligning AI behaviors with established learning theories, educators can ensure that technological interventions enhance instruction while maintaining educational quality, fostering environments that are engaging, adaptive, and responsive to diverse learner needs.

Frameworks for Systemic Integration and Ecosystem Design

Systemic Integration Frameworks

Systemic integration frameworks focus on embedding agentic AI into school systems in a structured and cohesive manner. These frameworks emphasize coordination among technology, pedagogy, and administration to maximize AI effectiveness while minimizing disruption to existing workflows. By integrating AI systematically, schools ensure that interventions support instructional goals, enhance learning outcomes, and streamline administrative processes.

A robust infrastructure is foundational to integration, including high-performance computing devices, secure servers, responsive AI platforms, and cloud solutions. Such infrastructure enables real-time analytics, adaptive learning, and seamless interaction between human users and AI agents. It also ensures reliability and scalability, accommodating growth in student populations, curricular complexity, and AI functionalities. A solid technical foundation is essential for both classroom-level applications and broader institutional management.

Effective integration relies on interoperable systems and strong data governance. AI must communicate seamlessly with LMS, SIS, assessment platforms, and digital resources. Governance policies must define data collection, storage, access, and ethical usage, ensuring security, privacy, and compliance with legal and ethical standards. Interoperability combined with governance allows AI to leverage data for actionable insights while maintaining stakeholder trust and transparency.

AI interventions must align with curriculum objectives, instructional strategies, and assessment practices. By supporting adaptive learning, formative assessment, and performance analytics, AI enhances pedagogical relevance and promotes meaningful engagement. This alignment ensures that AI acts as a facilitator of learning rather than a disruption, complementing teacher expertise and reinforcing educational goals.

Successful integration requires professional development, stakeholder communication, and culture-building. Teachers, administrators, and technical staff need training to interpret AI insights, adjust instructional strategies, and integrate AI into daily workflows. Change management also addresses resistance, encourages innovation, and fosters a school culture that embraces continuous improvement and effective use of AI tools.

Ecosystem Design Frameworks

Ecosystem design frameworks conceptualize schools as interconnected networks of human and AI agents. These frameworks emphasize collaboration, adaptability, and holistic resource integration, creating environments where AI enhances learning outcomes while complementing human expertise.

Active involvement of students, teachers, administrators, parents, and AI developers ensures that AI tools meet educational, ethical, and cultural expectations. Co-creation fosters ownership, engagement, and trust, improving relevance, usability, and adoption across diverse learning contexts. AI ecosystems integrate continuous feedback from students, teachers, and system performance metrics, enabling real-time adjustments to learning pathways, teaching strategies, and AI behaviors. Iterative improvement ensures that AI remains responsive, effective, and aligned with evolving educational needs.

Coordinated use of digital platforms, content repositories, and AI tools creates seamless learning experiences, reduces redundancy, and enhances instructional efficiency. Resource integration ensures that students and educators have access to the right materials and analytics at the right time. Sustainable AI ecosystems prioritize equity, inclusivity, and ethical compliance. Ethical frameworks guide responsible decision-making, prevent bias, and maintain accountability, while sustainability strategies ensure long-term operation, scalability, and continuous improvement.

By combining systemic integration with ecosystem design, schools establish robust, adaptive environments where agentic AI enhances individual learning, instructional effectiveness, and institutional efficiency. This integrated approach provides a foundation for evaluating impact, scaling interventions, and sustaining ethically aligned innovation across educational ecosystems.

SYSTEMIC INTEGRATION INFRASTRUCTURE

The successful deployment of agentic AI in schools depends on a robust systemic integration infrastructure. This infrastructure encompasses the technical, organizational, and operational elements necessary to support AI systems while ensuring alignment with pedagogical objectives and institutional workflows. A systemic perspective ensures that AI tools are not isolated technologies but part of an interconnected ecosystem capable of enhancing learning outcomes and operational efficiency.

Technical Infrastructure Requirements

A robust and scalable hardware foundation is critical for effective deployment of agentic AI in schools (Bandi et al., 2025; Huang, 2025). Beyond high-performance computing devices such as servers, teacher and student workstations, interactive whiteboards, and AI-enabled classroom tools, schools may also require specialized devices for immersive learning, such as tablets, AR/VR equipment, and smart projectors. These devices must handle real-time AI computations, large datasets for predictive analytics, and dynamic adaptive learning algorithms without latency, ensuring seamless classroom experiences. Scalable hardware also supports multi-user environments, enabling simultaneous AI-driven interactions across multiple classrooms. Proper hardware deployment minimizes technical disruptions, improves system responsiveness, and ensures that both teachers and students can engage fully with intelligent educational tools. Additionally, considerations such as device redundancy, durability, and compatibility with future AI upgrades are essential for long-term viability.

The software layer forms the operational core of agentic AI systems. AI platforms should support natural language processing, predictive analytics, personalized learning engines, and adaptive assessment mechanisms. Emphasis on modularity and interoperability allows schools to integrate new features, third-party educational apps, or updates without system-wide disruption. User-friendly interfaces are essential to reduce technical barriers for teachers and administrators, enabling them to leverage AI insights for lesson planning, progress monitoring, and instructional decision-making. Furthermore, software should include analytics dashboards that provide actionable insights, visualizations of student progress, and alert mechanisms for at-risk learners. A carefully curated software ecosystem ensures that AI enhances learning experiences while remaining pedagogically aligned and accessible.

Cloud computing enables centralized data storage, scalable model training, and collaborative access across school networks, while edge computing ensures low-latency processing for real-time classroom interactions. A hybrid approach combines the strengths of both: cloud-based AI models provide high computational power and continuous updates, whereas edge devices handle immediate feedback and interactive applications locally. This configuration ensures high responsiveness, minimal delays, and seamless operation even during peak usage. Additionally, hybrid architectures allow schools to optimize costs, scale infrastructure efficiently, and implement robust backup and disaster recovery protocols. The combination of cloud and edge computing also supports data-driven insights at both individual and institutional levels, enhancing both classroom instruction and school-wide decision-making.

High-speed, reliable network connectivity is the backbone of AI-enabled schools. Secure wired and wireless networks, robust LANs, and redundant internet connections are essential to ensure uninterrupted AI operations, facilitate collaboration, and enable access to cloud-based platforms. Network design must account for simultaneous multi-device usage, real-time data transmission, and cybersecurity safeguards. Features such as bandwidth prioritization, failover protocols, and secure VPN access enhance reliability, especially in large schools or multi-campus networks. A well-engineered network infrastructure ensures that AI tools function optimally, supporting consistent learning experiences and uninterrupted teacher-student interactions.

Data Management, Interoperability, and Security Considerations

Implementing agentic AI requires comprehensive data governance policies that define how student, teacher, and institutional data are collected, stored, processed, and shared. These policies must comply with local regulations and international standards such as GDPR or ISO guidelines for educational data protection. Effective governance includes clear roles and responsibilities, consent management protocols, and mechanisms for auditing data access and usage. Establishing such frameworks ensures transparency, accountability, and trust, while also guiding schools in responsibly leveraging AI-driven analytics for instructional and administrative decision-making (Pati, 2025; Reddy et al., 2025).

Interoperability ensures that AI tools seamlessly integrate with existing educational technologies such as LMS, SIS, assessment platforms, and content repositories. Standardized APIs, communication protocols, and data formats enable smooth information exchange, preventing data silos and redundancy. This integration allows AI to analyze student performance, recommend personalized learning pathways, and generate actionable insights without disrupting established workflows. Interoperable systems also facilitate the addition of new AI modules or third-party applications over time, ensuring scalability and adaptability within dynamic educational environments.

Robust security frameworks are essential to protect sensitive educational data against unauthorized access, cyberattacks, or breaches (Huang & Hughes, 2025a, 2025b). Security measures should include encryption of data at rest and in transit, multi-factor authentication, role-based access control, and continuous monitoring of network and system activity. Audit trails enable administrators to track interactions with data, ensuring accountability and transparency. Multi-layered security, encompassing hardware, software, and network components, safeguards both institutional and personal information, fostering trust among teachers, students, and parents while complying with legal and ethical standards.

High-quality, reliable data underpins effective AI-driven decision-making. Schools must implement continuous data validation, cleansing, and updating protocols to maintain accurate student performance records, engagement metrics, and institutional data. Ensuring integrity minimizes errors in AI-generated recommendations, supports precise predictive analytics, and enhances evidence-based instructional and administrative decisions. High-quality data also enables adaptive learning algorithms to function optimally, delivering accurate and personalized learning experiences while building confidence in AI-assisted educational practices.

Integration with Existing School Systems

AI integration with LMS platforms allows for personalized content recommendations, automated assessments, and real-time feedback directly within the digital learning environment. By analyzing student engagement, interaction patterns, and performance trends, AI can tailor instruction to individual needs while providing teachers with actionable insights. Such integration supports differentiated learning without disrupting established workflows, creating a seamless and responsive instructional ecosystem. Advanced analytics can also help educators track long-term learning trajectories and identify areas requiring intervention.

Integration with SIS enables AI to process enrollment, attendance, and performance data to identify trends, predict learning outcomes, and inform administrative decisions. Historical and real-time data allow AI to optimize resource allocation, anticipate student needs, and trigger proactive interventions for learners at risk. This data-driven approach enhances institutional planning, instructional efficiency, and evidence-based policy implementation, ensuring that school operations are responsive to both pedagogical and administrative requirements.

Agentic AI should be compatible with a range of digital learning tools, including collaboration platforms, assessment software, virtual labs, and content repositories. Seamless interoperability enables teachers and students to transition across platforms without disruptions, maintaining consistent learning experiences. Proper alignment ensures AI enhances the pedagogical value of existing resources, supports differentiated instruction, and fosters student engagement through interactive and immersive technologies.

Successful integration requires designing AI interfaces that align with teacher routines, student learning patterns, and institutional workflows. Usability-focused design reduces cognitive and operational barriers, enhancing adoption rates and ensuring that AI complements rather than disrupts educational practices. By prioritizing intuitive functionality, AI becomes an embedded part of teaching and learning processes, supporting seamless collaboration, instructional efficiency, and pedagogical effectiveness.

Scalability, Maintenance, and Sustainability Aspects

AI infrastructure must be capable of scaling to accommodate increases in student population, curriculum complexity, and additional AI modules (Dwivedi et al., 2025; Neelu et al., 2025). Modular architecture, cloud-based resources, and standardized protocols facilitate expansion without major system overhauls. Scalable design ensures that AI continues to deliver responsive, personalized learning as school needs evolve, supporting long-term institutional growth and adaptive educational practices.

Maintaining AI systems involves regular monitoring, updates, troubleshooting, and performance optimization. Technical teams must be trained to manage software, hardware, and network components effectively. Proactive maintenance strategies, including predictive diagnostics and automated alerts, reduce downtime, maintain system reliability, and ensure uninterrupted access to AI tools, thereby safeguarding continuity in teaching and learning.

Long-term sustainability encompasses energy-efficient hardware, cost-effective cloud solutions, and scalable licensing models, reducing operational costs while maintaining system effectiveness. Equally important is professional development for educators, ensuring AI tools are used effectively, pedagogically aligned, and adaptable to evolving teaching strategies. Sustainable practices also include upgrading infrastructure responsibly, managing digital resources efficiently, and planning for ecosystem growth over time.

By developing a comprehensive, resilient, and adaptable infrastructure, schools can ensure that agentic AI functions reliably, enhances instructional quality, and supports administrative objectives. This foundation enables seamless integration with broader learning ecosystems, facilitates collaboration between human and AI agents, and creates a responsive, student-centered environment. A well-designed infrastructure ensures that technological innovation drives meaningful educational outcomes while remaining sustainable, scalable, and pedagogically aligned.

ECOSYSTEM DESIGN FOR AGENTIC AI

The integration of agentic AI into schools extends beyond technical infrastructure; it requires the creation of collaborative ecosystems where human and artificial agents interact seamlessly to enhance teaching, learning, and administrative processes. Ecosystem design focuses on the organizational, pedagogical, and social dimensions of AI deployment, ensuring that intelligent systems operate effectively within the school context while supporting adaptive, student-centered learning.

Designing Collaborative Ecosystems

In a collaborative AI ecosystem, teachers function as guides, interpreters, and co-designers, leveraging AI-generated insights to inform instructional decisions and optimize learning outcomes. Beyond automating routine tasks such as grading, attendance tracking, and scheduling, AI agents provide real-time analytics, predictive alerts, and pedagogical recommendations (Ding et al., 2025; Kim, 2024b; Kim, 2024a). For instance, AI can highlight students at risk of falling behind or suggest differentiated interventions tailored to individual learning profiles. This partnership allows teachers to devote more time to creative instruction, mentorship, and reflective practice, designing innovative activities that foster critical thinking, collaboration, and inquiry-based learning. Importantly, integrating AI as a supportive collaborator, rather than a replacement, maintains teacher agency, enhances professional satisfaction, and ensures that pedagogical expertise remains central to the learning process.

Students engage directly with AI agents through personalized learning pathways, adaptive problem-solving tasks, and collaborative activities. AI systems provide immediate feedback, scaffold complex tasks, and encourage self-directed exploration, fostering autonomy and intrinsic motivation. By tailoring instruction to each learner's pace, preferences, and prior knowledge, AI promotes differentiated learning, critical thinking, curiosity, and sustained engagement. Students can explore simulations, participate in AI-facilitated discussions, and track their own progress, developing a sense of ownership over their learning journey. These interactions transform classrooms into active, responsive, and student-centered environments, where learners become active participants in co-constructing knowledge rather than passive recipients of instruction.

Administrators leverage AI for decision support, resource management, and operational oversight, enabling data-informed management of school operations. AI can optimize classroom scheduling, forecast resource needs, and anticipate infrastructure maintenance requirements. Predictive analytics also support strategic staffing, curriculum adjustments, and allocation of learning materials, ensuring efficiency and responsiveness. By embedding AI into administrative workflows, schools can improve institutional planning, reduce operational bottlenecks, and enhance overall organizational capacity. This integration empowers administrators to focus on strategic goals, long-term development, and evidence-based policymaking that benefits both educators and students.

Effective AI ecosystems depend on inter-agent communication, enabling multiple AI systems to coordinate with one another and with human users. Such interactions allow AI modules to synchronize instructional strategies, share insights, and maintain consistency across different learning contexts. For example, an AI agent monitoring student performance in mathematics can communicate with another supporting science or language arts to provide a holistic view of learner progress. Inter-agent communication ensures coherence in learning experiences, harmonizes feedback across platforms, and enables adaptive cross-disciplinary interventions, creating a seamless ecosystem where AI collectively supports pedagogy, assessment, and administrative decisions.

Role of Stakeholders in Co-Creation and Governance

Teachers play a central role in co-creating AI-supported learning environments by designing lesson plans, defining learning objectives, and providing ongoing feedback on AI recommendations. Their involvement ensures that AI tools are pedagogically sound, curriculum-aligned, and responsive to diverse student needs. Teachers also act as intermediaries between AI systems and learners, interpreting AI-generated data and integrating insights into classroom practice. Active teacher participation in AI co-design fosters trust, usability, and adoption, ensuring that technology enhances instruction without undermining professional expertise.

Students contribute crucial insights regarding AI usability, learning preferences, and assessment experiences. Their feedback informs AI design to better accommodate individual engagement patterns, motivational factors, and diverse learning styles. By participating in co-creation, students become active stakeholders in shaping their educational environment, fostering autonomy, ownership, and a sense of responsibility for their learning. Student involvement ensures that AI tools are learner-centered, relevant, and accessible, supporting meaningful engagement and positive educational outcomes.

Administrators oversee governance, ethical compliance, and strategic integration of AI into school operations. Their responsibilities include establishing policies for data use, evaluating system performance, and ensuring AI adoption aligns with institutional priorities. By coordinating stakeholder engagement, administrators facilitate sustainable and systemic AI implementation, balancing operational efficiency with pedagogical goals. Their leadership maintains accountability, mitigates risks, and ensures that AI ecosystems evolve in line with ethical standards and strategic objectives.

Developers work collaboratively with schools to customize AI algorithms, ensure interoperability, and maintain transparency in decision-making processes. They adapt AI tools to local educational contexts, support seamless integration with existing platforms, and respond to evolving pedagogical needs. Continuous collaboration ensures that AI solutions remain technically robust, ethically responsible, and pedagogically effective. Developers also provide ongoing updates, technical support, and guidance to maintain ecosystem resilience and sustainability.

Parents and community members offer perspectives on expectations, ethical considerations, and cultural alignment of AI interventions. Engaging these stakeholders ensures that AI deployment respects community values, promotes equity, and fosters trust. Their participation helps shape learning ecosystems that are socially responsible, culturally relevant, and broadly supported, reinforcing the legitimacy and sustainability of AI integration.

Robust governance frameworks establish clear guidelines for data use, ethical standards, accountability, and decision-making. These frameworks define roles and responsibilities for all stakeholders, ensuring equitable and inclusive outcomes. By providing structured oversight, governance mechanisms enable schools to integrate AI responsibly, maintain transparency, and sustain long-term ecosystem functionality.

Strategies for Embedding AI in Pedagogical Workflows and Curricula

Embedding agentic AI begins with curriculum mapping, identifying points where AI can meaningfully enhance instruction. This may include personalized learning modules, formative assessments, simulations, or adaptive problem-solving tasks. Aligning AI functionalities with curricular goals ensures that technology reinforces educational objectives, supports differentiated learning, and integrates seamlessly into existing instructional plans. Mapping also identifies opportunities for cross-disciplinary learning and scaffolds progressive skill development over time.

AI tools support lesson planning, recommend differentiated tasks, and monitor student progress, providing actionable insights to teachers while complementing professional expertise. Integrating AI into workflows allows teachers to focus on higher-order instructional activities such as mentoring, discussion facilitation, and designing innovative learning experiences. Simultaneously, AI manages repetitive or data-intensive tasks, enabling more efficient, targeted, and student-centered instruction.

Agentic AI enhances project-based and experiential learning by facilitating collaborative projects, simulating real-world scenarios, and delivering instant performance feedback. AI can guide students through complex problem-solving tasks, model real-world decision-making, and track progress toward learning outcomes. Such AI-driven experiences encourage critical thinking, creativity, teamwork, and practical application of knowledge, creating engaging, interactive, and authentic learning environments.

Ongoing professional development ensures that educators can leverage AI effectively, interpret insights, and integrate technology into pedagogy. Training equips teachers to navigate AI interfaces, apply data-driven recommendations, and adapt instructional workflows dynamically. Continuous support fosters confidence, encourages experimentation, and ensures that AI becomes a trusted partner rather than a disruptive force, enhancing curricular and instructional quality.

Feedback Loops, Adaptation, and Continuous Improvement Mechanisms

Adaptive learning feedback enables AI to continuously monitor student engagement, comprehension, and outcomes, adjusting instructional pathways in real time. By personalizing content difficulty, pacing, and learning strategies, AI ensures that instruction remains effective, individualized, and aligned with evolving learner needs. This responsiveness fosters mastery, motivation, and sustained academic progress. Teachers contribute critical input through feedback loops, evaluating AI recommendations, identifying errors or biases, and suggesting improvements. This collaborative process ensures that automated interventions remain pedagogically appropriate, contextually relevant, and aligned with curriculum goals. Teacher guidance is essential for maintaining educational integrity and reinforcing trust in AI-assisted instruction.

Administrators continuously monitor system performance, data integrity, and infrastructure reliability to ensure seamless AI operation. Monitoring enables proactive troubleshooting, efficient resource allocation, and sustained functionality across classrooms. Performance tracking supports evidence-based decision-making for system upgrades, maintenance, and long-term scalability. Agentic AI ecosystems rely on iterative refinement to evolve dynamically in response to new data, pedagogical practices, and stakeholder feedback. Continuous cycles of evaluation integrate quantitative analytics and qualitative insights, allowing AI models, instructional strategies, and workflows to improve over time. Iterative improvement fosters resilient, adaptive learning environments that can respond to technological, educational, and societal changes while maintaining high-quality student outcomes.

DISCUSSION AND IMPLICATIONS

The deployment of agentic AI in schools represents a transformative shift in education, with implications that span pedagogy, administration, ethics, and policy. This section synthesizes the insights from systemic integration and ecosystem design, examining their effects on teaching and learning, addressing broader societal considerations, and offering recommendations for future development and research.

Impact on Teaching, Learning, and School Operations

Agentic AI enables highly personalized learning experiences by continuously adapting instructional content, pacing, and assessments to the unique profiles of individual students. Advanced AI-driven systems monitor student engagement, comprehension, and performance in real time, providing dynamic interventions and tailored learning paths. These interventions can include additional practice on challenging topics, accelerated progression for advanced learners, or adaptive simulations that cater to specific learning styles. Beyond academic content, AI can also support social-emotional learning, adjusting tasks to build confidence, motivation, and resilience. By offering a deeply individualized approach, AI helps students progress at their own pace, supports mastery learning, and fosters sustained engagement, ultimately contributing to improved long-term academic outcomes and holistic development.

By automating routine administrative and instructional tasks—such as grading, attendance tracking, scheduling, and performance monitoring—agentic AI frees teachers to concentrate on creative, higher-order instructional activities. AI-generated analytics provide actionable insights, helping teachers identify learning gaps, optimize lesson plans, and implement evidence-based interventions. This data-driven support enables personalized guidance for each student, improving instructional quality and teaching effectiveness. Additionally, teachers can use AI insights to reflect on their own practice, experiment with new pedagogical strategies, and collaborate with colleagues in professional learning communities. Over time, this integration fosters continuous professional growth, enhances instructional confidence, and positions teachers as facilitators of AI-augmented learning rather than passive operators of technology.

At the institutional level, agentic AI enhances school operations through predictive analytics, optimized resource allocation, and proactive infrastructure management. Administrators can leverage AI insights to make data-informed decisions regarding staffing, classroom scheduling, curriculum adjustments, and allocation of teaching materials. Predictive analytics can anticipate trends such as resource shortages, enrollment shifts, or maintenance needs, enabling preemptive planning and reducing operational disruptions. By streamlining administrative workflows and optimizing resource utilization, schools can focus more on pedagogical priorities, improve coordination among departments, and create a more organized, responsive, and sustainable learning environment.

Agentic AI fosters collaborative and inquiry-based learning by mediating interactions among students and between students and teachers. AI agents can facilitate group problem-solving, scaffold discussion, and guide inquiry-based projects, ensuring that each learner is actively engaged. By providing real-time feedback and adaptive challenges, AI encourages peer-to-peer learning and helps students develop critical thinking, communication, teamwork, and adaptive problem-solving skills. This approach not only strengthens collaboration but also enhances student agency, enabling learners to take ownership of their learning journey while developing competencies crucial for success in the 21st century.

The cumulative effects of agentic AI create dynamic, responsive, and efficient educational environments. Enhanced personalization improves learning outcomes, teacher support fosters professional growth, operational efficiency streamlines school management, and collaborative AI-mediated interactions cultivate student agency. Together, these impacts enable schools to adapt to evolving pedagogical, technological, and societal demands, preparing students for the challenges and opportunities of the modern world while promoting innovation, equity, and engagement across the educational ecosystem.

Ethical, Social, and Policy Considerations

Ensuring the privacy and security of student, teacher, and institutional data is a critical ethical requirement for AI-enabled schools. Agentic AI systems must adhere to strict privacy policies, secure storage protocols, and controlled access mechanisms to prevent unauthorized access, breaches, or misuse of personal information (Camilleri, 2024). Compliance with local laws, regional regulations, and international standards such as GDPR enhances stakeholder trust and supports responsible data stewardship. Beyond technical safeguards, schools should also foster a culture of digital responsibility, educating teachers and students about ethical data use and emphasizing transparency in data collection, storage, and utilization.

AI systems must be designed to promote equitable access to learning opportunities and avoid perpetuating systemic biases (Cachat-Rosset & Klarsfeld, 2023). Careful attention to dataset diversity, algorithmic fairness, and accessibility features is essential to ensure that students from different socioeconomic, cultural, or ability backgrounds benefit equally from AI interventions. Inclusive AI design can address disparities in learning by providing targeted support for underrepresented or struggling students, while avoiding unintended reinforcement of preexisting inequities. By prioritizing equity, AI fosters a level playing field that supports inclusive, high-quality education for all learners.

For AI adoption to succeed, the decision-making processes of AI agents must be transparent and explainable. Teachers, students, and administrators need to understand how AI generates recommendations, adjusts content, or modifies learning pathways. Clear accountability frameworks define responsibility for AI-driven decisions, ensuring that humans remain in control and can intervene when necessary. Transparency also allows stakeholders to evaluate AI effectiveness, identify biases, and maintain ethical and pedagogical standards. By fostering openness, accountability, and trust, schools can integrate AI as a collaborative partner rather than an opaque, uncontrollable tool.

Effective AI deployment requires alignment with policy frameworks at school, district, and national levels. Policies should guide ethical AI use, standardize interoperability across digital platforms, and inform professional development initiatives for educators and administrators. Governance mechanisms must ensure continuous monitoring, evaluation, and compliance, maintaining public confidence and legitimacy. Policies should also anticipate emerging technologies, providing a roadmap for sustainable AI adoption and enabling schools to integrate AI responsibly in ways that enhance learning outcomes, institutional efficiency, and societal trust.

Addressing ethical, social, and policy dimensions is essential to prevent unintended consequences and maintain confidence among all stakeholders. By prioritizing privacy, inclusion, transparency, and governance, schools can responsibly integrate agentic AI, ensuring that technological innovation enhances education without compromising ethical, social, or institutional standards. Such a proactive approach establishes a foundation for equitable, accountable, and sustainable AI-enabled learning environments.

Recommendations for Future Research, Infrastructure Investment, and Ecosystem Evolution

Sustaining the effective integration of agentic AI in schools requires a robust research agenda that examines both immediate and long-term impacts on learning outcomes, teaching practices, and institutional efficiency. Future studies should investigate adaptive AI models that dynamically respond to diverse learner profiles and evolving pedagogical contexts. Research should also explore human-AI collaboration, analyzing how AI can complement teacher expertise, enhance student agency, and facilitate more equitable classroom interactions. Additionally, ethical dimensions—such as bias mitigation, data privacy, and accountability—must be examined in depth within educational settings to ensure that AI applications are not only effective but socially responsible. Comparative studies across schools with different demographic and resource contexts can further illuminate best practices and inform scalable implementation strategies. Longitudinal research tracking student development, teacher adoption, and systemic outcomes will provide critical insights into the sustained value and limitations of agentic AI.

Robust, future-ready infrastructure is foundational for the long-term success of AI integration. Schools should prioritize investments in high-performance computing, secure cloud platforms, and reliable network systems, ensuring that AI tools operate seamlessly and efficiently. Investment planning must include data management solutions that protect sensitive student and institutional information while enabling interoperability across Learning Management Systems, Student Information Systems, and other digital tools. Continuous upgrades, maintenance schedules, and redundancy protocols are essential to sustain performance, prevent system downtime, and accommodate growing computational demands. Infrastructure planning should also consider scalability and adaptability, allowing schools to expand AI capabilities as student populations grow, curricula evolve, and new AI functionalities emerge. Strategic investments should be accompanied by cost-benefit analyses and sustainability assessments to ensure that AI adoption is economically viable and environmentally responsible over time.

The effective use of agentic AI hinges on continuous professional development that strengthens AI literacy, pedagogical integration, and ethical understanding among educators. Training programs should be designed to enable teachers to interpret AI-generated insights, personalize instruction based on data, and integrate AI tools into lesson planning and classroom management. Beyond technical skills, professional development must address ethical awareness, bias detection, and responsible AI use, empowering educators to make informed decisions and advocate for equitable practices. Stakeholders—including administrators, IT personnel, and curriculum designers—should also participate in training to foster collaborative ecosystem management and shared ownership of AI-driven learning environments. Ongoing support mechanisms, mentoring programs, and communities of practice can reinforce skill acquisition and encourage innovation, ensuring that AI adoption evolves in alignment with pedagogical goals.

Agentic AI ecosystems should be designed with iterative evolution as a central principle, allowing continuous refinement of AI systems, pedagogical strategies, and institutional processes. Stakeholder participation is essential at every stage, with teachers, students, administrators, and technology developers contributing feedback on usability, effectiveness, and alignment with educational objectives. Built-in feedback loops enable AI to adapt dynamically to learner needs, while administrators monitor system performance, data integrity, and resource utilization. Iterative evaluation cycles support evidence-based improvements, ensuring that both AI tools and broader ecosystem structures remain responsive, resilient, and sustainable. Ecosystem evolution should also consider emerging technologies, curricular innovations, and changing societal expectations, enabling schools to anticipate and respond proactively to future educational challenges.

Sustainable AI adoption requires comprehensive policy frameworks that establish ethical standards, interoperability requirements, and accountability mechanisms. Policies should clarify roles and responsibilities for educators, administrators, developers, and other stakeholders, ensuring transparent decision-making and responsible use of AI systems. Collaboration between policymakers, educators, and technology providers is essential to create coherent governance structures that support both innovation and protection of student rights. Policies should also provide guidance on data management, professional development, and equitable access, ensuring that AI contributes to inclusive and high-quality education. Continuous oversight, auditing, and policy review processes help maintain compliance, trust, and legitimacy, creating an environment in which AI can thrive while minimizing potential risks.

By addressing research priorities, infrastructure needs, professional development, ecosystem evolution, and policy governance in a coordinated manner, schools can maximize the benefits of agentic AI while mitigating associated risks. These strategies collectively foster educational ecosystems that are adaptive, equitable, resilient, and sustainable, enabling AI to function as a transformative force that enhances learning outcomes, supports teacher effectiveness, and strengthens institutional capacity for the challenges of the 21st century.

CONCLUSION

The integration of agentic AI in schools represents a paradigm shift in education, combining technological innovation with pedagogical transformation. This chapter explores the conceptual foundations, systemic infrastructure, and ecosystem design necessary to harness the potential of AI agents in learning environments. A synthesis of the key insights highlights the multifaceted nature of this integration:

- Unlike conventional educational technologies, agentic AI operates autonomously, adapting to student needs, supporting teachers, and optimizing administrative processes. Its capacity to personalize learning, provide real-time feedback, and enhance decision-making positions it as a catalyst for meaningful educational innovation.
- Robust technical infrastructure—including hardware, software, cloud systems, and secure networks—is essential for reliable AI performance. Interoperability with existing school systems, comprehensive data management, and sustainable maintenance strategies ensure that AI deployment is both scalable and resilient.
- Schools function optimally when AI agents, teachers, students, administrators, and other stakeholders interact within well-designed ecosystems. Co-creation, governance frameworks, adaptive feedback loops, and continuous improvement mechanisms ensure that AI enhances learning while maintaining ethical and pedagogical alignment.

- The deployment of AI must prioritize data privacy, equity, transparency, and accountability. Policy frameworks, professional development, and inclusive design are critical to safeguard ethical standards and build stakeholder trust.

Looking forward, the vision for fully integrated agentic AI ecosystems envisions schools as adaptive, responsive learning environments where intelligent agents complement human expertise to foster personalized, collaborative, and engaging education. Such ecosystems are characterized by seamless interaction between human and AI agents, continuous adaptation to evolving educational needs, and a culture of innovation and reflective practice.

Finally, reflections on scalability, sustainability, and transformative potential underscore the importance of long-term planning. Scalable AI solutions, sustainable infrastructure, and iterative ecosystem design are crucial for maximizing benefits while minimizing risks. By adopting a systemic and ecosystem-oriented approach, schools can leverage agentic AI not merely as a technological tool, but as a transformative force that reshapes teaching, learning, and school operations, ultimately preparing students for the challenges and opportunities of the 21st century.

REFERENCES

Acharya, D. B., Kuppan, K., & Divya, B. (2025). Agentic AI: Autonomous Intelligence for Complex Goals - A Comprehensive Survey. *IEEE Access : Practical Innovations, Open Solutions*, *13*, 18912–18936. DOI: 10.1109/ACCESS.2025.3532853

Ashwani, S. (2025). *Agentic AI in Education: Transforming Pedagogy and Personalized Learning*. 321–332. DOI: 10.1007/978-3-031-89424-4_21

Bandi, A., Kongari, B., Naguru, R., Pasnoor, S., & Vilipala, S. V. (2025). The Rise of Agentic AI: A Review of Definitions, Frameworks, Architectures, Applications, Evaluation Metrics, and Challenges. *Future Internet 2025, Vol. 17, Page 404*, *17*(9), 404. DOI: 10.3390/fi17090404

Bandura, A., & Walters, R. H. (1977). *Social learning theory* (Vol. 1). Prentice hall Englewood Cliffs, NJ.

Berisha Qehaja, A. (2025). Strategic integration of artificial intelligence solutions to transform teaching practices in higher education. *Foresight*, *27*(5), 970–991. DOI: 10.1108/FS-04-2024-0079

Cachat-Rosset, G., & Klarsfeld, A. (2023). Diversity, Equity, and Inclusion in Artificial Intelligence: An Evaluation of Guidelines. *Applied Artificial Intelligence*, *37*(1), 2176618. Advance online publication. DOI: 10.1080/08839514.2023.2176618

Camilleri, M. A. (2024). Artificial intelligence governance: Ethical considerations and implications for social responsibility. *Expert Systems: International Journal of Knowledge Engineering and Neural Networks*, *41*(7), e13406. DOI: 10.1111/exsy.13406

Daher, R. (2025). Integrating AI literacy into teacher education: A critical perspective paper. *Discover Artificial Intelligence*, *5*(1), 1–20. DOI: 10.1007/s44163-025-00475-7

Ding, L. J., Li, J. M., & Hui, B. H. (2025). Will Teacher-AI Collaboration Enhance Teaching Engagement? *Behavioral Sciences 2025, Vol. 15, Page 866*, *15*(7), 866. DOI: 10.3390/bs15070866

Dwivedi, Y. K., Helal, M. Y. I., Elgendy, I. A., Albashrawi, M. A., Hughes, L., Shawosh, M., Dutot, V., & Jeon, I. (2025). Artificial intelligence agents and agentic systems in hospitality and tourism: Challenges, opportunities and research agenda. *International Journal of Contemporary Hospitality Management*. Advance online publication. DOI: 10.1108/IJCHM-02-2025-0287

Edwards, J., Nguyen, A., Lämsä, J., Sobocinski, M., Whitehead, R., Dang, B., Roberts, A. S., & Järvelä, S. (2025). Human-AI collaboration: Designing artificial agents to facilitate socially shared regulation among learners. *British Journal of Educational Technology*, *56*(2), 712–733. DOI: 10.1111/bjet.13534

Hein, G. E. (1991). Constructivist learning theory. *Institute for Inquiry, 14*.

Huang, K. (2025). *Agentic AI*. Springer. DOI: 10.1007/978-3-031-90026-6

Huang, K., & Hughes, C. (2025a). *Agentic AI Capability and Security Benchmark*. 145–167. DOI: 10.1007/978-3-032-02130-4_6

Huang, K., & Hughes, C. (2025b). *Agentic AI Communication Protocols and Security*. 81–110. DOI: 10.1007/978-3-032-02130-4_4

Hughes, L., Dwivedi, Y. K., Malik, T., Shawosh, M., Albashrawi, M. A., Jeon, I., Dutot, V., Appanderanda, M., Crick, T., De', R., Fenwick, M., Gunaratnege, S. M., Jurcys, P., Kar, A. K., Kshetri, N., Li, K., Mutasa, S., Samothrakis, S., Wade, M., & Walton, P. (2025). AI Agents and Agentic Systems: A Multi-Expert Analysis. *Journal of Computer Information Systems*, *65*(4), 489–517. DOI: 10.1080/08874417.2025.2483832

Kaswan, K. S., Dhatterwal, J. S., & Ojha, R. P. (2024). AI in personalized learning. *Advances in Technological Innovations in Higher Education: Theory and Practices*, 103–117. /DOI: 10.1201/9781003376699-9

Kayal, A. (2024). *Transformative Pedagogy: A Comprehensive Framework for AI Integration in Education*. 247–270. DOI: 10.1007/978-3-031-72410-7_14

Kim, J. (2024a). Leading teachers' perspective on teacher-AI collaboration in education. *Education and Information Technologies*, *29*(7), 8693–8724. DOI: 10.1007/s10639-023-12109-5

Kim, J. (2024b). Types of teacher-AI collaboration in K-12 classroom instruction: Chinese teachers' perspective. *Education and Information Technologies*, *29*(13), 17433–17465. DOI: 10.1007/s10639-024-12523-3

Kotsis, K. T. (n.d.). *Integrating Artificial Intelligence into Higher Education Curricula: Challenges and Opportunities for Science-Based Programs*. DOI: 10.54660/IJAIET.2025.6.1.04-12

Liu, J., Chu, C., Zhao, Y., Aoki, G., & Xiao, Z. (2025). Agentic AI for Sustainable Development: Leveraging Large Language Model-Enhanced Agent-Based Modeling for Complex Policy Strategies. *Emerging Media*, *3*(3), 401–413. DOI: 10.1177/27523543251365678

Neelu, A., Pramod, J. P., & Lahari, A. (2025). *Optimizing Networks Using AI and Machine Learning: The Role of Agentic AI in Transforming Network Management*. 229–254. DOI: 10.1007/978-3-031-89424-4_16

Ouwehand, K., Lespiau, F., Tricot, A., & Paas, F. (2025). Cognitive Load Theory: Emerging Trends and Innovations. *Education Sciences 2025, Vol. 15, Page 458, 15*(4), 458. DOI: 10.3390/educsci15040458

Pati, A. K. (2025). Agentic AI: A Comprehensive Survey of Technologies, Applications, and Societal Implications. *IEEE Access : Practical Innovations, Open Solutions, 13*, 151824–151837. DOI: 10.1109/ACCESS.2025.3585609

Reddy, C. K. K., Joseph, S., Joshi, H., Doss, S., & Ouaissa, M. (Eds.). (2025). *The Power of Agentic AI: Redefining Human Life and Decision-Making*. DOI: 10.1007/978-3-031-89424-4

Sweller, J., & Chandler, P. (1991). Evidence for Cognitive Load Theory. *Cognition and Instruction, 8*(4), 351–362. Advance online publication. DOI: 10.1207/s1532690xci0804_5

Wang, H., Wang, C., Chen, Z., Liu, F., Bao, C., & Xu, X. (2025). Impact of AI-agent-supported collaborative learning on the learning outcomes of University programming courses. *Education and Information Technologies, 30*(12), 17717–17749. DOI: 10.1007/s10639-025-13487-8

Xiao, K., & He, Y. (2025).. . *Adaptive AI Agent Systems for Personalized Learning: Frameworks, Algorithms, and Practical Applications in Education, 108–112*, 108–112. Advance online publication. DOI: 10.1109/ICAIE64856.2025.11158641

Chapter 9
Regulatory Frameworks for Agentic AI in Education

S. Ida Evangeline
https://orcid.org/0000-0003-2997-7897
Government College of Engineering, Tirunelveli, India

ABSTRACT

As agentic artificial intelligence (AI) systems become increasingly embedded in educational technologies—ranging from adaptive learning platforms to predictive assessment tools—they introduce not only new pedagogical possibilities but also profound regulatory challenges. This chapter critically examines the urgent need for robust governance frameworks tailored to the distinctive features of agentic AI: autonomy, context sensitivity, and real-time decision-making. Moving beyond general data protection laws and ethical codes, it proposes a multi-layered regulatory model that addresses legal accountability, data governance, bias mitigation, and systemic equity. Informed conceptual analysis, international case sharing, and comparative policy lessons help the chapter identify the ways that, poorly regulated, agentic AI can worsen educational inequality, inhibit the agency of learners, and damage institutional trust. It proposes practical guidelines on risk-based supervision, audit of algorithms, involving of stakeholders and harmonization on a global basis.

INTRODUCTION: THE RISE OF AGENTIC AI IN EDUCATION

The integration of artificial intelligence (AI) into educational systems marks a transformative moment in the evolution of teaching and learning. Among the most consequential developments within this domain is the emergence of agentic AI—

DOI: 10.4018/979-8-3373-4621-2.ch009

systems that possess a degree of autonomy, adaptability, and contextual awareness, enabling them to engage in complex, interactive, and often decision-making behaviors in real time. In contrast to more conventional forms of rule-based or narrowly assistive AI tools that can be applied within a set of parameters, agentic AI systems can adjust themselves to outputs based on subtleised interpretations of student inputs, learning surroundings and dynamically changing pedagogical objectives. The transition poses significant opportunities as well as poses an alarming concern to the control, responsibility and ethical usage of such systems within formal education (Zhang & Aslan, 2021).

Over the past decade, schools and universities have increasingly adopted AI-driven technologies for a range of functions: adaptive learning platforms tailor instructional materials based on student performance; automated grading tools provide rapid assessment and feedback; and intelligent tutoring systems simulate human-like interaction to support personalized learning. Such developments have been heralded as a means of improving access to and the effectiveness and responsiveness of education. But using AI tools with agentic properties, which refers to those that not only react to learner actions but also undertake pedagogical decisions, brings a new complication into the picture that current policies and regulations fail to accommodate (Zhai et al. 2021).

Agentic AI, by virtue of its quasi-autonomous nature, challenges foundational assumptions about the roles of teachers, learners, and institutions in the educational process. It brings important questions on how to handle situations when an AI system makes a wrong assessment and, in this case, any harm on the learner, who is responsible? How will remedy work in the workings of an automated decision that has acted negatively on a student career program? What can we do to make sure the data that these systems gather is ethically used and not introduced in methods that interfere with student privacy or increase social divisions? These inquiries are not hypothetical they are already occurring in the context of classrooms where AI is being deployed to suggest placements of students or identify those who are at risk or even proffering interventions of a behavioral nature (Dai et al. 2024).

The current state of the regulatory environment that governs educational AI is disjointed and reactive. Although some nations have enacted general principles of ethics in AI and data protection legislation (i.e. the European Union General Data Protection Regulation, GDPR, in the EU, or the Children Online Privacy Protection Act of 1998, COPPA, in the US), these policies have not been tailored to fit the specifics of an agentic educational AI context. Moreover, those mechanisms tend to be of limited applicability by lacking enforceable mechanisms specifically corresponding to the needs of the pedagogical scenario and leaving schools and developers to traverse a regulatory patchwork that is haphazard, largely undeveloped and not substantively prepared to deal with the capabilities of emerging systems (Mouta et al. 2025).

The aim of this chapter is to fill that regulatory gap. It presents an in-depth discussion on the way the existing legal and ethical frameworks overlap with the reality of agentic AI in education and suggests a way forward in creating a model that balances innovation and regulation. Based on interdisciplinary inquiries into the history and ethics of AI, education policy, and cross-national comparative law, the chapter proposes a flexible and overlapping system of regulation that aims to keep pace with technological development and satisfy educational requirements at the same time as fostering justice, fairness, and democratic accountability within educational settings.

It is not just a technical and legal question, it is an educational one on a deeper level The introduction of agentic AI systems in the classroom can affect not only the subject matter students are taught but how they will be educated, classified, and treated by the institution. These systems, left without effective regulatory schemes run the risk of entrenching inequalities, unnaturally ousting the human decision-making process and damaging the trust necessary to perform effective education. As a counter-argument to that, the chapter attempts to introduce the base of regulatory design that should both acknowledge the potential and the pitfalls of agentic AI so that the future of education could remain not only smart but also not unjust.

DEFINING AGENTIC AI IN EDUCATIONAL CONTEXTS

To comprehend what agentic artificial intelligence is in educational systems, it is important to differentiate clearly between the new type of AI and previous generations of automated systems. Although the concept of AI in education is not new fortune-computer-assisted instruction and intelligent tutoring systems have been developed and used since the 1970s- the telling aspect of agentic AI is that it can autonomously take context-sensitive decisions that may shape learning processes, without human intervention at each point. This aspect of agency contrasts with more fixed/narrowly-programmed systems, and it provides conceptual and regulatory tensions (Brohi et al. 2025).

Agentic AI systems work in more than a rule-expressive manner. They employ complex machine learning, natural language processing, and predictive analytics to interpret a variety of input types including (but not limited to) student behavior, emotional body language, previous performance records, and metadata of related contexts, after which they act autonomously to make pedagogical decisions. These can cover such options as customizing the instructional content, triggering feedback, adjusting assessment practices, or changing the learning pace and task modality in order to better correspond to the inferred student needs. By so doing, the agentic AI systems start to model the function typically held by the educators: the diagnostician, tutor, assessor; occasionally even mentor.

A more concrete example would be a personalized learning system that adapts both problem difficulty and the mechanism of student response to student performance (adjusting difficulty based on the response) but also monitors individual student engagement (including by the pattern of keystrokes, monitor gaze, expressions) and intervenes, perhaps by adjusting the curriculum on the fly, to re-engage the learner. Or take an artificial intelligence-based essay grading application that will analyze the type of argumentation used by the student, identify logical fallacies, and recommending to the student what can be done to reorganize his or her thinking, and never requiring a human to take a look at it. The systems are not supporting instructions as mere adjuncts to the teacher but are autonomous agents within the instruction itself (Katsenou et al. 2025).

In such a manner, agentic AI upheaves pre-existing pedagogical hierarchies and presents alternative sites of power in the learning space. The previous passive role of the AI system is over; it is an actor with massive power on what and how students learn. This begs both philosophical and practical issues on the extent to which educational settings hand off agency to machines when the system or tool is unwilling to disclose itself, explains itself, and is prejudiced in its decision-making.

The question of context sensitivity is also worth attention as it is the property the agentic AI lacks as opposed to traditional automation. Whereas older systems are based on a linear and rule-based logic agents AI applies probabilist models, trained on extensive data, and can make inferences on the cognitive states, socio-emotional preparedness or even long term fulfillment of the learner. It is this contextual intelligence that allows the system to be responsive to individuals--but it is also the thing that makes its actions harder to anticipate, or outright impossible to audit. The danger is that potentially suboptimal or harmful system decisions may be based on incomplete, biased, or culturally misaligned data and that they may go unchallenged and uncorrected (Liu et al. 2025).

Additionally, it is not always very clear what marks the boundaries between assistive and agentic AI. Several commercial learning systems sold as such as adaptive or smart learning contain some assistive elements and agents. What appears like a harmless recommendation engine can eventually build enough power to reframe the academic route of a student- through suggesting or deterring specific courses, and re-channelling towards specific careers. Gradual and embedded, in this sense, the agency of the system is hence all the more needed to be subjected to examination by regulators and educators alike: in what specificities of places and times such agency will be fulfilled.

In regulatory terms, in other words, agentic AI does not constitute a technological enhancement but an institutional transformation in the distribution, application, and subjectivity of educational powers. It makes conventional understandings of instructional design, learner autonomy and institutional responsibility complicated. In order to be artful rulers of such systems, A single clear-focused knowledge of the nature that makes them agentic; that, they have the ability to make autonomous decisions, responsiveness to situation and influential affect in the context of learning.

REVIEW OF EXISTING REGULATORY LANDSCAPES

As the process of implementing agentic AI in the field of education continues at an increasing pace, regulatory bodies and policy makers are presented with an extreme level of adjustment to the current legal framework in order to accommodate a whole new category of risks and liability. Nevertheless, the existing body of regulation of educational AI can be aptly described as a patchwork because it combines ordinary laws on data protection, codes of conduct and morals on one hand and on the other, industry-specific regulations. This segment will briefly overview the key international and national frameworks already present, review their applicability to AI systems specific to learning, and draw attention to glaring gaps that need to be filled with the implementation of relevant regulatory reform (García-López & Trujillo-Liñán, 2025).

Higher up, on the international front, some of the leading efforts have been to put some ethical and legal guardrails around AI development at large. The most comprehensive and fully enforceable legal framework touching on data protection and algorithmic transparency is the General Data Protection Regulation (GDPR) that is developed by the European Union. It makes compliance to data processing by clear consent, data minimization and explains the right to make a decision by automated means. Although GDPR provides some protection to learners (the regulations concerning data pertaining to children, in particular), they are not the GDPR primary target, and the consequences of pedagogical concerns and implications are lacking specificity in them. In addition, its protections are frequently dysfunctional when AI judgments are buried in multi-user education systems and platforms that fail to offer students substantive opt-out opportunities (Molenaar, 2022).

The United States CCPA presents a different hole in the security net, namely the Children Online Privacy Protection Act (COPPA), in that, it is specifically designed to inhibit the collection of data on children younger than 13 due to the existence of the United States CCPA. Nonetheless, COPPA is not only narrowly construed but also technologically oriented and pre-adaptive, continuous, and inferential characteristics of agentic AI systems; COPPA is not parentally focused but instead focused on systemized responsibilities. The most important concern is that it does not dwell upon the self-determination of AI systems or the institutional implications of the implementation use of AI in learning settings.

Multilateral organizations have also issued ethical guidelines including the Recommendation on the Ethics of Artificial Intelligence by UNESCO and OECD AI Principles, the latter of which emphasis values of fairness, explainability, deciding responsibility, and human-centric design. This type of frameworks provides desirable (aspirational) standards of AI governance and is not legally binding. They are powerful in defining national agendas, and creating global cooperation, but they do not create legal commitments on either educational institutions or technology vendors. Although the UNESCO framework is admirable in its conceptual vision, it fails to set out education-related provisions in the detail necessary to inform practical practice within education systems, at university level or in schools (Järvelä et al. 2023).

Policies responses at the national level can hardly be more disparate in scope and sophistication. States such as Canada, Australia, and the United Kingdom have implemented AI plans that recognize the application of AI in education, yet they are typically integrated into larger innovation plans without establishment of defined regulatory frameworks. In the United States, state control over educational technology is uneven across state boundaries, and there is no attempt to coordinate regulation at the federal level, leaving a regulatory vacuum that is especially attractive to commercial edtech vendors interested in evading regulation.

One such case is the 2021 guidance issued by the UK Department for Education (DfE) on the use of AI in schools, where it stressed the need to have human oversight and that such systems may be biased. This recommendation, however, is not binding and leaves scarce clarity in the issue of accountability processes. Equally, the AI Ethics Framework of Australia is only partly prescriptive in what needs to be done, leaving it largely up to educational institutions to include their own safeguards into their system, with little legal or technical expertise to what that means (Schiff, 2022).

Leading regulatory regimes in countries with more advanced policies on digital learning, e.g., Finland or Singapore, are focused on infrastructure and access instead of algorithmic regulation or the rights of learners. These inconsistencies speak to the lack of a unified regulatory framework that would be able to regulate the peculiarities of agentic AI, especially as systems become more than the tools they are currently, shifting into becoming semi-autonomous agents within the educational paradigm.

The other complication is due to the growing importance of public-private partnership involving educational technology. Most agentic AI systems are being designed and deployed by private corporations that are present in multiple jurisdictions, and such systems epitomize regulatory enforcement difficulties by national regulators. Licensing agreements, proprietary algorithms, and trade secrecy claims often prevent such systems entering meaningful scrutiny, such that it is challenging to allow educational establishments to audit, or challenge the decision of, such systems even when the decision involves a person. The dynamic intensifies existing power imbalances among learners, teachers and the providers of technology, and adds to difficulties in imposing regulatory oversight (Chan, 2023).

Overall, though, the international regulatory environment has a number of valuable building blocks, including data protection legislation, codes of ethics, and educational edtech standards, been much too slow to react, disparate, and inadequately relevant to the realities of agentic AI in learning. They fail to properly answer the questions of systemic accountability, student agency and pedagogical alignment. As this book will explain in the following sections, these gaps play out in practice and there must be regulatory mechanisms designed to go beyond general principles to enforceable education-specific structures of governance.

ACCOUNTABILITY, LIABILITY, AND REDRESS MECHANISMS

With agentic AI becoming more involved in making decisions in an educational setting, the issue of accountability is getting more pressing. In contrast to conventional tools that only enable teaching or learning, agentic AI tools can grade assignments, suggest interventions, implement and report on behavioral concerns, or re-route the curricular path. Such actions- which may, in many cases, be well-meant to benefit the learners, might bring about unintended or negative side-effects. However, in the case that such results may come about, it is often left uncertain, the software designer or developer, the school, the instructor, or even the artificial intelligence system itself? (Memarian & Doleck, 2023).

Figure 1. Accountability and redress flow in agentic AI-driven educational decisions

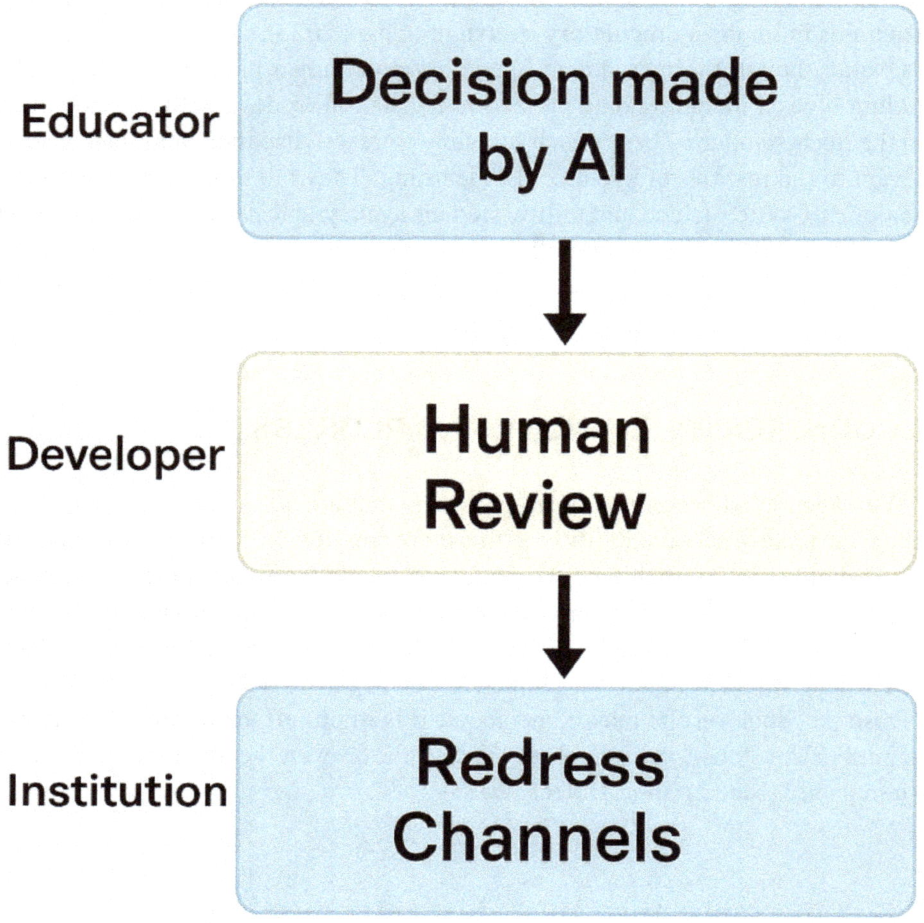

Such lack of clarity is partly due to the diffuser agency that such systems have. Human educators once made decisions about education, but decisions in the education sector are now the result of many roundtrip algorithmic processes, including proprietary code, uninterpretable machine learning models and real time behavioral information. The student who is a subject of an AI judgment, such as a low grade, an incorrect identified learning need, or an educational recommendation that has a long-term academic consequence, is unlikely to know how that judgment was reached, and is unlikely to know what to do about challenging the judgment. Such a lack of accountability may be regarded as one of the most urgent ethical and legal issues of the introduction of the agents of AI to educational systems.

Figure 1 shows the accountability and redress flow in agentic ai-driven educational decisions. This flowchart maps the key actors (educators, developers, institutions) and procedural stages involved in handling AI-generated decisions—from algorithmic outputs to human oversight, and ultimately to redress mechanisms accessible to students.

As far as the legislation is concerned, AI has not yet been considered as a responsible agent. Neither autonomous nor non-autonomous AI systems are accepted as legal persons, whose direct liability to causal harm can be imposed. Rather, liability is broadly shared by both humans and institutions- most of the times in ambiguous or unproven manners. Software developers can add clauses of indemnity under which they avoid liability after the school adoption of a product. The teachers might use AI results but refrain to take responsibility regarding the reasonings of the algorithms. Institutions can claim limits in the contracts with suppliers. Consequently, the aggrieved student is usually left without a clear redress mechanism, and damages go unsurmounted or unmapped (Bogina et al. 2022).

Without direct liability, researchers and policy experts have put forth multiple schemes of allocating responsibility when AI is involved in making a decision. Human-in-the-loop governance combining the human element is one such model, allowing that the reasoning and judicious choices made by the AI be instructive to retain a finger on the pulse of what ultimately happens. In the educational setting, this can mean, first, that all AI-generated high-stakes assessments or recommendations of placement should be reviewed and confirmed by credentialed educators. Theoretically, the approach is sound, but it could only be practically applied with certain amount of training by educators in how the system works, how to override the results, and backed up by institutional practices that promoted questioning and evaluating the results of the algorithm over and above mechanically accepting and leaving it to run on its own (Volin et al. 2025).

A further suggested system is referred to as algorithmic accountability by design and is intended to incorporate transparency and traceability in the architecture of an AI system. In terms of education, that would imply that all automated decisions, e.g. responding to a student with a remedial track, would be the subject to audit, explanation, and dispute. Classification of AI systems based on risks and documentation of how decisions are made has been included in some jurisdictions (e.g. the European Union with their future AI Act). Nevertheless, these requirements still have not been translated into education-specific regulation and a majority of existing commercial edtech platforms tend to remain black boxes.

It is also very essential to have sounds redress gaps in place to deal with students. During the training, the educational facilities must have guidelines on the ways in which students (or their guardians) can appeal against decisions made by an AI system. This goes beyond just appeals on grades but also appeals on behavioural assessment, intervention suggestion or even algorithm mediated feedback that might impact on the emotional well-being or the academic identity of the student. Such processes should be proximable and responsive whereby students know why the decision has been made, be given the hearing to contradict the claim/evidence and have the human decision-makers give prompt response (Buiten, 2024).

More so, it should not be imposed on individual learners and teachers that much of the accountability should depend on them. Regulatory authorities and accreditation agencies have a role to play to establish industry-level norms of auditability, surveillance and remedy of complaints. It can include establishing independent review boards on AI-related complaints to education, developing certification standards on AI tools to be used in high-stakes educational-related activities or using uniform audit processes to evaluate algorithmic equitability and dependability.

Lastly, the ethics of redress should not have the assumption that redress should be made only after the harm has been perpetrated. An effective accountability mechanism must also have a preventive role of ensuring that AI systems are configured, purchased, and implemented with accountability as a priority. These will include strict pre-deployment testing; impact measures of the vulnerable populations and consistent post-deployment surveillance. Indeed, so important is the educational judgment that without restraint, institutions run the risk of normalizing the incursion of arbitrary systems into their educational course and of redundantly subjecting their students to algorithmic control without appeal (Schiff, 2022).

In short, case with agentic AI in education is a paradigm to reconsider accountability frameworks. Conventional theories of institutional responsibility and teacher autonomy do not deal well with the new complexities brought out by semi-autonome systems. A new framework in regulation must be developed one that is accountable, has transparency and ensures that learners have the voice and protection in the ever-changing learning environment dominated by technology.

DATA GOVERNANCE AND PRIVACY IN REAL-TIME AI SYSTEMS

Agentic AI can only survive on data. These systems operate on endless, fine-grained flows of data- academic performance, behavioral trends, emotional indicators, demographic data, device usage, and in some cases even biometric data - to make subjective modifications to decision-making. Although such real-time responsiveness is the distinguishing strength of agentic AI in an educational environment, it poses significant new data security, learner privacy, and ethical management challenges like never before. What we have is old models of educational data protection that fail to sufficiently address an era where AI systems make decision on behalf of students, on behalf of students often without the full awareness much less consent of the students involved (Filgueiras, 2024).

In contrast with more traditional forms of data collection (the end of term grade, paper-based assessments), agentic AI allows the exploitation of continuous monitoring of cognitive and behavioral cues embedded in the cognitive and behavioral data collected on learners. This involves clickstreams, the amount of time that is spent on any content, eye tracking, speech, and variations in performance to deduce states such as confusion, lack of engagement or mastery. This kind of data is not simply accumulated, but algorithmically interpreted to make subsequent pedagogical, pacing or intervention decisions. This interpretive application of the data gives an additional qualitative dimension to the risk of privacy, in that students are no longer mere objects of data, but datafied students, continuously profiled by intelligent systems.

Policies such as the General Data Protection Regulation (GDPR) and FERPA (Family Educational Rights and Privacy Act) establish fundamental protection, such as the right of access, correction, and consent. Such laws are however inadequate when they are put to reality of being opaque and complicated to the flow of real-time data inside AI systems. As an example, the GDPR right to explanation is seldom applicable when applied to black-box AI models used in education wherein even the developers cannot be completely clear how a decision was made. In the same regard, FERPA was implemented in the systems of static records and did not apply in the spheres of predictive analytics and behavioral inference, as well as pertains to third-party vendors, who may collect data on behalf of educational establishments (Ghimire & Edwards, 2024).

One of the issues in this regard is informed consent. At a majority of schools, consent is given at the start of the academic year based on a blanket consent form that may not provide detailed information about which type of data is being obtained, or which actions are being made by AI. This strategy compromises the principles of meaningful consent especially among the minors who could not possibly understand what constant monitoring by the algorithms means. In addition, parents and guardians will have little control over how their child data is used, in which locations they are deposited, and by who and especially in the case of using cloud-based services or selling to overseas companies.

New concern is the one of data minimisation, a concept that appears in most privacy legislation and requires that only data essential in a particular process should be received and kept. Agentic AI applications are likely to flaunt this principle in operation by scooping up huge amounts of data to leverage their training data, customize their outputs, or do predictive modelling. Not only is achievement of additional pressure technological, but also commercial- data fuels the variety in algorithms and leads to competitive edge of AI vendors. In this sense, therefore, lies a degree of conflict between personalization and privacy: the more specific the AI is, the more invasive its data will be required to be.

Besides privacy there is an emerging issue of data equity. The data utilized to train and run agentic AI systems are typically biased- socioeconomic, racial, linguistic or regional bias. Such biases can be imported into the artificial intelligence outputs and cause it to continue perpetuating education disparity under the guise of individualization. As another example, predictive models learn how to use past academic performance to predict future performance, perhaps reinforcing the stigmatization of students of marginalized backgrounds, systematically biasing expectations or even limiting access to advanced opportunities. Data-driven discrimination becomes a structural and hidden aspect when it is supported without any regulatory check (Chan, 2023).

To overcome these challenges, educational systems require powerful data governance frameworks beyond juvenile-compliance checklists and require active supervision, openness, and responsibility. This includes defining clear guidelines on data collection, data retention, and data deletion; applying privacy-by-design and equity-by-design principles to data driven AI development; and providing educators and students with privacy and control. Noteworthy, data governance should be institutionalized, rather than delegated to individual schools and districts, but boosted by national regulatory bodies that can audit, enforce and inform proper ethics of using data.

The establishment of learner data trusts or data stewardship councils is one possible version of this approach in which student data is treated as a common good that can be governed by general consent, instead of it privately ownership. These models can aid in mediating between privacy and innovation so that education can make use of the data without infringing on the rights of the individuals. The next strategy is to compare some form of impact assessment of any AI system prior to its deployment, the assessment outlining its risks to privacy, equity, and autonomy, and a mitigation plan imposed (Gulson & Witzenberger, 2022).

Overall, the practices of data that enabled agentic AI systems require rethinking the fundamentals of educational privacy protection. Student data can no longer be treated as mere information stored on the files. Rather, it should be viewed as direct contribution to user-generated educational futures that can be constructive at any point in time. The need to protect this information is not only legal and technical but also educational justice.

BIAS, EQUITY, AND INCLUSION

In contrast to the agentic AI that claims to have a superiorly more personalized and efficient educative process, an exclusive disadvantage is the eventuality that agentic AI might merely reify or rather reinforce pre-existing structural disparities. These systems operate on data using algorithms that themselves are frequently trained on past biased or out of context datasets and therefore continue to be used to contribute to the marginalization of learners already on the edge. Since the agentic AI systems become increasingly influential in shaping student assessment, placement and support, the ethical and regulatory requirement of the need to be inclusive and fair is no longer desirable, but mandatory (Viberg et al. 2024).

Bias in education could be in a number of ways and subtle in nature. It is possible to imagine an AI powered early warning system that identifies students as at risk over attendance, grades, and other behavioral indicators. Such a system might then exhibit bias against, and flag, students of some racial, linguistic, or economic demographic even as they are academically successful--simply because that system was trained on, or disproportionately punishes, non-conformity in previously under-resourced schools or schools with a disproportionate number of low-income students. In the same way, predictive models that determine learning path/course will push female students away in the direction of STEM subjects or English learners into lower tracks and in essence limit the opportunity in the name of personalization.

Such results are not out of the ordinary, but rather it is the consequence of deeply engrained biases in training data, model structure, and feedback loops. AI systems in the education sector tend to amplify prevailing cultural and evaluation standards and gives precedence to those students who do not conform to them. This issue is also complicated by the fact that many AI models are opaque, and it has been hard to identify or even make sense on why such decisions were made- leave alone questioning them, whether by a teacher, students or the government as regulators. This obscurity is the engine of what other scholars have described as the automation of inequality, in which algorithmic decisions develop a deceptive rationality and legitimacy, despite being wildly erroneous (Roshanaei, 2024).

The regulatory framework should therefore get out of stating generic promises of fairness and adopt concrete bias reduction and inclusion mechanisms. The key step is the requirement of algorithmic impact assessment, especially when using AI tools in high-stakes educational settings. These tests are supposed to compare the performance of the models across the various demographic sets and recognize disparities prevailing within those differences and remediate them before deployment. In addition to that, such evaluations should be iterative, in other words, they should be repeated periodically, as an A/B model behavior changes with the further learning and new data inputs.

Disclosure is also a major factor in making equity possible. Regulators should demand that AI designers and institutions that educate them reveal the data set, training hypotheses, and performance standards of their tools. When biases are identified in these cases there must be binding requirements to re-calibrate or eliminate the AI tool as a usage requirement. The third-party audits have a strong third-party check point that provides a third-party viewpoint on fairness and technical validation. Audits are not always quantitative with emphasis being made on qualitative tests taking the attitude of the educator, the students and the community stakeholders (Roscoe et al. 2022).

Key, the notion of inclusion should also be constructed as the principle of design. The inclusive AI design has required that the systems are created to consider diverse learners rather than as an afterthought. This involves catering to neurodiverse students, multilingual students and culturally diverse students. By way of example, an AI language model used in tasks such as grading or tutoring is expected to understand a variety of dialects and forms of rhetoric used, instead of strictly following dominant norms of language. As with most learning features, the approach to adaptive learning systems should be customisable, as opposed to ensuring there is a single model of advancement.

Regulation based on equity needs to be attendant to the wider institutional environment within which AI will be employed. The schools with marginalised groups under-represented can neither afford the technical insight, nor appropriate support, finances or autonomy to investigate or adopt custom AI systems. The outcomes of AI governance without systematic support the creation of the same inequities of access and opportunity that already exist in schools: lack of centralized technical assistance, funding of inclusive procurement practices, and training of educators that will reflect and, without additional support, likely expand those inequities in education (Cachat-Rosset & Klarsfeld, 2023).

In response, regulators can encourage equity-based procurement criteria that would encourage vendors to show that their AI tools are not only truly effective but that they are also invested in delivering equitable results. Student agency and demonstrable bias audits, accessibility features, and means of securing public funding and procurement should be contingent. Similarly, regulators may require that students and communities should play a role in AI oversight activities, as algorithmic decisions can most injuriously affect those, they most affect, they should be able to sit on the table as their systems are vetted and regulated.

In sum, agentic AI requires proactive design, implementation and enforcement of fairness: it does not occur by default. A system of educational practice and technologies that ignore the regulations, by adopting these technologies generates the possibility of converting the efficiency of algorithms into a kind of structural discrimination. Equitable and dignified AI-driven education system needs to be responsible not only regarding its accuracy, but also its effect on equality, fairness and inclusion- providing all students with a possibility to excel, irrespective of their origin.

DESIGNING A REGULATORY FRAMEWORK

After discussing the theoretical, ethical, and legal tensions of agentic AI in education, the present section suggests a specialized regulatory framework accountable to the unique set of risks and dynamics of such systems. Agentinic AI, unlike traditional AI applications, needs models of governance capable of discussing its self-determination, flexibility, and the ability of enclosed decision-making in the learning environment. Such regulation should thus be multi-layered, fact-sensitive, and prospective, being able to balance innovation against protectionism and flexibility against enforcement ability (Molenaar, 2022). To operationalize these principles, the chapter proposes a multi-layered regulatory model that distributes oversight across institutional, national, and international levels. This structure ensures that accountability, transparency, and pedagogical alignment are embedded at each stage of educational AI implementation. Figure 2 illustrates this layered framework and the key responsibilities associated with each tier.

Figure 2. Multi-layered regulatory framework for agentic AI in education

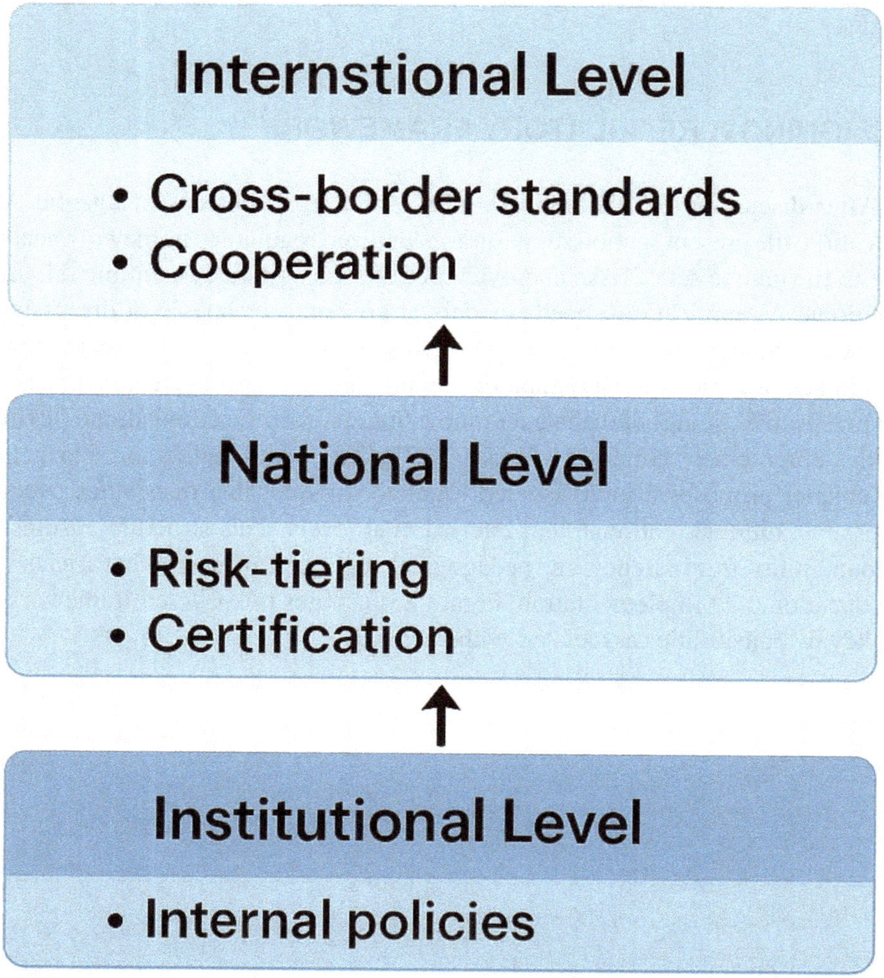

The many tiers of multi-layered structure acknowledges that there is no one party capable of handling all the burden of regulation: it may be the developer, it may be the school, or it may be the state. Rather, the control should be exercised on many levels both institutional, national, and international. On the institutional level, schools, universities, and education officials must be mandated into formulating internal regulations when it comes to the use of the AI systems, such as the protocols of educator supervision, student consent, and monitoring after operationalization. Such policies need to specify lines of responsibility: who authorizes use of a particular

AI tool, who certifies its accuracy and fairness in action, and who takes student complaints in the event of harms (Järvelä et al. 2023).

The national decision-makers need to set standards of AI tools used in education by instituting appropriate ministries of education and regulatory bodies through binding measures. The criteria used by these standards should be certification on the basis of the existence of algorithmic transparency, reduction on bias, explainability, and protection of student data. Using templates such as the EU AI Act, two countries can implement risk tiering, in which AI systems can be divided into risk categories based on the potential harm that they may cause. As an example, systems that carry high value such as systems that are used in grading, placement, and behavior prediction should be demanding in auditing externally and continuous performance evaluation whereas those that have lesser risk might be guided with less supervision.

Figure 3 shows the risk-based classification of ai systems in education. This pyramid model categorizes AI tools based on their level of impact and required regulatory scrutiny—from low-risk supplementary tools at the base, to high-risk systems used for grading, placement, or behavioral prediction at the top.

Figure 3. Risk-based classification of AI systems in education

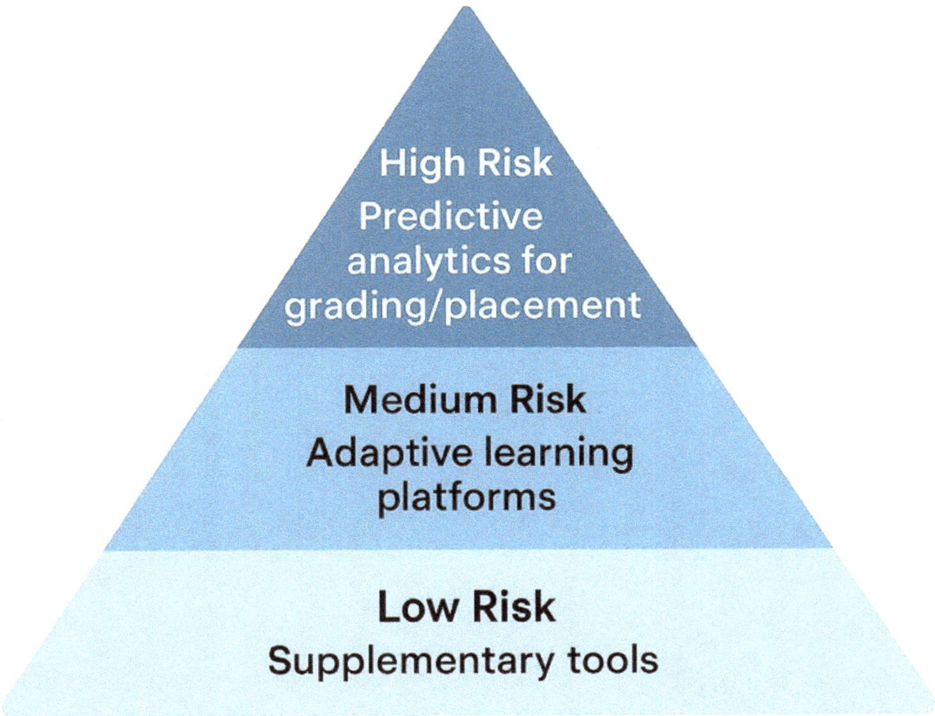

Third party accreditation and auditing organizations are also important in this set-up. These independent bodies would evaluate the education AI goods both before implementation and after making sure they are within the regulatory requirements, benchmarks on fairness, and have paths to meaningful explanation and redress. Such organizations would also have to have the capability to send warnings, recall products, or make recommendations in case during its evaluation an AI system is determined to be causing disproportional harm to one or more groups of learners or operates continually outside of acceptable standards (Smuha, 2021).

To ground our regulatory recommendations in international practice, Table 1 offers a comparative look at how different countries or regions are approaching AI regulation in education. It shows variation in whether legal frameworks exist, how risk classification is being applied (or not), what redress or appeals mechanisms are available to students, and how equity and bias are addressed. These comparisons help illustrate both gaps and promising approaches—offering guidance for how more coherent and enforceable frameworks might be built.

Table 1. National approaches to AI regulation in education

Country / Region	AI Regulation Status in Education	Risk-Tiering / Classification Framework	Redress Mechanisms / Student Appeal	Equity & Bias Safeguards
European Union	Working on the AI Act which covers high-risk AI systems. Some member states have specific guidelines for educational AI.	Yes — high risk, limited risk categories are defined; educational tools likely fall under "high-risk" if used in assessment or placement.	Provisions for liability, transparency. Students can appeal or require explanations under GDPR-like provisions.	Strong emphasis on fairness, non-discrimination, bias in data; audits and oversight are required.
United States	No unified federal AI law specific to education; patchwork of state, district policies.	Some institutions and districts classify or restrict certain AI tools, but no broad risk-classification law yet.	Student grievance/ appeal mechanisms vary by school or district; some states have privacy / education rights laws.	Equity concerns increasingly discussed; some juries and research focus on biases in AI-EdTech, but less formal regulation compared to EU.
China	Has released "Interim Measures for the Management of Generative AI Services" governing public-facing AI, including education regionally.	Some classification of AI tools under regulation of "generative" vs non-generative; high-visibility regulation of tools affecting public discourse. Education-specific classification less explicit.	State/government oversight; less transparent appeal processes compared to Western democracies. Individual redress may be limited in practice.	Emphasis on controlling content and avoiding societal risk; less public debate on bias or fairness than in EU/ US, though these issues are being raised.
Japan	Developing national guidelines; has pilot programs and frameworks for generative AI in education.	Moderate — not all tools are classified; government documents usually provide guidance rather than strict regulation.	Some regulatory fallback, oversight; education ministries often set policy rather than courts. Student redress tends to be institution driven.	Equity and bias are recognized; privacy/ data protection also emphasized in policy documents.

Above national boundaries, edtech buyers are increasingly globalised and international data flows depend on international cooperation. A regulatory framework cannot exist in a silo, especially when schools use the AI-based tools created by multinational corporations whose activities go beyond the national jurisdictions. An intersectionality of regulation, which bridges intergovernmental agreements, ethical pacts and standards convergence, which may be achieved through UNESCO, OECD, or regional blocs efforts, may lead to accountability without cluttering innovation. The transnational harmonization of important principles (such as transparency of algorithms or the sovereignty of data) can act as a threshold of policies nationally and in ensuring the safety of learners whose data spill over across borders.

The institutionalization of human oversight is another necessary cake layer in this structure. The agentic AI systems should also not respond in pedagogical isolation. It is important that educators are empowered to not only decipher AI outputs, but to indeed override them in the event of conflict with professional judgment or student welfare. This requires long-term care in teacher training--not only technical training, but pedagogical integration and moral literacy. Educational institutions will also need to ensure that students/families are aware of the impact of AI systems on learning and are provided with actual possibilities to appeal to conclusions (Lim et al. 2023).

In terms of practical implementation, the proposed regulatory framework would include:

- Mandatory pre-deployment testing of AI systems for bias, reliability, and explainability.
- Data governance protocols, including real-time logging, anonymization, and rights to data access and deletion.
- Impact assessments evaluating the potential consequences of AI deployment on learner outcomes, equity, and institutional capacity.
- Redress mechanisms that are clearly articulated, timely, and accessible to all students.
- Stakeholder engagement requirements, mandating consultation with teachers, students, parents, and community representatives before system-wide adoption of agentic AI tools.

This sort of the framework is not designed to limit the (educational) potential of AI, would rather encompass it in a responsible manner. A focus on putting in place the appropriate expectations and enforcement capacity with an ethical innovation culture embedded into the education systems will result in equitable distribution of the benefits of agentic AI, and systemic prevention or redress of harms. This takes this governance out of principles to practice, to a model in which AI augments the human aspects of instruction and learning, instead of replacing it.

CASE ILLUSTRATIONS AND COMPARATIVE POLICY ANALYSIS

To inform the regulatory challenges and opportunities confronting agentic AI in education, this area discusses a set of case studies as well as a comparative examination of national practices. These illustrations are critical in demonstrating the difference and power of regulatory foresight in establishing education and ethical impacts of any AI implementation. They also indicate the practical reflections of the previous conceptual treatments on the issue of accountability, equity and data governance when translated into the practical situation of education.

Case Study 1: Algorithmic Grading in the United Kingdom

Among the most popular disputes related to AI in the education sector is the case that happened in the United Kingdom in the context of the COVID-19 pandemic involving the Office of Qualifications and Examinations Regulation (Ofqual), which introduced an automatic system to rate learners where standardized exams were not provided. The model was supposed to ensure consistency and guard against grade inflation, based upon previous performance data at the school and statistical normalization of it.

The outcome was a large negative change to students in historically low performing schools, many but not all of which served working-class and minority communities. Students with higher statuses tended to improve or score as expected on the other hand. The major issue with the algorithmic results and grade changes caused a strong outcry in society that led the government to change their mind and revert the results on teacher-assessed grades (Aloisi, 2023).

This case presents the risks of high-stakes agentic AI systems deployed with improper bias testing, transparency or redress mechanisms. It also demonstrates the necessity of previous deployment equity testing and consultation with stakeholders that would have avoided large scale injury and institutional indignity.

Case Study 2: AI-Powered Early Warning Systems in the United States

With AI-based early warning systems (EWS), at-risk students are identified to prevent dropout across many U.S. school districts. These systems combine people on the attendance, behavior and academic and create a risk score and mark students at-risk to be intervened upon. Although usually positioned as supportive, the models have also caused concern about false positives and disparities depending on race, as well as transparency in the algorithm behind calculating the risk scores.

These systems unfairly reported black and Latino students, according to a 2020 report by the Center on Privacy & Technology at Georgetown Law--a replay of the past over-monitoring and disciplining of these groups. In addition, the algorithm use was hardly explained to affected students and families, the scores could not be accessed by the students and families, and they did not have a chance to challenge or explain the predictions in any way (Aldous & Ismail, 2025).

The case highlights the necessity of explaining requirements and mechanisms of student consent as well as all-inclusive governance framework that can block the way to predictive tools as automated stigmatizing tools.

Case Study 3: Adaptive Learning Platforms in Finland

The opposition demonstrates a pro-active approach to the integration of AI, however, in accordance with effective governance in Finland. It has also enacted national digital education policies that all vendors of edtech products, including those that use AI, must respect the strict standards of data minimization, teacher control, and alignment to the curriculum.

A particular example is by using adaptive mathematics platforms whereby they always adapt according to the performance of the students. These aids are incorporated in a pedagogical system whereby teachers are not edged out as the key decision-makers. In addition, Finland requires impact assessment even prior to the adoption of the tool in large quantities, with the participation of teachers and the student representation in the consideration process (Strielkowski et al. 2025).

The Finnish example illustrates how co-design with teachers, explicit regulatory requirements, and centralized authority could reduce the risks to drive innovation.

Comparative Policy Insights

Analyzing these cases reveals stark differences in how countries approach the governance of agentic AI in education:

- **Regulatory Proactivity**: Nations like Finland and Singapore embed AI oversight within national education strategies, while countries like the U.S. and UK often respond reactively to crises.
- **Stakeholder Involvement**: Participatory models that involve educators, students, and communities (e.g., Finland) outperform top-down implementations in terms of trust and legitimacy.
- **Transparency and Access**: Jurisdictions that mandate clear communication of algorithmic logic and provide access to decision records foster greater accountability.
- **Bias Mitigation**: Impact assessments and fairness audits are unevenly applied across countries, with most lacking enforcement mechanisms for equity-oriented standards.

These comparative lessons act to support the necessity of internationally experienced yet locally responsive, regulatory structures. Although very different educational settings are involved, dangers of agentic AI are remarkably similar: lack of transparency in decision-making, disproportionate consequences, and ineffective means of complaint. Case-based learning thus has the potential to inform the design of regulation, which in turn would enable jurisdictions to learn not just on what paths to take but the paths to avoid.

RECOMMENDATIONS AND FUTURE DIRECTIONS

Introducing agentic AI in the field of education is an issue that requires not only an analytical approach but a future-proof and practical step. As the foregoing sections have illustrated, the regulatory regimes in place do not often align well with the complex, autonomous and powerful nature of agentic AI. What is needed now is the move beyond compliance piece in the puzzle to systemic, proactive governance that will grant rights to learners, promote pedagogical integrity, and technological accountability (Ng et al. 2025).

Develop Risk-Driven Regulatory Categories

The classification of AI systems in relation to their potential on both the learners and educational outcomes should be done. Systems that have a high risk of impacting on grading, placement, or behavior monitoring should have compulsory certification, third party, as well as sustained monitoring. The less risky systems are likely to be subject to special regulatory tracks, even though they are also expected to comply with base standards in privacy protection, transparency and public access.

Pre-Deployment and Continuous Impact Assessments Pre-Deployment Requirements

Algorithmic impact assessment (AIA) should be applied to all agentic AI means that are introduced into education before their adoption. These must discuss the possibility of bias and data misuse, misclassification, and pedagogical misfit in the tool. These evaluations should be an iterative process, returning to it periodically as the tool evolves or as new data sets and contexts of use become present.

Design in Embed Explainability and Contestability Embed Explainability and Contestability

The AI systems that are agentic need to be testable and challengeable. Learners, parents, and teachers must be able to get readable explanations of how AI decisions arrived upon and must be given clear routes with which to dispute, override or appeal the decisions. This is specially so when determination is high-stakes like course recommendations, assessments, or behavioral flags.

Include Participatory Development

The proliferation, acquisition and implementation of artificial intelligence should be inclusive. Learners, educators, parents, and community stakeholders should be directly not only in the testing phase, but also in defining the purposes, assumptions, and criteria of assessment by intelligent systems. This will make sure that the technologies represent a variety of educational values, cultural backgrounds and learner demands.

Establish Institutional AI Governance Infrastructure

The educational establishments must establish an AI oversight panel or ethics committee with the aim of assessing the application of AI technologies in their area of interest. These should be interdisciplinary with expertise in law, technology, pedagogy who may approve, suspend or withdraw AI tools which are failing to perform, are ethically questionable, or are generating feedback complaints of students.

Build Capacity by Training and Public Education

Even the regulation is not very good without informed actors. There is a need to provide educators with professional development on the aspects related to the pedagogy, ethical, and operational concerns regarding AI. The families and students must have information accessible concerning the impact of AI systems on the learning process and rights of the individual. Regulatory frameworks have to go hand in hand with effective capacity building programs which are facilitated by public agencies as well as academic institutions.

Advance International Coordination and Share Knowledge

Since educational AI markets are effectively transnational, national regulators would be prudent to aim at internationally harmonized educational AI governance standards. This also entails the collaboration with such organizations as UNESCO, OECD and the council of Europe to devise common standards of fairness, audit and data protection. An opportunity to learn both good policy and implementation failure can be facilitated by the knowledge-sharing networks.

Looking Ahead

Due to increasing prevalence of AI in classrooms, it does not suffice to control a technology- it is a social-technological change that has to be controlled. Educational AI regulatory frameworks of the future have to keep pace with the technology itself: flexible, data-driven, and human dignity- and learner empowerment-focused.

More importantly, policymakers should be interested in the idea that educational situations are not merely the facilities where knowledge transfers, but rather, the places where identities, social inclusion, and democratic growth happen. The choices of the agentic AI systems may affect not only academic performance but self-concept, desire, and opportunity. A regulatory framework that does not take into consideration these dimensions has the potential to cause greater inequality, reduce trust, and fail its own mission of education (Li et al. 2024).

Rather, future government should adhere to a vision of just, accountable and learner-driven AI: an approach that upholds rights, establishes trust and cultivates a shared ability to influence the future technologies that will serve, rather than disturb, our collective education futures.

CONCLUSION

Agentic AI represents one of the most significant shifts in the educational landscape since the digital revolution. Its capacity to adapt, infer, and act upon complex streams of learner data offers real potential to personalize instruction, streamline administrative processes, and democratize access to high-quality educational experiences. Yet these same features also introduce profound risks—of opacity, bias, exclusion, and unaccountable decision-making—that challenge the very principles upon which equitable education is built.

This chapter posited that the regulation of agentic AI in education is a question not only of technical and/or procedural management, but of normative necessity. More than data protection laws or mere ethical principles that are not grounded in reality, the implementation of semi-autonomous systems in the classrooms requires. It necessitates an ardent, tiered regulatory plan that is based on equity, openness, and supremacy of human educational relationships.

Tracing the unique essence of the agentic AI and the real time decision-making capabilities it brings, identifying regulatory gaps, and suggesting specific governance plans, the chapter has traced the risks and the paths to responsible regulation. It has demonstrated the role of regulation in institutionalizing damage or the potential to use AI to achieve good through international case studies and the comparative policy analysis to assess the potential of AI as commonly perceived to regulate their intended use.

And finally, with changing education systems and emerging intelligent technologies the question less concerns whether to regulate, but how. The ambition should then be the alignment of technological innovation in line with democratic responsibility, empowerment of learners and relevance of equity in the system. Governing agentic AI is about this: being able to govern the progress, rather than curbing it, so that it is directed toward human flourishing.

REFERENCES

Aldous, S. M., & Ismail, G. A. (2025). AI for Sustainable Emergency Preparedness and Response in Schools. In *Convergence of AI, Education, and Business for Sustainability* (pp. 51-74). IGI Global Scientific Publishing. DOI: 10.4018/979-8-3373-1917-9.ch003

Aloisi, C. (2023). The future of standardised assessment: Validity and trust in algorithms for assessment and scoring. *European Journal of Education*, *58*(1), 98–110. DOI: 10.1111/ejed.12542

Bogina, V., Hartman, A., Kuflik, T., & Shulner-Tal, A. (2022). Educating software and AI stakeholders about algorithmic fairness, accountability, transparency and ethics. *International Journal of Artificial Intelligence in Education*, *32*(3), 808–833. DOI: 10.1007/s40593-021-00248-0

Brohi, S., Mastoi, Q. U. A., Jhanjhi, N. Z., & Pillai, T. R. (2025). A Research Landscape of Agentic AI and Large Language Models: Applications, Challenges and Future Directions. *Algorithms*, *18*(8), 499. DOI: 10.3390/a18080499

Buiten, M. C. (2024). Product liability for defective AI. *European Journal of Law and Economics*, *57*(1), 239–273. DOI: 10.1007/s10657-024-09794-z

Cachat-Rosset, G., & Klarsfeld, A. (2023). Diversity, equity, and inclusion in artificial intelligence: An evaluation of guidelines. *Applied Artificial Intelligence*, *37*(1), 2176618. DOI: 10.1080/08839514.2023.2176618

Chan, C. K. Y. (2023). A comprehensive AI policy education framework for university teaching and learning. *International Journal of Educational Technology in Higher Education*, *20*(1), 38. DOI: 10.1186/s41239-023-00408-3

Dai, L., Jiang, Y. H., Chen, Y., Guo, Z., Liu, T. Y., & Shao, X. (2024, November). Agent4EDU: Advancing AI for Education with Agentic Workflows. In *Proceedings of the 2024 3rd International Conference on Artificial Intelligence and Education* (pp. 180-185). DOI: 10.1145/3722237.3722268

Filgueiras, F. (2024). Artificial intelligence and education governance. *Education, Citizenship and Social Justice*, *19*(3), 349–361. DOI: 10.1177/17461979231160674

García-López, I. M., & Trujillo-Liñán, L. (2025). Generative Artificial Intelligence in Education: Ethical Challenges, Regulatory Frameworks and Educational Quality in a Systematic Review of the Literature. [). Frontiers.]. *Frontiers in Education*, *10*, 1565938. DOI: 10.3389/feduc.2025.1565938

Ghimire, A., & Edwards, J. (2024, July). From guidelines to governance: A study of ai policies in education. In *International Conference on Artificial Intelligence in Education* (pp. 299-307). Cham: Springer Nature Switzerland. DOI: 10.1007/978-3-031-64312-5_36

Gulson, K. N., & Witzenberger, K. (2022). Repackaging authority: Artificial intelligence, automated governance and education trade shows. *Journal of Education Policy*, *37*(1), 145–160. DOI: 10.1080/02680939.2020.1785552

Järvelä, S., Nguyen, A., & Hadwin, A. (2023). Human and artificial intelligence collaboration for socially shared regulation in learning. *British Journal of Educational Technology*, *54*(5), 1057–1076. DOI: 10.1111/bjet.13325

Katsenou, R., Kotsidis, K., Papadopoulou, A., Anastasiadis, P., & Deliyannis, I. (2025). Beyond Assistance: Embracing AI as a Collaborative Co-Agent in Education. *Education Sciences*, *15*(8), 1006. DOI: 10.3390/educsci15081006

Li, L., Yu, F., & Zhang, E. (2024). A systematic review of learning task design for K-12 AI education: Trends, challenges, and opportunities. *Computers and Education: Artificial Intelligence*, *6*, 100217. DOI: 10.1016/j.caeai.2024.100217

Lim, W. M., Gunasekara, A., Pallant, J. L., Pallant, J. I., & Pechenkina, E. (2023). Generative AI and the future of education: Ragnarök or reformation? A paradoxical perspective from management educators. *International Journal of Management Education*, *21*(2), 100790. DOI: 10.1016/j.ijme.2023.100790

Liu, G. L., Lee, J. S., & Zhao, X. (2025). Critical digital literacies, agentic practices, and AI-mediated informal digital learning of English. *System*, *134*, 103797. DOI: 10.1016/j.system.2025.103797

Memarian, B., & Doleck, T. (2023). Fairness, Accountability, Transparency, and Ethics (FATE) in Artificial Intelligence (AI) and higher education: A systematic review. *Computers and Education: Artificial Intelligence*, *5*, 100152. DOI: 10.1016/j.caeai.2023.100152

Molenaar, I. (2022). The concept of hybrid human-AI regulation: Exemplifying how to support young learners' self-regulated learning. *Computers and Education: Artificial Intelligence*, *3*, 100070. DOI: 10.1016/j.caeai.2022.100070

Mouta, A., Pinto-Llorente, A. M., & Torrecilla-Sánchez, E. M. (2025). "Where is Agency Moving to?": Exploring the Interplay between AI Technologies in Education and Human Agency. *Digital Society : Ethics, Socio-Legal and Governance of Digital Technology*, *4*(2), 49. DOI: 10.1007/s44206-025-00203-9

Ng, D. T. K., Chan, E. K. C., & Lo, C. K. (2025). Opportunities, challenges and school strategies for integrating generative AI in education. *Computers and Education: Artificial Intelligence*, 100373.

Roscoe, R. D., Salehi, S., Nixon, N., Worsley, M., Piech, C., & Luckin, R. (2022). Inclusion and equity as a paradigm shift for artificial intelligence in education. In *Artificial Intelligence in STEM Education* (pp. 359–374). CRC Press. DOI: 10.1201/9781003181187-28

Roshanaei, M. (2024). Towards best practices for mitigating artificial intelligence implicit bias in shaping diversity, inclusion and equity in higher education. *Education and Information Technologies*, *29*(14), 18959–18984. DOI: 10.1007/s10639-024-12605-2

Schiff, D. (2022). Education for AI, not AI for education: The role of education and ethics in national AI policy strategies. *International Journal of Artificial Intelligence in Education*, *32*(3), 527–563. DOI: 10.1007/s40593-021-00270-2

Smuha, N. A. (2021). From a 'race to AI'to a 'race to AI regulation': Regulatory competition for artificial intelligence. *Law, Innovation and Technology*, *13*(1), 57–84. DOI: 10.1080/17579961.2021.1898300

Strielkowski, W., Grebennikova, V., Lisovskiy, A., Rakhimova, G., & Vasileva, T. (2025). AI-driven adaptive learning for sustainable educational transformation. *Sustainable Development (Bradford)*, *33*(2), 1921–1947. DOI: 10.1002/sd.3221

Viberg, O., Kizilcec, R. F., Wise, A. F., Jivet, I., & Nixon, N. (2024). Advancing equity and inclusion in educational practices with AI-powered educational decision support systems (AI-EDSS). *British Journal of Educational Technology*, *55*(5), 1974–1981. DOI: 10.1111/bjet.13507

Volin, J., van Assen, M., Bala, W., Safdar, N., & Balthazar, P. (2025). Artificial Intelligence and Its Effect on Radiology Residency Education: Current Challenges, Opportunities, and Future Directions. *Journal of the American College of Radiology*, *22*(11), 1264–1270. Advance online publication. DOI: 10.1016/j.jacr.2025.07.004 PMID: 40659237

Zhai, X., Chu, X., Chai, C. S., Jong, M. S. Y., Istenic, A., Spector, M., & Li, Y. (2021). A Review of Artificial Intelligence (AI) in Education from 2010 to 2020. *Complexity*, *2021*(1), 8812542. DOI: 10.1155/2021/8812542

Zhang, K., & Aslan, A. B. (2021). AI technologies for education: Recent research & future directions. *Computers and education. Artificial Intelligence*, *2*, 100025.

ADDITIONAL READING

Garg, V. (2025). Designing the Mind: How Agentic Frameworks Are Shaping the Future of AI Behavior. *Journal of Computer Science and Technology Studies*, *7*(5), 182–193. DOI: 10.32996/jcsts.2025.7.5.24

Murugesan, S. (2025). The rise of agentic AI: Implications, concerns, and the path forward. *IEEE Intelligent Systems*, *40*(2), 8–14. DOI: 10.1109/MIS.2025.3544940

Sargsyan, L. (2025). Integrating agentic ai in higher education: Balancing opportunities, challenges, and ethical imperatives. *Foreign Languages in Higher Education*, *29*(1 (38)), 87–100. DOI: 10.46991/FLHE.2025.29.1.087

KEY TERMS AND DEFINITIONS

Agentic AI: Artificial intelligence systems capable of autonomous, context-sensitive decision-making, particularly in real-time environments. In education, these systems go beyond assistive functions to actively shape learning trajectories, assessments, and pedagogical interactions.

Algorithmic Accountability: The principle and practice of ensuring that the decisions made by algorithms, especially in high-stakes domains like education, can be traced, explained, evaluated, and—if necessary—challenged or corrected.

Bias in AI: Systematic and unfair discrimination embedded in AI systems, often stemming from biased training data, model design, or deployment contexts. In education, this can result in the unfair treatment of students based on race, gender, language, or socioeconomic background.

Data Governance: The policies, standards, and practices that regulate how data is collected, stored, shared, and used. In educational AI systems, this includes protections for learner privacy, consent procedures, and data minimization strategies.

Educational Equity: The principle of fair and inclusive access to learning opportunities, irrespective of background or identity of a given learner. Regulations of AI should prevent the use of technologies that worsen current disparities in education.

Explainability (or Interpretability): The degree to which the internal mechanics of an AI system or its decision-making logic can be understood by humans. Explainability is crucial in educational contexts where decisions impact learning outcomes and must be justified to students, educators, and parents.

Human-in-the-Loop (HITL): A governance model where human educators retain ultimate authority over AI-generated decisions, ensuring that automation supports—rather than replaces—professional judgment and student engagement.

Impact Assessment (Algorithmic Impact Assessment): A formal evaluation conducted before and during the deployment of AI systems to assess their ethical, legal, and social implications, including potential risks to privacy, equity, and learner autonomy.

Redress Mechanism: The mechanisms that enable people to appeal/gain redress to a decision made by an AI system. These are crucial mechanisms of upholding student rights as well as institutional accountability within an AI-mediated environment.

Risk-Based Regulation: A regulatory framework that can classify AI systems and authorize more rigorous oversight on systems with a higher risk of potential harm or impact, such as a grading or behavioral prediction tool.

Chapter 10
Teacher-AI:
A Collaborative Approach to Transforming Education

Kashvi Chaturvedi
https://orcid.org/0009-0005-3192-3400
Ajeenkya D.Y. Patil University, India

Arihant Prashant Chobharkar
Ajeenkya D.Y. Patil University, India

Aditya Shrivastav
https://orcid.org/0009-0000-8461-8171
Ajeenkya D.Y. Patil University, India

Sunil Sankathala
https://orcid.org/0009-0004-7809-7647
Ajeenkya D.Y. Patil University, India

Susanta Das
https://orcid.org/0000-0002-9314-3988
Ajeenkya D.Y. Patil University, India

ABSTRACT

This chapter reviews the changing role of teachers in K-12 and college lecture rooms as ChatGPT, intelligent tutoring systems and adaptive learning systems become trendier. It also points out the advantages of Artificial Intelligence (AI), i.e., the relief of teachers, individualization of the lesson and valuable data about business. The topics of interest are the willingness to teach, qualified tuition programs, and the effects that it may have on relationships between students and their teachers and AI-based teaching methods. These insights are collected with the help of research

DOI: 10.4018/979-8-3373-4621-2.ch010

techniques that range between surveys, focus groups, literature reviews, and case studies. This review points to the significance of listening to the voices of teachers, acknowledging their concerns, and giving them the resources, training, and guidance on successful integration of AI. It also calls to the ethical design and deployment of AI, with the emphasis on fairness, openness and accountability.

INTRODUCTION

The Education is talking about the boom of deep AI, in particular, of the ChatGPT and other instruments of similar types. In one hand, AI can add opportunities to enhance the teaching-learning aspects unfamiliar to the educators; in other hand, these tools cannot be called disruptive since the educator is afraid of plagiarism and exacerbation of student-teacher relationship. Although they raise concerns issued by the opinion that the ChatGPT can collect complex tests, the authors have ended up stating that AI is not always a threat. Rather, it ought to be highly incorporated so as to support the conventional teaching. The teachers will be able to concentrate on building on quality learning experiences since functions, like manning extensions and attendance checking, will be handled by the computers with the aid of AI (Al-Mughairi & Bhaskar, 2024).

Teachers lack the facilities and expertise to enable Student-AI Collaboration (SAC). This is a dynamic interaction and adaptation which cause pedagogical challenges with AI compared to traditional tools. The teachers should develop effective connections between students and AI without specific guidelines. This study attempts to narrow that gap by exploring how leading Korean teachers conceptualize a successful design with AI in the role of a co-learner. Their ideas could help not only in curriculum development and teacher preparation but also in educational policies and classroom environments where an AI would augment but not replace student learning (Venugopal & Mamatha, 2023).

With the spread of spam-bots, virtual assistants, and self-driving cars, AI technologies, educational systems need to prepare students to live in the world driven by AI. Other countries such as Germany are in the process to implement AI in K-12. With the spread of spam-bots, virtual assistants, and self-driving cars, AI technologies, educational systems need to prepare students to live in the world driven by AI. Germany and other countries have initiated the plans to incorporate AI in K-12 education. The teacher preparation is however, crucial towards successful integration as much as the curriculum and resources. Many teaching materials are not exploited as they fail to consider the views, requirements and expertise of the teachers. This paper outlines the importance of ensuring that the opinion of teachers is factored in making the AI curricula. To explore this, the authors surveyed German computer science lecturers in order to find out about their current knowledge, aims, and the perceived challenges of teaching AI. The study aims to give directions on how to improve teacher preparation and help in the effective teaching of AI (Fahimirad & Kotamjani, 2018).

It points to the challenges faced by educators because of subpar infrastructure and training of AI in education (AIED). The framework of distributed cognition is used to see learning settings, filtered contact with AI, the curriculum organization, and the progression of SAC. The assumptions about imagining AI as a collaborative agent as opposed to an object that should merely be used serve the goal of informing teaching strategies, educational policies, and the design of AI to enhance SAC (Kolchenko, 2018).

AI is a part of computer science that enables machines to perform such functions as speech recognition, decision-making with the help of analysing large volumes of data. The aspect AI in education brings is that intelligent tutoring and adaptive reviews, and custom learning become feasible, bringing focus out of the teacher-centric approach to a more student-centric approach. Despite the power it gives the teachers and interactive learning, it has its setbacks such as prohibitive costs, inexperience, and ethical issues such as prejudice and privacy. Schools have to work on human skills and higher-order thinking to complement AI and represent a balance between technical and interpersonal skills, where the displacement of the workforce is avoided (Kim et al., 2022).

By putting emphasis on the design frames of successful AI instructional strategies, teachers perceive teaching sustainable AI within K-12 environments. The lack of adequate knowledge of AI, outdated methods of educating technology, and other barriers prevents the effective work of teachers even though the increasing influence of AI on many aspects of social life makes its teaching desirable to become part of school curricular and it is possible to achieve through the results to enhance AI education, offer curriculum construction recommendations, and support the working progress of teachers (Celik et al., 2022).

Through its personal assistance, ChatGPT assists teachers in creating lesson plans, individual tasks, and research questions on different subjects. It can increase engagement and the effectiveness of teaching, but, at the same time, it evokes concerns concerning the lack of human interaction, ethical issues, and over-dependence, which, possibly, will influence collaboration and teacher-student relationships. To educate policymakers and service providers and ensure that the benefits of ChatGPT are maximized without compromising the quality of education, the study tries to determine the issues that affect its adoption. Through addressing these dynamics, aiming at guiding the integration of ChatGPT and other AI tools to facilitate creative and effective teaching processes to accomplish success in higher education. The abovementioned feelings can be described as the feeling of not fitting in and the feeling of being overwhelmed by the weight of life (Celik et al., 2022).

Analysing the transformative possibility of AI in college education in terms of its application in the teaching and learning processes, explores the powerful uses of AI in universities. An example of how AI in the form of systems that imitate human-like operations such as learning and decision-making is transforming the educational practices is machine learning and intelligent tutoring. It suggests that Deakin University approach with IBM Watson as a student advising tool indicates how AI can be used to enhance the quality of services. It examines the opportunity of AI to promote the efficiency of the institution, automation, and personalization of learning. However, these disadvantages include high costs and other ethical issues (Popenici & Kerr, 2017).

The article by Popenici and Kerr (2017) studies the changes in the sphere of higher education led by the revolutionary power of AI. The concept behind AI, that is, systems that emulate the processes of human beings i.e. learning and problem-solving, is transforming pedagogy as well as the service offered by the universities. The demonstration of the capability of AI to enhance administrative efficiency is given by such tools as Watson presented by IBM at the Deakin University, whereas the advancement in the area of machine learning (such as the production of AlphaGo), suggests possible applications in the sphere of education in the future (Popenici & Kerr, 2017). Individually-tailored resources and pace, where AI, computing that replicates human processes such as thinking and learning, is defined, will allow personalized learning. Applications like intelligent tutoring systems are aimed at acting as virtual tutors and being able to adapt to the requirements of every specific student. Education is an intricate combination that requires human intelligence, although AI demonstrates its perfection in applications, such as radiology and chess (Lin et al., 2022). Teachers can resort to focused interventions by using AI and observe students. To determine classroom dynamics with the use of story completion technique of AI, students and teachers. It points to three problems: the decontextualization of AI-teacher collaboration that poses the question of bias and power unbalances; and impact of AI on student behaviour that can isolate its success (Lindner et al., 2019).

This chapter examines how AI and teachers could work together to improve the learning environment and make it more efficient and interesting. Through more individualized and engaging learning experiences, the interaction between teachers and students can be improved by incorporating AI into the educational process. The chapter also mentions new idea of Student-AI Collaboration (SAC), in which AI is viewed as a cognitive partner that facilitates the formation of shared knowledge amongst intelligent systems, professors, and students rather than merely as a tool. A bibliometric analysis that charts the research landscape on this developing collaboration is also included in the chapter, emphasizing significant publications, emerging trends, and potential paths for AI-assisted education. In the end, the chapter also presents a bibliometric analysis that highlights the interdisciplinary evolution of teacher-AI collaboration, emphasizing pedagogical innovation, AI ethics, and teacher training as key research clusters from 1989 to 2025 by taking the data from Lens and using software like VOSViewer and Origin for figure generation.

LITERATURE REVIEW

AI in education first occurred in the 1960s when the first interactive learning systems such as the PLATO and ELIZA were developed. These tools gave the basis to modern AI uses, such as individual content delivery, dynamic online educational platforms, and immediate feedback mechanisms. The current situation is that AI is used by educators to identify learning gaps, individualize materials and speed up the evaluation process. However, the literature notes that much of the AI tools nowadays become available are represented as the so-called one-size-fits-all and are not ground-based on pedagogical aspects. It is feared that this over-reliance on AI could curtail critical thinking, inventiveness and the human aspects of lesson delivery that are unique to students. Specifically, when it comes to such aspects of education as motivation and pastoral care, this shows the need to develop a balance between the effectiveness of AI, and the emotional intelligence and situational awareness of human educators (Al-Mughairi & Bhaskar, 2024). In the context of the levels of the remembering and applying of knowledge (Bloom Taxonomy), they propose that the teaching activities, using the preceding conference article, can be categorized into two major levels. These tasks are then plotted on a Teacher-AI Task Spectrum that divides up the tasks that cannot be automated and those that can be based on how much of a human touch they need. A case in point is an audience in which human teachers are necessitated in the low mentality order and management roles though creativity, evaluation, and emotional services and support still require human teacher. The model recommends co-led areas, particularly, in the concept analysis and application. The objective is to find the optimal forms of collaboration between AI and educators in order to facilitate a more individualized, efficient and learner-driven teaching practice within a fast-tracking digital learning landscape (Al-Mughairi & Bhaskar, 2024). International communities are increasingly accepting the notion that young people must be educated on the use of AI at an early age as it continues to permeate the society. But the preparedness and the willingness of teachers in teaching AI will be a significant factor in implementing AI in the school curriculums. Since most teachers are not trained and experienced in teaching AI, the study investigates the aspects impacting teacher intention and willingness to teach AI, such as perceived usefulness, teacher attitudes, and confidence (Ayanwale et al., 2022). That is with an emphasis on how countries such as China and the UK are currently implementing AI into their K-12 curriculum already, begins by examining the evolution of AI in the world and the increased presence in education. Similar to the case of traditional literacy in terms of reading or math, AI is cited in the literature where it is important in future careers. Nevertheless, there is still insufficient AI education in most institutions especially in Africa. As research has shown, even in instances whereby educational tools and resources are present, teachers still feel ill-equipped to impart knowledge on the concepts of AI. Adversities include a shortage of professional growth, poor incorporation of curriculum, and fear of technology. The perspectives of teachers are often not considered in studies in the field of AI education, although the opinions of students are taken into consideration (Ayanwale et al., 2022). About 350 elementary to high school teachers were surveyed in the context of a study, which was quantitatively focused. The participants were of diverse origin (rural and urban), type of school (private and public), and backgrounds of teaching experiences. To assess variables, such as AI anxiety, AI perceived usefulness, AI to social good, confidence in teaching AI, and behavioural intention to teach AI, used a questionnaire, which had been designed in a structured form and adapted based on validated studies. The data were analysed and examined in terms of their relation to other variables with the help of Partial Least Squares Structural Equation Modelling (PLS-SEM). The results were that readiness and intentions to teach AI were greatly anticipated using perceived relevance, favourable feeling, and confidence in teaching AI. Surprising, the social good and AI anxiety were not predictors of outcomes (Ayanwale et al., 2022). The two major ways in which AI can be used in education that are reported in the literature are teaching using AI and teaching about AI. However, this approach to AI based on tools overlooks its cooperative, social, and interacting capabilities. The paper then changes to Student-AI Collaboration (SAC) where AI is seen as a tool in the distributed cognition where the knowledge will be shared among teachers, students and in the AI. To be based on the aspects of interaction, environment and co-evolution, four dimensions of new model curriculum in relation to SAC is proposed. Students adopt the role of active problem solvers as opposed to that of passive learners. The role of IH has also changed in form of being a learning agent rather than a toolbox. The problem of AI in the classroom continues to have teachers at its core. Along with offering a fixed material, this model can allow to have a look at the role of the AI in supporting the more significant, personal, and interactive learning (Venugopal & Mamatha, 2023). Schools related to AI have a better understanding of whether AI can be well implemented in the classroom or not. Both primary and secondary teachers composed it using purposeful snowball sampling technique, and they had prior exposure to AI in education. The 90 to 120 minutes of semi-structured interviews were conducted either face to face or through zoom. Both deductive and inductive thematic analysis evaluated and recorded these. The four domains of insight coded by researchers were learning environment, student-AI interaction, curriculum design, and the creation of SAC. Their transcripts were cross-checked by trailers. This is based on their practical classroom experiences in identifying the challenges, essential resources, and imagination processes in the generation of AI inclusive experiences in developing in the K-12 scenario (Venugopal & Mamatha, 2023). The broadness of approaches in AI as machine learning, logic, and natural language processing, makes it hard to define. AI is often scaled down by the layperson to machine learning, even though it also involves larger concepts, such as knowledge representation, reasoning and symbolic vs. sub-symbolic systems. AI, such as neural networks, works with implicit knowledge representation, as does the symbolic AI, such as the rules within an expert system. Most of the learning resources overlook the essential precepts and focus on the latest topics such as machine learning. Also, there is a lack of evidence on the attitude from a secondary teacher about AI. This underlines the necessity to study the perception and application of AI in the classroom by educators so that to shape equitable and effective instructional strategies. Its focus on dynamic, social interactions contrasts to traditional view of AI as a tool ("learning with AI" or "learning about AI"). SAC model includes curriculum (learning objectives, content, and assessment), student-AI interactions (cognitive, socio-emotional, and artifact-centered), environments (learning spaces, institutions and culture), and temporal change. Due to the autonomy and human-like features, AI can serve as peers or tutors as they encourage cognitive and emotional development. Educators remain fundamental participants in assisting SAC in maintaining a balance between human opinions and AI-generated data information. It shows how interdisciplinary curricula, computational thinking, and supportive environment can help the optimal SAC to be developed (Kolchenko, 2018). Qualitative methodology in the study was based on semi-structured interviews with ten Korean teachers that were selectively and snowball-sampled by the authors. As a result of COVID-19, the 90-120-minute interviews were conducted mostly over Zoom, with two of them in person. A hybrid inductive-deductive thematic analysis appealing to the components of the SAC model (curriculum, interaction, environment, and evolution) was used to analyze the transcripts. There were new themes identified through inductive theme identification following the deductive derivation of the initial codes. Researchers revealed themes iteratively and achieved reliability by having discussions with team members, including the verification of transcripts of the participants. Informed consent and the ethical approval were obtained. The analysis yielded 23 themes addressing four research questions and provided insights on how to design SAC in K-12 education (Kolchenko, 2018). There are six types of TAC that are identified: (One Teach, One Observe, One Teach, One Assist, Co-teaching in Stations, Parallel Teaching). The teachers have a sense that TAC is improving their professional growth, teaching design and pedagogy of instructions, and getting rid of grades. The barriers are dominance of business-based AI, imprecise bases of curricula, the deficit of ethical frameworks, and the poor mindsets of instructors towards AI, however (Koh et al., 2023). Intelligent tutoring, adaptive systems, profiling, and associated assessments, which are AI powered educational tools (Zawacki-Richter et al., 2019). It refers to classroom AI-based analysis tools that monitor a student behavior as a guidance of instruction, including facial and emotional recognition (Holstein et al., 2018). Privacy, bias, and fairness are the primary ethical issues (Tsai et al., 2020), whereas less research is known regarding the socio-technical effects on students (McKay et al., 2021). It also highlights a research gap in relation to student perspectives and endorses the user-driven and HCI-inspired research to prevent some unanticipated effects and ensure a moral transition to AI in education (Lindner et al., 2019). Even though TAC helps ensure better teacher efficacy and individual learning, its challenges comprise teacher illiteracy to AI and AI contextual shortcomings (Crescenzi-Lanna, 2023). Ethical concerns, such as bias and data privacy, are also essential, even though they have been insufficiently studied (Holmes et al., 2022). To ensure that educators do not lose control when harnessing the benefits of AI to deliver effective classroom experience, that highlights that there is a gap in workable TAC (Type Allocation Code) models as well as encourages human-centric design of AI (Koh et al., 2023). Six types of TAC and related benefits and drawbacks were considered using eflective thematic analysis of the conversational Chinese interviews that were held between March and April 2023. The scenarios included the coverage of AI tools, like dashboards and intelligent tutoring systems. With the proofs given by professionals and validation by respondents, ethical consent was ensured and reliability in data was accomplished. This allows controlling the sample size restrictions and the lack of direct AI contact without testing AI in the real world but focusing on how teachers perceive TAC in order to construct them in the future (Koh et al., 2023). Nevertheless, this very concept of applying robots based on AI as teachers is still regaining its grounds in the background of the strides in the development of the sphere of robotics and AI, though, in view of the emergence of ChatGPT. The authors believe that AI teachers will enable the flexibility of the teaching to be increased, learning levels become more equal, and will help solve the teacher shortage crisis that has been witnessed globally. In spite of this, their efficacy, morality and the end result they have on social development of students comes into question (Malik & Shah, 2025). Early history of teaching robot is also mentioned, beginning with the LOGO Turtle in 1970s and advancing to present-day human like robots, such as Pepper, Kaspar, Keeko, and Iris. Japan, China, Korea, and India use robots in the classrooms to instruct language, narrate stories as well as interrelate with students with special needs. Such division categorizes the functions of AI in education into two primary categories: AI as a teacher (a teacher robot that provides knowledge directly) and the other as a tool (such as digital assistants or learning platforms). Former has received quite a number of studies but on the latter, not so much has been done (Malik & Shah, 2025). The theories and informal practices formulated and the existing bodies of knowledge are put together to measure the role played by AIs in the capacity of teachers. They divide the categories of AI use into a model that describes different AI roles, which include teaching aides to an individual classroom teacher, and discuss certain case studies in different countries. This is capped off with four suggested strategies of co-teaching with human and AI teachers including (1) human teaching with the assistant of AI, (2) team teaching, (3) instruction with AI and human support in case of struggling learners, and (4) AI that acts as the main teacher, with the human teacher acting as an observer and providing a backup. The purpose of these models is to take the best experiences of both entities and reduce the weakness of these entities to the maximum (Malik & Shah, 2025). AI makes the applications such as chatbots, virtual reality, and personalized learning platforms such as possible, including rule-based systems, machine learning, and deep learning. Such resources provide data-based information, enhance student engagement and differentiate instruction. Nevertheless, some challenges exist regarding ethical issues, which are algorithm bias, data privacy, and job destruction. This identifies the role played by AI in propelling education towards student centered approaches, including the fact that AI is assisting in intelligent tutoring and adaptive assessments. It similarly focuses on fair access and moral application to deal with disparities. To ensure that AI complements the human capacities and builds a balanced educational ecosystem that maximizes the learning process, teachers can foster creativity and critical thinking of their students (Kim et al., 2022). It compiles the results of reports, case studies, and scholarly journals in order to explore the issue of AI application, such as intelligent tutoring and personalized learning. The methodology is devoted to establishing the benefits, challenges, and ethical inferences of adopting AI. Ensuring the information was relevant to the context of India, the data were collected based on reputable sources, which include the reports published by institutions and materials on educational technology. They were used in categorizing the results of the study (using thematic analysis) into themes such as; implementation barriers, faculty empowerment and student engagement. Nevertheless, despite some limitations of the study such as its use of secondary data, the research presents a valid foundation of understanding the revolutionary character of AI in postsecondary teaching and learning (Kim et al., 2022). Effective AI lesson schemes in the process of exploring the teachers experience design in technology learning. It highlights the unique socio-technical needs of AI that render traditional technology teaching and learning methods (problem-based and cooperative learning, etc.) inadequate in teaching AI. The design frames like pedagogical and knowledge-based approaches are meant to help the teachers surmount nonroutine AI teaching problems. Based on new research, to encourage student engagement, the learning community needs to place an exceptional emphasis on the ethical consequences of AI and its social rewards. To find the ways to integrate current practices into the AI pedagogy, the review also points to the deficiencies of our knowledge about the teachers-specific design knowledge about AI and offers such frameworks like TPACK. Although AI has already begun to transform education with the technologies of chatbots, dashboards, intelligent tutoring systems, and automated assessments, not all teachers have enough knowledge to employ such tools successfully and ethically. To seal this gap, the intends to append an ethical dimension to the widely used TPACK (Technological Pedagogical Content Knowledge) framework. Out of this there emerges a different structure which the terms as the Intelligent-TPACK. This enlarged framework points out that instructors should understand how to determine the fairness, transparency, inclusivity, accountability of AI tools besides understanding how to use them in instruction. To develop transferable AI teaching instructions that render support to a long-term goal in education, grounded theory is proposed as a method to research the changing experiences of teachers (Celik et al., 2022). To familiarize ourselves with the behavioral intentions of teachers regarding new tools, such as ChatGPT, the literature review has employed models, such as TAM, UTAUT, and DOI to study the technologies adoption in the sphere of education, particularly post-COVID-19. The adoption of ChatGPT by teachers has been rather underexplored, yet the recent studies highlight the benefits of using it, including automation of time-consuming processes and individual learning. There are mixed views regarding ChatGPT; qualitative and quantitative research show that some individuals are thankful to the practicality and usability of ChatGPT, whereas others are dissatisfied due to ethical and reliability concerns. To create a conceptual framework on future studies of the AI implementation into education, the review identifies the necessity to explore certain motivators and obstacles to the use of ChatGPT by teachers (Celik et al., 2022). The literature review traces the history of AI in education beginning with Turing intelligence tests in the 50s and continuing to include the use of AI such as IBM Watson and Google DeepMind. AI enables pattern recognition and adaptive learning, and practices such technologies as smartphones, driverless vehicles, and machine learning. At a higher education level, AI is employed in automation of most administration functions, and extension of individual learning or assistance of students with disabilities by means of the use of brain-computer interfaces. According to the research, AI can enhance learning interest, provide feedback, and transform the work of teachers into a role of facilitators. Nonetheless, the misalignment between pedagogy and cultural resistance in combination with the cost of implementation, as shown by the ludicrous claim of MOOCs, present obstacles. The review focuses on the necessity to find the middle ground between the technological complexity of AI and ethically responsible and innovative learning goals being human-centric (Popenici & Kerr, 2017). The literature review of the paper by Popenici & Kerr (2017) reflects the role of AI in higher education using historical and current sources. It tracks the history of the development of AI, through the imitation game developed in the 1950s by Turing to modern-day machine learning based on an example of DeepMind by Google. The studies say that AI can automate the administrative work and make learning personal, but there are also potential harms such as the inability to handle irony or moral complications. The review criticizes the inflation of expectations by citing unsuccessful attempts in AI like the Tay bot created by Microsoft. It underlines the importance of keeping a sceptic spirit to avoid placing algorithms-based solutions to replace education-based on humans. There is no research in the pedagogical impact of AI and the role of teachers, so it is time to explore the ways in which AI could assist human teachers and not substitute them (Popenici & Kerr, 2017). Drawn upon academic literature, case studies (IBM Watson and Georgia Tech Jill Watson), and media accounts, it draws an overview of the existing body of research on AI in higher education. The evaluation of the applications of AI, as well as their impact on education, learning, and the operation of universities is critical; in this case, it means data gathering. Adopting the humanistic approach, the authors outline the pedagogical and moral implications and propose the future research directions. In finding the benefits and limitations of implementing AI, this inductive strategy aims at giving an impressionable opinion which will assist colleges in applying AI in a responsible manner (Popenici & Kerr, 2017). It can be referred to as the history of AI, beginning with neural networks up to individualized educational programs such as intelligent tutoring systems (Burton et al., 1982). Studies focus on the ability of AI to differentiate education, however, the disadvantages, including the data should be high quality, and a lack of pedagogical knowledge are also noted (Brusilovsky & Peylo, 2003). Their apprehensions as to the unrealistic promises of AI and the growth of gaps in accomplishment (Daniel et al., 2015). It asks that AI systems be made more student-centric and focused on the context and identifies a knowledge gap in the focus on investigating the impact of AI on educational inequity (Lin et al., 2022). The methodology includes the analysis of the interactions that students have with adaptive learning (AL) programs provided by publishers across multiple semesters. The area of data collection is the difference in engagement of motivated/distracted students and it is determined by student surveys, observations in the classroom and trends in the AL use. This highlights the data-driven aspect of AI and its weaknesses in using inputs of low quality through the inclusion of literature to inform against the backdrop of the findings. This exploratory procedure aims to attract attention to the issues of AI-driven education in the real world and offer some recommendations to future research concerning the equitable AA design (Lin et al., 2022). Although AIEd enhances evaluation, individualization, and prophesy, privacy, bias, and justice are the primary moral risks. But most of these discussions overlook student opinions and are not empirical-based. The HCI and CSCW research disclose the unintentional sociotechnical consequences, including easier-to-read student data and increased biases, that are a part of unintended sociotechnical consequences. The gap in knowledge that needs to be filled with information about the broader implications of AIEd on classroom dynamics and academic results as well as requests user-empirical research to addressing these questions and ensuring that the use of AIEd is not only morally sound but as successful implementation that considers the demands of all stakeholders (Lindner et al., 2019). The SCM (School Management C) explore the concerns held by students about the AI-driven education in higher learning. There were three story completion tasks in the form of scenarios to elicit 65 narratives by college students. Facial recognition was one of the AI-powered technologies present at that point. Qualtrics helped to collect anonymous information among the Australian demographics. One of the ideas that were identified by applying reflexive thematic analysis concerned the contextual restrictions of AI and its relations to power. The method concentrates on the socially constructed perception of the students without involving the real-life test because it will cause ethical harm. With the help of the Ethics Committee of the University of Melbourne, it is also planned to outline the anticipated socio-technical issues in classroom interaction to be used in guiding ethical design of AI-driven design (Lindner et al., 2019). Three AIEd scenarios that involved facial recognition, emotion analysis, and personalized learning profiles were designed, and 65 people (recruited in China and Australia) completed narratives using them. The scenarios were developed to simulate with the ethical approval of The University of Melbourne ethically using scenarios on published AIEd literature. Speculative approach of SCM avoided testing AI in the real world, focusing instead his socially constructed concerns of the students. Among the limitations, there is the framing biases that manifest in potential scenarios, and a lack of younger students to participate; in the future studies, a broader scope of stakeholders and real-life conditions of AIEd should be considered (Lindner et al., 2019). Every student should be able to develop at least the basic knowledge of AI and understanding its consequences as the explosive development of the technology is transforming every industry as well as society. Nevertheless, there are not enough relevant curricula, national standards, and teacher preparation, which constitutes a barrier to access to AI education in schools. The designing and implementation of the AI Methods in Data Science (AIMSinDS) course and the professional development (PD) program that provide content knowledge and pedagogical skills to high school educators to teach AI to high school students. Its project aims at introducing AI into existing STEM education by applying an inclusive and age-appropriate approach (Lee et al., 2022). The theoretical background of this project is the intersection of data science, AI, science, technology, engineering, and mathematics education and ethics. Whereas AI is increasingly becoming pertinent, the authors also note that it has so far been covered strictly in the upper-level math-intensive courses that high school students can often not even have access to. Two of the recent frameworks that help to implement AI in K-12 learning along with the Next Generation Science Standards (NGSS) are the AI4K12. Nevertheless, it is not seen that much inculcating AI, a variety of reasons that can be attributed to the lack of proper preparation on behalf of teachers. Several studies on AI literacy reveal that students show promising results when concepts of AI are taught in interactive and hands-on form and connected with real-life use. Nevertheless, teaching AI in regular courses in the long run and bringing about equity in learning outcomes may be more effective than creating specialized electives (Lee et al., 2022). These five core courses of the curriculum: Data Analytics, Decision Trees, Machine Learning, Neural Networks and Transfer Learning were developed with undergraduate students. These units are driven by a scaffolded learning model introduce real-world learning progressing to a practical exercise of coding in Google Colab. The study took 19 STEM high school teachers located in different regions in the U.S. who were involved in two of one-week professional development workshops held in 2021. The data was obtained via pre- and post-tests, exit tickets to determine the daily performance, and attitude surveys. Teachers modified AI models through coding, explored ethical considerations, and participated in lessons as students. The results proved the educator's gained knowledge and skills regarding AI, particularly in such topics as neural networks (Lee et al., 2022). To ensure a successful adoption of AI-powered educational technology (AI-EdTech) to the classrooms, the proposed study determines how the implementation of AI-EdTech can make K-12 teachers trust the technology. Although AI continues to develop increasingly in the classroom, a significant group of educators remains skeptical or even against using AI, often due to misconceptions, fear of losing their jobs, and ignorance of how this technology functions. In those cases, when there is some question of technology such as automated grading systems, trust is all the more important. We need to unfold the value of AI but also help educators feel safe and in control till the use of these technologies. That is why the researchers designed the professional development program (PDP) that would introduce educators to AI-based assessment system (AI-Grader) in an attempt to enhance their understanding (Nazaretsky et al., 2022). There is the AI tool, which is called AI-Grader, the system that provides the analysis of open-ended responses by students in biology and is rooted in Natural Language Processing (NLP). It was deliberate to subject the intervention to an atmosphere of vulnerability and uncertainty as the teachers would be requested to deploy AI-graded reports to their own real students. This structure imitated decision-making, decision stakes, both of which are pre-eminent in investigating trust. In order to create awareness and become familiar with expectations, this program had descriptions of AI capabilities and limitations included, and a creative exercise was built around what they called a Masked Rater, where teachers were blinded to their grading being compared to other teachers, experts and AI system (Nazaretsky et al., 2022). To build the Intelligent-TPACK framework, some of the basic learning theories and studies regarding educational technology had to be employed. The traditional model of TPACK field incorporates three core areas of teacher knowledge: content knowledge (CK), pedagogical knowledge (PK) and technological knowledge (TK) and the interactions of these three areas (TCK, TPK and TPACK), in order to ensure that the general approach to AI integration is realized. However, these are not enough in the AI-powered learning environment. AI systems can bring such ethical concerns as bias in the making of decisions, lack of transparency, or equal accessibility. As such, the teachers should also possess an understanding of ethics, i.e., be in a position to question or argue the judgment made by AI (Celik, 2022). The research went through two main stages. In Stage 1, the Intelligent-TPACK scale, a new survey instrument to measure the knowledge of teachers consequently into five themes: TK, TPK, TCK, TPACK and Ethics, was developed and approved by the author. Stage 2 developed and tested a structural equation model (SEM) to explore the interdependencies between the Intelligent-TPACK components. The model tested was based on the scale, with EFA and CFA used to test the scale, and the result indicated the scale to have good internal consistency and validity. The model was tested on 219 teachers in the second sample (Celik, 2022). The perspectives of teachers form the knowledge gap since prior studies about the education about AI had been dominated by those focusing on the student side of the spectrum. This gap is explored by exploring the attitude of in-service teachers towards the implementation of AI education in classes as well as their experience of AI training of teachers, as the teachers are considered to be key personnel of K-12 learning. The information regarding general perceptions was collected through online survey The findings are significant illumination on teacher readiness and issues and the need to understand the perspective to ensure a successful implementation of the AI in classrooms (Lee et al., 2024). This argues the point that, teachers are vital in effective adoption of AI in K-12 learning and therefore, it is critical to understand their perceptions. It shows that the literature has a gap, which has been evident through the lack of focus on the real-life demands and challenges of educators in the process of using AI technologies and taking advantage of relevant training efforts. Consequently, the research places itself in a position to assist through providing an insight into this under-represented sphere (Lee et al., 2024). The two common tools in the methodology that were employed to collect data were a focus group interview and an online survey. aimed to measure the opinion of teachers regarding AI education as the means of teaching in the classroom setting. A smaller group of four teachers was then interviewed using focus group to explore further their thoughts and experiences with teacher training programs that use AI. The survey findings were analyzed as descriptive statistics and the focus group discussions were analyzed qualitatively which was likely to be thematic to identify critical perceptions and challenges (Lee et al., 2024). By focusing on the conceptualization of AI in the field, this tries to summarize the body of research about the impacts of AI in education. This gathers information through PRISMA model to bring some light on the way AI is perceived and integrated into the delivery of teaching methods. It also speaks about the significant role that educators play in this changing environment and it aims at getting them prepared with some knowledge on the possibilities and challenges of AI. The review provides educators, researchers, and policymakers with a basic knowledge level of the fast-growing phenomenon, AIED. It strives to prepare the groundwork of the following developments and ensure that AI can be effectively used to foster the teaching and learning process by shedding light on the theoretical frameworks (Lameras & Arnab, 2022). It examines conceptualization of AIED, such as intelligent tutoring and personalized learning system. Along with some valuable benefits, such as increasing efficiency and learning opportunities, the review talks about such negative aspects as the privacy issues of data, ethical issues, and the need to prepare teachers. Even though AI has the potential to act as a game-changer, its implementation requires a good understanding of its pedagogical implication and involvement of teachers (Lameras & Arnab, 2022). In order to have exhaustive evidence collection, a systematic approach was utilized by following PRISMA (Preferred Reporting Items for Systematic Reviews and Meta-Analyses) framework. The methodology involved drawing specific research questions to guide the literature search and subsequently, a wide search was conducted in the relevant databases. In selecting the studies that would be of relevance to the concept of AI in Education (AIED), there were inclusion and exclusion criteria. The primary objectives of the data extraction were related to finding significant themes, definitions, and effects of AI in education. To achieve this purpose, a robust systematic process aimed at synthesizing data and identifying frequent similarities and gaps in an existing body of literature (Lameras & Arnab, 2022). The psychological and educational factors that have impact on the readiness of K-12 teachers to use AI in their curriculum. The exploratory qualitative study was conducted among 66 teachers with 11 different disciplines in one of the private schools in Turkey. The participants attended a professional development course on AI enhanced instruction. According to the results of the analyses of online discussion forums and AI-supported learning activity design tasks, teachers valued the effectiveness, interactivity, and flexibility of AI, particularly when they used such tools as ChatGPT. However, they came up with some significant blockers, including cultural barriers, ethical issues, curriculum mismatch and technical issues. The paper arrives at the conclusion that to effectively roll out AI, funds and specific assistance must be present in order to overcome all these challenges (Filiz et al., 2025). Via its focus on the importance of studying the factors that can affect the preparedness among teachers in regards to AI, it can review the current situation implicitly. During the discussion, it is stated that, although AI can transform the field of education, the successful use of this trend presupposes adequate understanding and consideration of the voice of teachers. This incorporates their didactic and mental sides, the supposed benefits of AI-based instruments such as ChatGPT, and the challenges they face, which can be technical problems, ethical objections, or curriculum congruence, and are often overlooked in the broader debate about the use of AI in education (Filiz et al., 2025). One hundred and eleven private school teachers in Turkey with a K-12 background representing their subject areas sixty-six participated in a course on AI-based instruction as part of their professional learning. The data acquisition had two primary methods shared among AI-assisted learning activity design tasks that presented teachers with information about their real-life use of AI tools and online discussion forums where their opinions and experiences could be shared. As a qualitative approach, inductive thematic analysis allowed identifying some common themes and patterns related to teacher attitudes, problems, and needs regarding the application of AI in education due to the collected information (Filiz et al., 2025). In order to determine the view of teachers toward AI, a questionnaire will be that of the TPACK framework that passes a test regarding the knowledge of a teacher, whether content, pedagogical, or technological. The survey was also sent to 37 German secondary school instructors of computer science prior to them participating in an AI-teaching workshop. Participants represented regions and experienced different levels of expertise in AI. The online questionnaire had five core questions with the following topics: knowledge on the concepts of AI, experience in teaching, the preferred curriculum alterations, educational intentions, and the perceived barriers. Reputable textbooks were used to identify the keywords related to AI to test the knowledge of the contents and the distractor words to test the correctness in their answers. The expected outcome was to obtain general idea of teacher knowledge and to use it in further curriculum development and teacher training programs in the field of AI education (Fahimirad & Kotamjani, 2018).

BIBLIOMETRIC ANALYSIS

The network clustering visualization, which was made with VOSviewer and based on bibliometric data obtained from the Lens database for the years 1989 to 2025, is shown in Figure 1. The co-occurrence network of author keywords used in publications centered on teacher-AI collaboration is depicted in the image. Each node stands for a keyword, and its size indicates how frequently it appears in the dataset. The connecting lines, or edges, indicate how strongly keywords co-occur. The modularity-based algorithm in VOSviewer produced the color-coded clusters, which each represent a different thematic domain that together create the intellectual framework of the field of study. With phrases like "AI in education," "teacher collaboration," "pedagogical innovation," and "digital learning," the red cluster symbolizes the incorporation of AI into teaching and learning processes. Research examining how AI technologies enhance teaching methods, student-teacher interactions, and classroom innovation is highlighted in this cluster. The green cluster's main buzzwords include "machine learning," "data-driven education," "student performance," and "adaptive learning." It is focused on learning analytics, intelligent systems, and machine learning. It illustrates the analytical and computational aspects of teacher-AI collaboration, in which AI helps teachers analyze student learning patterns and tailor their lessons. With phrases like "teacher education," "AI literacy," "curriculum design," and "digital pedagogy," the blue cluster places a strong emphasis on professional development and training for teachers in AI environments. The efforts to get instructors ready for the successful integration of AI tools in the classroom are encapsulated in this theme. With phrases like "AI ethics," "education policy," and "human-AI interaction," the yellow cluster addresses the socio-ethical and regulatory aspects of implementing AI in education. It also focuses on ethics, policy, and human-centered design. When taken as a whole, these clusters show that research on teacher-AI collaboration covers a wide range of topics, including pedagogy, technology, and ethics, illustrating the development of a more interdisciplinary academic environment.

Figure 1. Bibliometric analysis on teacher AI collaboration with data from lens and made using VOSViewer: network clustering

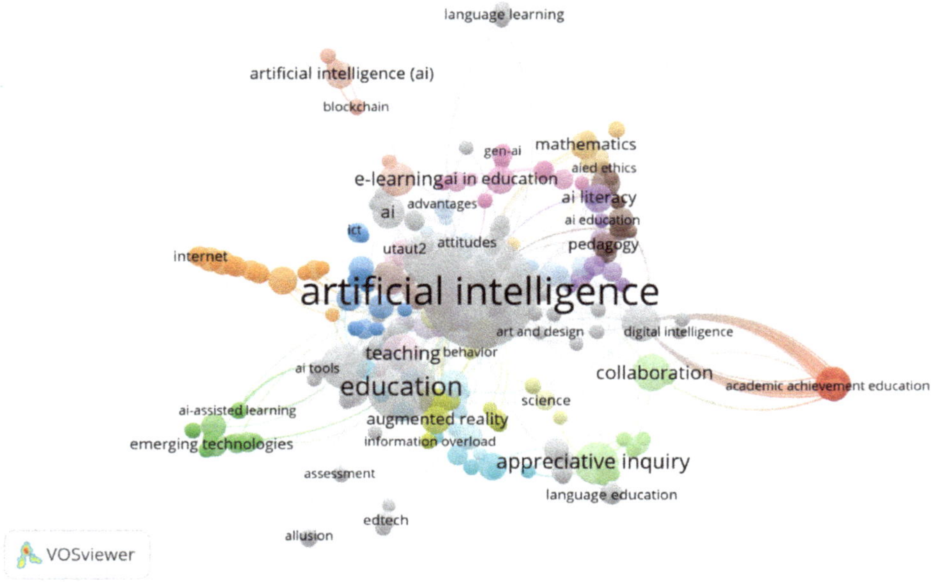

Based on the same dataset, Figure 2 shows a density visualization map created with VOSviewer that illustrates the distribution and level of research activity in the field of teacher–AI collaboration. A keyword is represented by each point on the map, and the color intensity shows how frequently and relevantly the term appears in the dataset. Regions with high keyword occurrence and strong interconnectedness are indicated by areas tinted in red and yellow, which indicate study topics that have drawn a lot of attention. On the other hand, blue and green areas indicate new or uncharted territory. According to the density graphic, terms like "AI in education," "machine learning," "teacher training," "pedagogical innovation," and "learning analytics" are where the most research activity is concentrated. As the main concepts guiding the literature on teacher-AI collaboration, these terms take up the majority of the map's central area. Areas such as "AI ethics," "emotional intelligence," "educational data mining," "digital pedagogy," and "adaptive assessment" are progressively becoming more prominent in peripheral locations. A dynamic shift in focus regions is reflected in the color gradient, which graphically conveys how some once-peripheral subjects have grown more important to modern research. As a result, this figure offers a visual representation of the field's intellectual density, highlighting areas of focus for scholarly research as well as emerging new areas.

Figure 2. Bibliometric analysis on teacher AI collaboration with data from lens and made using VOSViewer: density chart

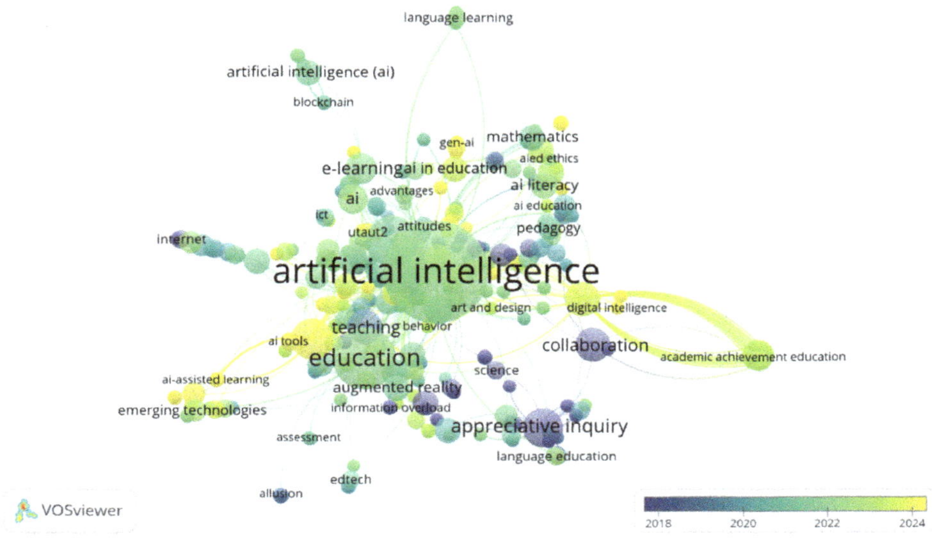

An overlay visualization created with VOSviewer is shown in Figure 3, which gives a chronological overview of the development of research themes in teacher-AI collaboration. Each keyword is color-coded in this graphic according to the average year of publication. More current or developing themes (post-2016) are shown in yellow, mid-phase advances (2005–2015) in green, and earlier study topics (usually from the 1990s to early 2000s) in blue. The overlay graphic makes it abundantly evident that the early stages of digital learning experiments were characterized by studies that concentrated on the fundamentals of computer-assisted instruction, teacher preparation, and educational technology. The shift to green-colored nodes signifies the increasing impact of AI applications in personalized learning and is a reflection of the growth of research on learning analytics, adaptive technologies, and intelligent tutoring systems. The most recent yellow patches, which stand for the continuous change of education through human-AI collaborations, correlate to keywords like “AI ethics,” “machine learning,” “teacher–AI collaboration,” “AI literacy,” and “data-driven pedagogy.” This temporal gradient shows how research goals have changed from simple automation to collaborative intelligence between teachers and AI systems, indicating a clear trend from technology adoption to AI integration.

Figure 3. Bibliometric analysis on teacher AI collaboration with data from lens and made using VOSViewer: density chart

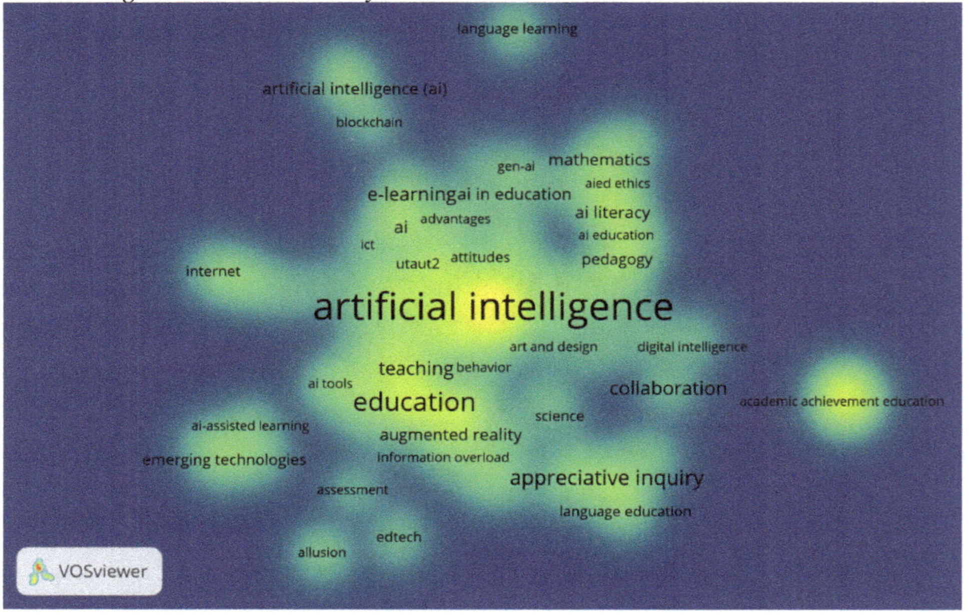

An area map created with Python and displaying the temporal trend of publications about teacher-AI collaboration from 1989 to 2025 is shown in Figure 4. Publication years are represented by the x-axis, while the quantity of documents released each year is shown by the y-axis. The steadily growing region highlights significant junctures of scholarly effort and topic development, reflecting the evolution of research output throughout time. According to the figure, there was comparatively little research activity during the early years (1989–2005), with publications mostly concentrating on the early applications of digital pedagogy and educational computing. There is a discernible increase from 2010 to 2015, which corresponds with the growth of data-driven teaching resources and the worldwide adoption of AI in education. Since 2016, when subjects like AI-assisted learning, teacher professional development in AI contexts, and human–AI collaboration attracted a lot of scholarly attention, the growth has been the sharpest. According to the figure, the years 2020–2025 saw an unparalleled surge in publications, which reflects the quickening of AI integration in education in the wake of the COVID-19 pandemic and other worldwide digital developments. This chart aptly illustrates the evolution of research interest in teacher-AI collaboration from specialized experiments to a high-impact, mainstream area.

Figure 4. Area chart on publications per year on teacher AI collaboration with data from lens

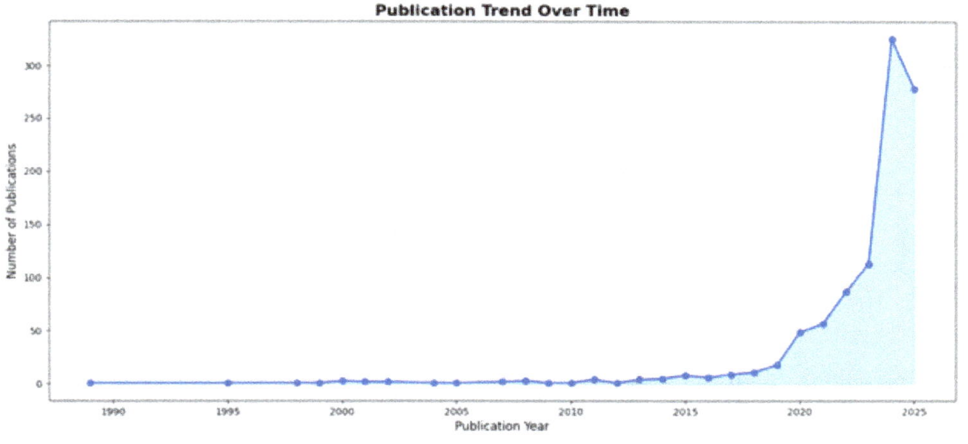

A tree map visualization created in Origin that illustrates the connection between publishing entities and publication years in research on teacher-AI collaboration is shown in Figure 5. The size of each rectangle, which stands for a publisher, reflects the total number of publications the publisher has contributed to the Lens collection. Different time periods are indicated by the color variations (if any) that show the development of publications across the decades. According to the graphic, the leading publishers in this field are Springer Nature, Elsevier, MDPI, IEEE, and Taylor & Francis, who together account for a sizeable amount of research distribution. Journals in computer-assisted learning, artificial intelligence, and educational technology are the main areas of their contributions. Publishers like Wiley, Frontiers, and IGI Global are represented by medium-sized rectangles. These companies have also become significant contributors to interdisciplinary studies that integrate education and artificial intelligence. Contributions from regional or specialist publications are represented by smaller rectangles, indicating a rise in scholarly interest in a variety of educational contexts. A wide and balanced distribution of knowledge across educational ecosystems is ensured by the treemap's structure, which shows that although major international publishers propel mainstream diffusion, specialized academic sources support regional advancements in AI pedagogy.

Figure 5. Word cloud on author keywords on teacher AI collaboration with data from lens

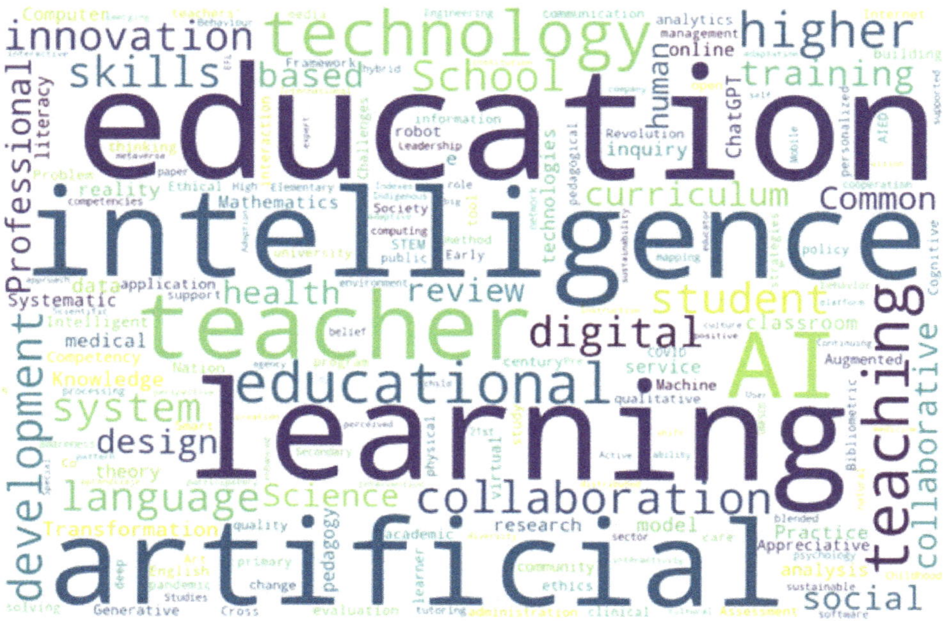

The frequency and significance of author-provided keywords in publications on teacher-AI collaboration are visualized in Figure 6, which is a word cloud created with Python. The size of each word reflects how frequently it occurs, providing a rapid visual comprehension of the key terms that define this field of study. The graphic is dominated by larger terms that indicate their importance in the field: "artificial intelligence," "teacher collaboration," "machine learning," "education," "AI in education," "pedagogical innovation," and "digital learning." Medium-sized phrases like "teacher training," "adaptive learning," "learning analytics," "educational data mining," "AI literacy," and "personalized education" surround these. Together, these terms highlight the pedagogical and technological nexus that characterizes the core of teacher-AI cooperation. Emerging fields of study concentrating on ethical AI integration and professional preparedness are shown by the existence of minor but important terminology like "AI ethics," "curriculum design," "digital transformation," and "human–AI interaction." All things considered, this word cloud illustrates the literature's diverse range of themes and the growing conceptual limits of artificial intelligence in education.

Figure 6. World graph on countries' contribution to teacher AI collaboration research with data from lens

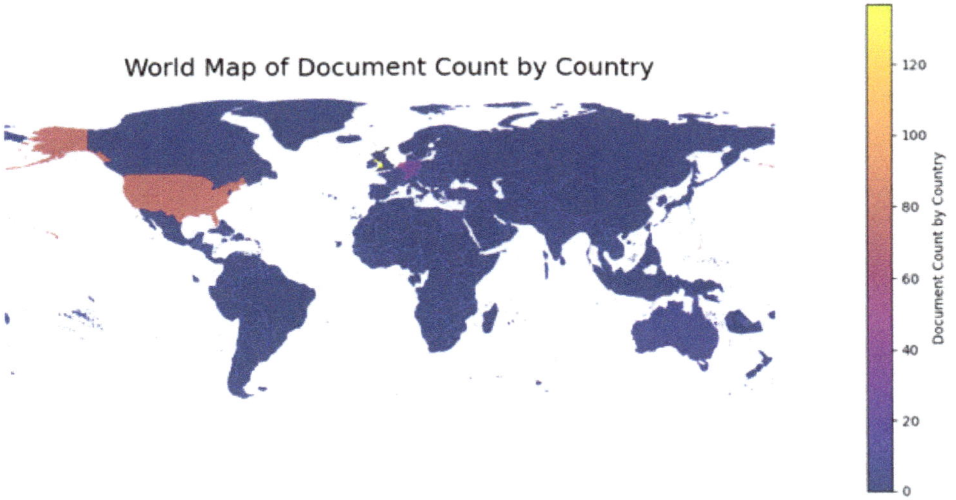

The historical distribution of teacher-AI cooperation papers from 1989 to 2025 across major publishers is shown in Figure 7, a treemap visualization made with Origin using data from Lens.org. With colors designating publishers and hues reflecting annual trends, tile size represents publication volume, with Springer Science and Business Media LLC leading at over 40% (5,329 publications), followed by Elsevier (2,093), SAGE (1,415), and Wiley (1,409). Growing contributions, particularly after 2016, from mid-tier publishers like Emerald (1,212) and IEEE (1,010) as well as specialized firms like Frontiers (490) demonstrate a trend toward human-AI co-teaching in the midst of the COVID-19 digital pivot. An evolutionary arc can be seen in the treemap: Elsevier's moderate early output (1989–2005) at about 100 per year, Springer and Wiley's mid-period spike (2005–2015) using learning analytics, and Springer, Elsevier, and IEEE's enormous post-2016 expansion (70% of volume). With new publishers indicating democratization, this expansion demonstrates a shift from solitary AI experimentation to a cooperative, morally driven sector. This graphic, which comes from Lens.org, highlights the dominance of publishers (Springer and Elsevier at about 60%) while promoting the inclusion of more voices from the Global South, which are underrepresented in AIEd research.

Figure 7. Tree map between publishing year and publishers with data from lens and made using origin

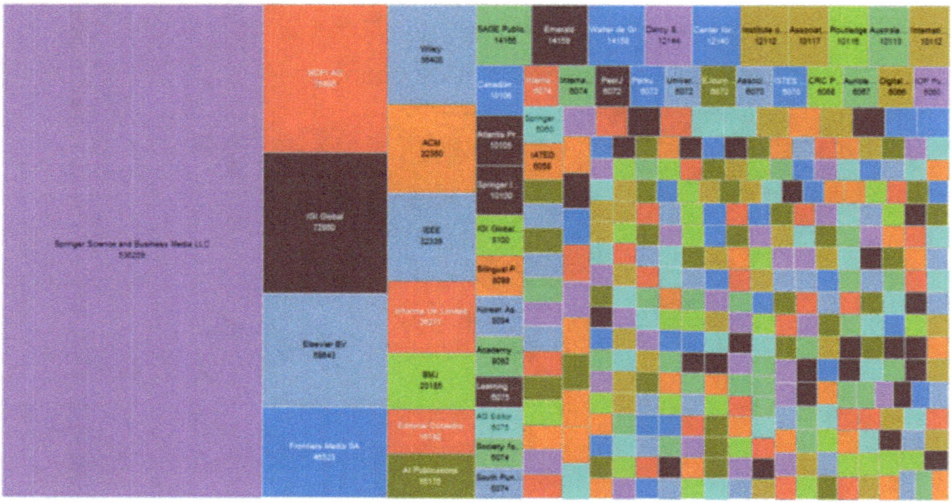

CONCLUSION

Combining, this study, in general, provides the significance of changes to the education caused by AI, as well as the value of exercising caution when introducing this approach, primarily on the side of the educator. Adding AI and making its monitoring a focus of attention, teachers will be able to personalize their teaching, less time is wasted on administration, and students have both immediate guidance and one massive pool of learning, a resource with which they can build their lives. Such advanced tools can allow educators to evaluate each of their students correctly, identify their strengths and areas of improvement, and adjust the classroom time in a way that is more appropriate to an individual. With the AI deployed to assist in the lesson planning, grading, provision of advice and creation of learning materials, teachers will have time to focus on taking care of students and applying their unique skills and expertise. The studies, however, demonstrate that it is necessary to address any issues that may be encountered by the teachers when implementing AI in the classroom actively. Such issues as the risk of biased AI algorithms, the necessity to take care of collecting student information safely, the possibility of using technology excessively, and the threat of AI multiplying inequalities that already exist in the world are all understandable concerns that should not be overlooked. The fact that educators should know the principles of AI and use it comprehensively and even the development of curriculum needs to include a lesson about the morality of AI is clear. Moreover, the studies always note that AI is expected and designed to improve human educators and make them even more efficient at work. Emotional supporting of students, stimulating their creativity, creation of strong relationships with students and adaptation to the needs of everyone are the types of skills that cannot be performed by machines. Teachers' ought to have adequate preparation to evaluate AI tools, alter their usage in their classrooms, and ensure that none of their pupils fails to benefit because of their learning styles. It seems that TAC is the framework worth utilizing to assist schools in working with the AI, treat AI not as a tool, but something useful and valuable as a tutor to teachers. In this manner, we underline that learning is both fast-moving and social, meaning that we need to focus on creating the environments that allow all members of the community such as public members, students, teachers, and AI to communicate, sharing what they know, and learn together as an enjoyable process. Effective AI in education is achieving it as a consideration of the needs of all stakeholders including; students, teachers, administrators, and the entire community. A person needs to be cautious in his or her planning process, often review the outcomes, and has to perform in an ethical and best practice manner, as well as, in response to AI development. With a human element where the resources provided by AI and teachers are combined, students find it easier to acquire essential skills and become prepared to enter the technological society of the future. Along with small-scale TAC models, investigations should be conducted on the practical and large-scale TAC models, addressing the ethical issues, considering the teacher factor, and investigating the impact of AI on the student learning outcomes and the sense of the teachers in the long term. The teachers should also be provided with constant training, guidance, and support to use AI in their practice, solve the arising problems, and become effective leaders in AI-assisted classrooms. The bibliometric analysis, that is performed in the end to understand more about the research trend and importance of some keywords on the related topic, underscores the exponential growth in teacher-AI collaboration research from 1989 to 2025, with emerging clusters in AI ethics, machine learning, and pedagogical innovation, illustrating the field's shift toward interdisciplinary and human-centered educational practices.

REFERENCES

Al-Mughairi, H., & Bhaskar, P. (2024). Exploring the factors affecting the adoption AI techniques in higher education: insights from teachers' perspectives on ChatGPT. *Journal of Research in Innovative Teaching & Learning*. DOI: 10.1108/JRIT-09-2023-0129

Ayanwale, M. A., Sanusi, I. T., Adelana, O. P., Aruleba, K. D., & Oyelere, S. S. (2022). Teachers' readiness and intention to teach artificial intelligence in schools. *Computers and Education Artificial Intelligence*, *3*, 100099. DOI: 10.1016/j.caeai.2022.100099

Brusilovsky, P., & Peylo, C. (2003). Adaptive and intelligent web-based educational systems. *International Journal of Artificial Intelligence in Education, 13*(2-4), 159–172. DOI: 10.3233/IRG-2003-13(2-4)02

Celik, I. (2022). Towards Intelligent-TPACK: An empirical study on teachers' professional knowledge to ethically integrate artificial intelligence (AI)-based tools into education. *Computers in Human Behavior*, *138*, 107468. DOI: 10.1016/j.chb.2022.107468

Celik, I., Dindar, M., Muukkonen, H., & Järvelä, S. (2022). The Promises and Challenges of Artificial Intelligence for Teachers: A Systematic Review of Research. *TechTrends*, *66*(4), 616–630. DOI: 10.1007/s11528-022-00715-y

Crescenzi-Lanna, L. (2023). Literature review of the reciprocal value of artificial and human intelligence in early childhood education. *Journal of Research on Technology in Education*, *55*(1), 21–33. DOI: 10.1080/15391523.2022.2128480

Daniel, R. M., De Stavola, B. L., Cousens, S. N., & Vansteelandt, S. (2015). Causal mediation analysis with multiple mediators. *Biometrics*, *71*(1), 1–14. DOI: 10.1111/biom.12248 PMID: 25351114

Fahimirad, M., & Kotamjani, S. S. (2018). A Review on Application of AI in Teaching and Learning in Educational Contexts. *International Journal of Learning and Development*, *8*(4), 106. DOI: 10.5296/ijld.v8i4.14057

Filiz, O., Kaya, M. H., & Adiguzel, T. (2025). Teachers and AI: Understanding the factors influencing AI integration in K-12 education. *Education and Information Technologies*, *30*(13), 17931–17967. Advance online publication. DOI: 10.1007/s10639-025-13463-2

Holmes, W., Persson, J., Chounta, I. A., Wasson, B., & Dimitrova, V. (2022). *Artificial intelligence and education: A critical view through the lens of human rights, democracy and the rule of law*. Council of Europe. Burton, R., Brown, J. S., & Sleeman, D. (1982). Intelligent tutoring systems.

Holstein, K., McLaren, B. M., & Aleven, V. (2018, June). Student learning benefits of a mixed-reality teacher awareness tool in AI-enhanced classrooms. In *International conference on artificial intelligence in education* (pp. 154-168). Cham: Springer International Publishing. DOI: 10.1007/978-3-319-93843-1_12

Kim, J., Lee, H., & Cho, Y. H. (2022). Learning design to support student-AI collaboration: Perspectives of leading teachers for AI in education. *Education and Information Technologies*, *27*(5), 6069–6104. DOI: 10.1007/s10639-021-10831-6

Koh, J., Cowling, M., Jha, M., & Sim, K. N. (2023). The human teacher, the AI teacher and the AIed-Teacher relationship. *Journal of Higher Education Theory and Practice*, *23*(17), 199–202. DOI: 10.33423/jhetp.v23i17.6543

Kolchenko, V. (2018). Can Modern AI replace teachers? Not so fast! AI and Adaptive Learning: Personalized Education in the AI age. *HAPS Educator*, *22*(3), 249–252. DOI: 10.21692/haps.2018.032

Lameras, P., & Arnab, S. (2022). Power to the Teachers: An Exploratory review on AI in education. In Kerres, M., & Agre, G. (Eds.), *Information* (Vol. 13–14)., DOI: 10.3390/info13010014

Lee, I., & Perret, B., & Education Development Center, Inc. (2022). Preparing High School Teachers to Integrate AI Methods into STEM Classrooms. In *The Thirty-Sixth AAAI Conference on AI (AAAI-22)*. DOI: 10.1609/aaai.v36i11.21557

Lee, Y. J., Davis, R. O., & Ryu, J. (2024). Korean In-Service Teachers' perceptions of implementing artificial intelligence (AI) education for teaching in schools and their AI teacher training programs. *International Journal of Information and Education Technology (IJIET)*, *14*(2), 214–219. DOI: 10.18178/ijiet.2024.14.2.2042

Lens, (2025). *Teacher AI collaboration*. https://www.lens.org/lens/search/scholar/list?q=Teacher-AI%20collaboration

Lin, X., Chen, L., Chan, K. K., Peng, S., Chen, X., Xie, S., Liu, J., & Hu, Q. (2022). Teachers' perceptions of teaching Sustainable AI: A Design frame perspective. *Sustainability*, *14*(13), 7811. DOI: 10.3390/su14137811

Lindner, A., & Romeike, R. (2019). Teachers' perspectives on AI. ISSEP 2019: 12th International conference on informatics in schools. Situation, evaluation and perspectives. Cyprus

Malik, M. A., & Shah, R. (2025). AI teachers (AI-based robots as teachers): History, potential, concerns and recommendations. *Frontiers in Education*, *10*, 1–5. DOI: 10.3389/feduc.2025.1541543

McKay, A. K., Stellingwerff, T., Smith, E. S., Martin, D. T., Mujika, I., Goosey-Tolfrey, V. L., Sheppard, J., & Burke, L. M. (2021). Defining training and performance caliber: A participant classification framework. *International Journal of Sports Physiology and Performance*, *17*(2), 317–331. DOI: 10.1123/ijspp.2021-0451 PMID: 34965513

Nazaretsky, T., Ariely, M., Cukurova, M., & Alexandron, G. (2022). Teachers' trust in AI -powered educational technology and a professional development program to improve it. *British Journal of Educational Technology*, *53*(4), 914–931. DOI: 10.1111/bjet.13232

Origin, (2025). https://www.originlab.com/

Popenici, S. A. D., & Kerr, S. (2017). Exploring the impact of AI on teaching and learning in higher education. *Research and Practice in Technology Enhanced Learning*, *12*(1), 1–13. DOI: 10.1186/s41039-017-0062-8 PMID: 30613250

Tsai, S. T., Lu, M. K., San, S., & Tsai, C. H. (2020). The neurologic manifestations of coronavirus disease 2019 pandemic: A systemic review. *Frontiers in Neurology*, *11*, 498. DOI: 10.3389/fneur.2020.00498 PMID: 32574246

Venugopal, R., & Mamatha, V. (2023). Impact of artificial intelligence (AI) on teaching and learning in India's higher education sector. *IOSR Journal of Research & Method in Education (IOSRJRME)*, 1–6. https://doi.org/.DOI: 10.9790/7388-1305020106

VOSViewer. (2025). Retrieved October 2025. https://www.vosviewer.com/

Zawacki-Richter, O., Marín, V. I., Bond, M., & Gouverneur, F. (2019). Systematic review of research on artificial intelligence applications in higher education–where are the educators? *International Journal of Educational Technology in Higher Education*, *16*(1), 1–27. DOI: 10.1186/s41239-019-0171-0

ADDITIONAL READING

Kuzminov, Y., Sorokin, P., & Froumin, I. (2019). Generic and Specific Skills as Components of Human Capital: New Challenges for education Theory and practice. In National Research University Higher School of Economics, Foresight and STI Governance, *13*(2), 19–41. https://doi.org/DOI: 10.17323/2500-2597.2019.2.19.41

Moradbakhti, L., Schreibelmayr, S., & Mara, M. (2022). Do men have no need for "Feminist" AI? agentic and gendered voice assistants in the light of basic psychological needs. *Frontiers in Psychology*, *13*. Advance online publication. DOI: 10.3389/fpsyg.2022.855091 PMID: 35774945

Mouta, A., Torrecilla-Sánchez, E. M., & Pinto-Llorente, A. M. (2025). Comprehensive professional learning for teacher agency in addressing ethical challenges of AIED: Insights from educational design research. *Education and Information Technologies*, *30*(3), 3343–3387. DOI: 10.1007/s10639-024-12946-y

Nguyen, A., Ngo, H. N., Hong, Y., Dang, B., & Nguyen, B. T. (2022). Ethical principles for artificial intelligence in education. *Education and Information Technologies*, *28*(4), 4221–4241. DOI: 10.1007/s10639-022-11316-w PMID: 36254344

KEY TERMS AND DEFINITIONS

Adaptive Learning: In adaptive learning, students are given different types of information depending on their results throughout the course. It reviews the student's abilities and skills and adjusts the lesson material, how quickly it is delivered, and the difficulty accordingly. The aim of this personal approach is to boost learning by giving students the right help and challenges.

AI in Education (AIEd): AI for Education focuses on finding ways to use AI in teaching and learning. These applications are used in education, for instance, personal learning, expert tutoring, automated testing, and data analysis, to support fairness and help students succeed.

AI Integration: AI integration is when AI technology and tools are added to educational systems and practices that are already used. This means that AI-powered programs should be included in classes, teachers should be shown how to use AI tools, and rules should be created for the proper and responsible application of AI in education.

AI-Driven Analytics: AI-Driven Analytics is about using AI methods, for example machine learning and natural language processing, to examine educational information and find useful outcomes. Among the tasks are finding how students learn best, estimating their results, and advising teachers based on information from data.

Automated Assessment: Automated Assessment means letting AI and computer methods evaluate student essays, quizzes, and projects by itself without human help. They can deliver responses right away, point out strengths and weaknesses, and ease teachers' workload so they can pay more attention to other areas of teaching

Educational Technology: EdTech describes how technology is applied to make learning and teaching easier. Examples of these tools and resources are computers, software, online learning web sites, and mobile gadgets. With the help of AI, EdTech now gives learners more flexible and interactive learning opportunities.

Intelligent Tutoring Systems (ITS): Intelligent Tutoring Systems (ITS) provide students with one-on-one style instruction using computers and give them appropriate feedback. ITs make use of AI to identify where students are making errors, modify the course content, and give detailed help on the basics.

Personalized Learning: Personalized learning offers instruction specifically made to fit every student's special learning needs. It makes use of data and new tools to design personal routes that help students build their skills at their own rate and to focus on their disadvantages. Because of AI, many students can receive personalized education.

Technology in Education: Technology in Education: The phrase means using technology in schools to improve how lessons and classes are run. It may consist of using electronic tools for instruction, encouraging students to cooperate, evaluating their learning, and handling resources for education. AI in technology for education is growing fast and may change many parts of learning and teaching.

Chapter 11
Tutoring and Mentoring in the Age of AI:
An Academic Perspective

Geetha Manoharan
https://orcid.org/0000-0002-8644-8871
SR University, India

ABSTRACT

"Tutoring and Mentoring in the Age of AI: An Academic Perspective" is a part that talks about how AI is changing standard educational support systems by changing the roles of tutoring and mentoring". As AI-powered intelligent teaching systems (ITS) and virtual teachers become more popular, they offer personalized, flexible learning experiences that are tuned to each student's needs. Looking at AI's capability to actively help students, provide real-time feedback, and keep track of their academic progress, this chapter shows how these technologies support and improve the work of human teachers in promoting student success. It also talks about the problems with integrating AI tools, social issues, and how the relationship between AI tools and teachers is changing to facilitate effective academic mentoring. This chapter uses current events and real-life examples to give a fair academic view on using AI as a teaching aid, focusing on how it can help students learn on their own, stay motivated, and have equal access to good coaching and mentoring systems.

INTRODUCTION TO ARTIFICIAL INTELLIGENCE IN EDUCATION

The use of artificial intelligence in schools is quickly changing the way tutoring and mentoring work, which means that we need to completely rethink how we teach and what the moral consequences are (Nguyen & Barbieri, 2025). Bit et al. (2024)

DOI: 10.4018/979-8-3373-4621-2.ch011

say that artificial intelligence has the unique ability to tailor learning evaluations, give real-time feedback, and expand academic assistance. This might greatly improve student performance and make learning settings fairer. For instance, intelligent tutoring systems keep an eye on how students act, give them specific projects, provide them useful comments, and encourage them to communicate with other students through laptops (Zhai et al., 2021). AI systems are getting smarter, and their uses in education are growing. They can now help with personalized learning, smart tutoring, and advising policymakers (Huang et al., 2022). But when AI is used more in tutoring and mentoring, important concerns arise concerning the importance of human teachers, the possibility of bias in algorithms, and the necessity to learn important non-cognitive skills that AI might be able to help with. In this investigation, the advantages and disadvantages of employing intelligent machines in the classroom are examined, as well as the evolving dynamic between human instructors and intelligent machines. Also examined are the intricate consequences of AI on mentoring and tuition (Zhai et al., 2021).

In education, AI has been introduced because of enhanced data analytics, natural language processing, and device learning. These advancements have enabled the development of intricate tutoring systems that can accommodate the needs of both male and female students (Bulut et al., 2024). Tailoring mastery studies, automated assessment and commenting systems, and intelligent material delivery systems are all feasible with these technologies. All these things might change how teachers and students learn. The growing use of system-generated knowledge in many areas, such as education, raises moral questions that need to be thought about very carefully. To properly use AI in mentoring and instructing, one must comprehend the technology's capabilities and limits, as well as its educational, social, and moral consequences.

This article will discuss the pros and downsides of using AI in teaching and mentoring and its effects on training. This bankruptcy is meant to help teachers, policymakers, and researchers deal with the changing world of AI in education by looking at how AI could change things while also talking about the moral issues and reasonable demands that come with using it (Manoharan, 2026). To illuminate ethical, cultural, language, and privacy issues related to AI training, this research examines crucial topics, unpleasant scenarios, and fears. The advantages and bad of AI in tutoring and mentoring are shown to inspire responsible innovation and ensure all students receive a good education. Manoharan et al., 2025

The next portion of this chapter will examine academic artificial intelligence to better understand how it affects professors.

THE SYMBIOTIC RELATIONSHIP BETWEEN AI AND HUMAN TUTORS

Combining human and AI teachers, especially for college students from low-income backgrounds, might be a strategy to improve mastery effects (Thomas et al., 2024). AI-assisted tutoring models can aid human tutors by giving them more knowledge, personalizing lessons, and letting them focus on helping students reach greater cognitive and emotional goals (Thomas et al., 2024). While AI tutors can test students' knowledge, identify knowledge gaps, and suggest targeted answers, human tutors may offer more nuanced advise, emotional support, and mentorship that promotes critical thinking, creativity, and problem-solving abilities. Collaborative learning environments, in which AI tutors work with human educators, can generate more compelling and effective learning evaluations to address the diverse requirements and learning styles of college students (Holstein & Aleven, 2022). Despite the theoretical promise of tailored technology-better education and considerable financial investments in these research technologies (Bulathwela et al., 2021), practical outcomes have been limited. Instead of reducing the effectiveness of human educators through automation, AI must help them make decisions by providing important, fact-based insights (Cukurova et al., 2019). It is usually desirable to have the best academic alternative for a student's future.

NAVIGATING THE ETHICAL LANDSCAPE OF AI IN EDUCATION

Using AI in training poses a lot of ethical questions, especially around algorithmic bias, data privacy, and the possibility of more academic inequality (Bulathwela et al., 2024; Jian, 2023). Preventing educational disparities requires fair access to AI-powered learning materials (Harry & Sayudin, 2023). Data skewing or algorithm malfunctions can worsen socioeconomic inequality and lead to unfair student results. AI systems collecting and processing student data present privacy and security concerns, requiring strict information security and data governance. To address these ethical issues, educators, legislators, AI developers, and ethicists must work together to establish explicit norms and standards for the appropriate utilization of AI in education (Bettayeb et al., 2024). It involves meticulously evaluating the impact of AI on students' well-being, promoting transparency and accountability inside AI systems, and guaranteeing that AI is used to advance, rather than obstruct, the objectives of inclusive and equitable education (Delello et al., 2025). The shortage of transparency and responsibility in AI systems, blended with the ability for bias and discrimination in AI algorithms, increases worries amongst educators, mother and father, and policymakers (Akinwalere & Ivanov, 2022).

Figure 1. Ethical challenges in the education of AI

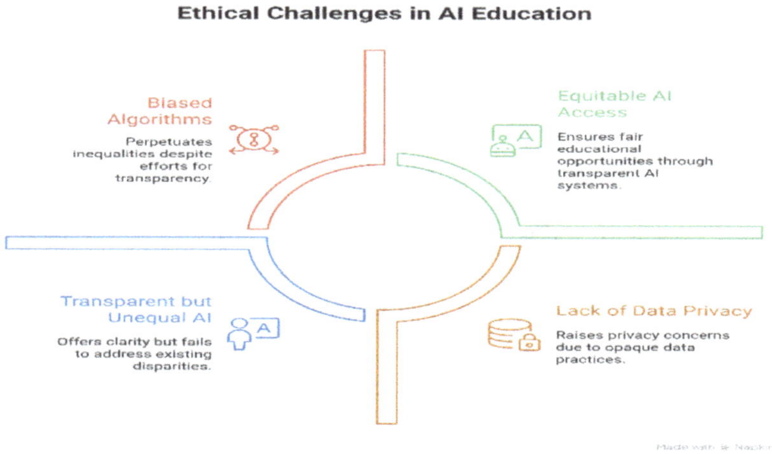

Therefore, it is far vital to have moral frameworks, transparency in AI utilization, and participation from all stakeholders to make certain truthful and equitable evaluation inside the educational placing (Grünberg, 2024).

The ethical perspective on the artificial intelligence towards the educational sector will lead to the academic integrity starting from the Montessori school education, primary year programmes, middle year programs, secondary year programmes and into higher education.

THE EVOLVING LANDSCAPE OF TUTORING AND MENTORING

In this phase we are going to discuss about the evolution of tutoring and mentoring in academia this will give us a clear insight for better understanding. There are such as follows below:

Conventional Tutoring and Mentoring Models

Traditionally, tutoring and mentoring have depended on human interaction, with experienced educators or mentors presenting individualized help and steering to freshmen. Human tutors provide personalised interest, adapting their coaching techniques to the precise desires and studying varieties of person college students (Kamalov & Gurrib, 2023). Powerful human tutors possess problem matter expertise, pedagogical abilities, and the capability to build rapport with students, developing a supportive and inspiring mastering environment. Mentoring, then again, focuses on presenting steering and guide for private and professional development, assisting college students navigate challenges, set desires, and increase essential lifestyles talents. According to Fakour and Imani (2025), the advantage of human tutors is their ability to identify the cognitive and emotive needs of their pupils. Additionally, human instructors modify their speech patterns to create a visually appealing learning environment that is customized for each student.

The Impact of Technology on Schooling

By introducing new opportunities for individualized instruction and more mastery stories, the integration of technology into education has transformed conventional coaching and learning methodologies (Ashtika et al., 2025). The prevalence of online learning platforms, educational software, and virtual resources has increased, giving students access to a wide range of learning resources and interactive technologies (Mallik & Gangopadhyay, 2023). College students may study at their own speed and access academic materials from anywhere in the world because to the ease and flexibility these digital resources offer. The integration of generations in education has also enabled new forms of communication and cooperation between students and instructors, allowing for remote learning and virtual classrooms (Resnick, 2024). Zou et al. (2025) assert that virtual reality, artificial intelligence, and other advanced technologies are transforming education, altering the traditional academic environment, and enhancing the learning experience.

Emergence of AI in Academic Settings

AI in education has completely changed how students do research and how teachers educate. Students are getting personalized help and assistance, while teachers' administrative tasks are being automated. AI-powered tutoring systems may analyse student data to identify areas in which they excel and subsequently offer personalized comments and guidance to accommodate their individual needs. AI may examine essays and research papers, providing helpful input (FİLİZ et al., 2025). AI saves educators time by automating evaluation, delivering individualized feedback, and developing student-specific learning materials (Bit et al., 2024). Teachers have more time for more extensive preparation and student involvement. Additionally, AI is being used to improve intelligent learning environments. These settings follow students' growth and provide individualized help learning about resources and activities. AI creates individualized learning reports that meet a variety of educational criteria and help students build critical thinking and computing skills (Walter, 2024). Phua et al. (2025) found that AI-enabled individualized narrative learning, fast feedback, and administrative support for instructors increased academic achievement. AI, VR, and other emerging technologies are changing education and improving learning (Zou et al., 2025).

The next section will examine AI's usage in tutoring, its effects, and AI-powered tutoring systems.

RESEARCH METHODOLOGY

In AI, the chapter examines mentorship and training using qualitative research. The chapter describes the use of artificial intelligence in tutoring and its effects to identify big trends, revelations, and emerging issues related to AI in mentoring, as well as its benefits, challenges, and moral implications. Ethical considerations are made to provide a complete understanding of how AI alters human mentoring relationships and to provide strategies to combine technological help with emotional and pedagogical guidance in the educational parts.

AI-POWERED TUTORING SYSTEMS

Adaptive Studying Platforms

Adaptive mastering systems use AI algorithms to research student overall performance statistics and regulate the difficulty level and content material of mastering substances to healthy character needs (Lizano-Sánchez et al., 2025). By way of continuously monitoring student progress, these structures can perceive areas in which students are struggling and provide centered assist and remediation. These structures provide customized learning studies via tailoring content material, pacing, and comments to man or woman college students' wishes and getting to know patterns (Dey, 2025). By using monitoring pupil enter and delivering appropriate obligations, those systems facilitate personalised studying (Zhai et al., 2021). Adaptive gaining knowledge of platforms maintains students fascinated and influenced by means of providing individualized gaining knowledge of studies that meet their requirements and hobbies (Kamalov & Gurrib, 2023). AI can examine students' emotional reactions, learning styles, and cognitive talents to supply custom designed training and assist via adaptive learning platforms (Akintayo et al., 2024).

Intelligent Tutoring Systems (ITS)

Sensible tutoring structures use AI strategies to simulate one-on-one tutoring, imparting college students with customized practise and feedback on precise topics or capabilities. Those structures can diagnose scholar mistakes, provide focused pointers and factors, and adapt the tempo of education to match character mastering speeds. By means of examining a pupil's interactions with an e-gaining knowledge of module, AI can spot trends that would point to a scholar's desired mastering approach or areas of difficulty (Jian, 2023). AI gives sources like support, comments, and tools that make private learning simpler for college students (Saputra et al., 2023). Moreover, tendencies in AI-powered chatbots and digital assistants have made personalised studying less difficult. These sources function as non-public tutors, offering prompt responses, addressing questions, or even recommending greater equipment based totally on the pupil's route (Jian, 2023; Lin et al., 2023). ITSs offer personalised getting to know enjoy in 4 fundamental approaches: tracking pupil's input, delivering appropriate tasks, offering powerful remarks and suggestions (Zhai et al., 2021). With the aid of taking advantage of AI/ML strategies, the educational platform exactly acquires the pupil's traits (Maghsudi et al., 2021). This allows the development of individualized instructional content for every pupil.

Customized Getting to Know Paths

Customized getting to know paths contain using AI algorithms to create individualized mastering plans for college students based totally on their strengths, weaknesses, and studying choices (Jian, 2023). These paths can contain a selection of studying sources and sports, together with on-line films, interactive simulations, and collaborative projects, to cater to exceptional studying patterns. AI-pushed systems monitor scholar interactions with mastering substances, check their comprehension, and adjust the presentation of content as important, imparting custom designed learning stories. AI algorithms may be used to research scholar facts and create personalized studying experiences for every scholar (Lin et al., 2023). By comparing scholar overall performance facts, AI can pinpoint weaknesses and offer greater help (Opesemowo & Adewuyi, 2024). AI structures compare every scholar's overall performance, options, and mastering fashion if you want to customise the gaining knowledge of direction, content, and pacing to match their specific wishes. AI is capable of offer custom designed mastering paths and guide based on college students' gaining knowledge of needs and characteristics (Ma et al., 2024).

The emergence of AI in education provides each possibility and challenges for the future of tutoring and mentoring. AI driven personalised gaining knowledge of has numerous difficulties and ethical issues, inclusive of algorithmic bias, statistics privateness, fairness, and the changing roles of teachers. It is vital that AI is used responsibly in education, paying near interest to moral problems and making certain that era supports and improves coaching, no longer replaces it. AI is also able to recommend the most appropriate content material from what is to be had, connecting freshmen and comparing performance (Maghsudi et al., 2021).

Table 1. Representing AI as a tutoring tool

Component	Functions / Features	Key Benefits
Adaptive Learning Platforms	• Monitor student progress continuously • Identify weak areas and provide targeted support. • Tailor content and feedback based on individual needs • Analyze emotional responses and cognitive abilities	• Personalized and engaging learning experiences • Increased motivation and retention • Supports diverse learning styles
Intelligent Tutoring Systems (ITS)	• Diagnose student errors • Provide corrective feedback and hints • Adapt teaching pace to student performance • Employ AI chatbots and digital assistants for instant responses	• Mimics personalized human tutoring. • Provides immediate support and explanations. • Enhances independent learning
Customized Learning Paths	• Develop personalized learning sequences • Integrate multimedia and collaborative activities • Adjust content presentation based on comprehension • Offer continuous performance-based adaptation	• Encourages self-paced, flexible learning • Improves understanding through targeted activities • Promotes learner autonomy

In the upcoming content phase, we will be discussing about the artificial intelligence in the mentoring aspect also it gives the insights on the influence and impact of various tools that can be utilised for better mentoring.

AI AS A MENTORING TOOL

AI-Pushed Remarks and Assessment

AI-powered equipment can offer college students fast and insightful feedback, that is one of the predominant blessings of the usage of AI in schooling (Kaledio et al., 2024). AI can automate grading and evaluation processes, offering students with immediate remarks on their paintings and liberating up teachers' time for greater individualized support (Bit et al., 2024). AI can assist instructors through automating monotonous operational tasks, generating exams and automating grading and remarks (AlTwijri & Alghizzi, 2024; Chaudhry & Kazim, 2021). However, it is critical to continue with caution when the use of AI for assessment responsibilities like grading or comments due to the fact evaluation is a fundamental teaching pastime that has a large effect on studying. Teachers are capable of offer insightful criticism and route with the aid of hastily evaluating student assignments way to AI algorithms.

Digital Mentors and Chatbots

AI-powered chatbots and virtual assistants can provide students with on-call for assist and steering, answering questions, offering assets, and providing encouragement. These digital mentors can be available 24/7, presenting students with get right of entry to aid each time they need it. AI also can assist college students with research and writing assignments through providing remarks, detecting plagiarism, and recommending resources. AI-powered virtual assistants and chatbots can provide customized steerage and guide to students, answering their questions and assisting them navigate the educational landscape. Virtual mentors offer individualized help to college students with the aid of offering sources, answering questions, and supplying encouragement.

AI for Talent Improvement and Profession Steering

AI also can be used to assist college students expand essential abilities and discover profession options. AI-powered systems can analyse scholar facts to perceive talent gaps and propose personalised gaining knowledge of assets to cope with the ones gaps. Additionally, AI can offer college students with insights into distinct profession paths and the talents and qualifications needed to reach the ones fields. AI can examine student facts to decide ability gaps and provide customized mastering resources to shut the ones gaps, further, to providing insights into numerous career paths and the skills and credentials required to succeed in the one's professions. Instructors can combine AI technology into their teaching, as an instance, with the aid of the usage of smart academic gear, customized studying software, or digital assistants, that can provide a greater personalised and interactive mastering enjoy (Ma et al., 2024).

Table 2. Representing AI as a mentoring tool

Component	Functions / Features	Key Benefits
AI-Driven Feedback and Assessment	• Automates grading and feedback processes • Generates assessments and evaluates student work • Provides immediate, personalized feedback • Supports teachers by reducing repetitive tasks	• Saves teachers' time for individualized mentoring • Provides instant, consistent feedback • Enhances learning through timely assessment insights
Digital Mentors and Chatbots	• Provide 24/7 guidance and assistance • Answer student queries and recommend resources • Offer writing feedback and detect plagiarism • Motivate and emotionally support learners	• Ensures continuous student support • Increases engagement and accessibility • Promotes self-directed learning
AI for Skill Development and Career Guidance	• Detects individual learning and skill gaps • Suggests learning materials to bridge gaps • Provides insights into relevant career paths and required skills • Integrates AI tools into teaching for interactive learning	• Supports holistic student development • Improves employability through personalized guidance • Aligns education with future workforce needs

The function of human educators will trade as AI will become extra included into training, necessitating modifications to teaching strategies and curricula. In the next aspect we are going to discuss about the different kinds of challenges and the ethical considerations that is found in the artificial intelligence towards the mentoring and tutoring criteria.

ETHICAL CONSIDERATIONS AND CHALLENGES

Records Privacy and Protection

AI systems rely on substantial quantities of information to feature effectively, raising concerns about statistics privateness and security (Davar et al., 2025). It is far important to make certain that scholar information is covered and used ethically, and that students and educators are privy to how their statistics is being used. AI-powered on-line mastering systems regularly operate across countrywide borders, elevating questions about jurisdiction and the applicability of countrywide regulations (Karpouzis, 2024). It is far vital to guard scholar data and utilize it morally.

Bias and Fairness in AI Algorithms

AI algorithms can perpetuate and extend existing biases if they are skilled on biased facts. this can cause unfair or discriminatory outcomes for college kids from sure demographic companies (Cordero et al., 2024). It is miles essential to address bias in AI algorithms and make certain that AI systems are truthful and equitable for all college students (Roshanaei et al., 2023). Bias must be addressed in AI algorithms to guarantee that AI structures are just and equitable for all college students, as AI algorithms might also expand present biases if trained on prejudiced facts (Poornesh, 2024). In their training materials, AI algorithms may reflect social prejudices, leading to algorithmic bias and discrimination against underrepresented student companies (Al-Zahrani, 2024).

The Role of Human Interplay

Although artificial intelligence (AI) has numerous educational advantages, it is crucial to remember the value of human connection and interaction. Teaching statistics is only one aspect of tutoring and mentoring; other goals include developing connections, encouraging trust, and providing emotional support (Sunitha Purushottamashtikar, Geetha Manoharan; 2024). S. P. Ashtikar and G. Manoharan (2024) argue that it is critical to strike a balance between AI-powered tools and human interaction to guarantee that students receive the assistance they need to succeed. Even though AI offers numerous advantages in education, human interaction and connection remain crucial in tutoring and mentoring. Tutoring and mentoring entails developing connections, building trust, and providing emotional support in addition to imparting knowledge.

A mix of AI-powered tools and human engagement is required for students to obtain the assistance they require to succeed (Chinta et al., 2024; Gutiérrez et al., 2025; Merino-Campos, 2025; Onesi-Ozigagun et al., 2024). To avoid unjust treatment of individual college students and the persistence of linked injustices, institutions must ensure that their AI systems are impartial and maintain current standards (Harry & Sayudin, 2023). These are all the most important ethical considerations and the challenges that often can be witnessed in the professional aspects of artificial intelligence with regards to tutoring and mentoring. Furthermore, the future directions and the opportunities can be discussed as follows below.

FUTURE DIRECTIONS AND OPPORTUNITIES

Integrating AI with Human Understanding

The maximum promising method to tutoring and mentoring within the age of AI entails integrating AI-powered gear with human expertise. AI can deal with repetitive duties and offer personalized mastering reviews, even as human tutors and mentors can attention on imparting emotional support, steering, and mentorship. AI has the capability to enhance individualized learning stories and manipulate repetitive tasks. Human tutors and mentors can provide advice, emotional aid, and mentorship while AI handles customized studying reviews and repetitive duties.

Developing AI for Diverse Freshmen

AI systems need to be designed to fulfil the needs of various beginners, consisting of college students with disabilities, college students from exceptional cultural backgrounds, and students who communicate one-of-a-kind languages. For AI systems to be practical, inclusive, and culturally sensitive, their design and deployment must be carefully planned. AI systems must be accessible, inclusive, and culturally sensitive, which requires careful planning and execution. This is because AI systems should be built to suit the demands of a wide range of novice users, including college students who speak various languages, students with impairments, and students from diverse cultural backgrounds.

After learning about the functional aspects, the following portion of this chapter will discuss the enhanced effect on students' academic and maintenance results.

IMPACT ON STUDENT OUTCOMES

1. AI tutoring and mentorship programs have been found to improve student results in some academic subjects. The study found higher educational performance when grade factor averages climbed, and observer hours declined. Scholarly preferences include adaptive look-at adjustments, tailored learning, and real-time lecture room evaluation (Ward et al., 2025).
2. Artificial intelligence tutoring improves students' test scores, grades, and academic achievement (Merino-Campos, 2025). These advances may be attributed to personalized training, targeted feedback, and adaptive learning routes supplied by AI structures that match individual student preferences and learning styles.
3. AI tutoring systems can boost student motivation, engagement, and self-esteem.

4. AI systems may provide a sense of accomplishment and inspire college students to continue through thick fabric by providing prompt feedback and assistance. However, a study found that an excessive dependence on AI technology may hinder critical thinking and problem-solving skills, and concerns have been expressed over the virtual gap and fair access to the modern world. It is critical to recognize that the use of AI in education presents significant ethical issues that warrant careful consideration. These issues include algorithmic bias, privacy of information, rights to intellectual property, and educational integrity (Maphalala & Ajani, 2025).

AI's function as an assistant in place of an alternative for teachers emphasizes its capacity to reinforce human talents. The upcoming chapter phase the innovativeness towards research in artificial intelligence enhanced education system in the latest trend can be discussed along with the example for the successful implementation of artificial intelligence in the successful tutoring.

RESEARCH AND INNOVATION IN AI-ENHANCED EDUCATION

Sustained investment in studies and innovation is essential for understanding the whole capacity of AI in schooling, Peddi, S. & Manoharan, G. (2025). This consists of studies at the effectiveness of AI-powered tutoring and mentoring structures, the improvement of new AI gear and strategies, and the exploration of moral and societal implications of AI in schooling (Mello et al., 2023). AI in schooling must be explored for its moral and social implications, and new AI technologies and tools must be created, alongside research on the efficacy of AI-powered tutoring and mentoring systems (Jose et al., 2025). Future studies need to use longitudinal designs to acquire an intensive picture of AI's lengthy-time period consequences on education.

Furthermore, interdisciplinary research projects must be promoted so that it will sell cooperation between educators, AI developers, and ethicists so one can address the complex problems supplied by means of AI in tutoring and mentoring. AI gives a spread of alternatives for reinforcing coaching and mastering, such as language acquisition, studies and writing help, and trainer professional improvement (FİLİZ et al., 2025). But concerns approximately data privateness, set of rules bias, and the need of human connection need to be taken under consideration. As AI generation develops, it has the potential to convert verbal exchange, life, and work environments, in education (FİLİZ et al., 2025). Via utilising AI's skills and thoroughly thinking about its effects, educators, legislators, and researchers can create a future in which AI improves academic possibilities and effects for all college students.

EXAMPLE ON SUCCESSFUL IMPLEMENTATIONS OF AI TUTORING

Wise tutoring structures have emerged as a pivotal application of AI in education, providing customized gaining knowledge of stories tailor-made to person student wishes. Those structures examine pupil overall performance records to become aware of understanding gaps and studying patterns, dynamically adjusting the difficulty stage and content to optimize mastering outcomes (Ullrich et al., 2022). Several research have verified the effectiveness of ITSs in enhancing student achievement in subjects along with arithmetic, technological know-how, and language arts (Malik et al., 2018). Their satisfaction is derived from ITS's ability to provide personalized assistance, initiate conversations, and allow individuals to determine their own learning paths. Lai et al. (2023) have demonstrated that a community tutoring system that generates an appropriate learning environment has a beneficial impact on the longevity of education. In addition, the adaptability of ITSs allows them to accommodate a wide range of learning styles and preferences, thereby increasing student engagement and motivation.

Further discussion of the obstacles associated with the implementation of AI in tutoring and mentoring could be conducted on the subsequent page of this chapter.

Despite AI tutoring systems' hopeful findings, worldwide deployments have produced complicated circumstances and training insights. Bias in AI systems might prevent education inequities from being closed. Through biased educational records, algorithm mistakes, or prejudicial design decisions, bias can cause unfair or discriminating outcomes for some student groups. We must eradicate bias through legislation, rigorous record-keeping, and periodic audits to treat everyone equitably. Another problem is integrating AI instructional frameworks into present teaching approaches. AI can change instructional technology in many classroom applications. Instructors can use computer-based evaluation tools, tailored learning frameworks, and facial recognition technologies to monitor student conduct. To maximize AI's potential, teachers must integrate it into their instruction. Protecting student data and respecting AI systems requires addressing data privacy and security concerns. Academic institutions must develop transparent fact governance policies and follow ethical norms to preserve student data. AI education may bring hazards relative to its capabilities, say some experts. In addition, using intelligent generation to collect novices' statistics may raise ethical and security problems due to information leakage (Lai et al., 2023).

DISCUSSION AND CONCLUSION

AI can increase learning and efficiency, but it also raises ethical, justice, and coaching challenges. Teachers found pupils utilizing ChatGPT and other AI applications. Coaching now emphasises critical thinking over reliance (Delello et al., 2025). By addressing ethical problems, improving teacher training, and providing equal access, schools can help students understand AI's revolutionary potential. The debate over AI in education must transcend age groups and focus on society, morality, and education. Koç and Greenhow (2021); Vidarre et al. (2024). The goal of this study is to summarize AI's current, future, and challenges in education. It underscores the necessity of strategic integration and ongoing research to guarantee that AI improves academic outcomes for all students (Kamalov & Gurrib, 2023; Lampou, 2023). To deal with the problems that AI brings up and make the most of its potential to improve education and, eventually, society (Nguyen, 2025) (Yu & Yu, 2023) (Vieriu & Petrea, 2025) (Maphalala & Ajani, 2025), we need to keep doing research and talking to each other.

To fully fulfill AI's revolutionary potential, educational institutions must apply complete strategies that handle ethical challenges, stimulate teacher training, and ensure equal access (Chan, 2023; Dey, 2025; Kalniņa et al., 2024).Policymakers and educational institutions should reassess their current rules to account for technological improvements in artificial intelligence (AI), which is increasingly being integrated into academic frameworks (Azzam & Charles, 2024). Regulations will no longer be able to adequately finance, modify, or recall the moral implications of AI in education if they continue to focus on AI readiness while disregarding the ethical challenges and promise of AI in education (Chan, 2023; Ojha et al., 2023). The increased use of AI in education has far-reaching implications for teachers and institutions, necessitating a paradigm shift in teaching methodologies, curriculum creation, and institutional policies. Teachers must take on new roles as information gatherers, assisting students in using AI-powered tools and resources while developing critical thinking, creativity, and problem-solving abilities (Dey, 2025). Instructors need ongoing training to integrate AI into their lesson preparations. AI literacy and ethics must be included in curriculum to prepare students to utilize AI responsibly (Delello et al., 2025).

AI in education improves efficiency and personalizes learning, but it also poses ethical, egalitarian, and human issues. AI literacy, critical thinking, and professional development must be prioritized by educators to promote responsible AI integration. According to the tables, ethically acceptable and efficient AI-powered education, mentorship, evaluation, and career advice have pros and cons. Schools must invest in user-friendly data control systems, powerful computers, and high-quality data to create AI-powered learning environments. In addition, universities must adopt specific AI ethics standards for academic integrity, data protection, and algorithmic prejudice. Nguyen et al. (2022) claim that unified ethical criteria for AIED allows the field's research timeline to accept extensive training digitization.

REFERENCES

Akintayo, O. T., Eden, C. A., Ayeni, O. O., & Onyebuchi, N. C. (2024). Integrating AI with emotional and social learning in primary education: Developing a holistic adaptive learning ecosystem. *Computer Science & IT Research Journal*, *5*(5), 1076–1089. DOI: 10.51594/csitrj.v5i5.1116

Akinwalere, S. N., & Ivanov, V. (2022). Artificial Intelligence in Higher Education: Challenges and Opportunities. *BORDER CROSSING*, *12*(1), 1–15. DOI: 10.33182/bc.v12i1.2015

Al-Zahrani, A. M. (2024). Unveiling the shadows: Beyond the hype of AI in education. *Heliyon*, *10*(9), e30696. Advance online publication. DOI: 10.1016/j.heliyon.2024.e30696

. AlTwijri, L., & Alghizzi, T. M. (2024). Investigating the integration of artificial intelligence in English as foreign language classes for enhancing learners' affective factors: A systematic review [Review of Investigating the integration of artificial intelligence in English as foreign language classes for enhancing learners' affective factors: A systematic review]. Heliyon, 10(10). Elsevier BV. https://doi.org/DOI: 10.1016/j.heliyon.2024.e31053

Ashtikar, S. P., & Manoharan, G. (2024). "Work-Load Management and Job Gratification: A Study on the Work-life Equilibrium of Higher Education Instructors," *2024 3rd International Conference on Computational Modelling, Simulation and Optimization (ICCMSO)*, Phuket, Thailand, pp. 193-197, doi: https://doi.org/DOI: 10.1109/ICCMSO61761.2024.00048

. Azzam, A., & Charles, T. (2024). A Review of Artificial Intelligence in K-12 Education [Review of A Review of Artificial Intelligence in K-12 Education]. Open Journal of Applied Sciences, 14(8), 2088. Scientific Research Publishing. https://doi.org/DOI: 10.4236/ojapps.2024.148137

Bettayeb, A. M., Talib, M. A., Altayasinah, A. Z. S., & Dakalbab, F. (2024). Exploring the impact of ChatGPT: Conversational AI in education. *Frontiers in Education*, *9*, 1379796. Advance online publication. DOI: 10.3389/feduc.2024.1379796

Bit, D., Biswas, S., & Nag, M. (2024). The Impact of Artificial Intelligence in Educational System. *International Journal of Scientific Research in Science and Technology*, *11*(4), 419–427. DOI: 10.32628/IJSRST2411424

Bulathwela, S., Pérez-Ortiz, M., Holloway, C., Cukurova, M., & Shawe-Taylor, J. (2024). Artificial Intelligence Alone Will Not Democratise Education: On Educational Inequality, Techno-Solutionism, and Inclusive Tools. *Sustainability (Basel)*, *16*(2), 781. DOI: 10.3390/su16020781

Bulathwela, S., Pérez-Ortiz, M., Holloway, C., & Shawe-Taylor, J. (2021). Could AI Democratise Education? Socio-Technical Imaginaries of an EdTech Revolution. arXiv (Cornell University). https://doi.org//arxiv.2112.02034DOI: 10.48550

Bulut, O., Beiting-Parrish, M., Casabianca, J. M., Slater, S. C., Jiao, H., Song, D., Ormerod, C. M., Fabiyi, D. G., Ivan, R., Walsh, C., Rios, O., Wilson, J. M., Yildirim-Erbasli, S. N., Wongvorachan, T., Liu, J. X., Tan, B., & Morilova, P. (2024). The Rise of Artificial Intelligence in Educational Measurement: Opportunities and Ethical Challenges. arXiv (Cornell University). https://doi.org//arxiv.2406.18900DOI: 10.48550

Chan, C. K. Y. (2023). A comprehensive AI policy education framework for university teaching and learning. *International Journal of Educational Technology in Higher Education*, *20*(1), 38. Advance online publication. DOI: 10.1186/s41239-023-00408-3

Chaudhry, M. A., & Kazim, E. (2021). Artificial Intelligence in Education (AIEd): A high-level academic and industry note 2021. *AI and Ethics*, *2*(1), 157–165. DOI: 10.1007/s43681-021-00074-z

Chinta, S. V., Wang, Z., Yin, Z., Hoang, N., Gonzalez, M., Quy, T. L., & Zhang, W. (2024). FairAIED: Navigating Fairness, Bias, and Ethics in Educational AI Applications. arXiv (Cornell University). https://doi.org//arxiv.2407.18745DOI: 10.48550

Cordero, J., Torres-Zambrano, J., & Cordero-Castillo, A. (2024). Integration of Generative Artificial Intelligence in Higher Education: Best Practices. *Education Sciences*, *15*(1), 32. DOI: 10.3390/educsci15010032

Cukurova, M., Kent, C., & Luckin, R. (2019). Artificial intelligence and multimodal data in the service of human decision-making: A case study in debate tutoring. *British Journal of Educational Technology*, *50*(6), 3032–3046. DOI: 10.1111/bjet.12829

Davar, N. F., Dewan, M. A. A., & Zhang, X. (2025). AI Chatbots in Education: Challenges and Opportunities. *Information (Basel)*, *16*(3), 235. DOI: 10.3390/info16030235

Delello, J. A., Sung, W., Mokhtari, K., Hebert, J., Bronson, A., & Giuseppe, T. D. (2025). AI in the Classroom: Insights from Educators on Usage, Challenges, and Mental Health. *Education Sciences*, *15*(2), 113. DOI: 10.3390/educsci15020113

Dey, D. (2025). Enhancing Educational Tools Through Artificial Intelligence in Perspective of Need of AI. https://doi.org/DOI: 10.2139/ssrn.5031275

Fakour, H., & Imani, M. (2025). Socratic wisdom in the age of AI: A comparative study of ChatGPT and human tutors in enhancing critical thinking skills. *Frontiers in Education*, *10*, 1528603. Advance online publication. DOI: 10.3389/feduc.2025.1528603

Grünberg, N. F. (2024). El uso de la inteligencia artificial en la evaluación educativa y sus desafíos (The use of artificial intelligence in educational evaluation and its challenges.). https://doi.org/DOI: 10.2139/ssrn.4920158

Gutiérrez, J. C. G., Chiappe, A., Rodríguez, D. F. B., & González-Pérez, L. I. (2025). The Transformative Journey of Artificial Intelligence Toward Personalized Learning. *New Educator*, *1*(3), 257–275. Advance online publication. DOI: 10.1080/1547688X.2025.2475811

Harry, A., & Sayudin, S. (2023). Role of AI in Education. [INJURITY]. *Interdiciplinary Journal and Hummanity*, *2*(3), 260–268. DOI: 10.58631/injurity.v2i3.52

Holstein, K., & Aleven, V. (2022). Designing for human–AI complementarity in K-12 education. *AI Magazine*, *43*(2), 239–248. DOI: 10.1002/aaai.12058

Huang, A. Y. Q., Lu, O. H. T., & Yang, S. J. H. (2022). Effects of artificial Intelligence–Enabled personalized recommendations on learners' learning engagement, motivation, and outcomes in a flipped classroom. *Computers & Education*, *194*, 104684. DOI: 10.1016/j.compedu.2022.104684

Jian, M. J. K. O. (2023). Personalized learning through AI. *Advances in Engineering Innovation*, *5*(1), 16–19. DOI: 10.54254/2977-3903/5/2023039

Jose, B., Cherian, J., Verghis, A. M., Varghise, S. M., Mumthas, S., & Joseph, S. (2025). The cognitive paradox of AI in education: Between enhancement and erosion. *Frontiers in Psychology*, *16*, 1550621. Advance online publication. DOI: 10.3389/fpsyg.2025.1550621

Kaledio, P., Robert, A., & Frank, L. A. (2024). The Impact of Artificial Intelligence on Students' Learning Experience. SSRN Electronic Journal. https://doi.org/DOI: 10.2139/ssrn.4716747

Kalniņa, D., Nīmante, D., & Baranova, S. (2024). Artificial intelligence for higher education: Benefits and challenges for pre-service teachers. *Frontiers in Education*, *9*, 1501819. Advance online publication. DOI: 10.3389/feduc.2024.1501819

Kamalov, F., & Gurrib, I. (2023). New Era of Artificial Intelligence in Education: Towards a Sustainable Multifaceted Revolution. arXiv (Cornell University). https://doi.org//arxiv.2305.18303DOI: 10.48550

Karpouzis, K. (2024). Artificial Intelligence in Education. *Ethical Considerations and Insights from Ancient Greek Philosophy.*, *1*, 1–7. Advance online publication. DOI: 10.1145/3688671.3688772

Lai, T., Xie, C., Ruan, M., Wang, Z., Lu, H., & Fu, S. (2023). Influence of artificial intelligence in education on adolescents' social adaptability: The mediatory role of social support. *PLoS One*, *18*(3), e0283170. Advance online publication. DOI: 10.1371/journal.pone.0283170

Lampou, R. (2023). The Integration of Artificial Intelligence in Education: Opportunities and Challenges. *Review of Artificial Intelligence in Education*, *4*(00), e015. Advance online publication. DOI: 10.37497/rev.artif.intell.educ.v4i00.15

. Lin, C.-C., Huang, A. Y. Q., & Lu, O. H. T. (2023). Artificial intelligence in intelligent tutoring systems toward sustainable education: a systematic review [Review of Artificial intelligence in intelligent tutoring systems toward sustainable education: a systematic review]. Smart Learning Environments, 10(1). Springer Nature. https://doi.org/DOI: 10.1186/s40561-023-00260-y

Lizano-Sánchez, F., Idoyaga, I., Orduña, P., Rodríguez-Gil, L., & Arguedas-Matarrita, C. (2025). Teachers' perspective on the use of artificial intelligence on remote experimentation. *Frontiers in Education*, *10*, 1518896. Advance online publication. DOI: 10.3389/feduc.2025.1518896

Ma, K., Zhang, Y., & Hui, B.-H. (2024). How Does AI Affect College? The Impact of AI Usage in College Teaching on Students' Innovative Behavior and Well-Being. *Behavioral Sciences (Basel, Switzerland)*, *14*(12), 1223. DOI: 10.3390/bs14121223

Maghsudi, S., Lan, A., Xu, J., & van der Schaar, M. (2021). Personalized Education in the Artificial Intelligence Era: What to Expect Next. *IEEE Signal Processing Magazine*, *38*(3), 37–50. DOI: 10.1109/MSP.2021.3055032

Malik, G., Tayal, D. K., & Vij, S. (2018). An Analysis of the Role of Artificial Intelligence in Education and Teaching. In *Advances in intelligent systems and computing* (p. 407). Springer Nature., DOI: 10.1007/978-981-10-8639-7_42

Mallik, S., & Gangopadhyay, A. (2023). Proactive and Reactive Engagement of Artificial Intelligence Methods for Education: A Review [Review of Proactive and Reactive Engagement of Artificial Intelligence Methods for Education: A Review]. arXiv (Cornell University). Cornell University. https://doi.org//arxiv.2301.10231DOI: 10.48550

Manoharan, G. (2026). Academic Research in the Age of Artificial Intelligence: A Revolutionary Look. In Tariq, M. (Ed.), *Improving Doctoral Education and Research Development for Sustainability* (pp. 363–388). IGI Global Scientific Publishing., DOI: 10.4018/979-8-3373-0225-6.ch012

Manoharan, G., Ashtikar, S. P., & Dudhagara, C. R. (2025). Ethics of AI in the Educational Sector - Navigating the Moral Landscape. In Rajagopal, S., Popat, K., Meva, D., Bajeja, S., & Mudholkar, P. (Eds.), *Artificial Intelligence Based Smart and Secured Applications. ASCIS 2024. Communications in Computer and Information Science* (Vol. 2427). Springer., DOI: 10.1007/978-3-031-86299-1_19

Maphalala, M. C., & Ajani, O. A. (2025). Leveraging artificial intelligence as a learning tool in higher education. *Interdisciplinary Journal of Education Research*, *7*(1), a01. Advance online publication. DOI: 10.38140/ijer-2025.vol7.1.01

Mello, R. F., Freitas, E., Pereira, F. D., Cabral, L., Tedesco, P., & Ramalho, G. (2023). Education in the age of Generative AI: Context and Recent Developments. arXiv (Cornell University). https://doi.org//arxiv.2309.12332DOI: 10.48550

. Merino-Campos, C. (2025). The Impact of Artificial Intelligence on Personalized Learning in Higher Education: A Systematic Review [Review of The Impact of Artificial Intelligence on Personalized Learning in Higher Education: A Systematic Review]. Trends in Higher Education, 4(2), 17. Multidisciplinary Digital Publishing Institute. https://doi.org/DOI: 10.3390/higheredu4020017

Nguyen, A., Ngo, H. N., Hong, Y., Dang, B., & Nguyen, B.-P. T. (2022). Ethical principles for artificial intelligence in education. *Education and Information Technologies*, *28*(4), 4221–4241. DOI: 10.1007/s10639-022-11316-w

Nguyen, N. N., & Barbieri, W. (2025). Mentorship in the Age of Generative AI: ChatGPT to Support Self-Regulated Learning of Pre-Service Teachers Before and During Placements. *Education Sciences*, *15*(6), 642. DOI: 10.3390/educsci15060642

Nguyen, V. (2025). The Use of Generative AI Tools in Higher Education: Ethical and Pedagogical Principles. *Journal of Academic Ethics*, *23*(3), 1435–1455. Advance online publication. DOI: 10.1007/s10805-025-09607-1

Ojha, S., Narendra, A., Mohapatra, S., & Misra, I. (2023). From Robots to Books: An Introduction to Smart Applications of AI in Education (AIEd). arXiv (Cornell University). https://doi.org//arxiv.2301.10026DOI: 10.48550

. Onesi-Ozigagun, O., Ololade, Y. J., Eyo-Udo, N. L., & Ogundipe, D. O. (2024). REVOLUTIONIZING EDUCATION THROUGH AI: A COMPREHENSIVE REVIEW OF ENHANCING LEARNING EXPERIENCES [Review of REVOLUTIONIZING EDUCATION THROUGH AI: A COMPREHENSIVE REVIEW OF ENHANCING LEARNING EXPERIENCES]. International Journal of Applied Research in Social Sciences, 6(4), 589. Fair East Publishers. https://doi.org/DOI: 10.51594/ijarss.v6i4.1011

. Opesemowo, O. A. G., & Adewuyi, H. O. (2024). A systematic review of artificial intelligence in mathematics education: The emergence of 4IR [Review of A systematic review of artificial intelligence in mathematics education: The emergence of 4IR]. Eurasia Journal of Mathematics Science and Technology Education, 20(7). Modestum Limited. https://doi.org/DOI: 10.29333/ejmste/14762

Peddi, S., & Manoharan, G. (2025). Research Issues and Challenges in Higher Education. In Mdikana, A. (Ed.), *Social Implications of Research in Higher Education* (pp. 297–326). IGI Global Scientific Publishing., DOI: 10.4018/979-8-3373-0654-4.ch011

Peddi, S., & Manoharan, G. (2025). Innovative Approaches to Staff Development in Education Using AI. In Morris, G., & Ye, J. (Eds.), *Training and Development in Transnational Higher Education* (pp. 347–368). IGI Global Scientific Publishing., DOI: 10.4018/979-8-3373-1897-4.ch017

Phua, J. T. K., Neo, H. F., & Teo, C.-C. (2025). Evaluating the Impact of Artificial Intelligence Tools on Enhancing Student Academic Performance: Efficacy Amidst Security and Privacy Concerns. *Big Data and Cognitive Computing*, *9*(5), 131. DOI: 10.3390/bdcc9050131

Poornesh, M. (2024). Through a Teacher's Lens: Combating Bias in AI-Powered Education for a Just Future. *The Clearing House: A Journal of Educational Strategies, Issues and Ideas*, *97*(4), 119–124. DOI: 10.1080/00098655.2024.2393153

Purushottamashtikar, S., & Manoharan, G. (2024, June 5). Emotional intelligence on higher education educators: A systematic literature review. *AIP Conference Proceedings*, *2971*(1), 030004. DOI: 10.1063/5.0195788

Resnick, M. (2024). *Generative AI and Creative Learning: Concerns*. Opportunities, and Choices., DOI: 10.21428/e4baedd9.cf3e35e5

Roshanaei, M., Olivares, H., & Lopez, R. R. (2023). Harnessing AI to Foster Equity in Education: Opportunities, Challenges, and Emerging Strategies. *Journal of Intelligent Learning Systems and Applications*, *15*(4), 123–143. DOI: 10.4236/jilsa.2023.154009

Saputra, I., Astuti, M., Sayuti, M., & Kusumastuti, D. (2023). Integration of Artificial Intelligence in Education: Opportunities, Challenges, Threats and Obstacles. A Literature Review. *Indonesian Journal of Computer Science*, *12*(4). Advance online publication. DOI: 10.33022/ijcs.v12i4.3266

. Thomas, D. R., Lin, J., Gatz, E., Gurung, A., Gupta, S., Norberg, K., Fancsali, S., Aleven, V., Branstetter, L., Brunskill, E., & Koedinger, K. R. (2024). Improving Student Learning with Hybrid Human-AI Tutoring: A Three-Study Quasi-Experimental Investigation. https://doi.org/DOI: 10.1145/3636555.3636896

Ullrich, A., Vladova, G., Eigelshoven, F., & Renz, A. (2022). Data mining of scientific research on artificial intelligence in teaching and administration in higher education institutions: A bibliometrics analysis and recommendation for future research. *Discover Artificial Intelligence*, *2*(1), 16. Advance online publication. DOI: 10.1007/s44163-022-00031-7

Vieriu, A. M., & Petrea, G. (2025). The Impact of Artificial Intelligence (AI) on Students' Academic Development. *Education Sciences*, *15*(3), 343. DOI: 10.3390/educsci15030343

Walter, Y. (2024). Embracing the future of Artificial Intelligence in the classroom: The relevance of AI literacy, prompt engineering, and critical thinking in modern education. *International Journal of Educational Technology in Higher Education*, *21*(1), 15. Advance online publication. DOI: 10.1186/s41239-024-00448-3

Ward, B., Bhati, D., Neha, F., & Guercio, A. (2025). Analyzing the Impact of AI Tools on Student Study Habits and Academic Performance. 2022 IEEE 12th Annual Computing and Communication Workshop and Conference (CCWC), 434. https://doi.org/DOI: 10.1109/CCWC62904.2025.10903692

Yu, L., & Yu, Z. (2023). Qualitative and quantitative analyses of artificial intelligence ethics in education using VOSviewer and CitNetExplorer. *Frontiers in Psychology*, *14*, 1061778. Advance online publication. DOI: 10.3389/fpsyg.2023.1061778

. Zhai, X., Chu, X., Chai, C. S., Jong, M. S., Starčič, A. I., Spector, M., Liu, J., Jing, Y., & Li, Y. (2021). A Review of Artificial Intelligence (AI) in Education from 2010 to 2020 [Review of A Review of Artificial Intelligence (AI) in Education from 2010 to 2020]. Complexity, 2021(1). Hindawi Publishing Corporation. https://doi.org/DOI: 10.1155/2021/8812542

Zou, Y. L., Kuek, F., Feng, W., & Cheng, X. (2025). Digital learning in the 21st century: Trends, challenges, and innovations in technology integration. *Frontiers in Education*, *10*, 1562391. Advance online publication. DOI: 10.3389/feduc.2025.1562391

Chapter 12
AI-Powered Career Guidance System for Students

Pancham Singh
https://orcid.org/0009-0005-0435-7941
Department of Information Technology, Ajay Kumar Garg Engineering College, Ghaziabad, India

Shivansh Sharma
Department of Information Technology, Ajay Kumar Garg Engineering College, Ghaziabad, India

Vansh Gupta
Department of Information Technology, Ajay Kumar Garg Engineering College, Ghaziabad, India

Siddharth Yadav
Department of Information Technology, Ajay Kumar Garg Engineering College, Ghaziabad, India

ABSTRACT

In today's fast-changing educational and career environment, many students face confusion and lack proper, personalized guidance when making important professional choices. Traditional career counseling methods, although beneficial, often fall short due to limited accessibility, inherent bias, and scalability challenges. As industries evolve, a growing need has emerged for intelligent, adaptive systems capable of providing accurate, individualized career paths. An AI-powered career guidance system addresses these issues by combining artificial intelligence, machine learning, and data analytics to deliver personalized recommendations aligned with

DOI: 10.4018/979-8-3373-4621-2.ch012

a student's academic background, skills, interests, and aspirations. The guiding concept behind such systems is to bridge the gap between students and quality career advice through smart, technology-driven solutions that adapt over time

INTRODUCTION

The most significant choice of a student's life is the selection of an appropriate career. Yet, such a decision is usually taken on the basis of peer pressure, parental pressure, or fashionable careers and not the individual's interest, talent, and objectives. In India, due to inadequate personalized career guidance and awareness, students tend to make inappropriate decisions, resulting in unhappiness, wasted talent, and multiple job changes (Kulugh et al., n.d.). Conventional school counselling, college counselling, or private professional counselling provides psychological guidance and emotional support. It falls short in coping with the fast-changing labour market and newer careers such as Artificial Intelligence, Data Science, and Digital Marketing. Additionally, limited numbers of trained professionals and the impossibility of scaling individual counselling to a large number of students point toward the necessity for a newer, scalable solution (Kulugh et al., n.d.).

This study suggests the creation of an AI-based Career Guidance System, employing Node.js for backend and React.js as the frontend. The system utilizes machine learning principles and statistical analysis methods for suggesting careers based on each student's profile. The system takes into account academic results, interests, strengths, personality characteristics, and socio-economic status to provide individualized and well-based career suggestions. AI has already demonstrated great promise in addressing real-world issues by automating processes, forecasting outcomes, and providing intelligent recommendations (Bećirović et al., 2025). In the context of career guidance, AI can compare vast amounts of data such as student records, past career success models, and current job market trends to provide timely and correct recommendations. The system is architected similar to recommendation engines utilized by online companies, recommending not just career routes but also college courses, certifications, and skills development programs as well. The business logic, data processing, and communication with AI models are undertaken by the backend, which was coded in Node.js. The frontend, designed based on React.js, is an intuitive profile creation interface for viewing results as well as feedback submission. A database with security for storing user data such as profiles, grades, and history of recommendations, designed based on Entity-Relationship (ER) diagrams, maintains clarity for the user information. The modular structure of the system is represented using UML diagrams class, sequence, and activity which also allow for future enhancements and scalability.

Privacy and ethical design are fundamental aspects of the system. Because sensitive student information is being used, rigorous privacy practices, user opt-in, and data protection procedures are implemented (Thakare et al., 2025). The AI models are designed to minimize bias and not perpetuate gender or socio-economic stereotypes, making recommendations fair and inclusive for all students. Accessibility is another significant advantage of being a web application; the system can serve students in remote or underserved areas, providing equal access to quality career guidance. It is more than a tool, though. This system aims to build a student-centred experience that develops with the student (Wang, 2024). With younger students, the system gives initial recommendations based on initial interests and academic patterns. The system presents increasingly sophisticated and focused career streams as students mature and learn more about themselves.

To validate its effectiveness, the system's recommendations are compared with those provided by experienced counsellors. Evaluation criteria include the accuracy of recommendations, student satisfaction, and response time. Initial results show that this system can match or even surpass conventional methods in providing personalized and reliable career advice (Westman et al., 2021). In summary, this study presents a technology-based solution to the multifaceted issue of career choice. By integrating Artificial Intelligence, intelligent data analysis, and new web technologies, the system offered in this study delivers precise, scalable, and personalized career advice (Pancham et al., 2025). It enables students to make informed decisions, boosts confidence, and facilitates lifelong career growth. In the end, this system shifts from advice based on a single size to adaptive guidance that adapts to the student.

The rest of this paper is structured as: Section 2 presents related works and existing systems; Section 3 explains system requirements and feasibility; Section 4 illustrates the system architecture and design; Section 5 addresses UML diagrams; Section 6 emphasizes database design; Section 7 describes the implementation approach; Section 8 discusses testing and outcomes; Section 9 identifies ethical concerns; and Section 10 concludes with future work.

KEY OBJECTIVE OF THIS PAPER

The main objective of this research is to develop and implement an AI-based career counseling system that utilizes machine learning algorithms to provide personalized career suggestions to students based on their strengths, abilities, and interests (Mehraj & Baba, 2019). The system will fill the gap between academic success and right career selection through data-driven insight to support student decision-making. In addition, it will offer an economically sustainable, affordable, and scalable solution that can be adopted by individuals and institutions alike. With the use of cutting-edge web technologies and artificial intelligence techniques, the research showcases the potential of intelligent automation to revolutionize traditional career counselling as an improved and personalized process.

RELATED WORK

Ong and Lim (2023) have analysed the use of machine learning techniques to suggest personalised skills based on job titles. Their suggested system, SkillRec, uses word embeddings coupled with deep neural networks to extract contextual meaning from job titles and then suggest relevant skills. The model is trained on a corpus of 6,000 actual job titles, enabling it to perform contextual analysis and vector space mapping to effectively relate job seekers, particularly students, to the dynamic skill demands of the market. The study highlights the capacity of SkillRec to enable users to find suitable career paths and predict future skill trends. The performance of the system was tested using F1-score and comparative performance metrics for different models, highlighting its precision and dependability in real-world use.

Westman et al. (2021) have researched the use of artificial intelligence for resume screening and career guidance via a platform called ResumAI. Using natural language processing and pattern recognition methodologies, the system automatically evaluates resumes, analyses their content, identifies missing information, and suggests enhancements based on individual skill sets of jobs. The research highlights the effectiveness of the system in rendering job-specific feedback on job applicants and enhancing their employability potential. Further, it discusses pertinent ethical issues such as transparency, fairness, and accountability regarding the use of AI in human resource technology, and highlights the necessity of developing responsible AI tools for recruitment and career development processes.

Wang (2024) has performed an analysis of an Indian graduate-specific career guidance system using decision tree and random forest algorithms. The system assesses a set of parameters, like students' academic performance, personal interest, career aspiration, and soft skills, to recommend appropriate career options, e.g., further studies, entrepreneurship, or jobs. Based on accessible student information, it delivers customized and adaptive career counselling. The project will allow educational institutions to provide one-on-one counselling, thus mapping students' aspirations with available career prospects and optimizing career decision-making in Indian education.

Trujillo et al. (2025) have carried out research on a job recommendation platform named GIRL (Generative Intelligent Recommendation for Labor), which uses large language models to produce personalized job recommendations and career advice. Unlike traditional keyword-based methods, GIRL uses generative AI to understand the natural language contained in resumes, thereby producing customized job descriptions and advice from users' individual profiles. The platform improves its performance by integrating user feedback and modelling career shifts, thereby allowing users to visualize likely job opportunities and make highly informed choices. It significantly contributes to improving user engagement through relevant and adaptive recommendations by utilizing advanced language processing methods.

Saini (2024) has compared the performance of an AI-facilitated hiring platform, JobHobe, that automates the recruitment process by intelligently matching resumes with job postings. The platform chooses qualifications over keyword matching, minimizing bias and enhancing candidate choice. By shortlisting the most suitable candidates based on skill and relevance, JobHobe enables recruiters to discover appropriate candidates within a shorter duration, thus optimizing the recruitment process. The study demonstrates how the platform is able to enhance recruitment accuracy, minimize time-to-hire, and enable merit-based hiring, thus offering a scalable solution to contemporary talent recruitment issues.

Kulugh et al. (n.d.) have studied the application of the WHO-RXGBoost model for predictive career guidance and entrepreneurial growth among university students. The AI model combines parameters such as educational qualification, demographic data, and experiential learning to recommend personalized career choices. More precise and easy to use than traditional machine learning models, WHO-RXGBoost demonstrates improved accuracy and user satisfaction. The paper documents its potential for not only improving students' employability but also entrepreneurship by offering actionable, data-based suggestions that adapt to users' changing profiles and interests.

Hartley et al. (n.d.) have conducted an analysis in the context of integrating artificial intelligence technologies into career guidance systems, with a focus on particularly guidance based on students. The research offers a framework based on machine learning algorithms to analyse educational records, personal interests, and cognitive characteristics for the presentation of personalized career options. Through the application of adaptive learning models, the system improves its recommendations through continuous user interaction and feedback. It emphasizes the need to ensure data privacy and ethical model training, with the aim of minimizing bias and maximizing transparency. This research contributes to the creation of scalable and student-centric guidance platforms with educational outcomes mapped to real-world employment requirements.

Kulugh et al. (n.d.) have discussed the possibility of agent-based interventions based on large language models to support career exploration through a novel letter-exchange intervention. The system, for young adults, evokes reflective thinking and emotional engagement through a simulated personalized dialogue. The study shows that this intervention enhances users' motivation and knowledge for career planning.

The AI-driven interaction not only provides necessary career-related information but also evokes emotional resilience, hence acting as an effective intervention to help individuals voice their aspirations and formulate concrete steps toward their career goals.

Michelson et al. (2021) have made a conceptual framework analysis of MentorAI, an AI-powered mentorship platform aimed at professional development through real-time mentoring. The platform is meant to offer customized recommendations based on users' unique profiles and professional aspirations while ensuring ethical implications of AI use. The study also addresses data privacy and algorithmic bias issues, with suggestions for ensuring transparency and accountability in its functioning. MentorAI is a case of an innovative approach to scalable and personalized mentorship, having been able to successfully combine traditional advisory models with smart automation.

Chen et al. (2025) have discussed the application of an Encoder-Decoder LSTM-based AI model to forecast and guide student career paths. The system evaluates academic background and self-stated ambitions to propose individualized career options, thus allowing students to align their talents with the appropriate opportunities. The model is unique in its forecasting capability and contextual understanding. Furthermore, the study discusses ethical issues, such as data privacy and AI-driven decision-making fairness, making the system technically feasible and socially acceptable within the career counselling domain.

Trujillo et al. (2025) have examined the application of artificial intelligence in enabling career guidance for young people through personalized observations of emerging job opportunities. Using large datasets and forecasting algorithms, the system offers personalized suggestions that allow people to make education and career choices. The study demonstrates the usefulness of AI in overcoming the shortcomings of traditional counselling, particularly for disadvantaged groups. It supports the contention that, if applied ethically, AI can level the playing field in access to quality career information and allow people to adapt to the forces of shifting labour market conditions.

Rao et al. (2020) have carried out a study on developing a Decision Support System based on Artificial Neural Networks (ANNs) to help students select suitable vocational career paths. The system, having learned from aptitude and knowledge-based test data, precisely suggests career options—resulting in a 91% concordance with Discriminant Function Analysis and an 81% agreement with human career guides. This is superior to that of conventional methods of career guidance and shows the potential of artificial intelligence in giving accurate career guidance. The study also indicates the feasibility of the system in educational institutions where professional career guides are not readily available.

Santos et al. (2025) have investigated the application of an artificial intelligence and big data analytics-based Talent Intelligence Solution through the Technology-Organization-Environment (TOE) model for career development and talent management. The system continuously matches the skills of employees with organizational needs to suggest customized career development plans. Structured machine learning methods are applied in the system to reconcile individual aspirations and corporate goals. This two-way process ensures both workforce planning and individual development are encompassed in account, and thus it is an omnibus tool for the modern talent environment.

METHODOLOGY

System Requirements and Feasibility

Developing a dependable AI-based Career Guidance System requires full understanding of the underlying technology, key qualities, and ways of implementing such a system for enduring success and valuable results. Originally designed for personal and end-user needs as well as educational institutions, the platform runs smoothly on everyday hardware configurations. The requirements from the client side are also minimal, only to require an Intel i3 processor, 4 GB of ram storage and 100 effectively unit storage and connectivity at least at 512 kb, or where appropriate higher speeds rendering such a system suitable for low resource institutions. In terms of server requirements, the system should better benefit from a Quad-Core processor (Intel i5 and above), 8 GB of RAM, and a 100 GB SSD. Servers are set to use reliable web servers such as Apache or Nginx, operating on systems as Ubuntu/Linux or Windows Server. From the software perspective, the system applies a modern web-based architecture approaching scalability and responsiveness. React.js propels the frontend, along with CSS3 frameworks Tailwind or Bootstrap managing the aesthetics, while JavaScript/TypeScript brings a touch of interactivity to produce a smooth user experience. The backend is built using Node.js and express.js - controlling the system logic and providing the ability to communicate with API. MongoDB is a No SQL- based configuration that manages unstructured outcomes such as student profiles and test outcomes giving flexibility and scalability (Pancham et al., 2025). TensorFlow is critical for building up the machine learning models which are the essence of the recommendation engine.

Several non-functional goals are relevant at the design of the system. Scalability of the system provides the guarantee of support for a substantial user population. Encryption and secure log in procedures are used to ensure security throughout the platform. Ease of use is emphasized through an uncomplicated design aimed at student users. The modularity of the codebase enables maintenance; the ability to add or change features in the future is easy. The system has technical viability, making use of tried tools such as Python, Node.js, TensorFlow, and MongoDB to save time during development and reduce risks. Cost effectiveness is realized with open-source software and affordable hosting options. Cloud service providers' educational discounts or free trials would go a long way of improving the financial projection of the project.

Technically, the system is designed to blend smoothly into educational settings requiring little modification or instruction. It complements existing routines and creates easy access for all the participants. Moreover, it is customizable for real-time analytics, a transparent integration of the job site, and resume preparation to create an all-in-one career planning resource (Morsy, 2024). Finally, the AI-driven Career Guidance System is a credible, cost-effective and significant system for career preparation. Providing custom recommendations, this system assists students in decision-making, and enables institutions to provide informed services, thereby transforming the traditional career counselling into a scalable and data-driven process, which resembles actual scenarios.

System Design and Architecture

The Student Career Recommendation System is built with utmost care to give users an intelligent and seamless environment in which to navigate proper career alternatives based on their interests, strengths, and academic background. The system is built following the Model-View-Controller (MVC) architectural pattern, which keeps the core logic (Controller), data storage (Model), and the user interface (View) separate. This separation of concerns keeps the system maintainable, scalable, and debuggable over a long period. At the centre of the architecture are three primary components: the frontend, the backend, and the database(Ong & Lim, 2023). The frontend is built using React.js, a mature JavaScript library to build fast, responsive, and component-based interfaces. Students interact with this layer to register, login, complete assessments, and receive career recommendations. Axios, a promise-based HTTP client library, facilitates smooth and efficient communication between the frontend and the backend. The backend is built using Node.js and Express.js, providing a scalable, event-driven architecture to process many concurrent requests efficiently. This layer processes all business logic, including input validation, processing test results, interaction with the AI recommendation engine, and sending responses to the frontend (Hartley et al., n.d.). Express.js handles routing, middleware functions, and APIs for student registration, quiz submission, and data retrieval. For storing data, the system uses MongoDB, a flexible and scalable NoSQL database. MongoDB facilitates efficient storage of heterogeneous data types such as student profiles, quiz responses, generated recommendations, and feedback. Its document-based nature makes it ideal for storing unstructured or semi-structured data, common in educational apps.

The most distinguishing feature of the system is an artificial intelligence-based recommendation engine. Upon collecting input from the students such as personal data, academic record, and feedback from the career assessment test—the system processes a series of pre-processing tasks such as data validation and classification of scores. The cleaned-up data is then input into the machine learning module, which uses techniques such as content-based filtering or decision trees to generate tailored career suggestions (Goel et al., 2025). The suggestions are not only generated based on unprocessed test scores but also take into account patterns, likes, and improvement areas of the student. The result is then presented in the form of a user-friendly interface providing actionable career suggestions, skill-building advice, and next-step suggestions. The entire end-to-end solution enables students to make sound career decisions based on real facts and tailored analysis (Fotea et al., 2019). The system is also crafted keeping usability, performance, and security in view. It provides rapid response times, secures user data by utilizing secure authentication and encryption methods, and is straightforward enough to be used easily by high school and college students. The modular structure also renders the system very easy to maintain and easy to update as shifting future needs change. Overall, the architecture allows for a strong, secure, and user-friendly platform to cater to the crucial requirement of career advice using modern-day web technologies and intelligent algorithms.

Interactions Between Modules

The Student Career Recommendation System uses RESTful APIs to seamlessly connect its React.js frontend and Node.js/Express.js backend, ensuring smooth communication. When a student inputs personal details, preferences, or assessment test responses through the intuitive interface, the frontend sends this data via secure POST requests to the server, where it's validated and processed shown in Figure 1. The backend interacts with a MongoDB database to retrieve or update student records, test configurations, or career mappings, while the integrated recommendation engine employs machine learning algorithms to analyse the input and generate tailored career suggestions (Wang, 2024). These personalized recommendations are sent back to the frontend through structured API responses, displaying actionable guidance to the student. By executing the recommendation logic server-side, the system maintains scalability, centralized control, and high performance, efficiently supporting a growing user base while empowering students with data-driven career paths aligned with their strengths and goals.

Figure 1. System architecture diagram

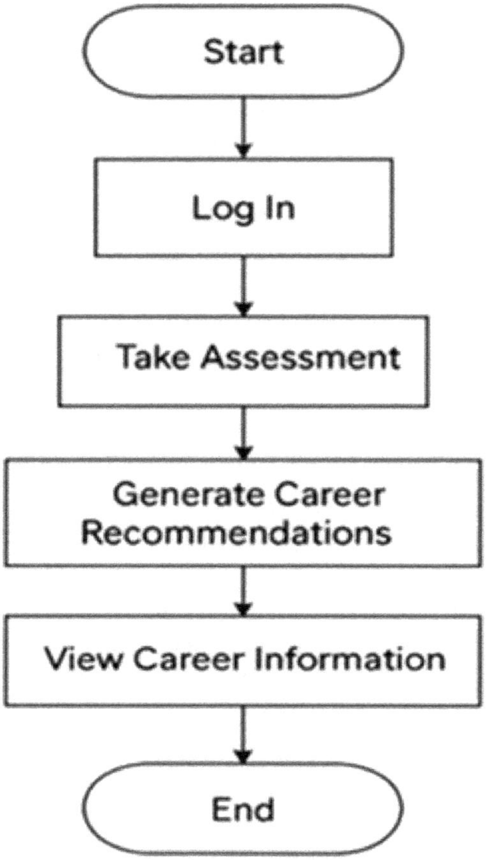

UML Diagrams

System Flowchart

The system flowchart for the AI Career Guidance platform offers a clear, step-by-step visual of how the system operates, from a student's first interaction to receiving personalized career recommendations. It highlights the key components: user input, data validation, AI processing, and output display. The journey begins when a student enters their details, preferences, or assessment responses through an easy-to-use interface. These inputs are then checked for accuracy during data validation to ensure reliable processing (Singh et al., 2024). Next, the AI engine, powered by advanced algorithms, analyses the validated data, drawing insights to match the student's profile with suitable career paths. Finally, the system presents tailored career suggestions in a clear, engaging format. This high-level overview simplifies the complex interplay between the platform's modules, making it easier to understand how each part works together to deliver a seamless, data-driven experience that guides students toward informed career choices. It is depicted in Figure 2.

Figure 2. System flow chat

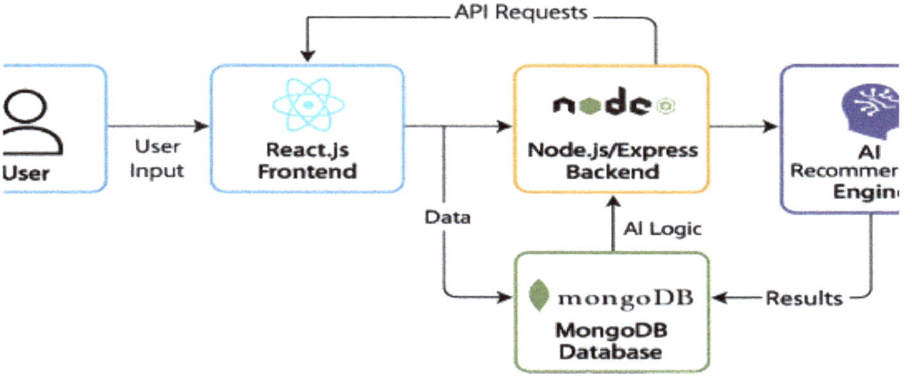

AI-Based Career Recommendation Process Flowchart

This flowchart shows the backend logic of how AI generates personalized career paths. Once the input data is received, the system performs pre-processing, applies the trained ML model, ranks career options based on fit, and sends the final recommendation to the frontend for display. The process flow diagram is shown in Figure 3.

Figure 3. Process flowchart

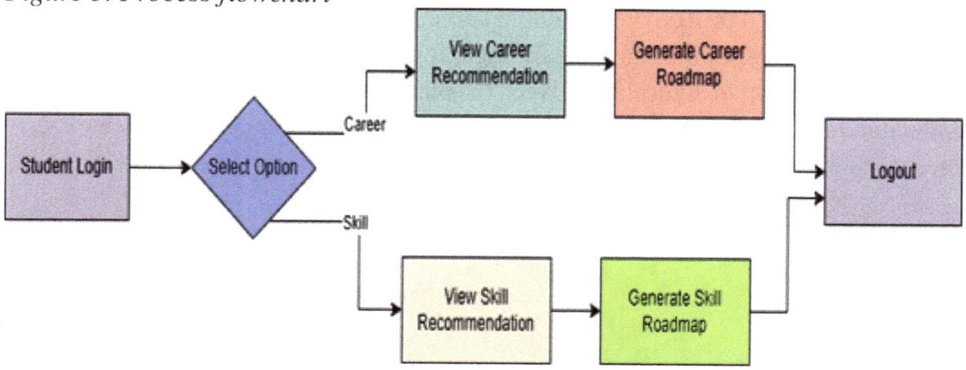

Database Design

The database is an important part of the career guidance system, facilitating proper data management and fast access to information. It is designed in such a manner that it is capable of holding and managing information on students, their test performance, career alternatives, skill suggestions, and personalized blueprints.

The primary entities within the system are Student, Career, Test Result, Recommendation, Skill, and Roadmap. Student records hold personal and academic details, while Test Result holds the result of aptitude or interest assessments. Based on test results, the system formulates a Recommendation, which can be in the form of a Career or a Skill. The recommendations have an associated Roadmap that gives a step-by-step path or collection of learning modules to reach the desired goal.

Relationships are explicitly defined a student can have more than one test result and recommendation. Each recommendation is associated with either a career or skill, and a career or skill can be linked to several roadmaps. This architecture enables personalized and dynamic recommendations per user.

Normalization is done up to the third normal form (3NF) to remove redundancy and maintain data integrity. For instance, instead of storing career information multiple times in different recommendations, they are stored once in the Career table and referenced through foreign keys.

This model of relationships provides scalability, querying efficiency, and consistency of data. An ER diagram is used to visually illustrate this structure, emphasizing entity attributes, primary keys, and foreign key relationships that enable the operation of the recommendation engine.

Implementation Details

The Career Guidance System was designed on a modular, scalable framework consisting of a responsive frontend with a smart backend logic for ensuring usability, flexibility, and computational effectiveness. The system aims to examine student interests, aptitude test scores, and individualized learning objectives to suggest appropriate career paths and formal skill development plans. The overall development strategy was component-based, where every one of the fundamental functionalities user registration, aptitude test, recommendation engine, and roadmap generation was built as a standalone module (Singh et al., 2024). This module-based structure enabled parallel development with ease, enhanced maintainability, and allowed scalability for future enhancements or feature addition. The frontend was built with React.js, a popular JavaScript library for its component-based structure, dynamic rendering, and reusability, which together provided a highly interactive and seamless user experience. Tailwind CSS was used to style the interface, taking advantage of its utility-first approach to apply responsive and uniform design patterns across different screen sizes and devices. The backend was created with Node.js and the Express.js framework, providing strong routing, effective middleware handling, and RESTful API construction necessary for managing data flow and user sessions. Frontend and backend communication was handled through RESTful APIs, which provided structured, secure, and efficient data transfer between client and server layers during user sign-up, test processing, and recommendation retrieval.

The database layer used MongoDB, a document-based NoSQL database chosen for its adaptability in storing varied and changing data structures. It was especially well-positioned to handle dynamic student profiles, aptitude test scores, interest tags, and the individualized roadmaps that the system produces. The schema was optimized to enable efficient querying and extensibility, and indexing strategies were adopted to improve performance on large datasets. The system's underlying intelligence is housed in its recommendation engine, which uses content-based filtering methods. This framework processes a student's test scores, stated interests, and academic history, and compares them to a hand-curated set of career paths and related competencies. A similarity-matching algorithm, combined with rule-based reasoning, calculates relevance scores and ranks the best-fit career choices for the student. Each suggested path is supplemented with a dynamically created roadmap of key skills, certifications, materials, and estimated timelines, enabling the student to see a distinct progression path.

Although the initial model employs deterministic logic, the system has been architected for extensibility, allowing for the incorporation of machine learning algorithms in subsequent releases. Suggested improvements are supervised models like decision trees and ensemble methods, and collaborative filtering methods that will utilize user feedback and historical data to enhance recommendation precision and personalization progressively. For the consistency and performance of the system, a comprehensive testing protocol was followed. This comprised unit testing of individual modules, integration testing to ensure cross-module interactions, and system-level testing to ensure overall stability and correctness. Certain test cases emulated real-world conditions such as new user registrations, varied aptitude test inputs, personalized recommendation generation, and roadmap rendering.

The system performed consistently well in the majority of test scenarios. Functional testing revealed that user flows from input to output were preserved with high integrity. Minor user interface issues faced during the initial testing stage were promptly fixed. Performance measurements were based on response time, system throughput, and scalability. The time required for generating personalized career suggestions averaged 2 to 3 seconds, proving the responsiveness of the system. Load testing affirmed that platform can support up to 100 concurrent users without performance degradation, suggesting the system's suitability for institutional deployment or wide public use. To establish the validity of the recommendation engine, system output was compared with expert career counsellor recommendations. Analysis revealed an 87% alignment between the system-provided career paths and human-expert-recommended career paths, affirming that the recommendation engine is accurate. This finding shows the strength and reliability of the AI-powered engine, particularly in providing consistent, objective, and timely recommendations. Furthermore, the platform was contrasted with other career guidance platforms, where it showed more personalization, transparency, and actionability through comprehensive skill roadmaps—a capability that most generic tools lack. Though human counsellors are still vital for empathy and subtle decision-making, the system augments these abilities with a scalable, data-driven solution that is especially well-suited for mass usage and digital-first consumers.

The overall implementation approach harmoniously integrates cutting-edge web development technologies with fundamental AI logic, resulting in a user-focused, flexible, and high-performance system. The use of open-source frameworks ensures cost-effectiveness and ease of community-driven improvement. The design of architecture, based on modularity and component independence, situates the Career Guidance System as a future-proof platform that can be adapted to incorporate emerging technologies like adaptive learning systems, real-time analysis, and support for multilingualism. Overall, the development process, design, and implementation of the Career Guidance System demonstrate a mature development process that is supported by both technical strength and educational grounding as a secure and intelligent tool for guided career decision-making.

RESULTS AND DISCUSSION

The suggested AI-powered Career Guidance System showed promising outcomes in offering personalized and data-driven advice to students. From input data academic performance, interests, and aptitude test scores the system could suggest appropriate career paths and skills-based learning pathways specifically tailored to the individual user.

Implications of Output, one of the key observations was the ability of the system to suggest career choices that closely match the strengths and interests of the user. Students who followed the suggestions expressed a clearer sense of direction about their future aspirations. The system also effectively offered step-by-step roadmaps, which encompassed essential skills, learning materials, and timeframes, thus helping students divide their aspirations into actionable steps. Additionally, the use of AI models (e.g., decision tree or content-based filtering) allowed the system to learn and modify its suggestions over time as more user data were gathered, increasing its intelligence and sophistication.

Limitations, although it has its benefits, the system is not without its limitations. First, the quality of the suggestions is highly dependent on the quality of the input data. Vague or wrong input can generate less relevant results. Second, although the system tries to eliminate bias, it is still based on the available data sets, which might not reflect real-world diversity or the dynamically changing character of the labour market. Moreover, another limitation is that emotional and psychological considerations, which are usually taken care of by human counsellors, are not adequately reflected in the system.

Benefits of the System, the system has numerous advantages, particularly in terms of scalability and availability. In contrast to human counsellors, who are not necessarily available or in other places, the platform is available 24/7, thereby making career counselling more accessible and cost-effective. Furthermore, the system provides consistency in guidance, as much as possible by eliminating human bias. It also facilitates continuous learning and improvement through feedback loop mechanisms and analysing data in real-time. Lastly, while the AI-powered Career Guidance System cannot completely replace human advisors, it is a powerful supplementary tool that provides data-driven, personalized advice to help students make better career and learning choices.

CONCLUSION AND FUTURE SCOPE

This research describes the development of an AI-based Career Guidance System, which has been specifically designed to offer personalized, data-based recommendations to students as they navigate their careers and academic courses. Through the processing of diverse inputs like aptitude test results, academic background, and user interests, the system recommends appropriate career options and skill-acquisition plans that are tailored to each individual. Artificial intelligence ensures flexibility and scalability, thereby providing standardized and sage advice to a diverse group of users. One of the main contributions of this work is in the automation of career guidance through artificial intelligence models, which can deliver efficient, unbiased, and scalable guidance. This is extremely important in schools that are constrained by limitations through limited trained human counsellors or due to large enrolments. The platform not only advises users in selecting a career but also recommends particular skills, courses, and timetables, thus allowing them to take concrete steps towards their aspirations.

In the future, the system can be further developed by incorporating real-time information on the labour market, such as job trends, compensation data, and emerging technologies, thus making the recommendations more relevant and timelier. Further development can also include the incorporation of psychological profiling and soft-skill testing to tackle concerns regarding emotional intelligence, creativity, and interpersonal skills. The system is scalable and can be used in schools, colleges, and government portals, allowing for wide usage across regions and socio-economic classes. Multilingual capabilities and mobile interfaces can also be added further. Feedback mechanisms and ongoing model training will allow the recommendations to improve over time, adapting to both learner progress and market demand.

REFERENCES

Bećirović, S., Polz, E., & Tinkel, I. (2025). Exploring students' AI literacy and its effects on their AI output quality, self-efficacy, and academic performance. *Smart Learning Environments*, *12*(1), 29. DOI: 10.1186/s40561-025-00384-3

Chen, S., Xie, J., Wang, G., Wang, H., Cheng, H., & Huang, Y. (2025). From Scores to Careers: Understanding AI's Role in Supporting Collaborative Family Decision-Making in Chinese College Applications. *Proceedings of the 2025 CHI Conference on Human Factors in Computing Systems*, 1–20. DOI: 10.1145/3706598.3713341

Fotea, S., Fotea, I., & undrea, E. (2019). *Artificial intelligence in education - romanian students' attitudes toward artificial intelligence and its impact on their career development*. 9330–9338. DOI: 10.21125/iceri.2019.2259

Goel, R., Jaiswal, U. K., Singh, P., Yadav, S. P., & Upadhyay, P. (2025). Deep Learning for Early Brain Tumor Detection: A Keras-Based Approach Using MRI and CT Imaging. In Mishra, A., Yadav, S. P., Kumar, M., Biju, S. M., & Deka, G. C. (Eds.), *Demystifying the Role of Natural Language Processing (NLP) in Mental Health* (pp. 145–180). IGI Global., DOI: 10.4018/979-8-3693-4203-9.ch009

Hartley, J. S., Jolevski, F., Melo, V., & Moore, B. (n.d.). *The Labor Market Effects of Generative Artificial Intelligence*.

Kulugh, V. E., Aondover, K. P., & Faki, A. S. (n.d.). Artificial Intelligence-Powered Personalised Career Guidance System. *Artificial Intelligence*.

Mehraj, T., & Baba, A. M. (2019). *Scrutinising Artificial Intelligence based Career Guidance and Counselling Systems: An Appraisal. 7*(1).

Michelson, R., DeWitt, A., Nagar, R., Hiniker, A., Yip, J., Munson, S. A., & Kientz, J. A. (2021). Parenting in a Pandemic: Juggling Multiple Roles and Managing Technology Use in Family Life During COVID-19 in the United States. *Proceedings of the ACM on Human-Computer Interaction, 5*(CSCW2), 1–39. DOI: 10.1145/3479546

Morsy, R. M. A. (2024). *The Impact of Expert Systems and Big Data Analytics Capabilities on Decision-Making in Private Higher Educational Sector in Egypt*.

Ong, X. Q., & Lim, K. H. (2023). *SkillRec: A Data-Driven Approach to Job Skill Recommendation for Career Insights* (No. arXiv:2302.09938). arXiv. /arXiv.2302.09938DOI: 10.1109/ICCAE56788.2023.10111438

Pancham, S., Updesh, K. J., Eshank, J., Nikhil, K., & Vimlesh, M. (2025). A Novel Methodology Utilizing Modern CCTV Cameras and Software as a Service Model for Crime Detection and Prediction. *International Journal of Performability Engineering, 21*(2), 112. DOI: 10.23940/ijpe.25.02.p6.112121

Rao, A. S., Kamath, B. S., & Kundar, R. K. (2020). Use of Artificial Neural Network in Developing a Personality Prediction Model for Career Guidance: A Boon for Career Counselors. *International Journal of Control and Automation, 13*(4).

Saini, A. (2024). IMPACT OF ARTIFICIAL INTELLIGENCE ON STUDENTS' SUSTAINABLE EDUCATION AND CAREER DEVELOPMENT USING EXTENDED TOE FRAMEWORK. *International Research Journal of Education and Technology, 6*(11), 224–243. DOI: 10.70127/irjedt.vol.7.issue02.243

Santos, F. M. D. A., Pereira, A., Shanches, A., Crespo, D., & Pala, H. (2025). The impacts of AI and automation on human resource management – systematic review. *Brazilian Journal of Development, 11*(2), e78003. DOI: 10.34117/bjdv11n2-079

Singh, P., Kansal, M., Singh, A. P., Verma, A., Tyagi, S., & Singh, A. V. (2024). Real-Time Symptomatic Disease Predictor Using Multi-Layer Perceptron. In Sharma, A. K., Chanderwal, N., Tyagi, S., & Upadhyay, P. (Eds.), (pp. 155–167). Advances in Medical Technologies and Clinical Practice. IGI Global., DOI: 10.4018/979-8-3693-2359-5.ch010

Thakare, Y. A., Satote, R. R., Kenkar, S. A., Nathile, S. R., Watane, S. A., & Hade, S. C. (2025). AI-based career counsellor: An AI driven career advisor. *International Journal of Science and Research Archive, 15*(1), 1013–1023. DOI: 10.30574/ijsra.2025.15.1.1088

Trujillo, F., Pozo, M., & Suntaxi, G. (2025). Artificial intelligence in education: A systematic literature review of machine learning approaches in student career prediction. *Journal of Technology and Science Education, 15*(1), 162. DOI: 10.3926/jotse.3124

Wang, W. (2024). Exploring the Attitudes of Higher Vocational College Students toward Artificial Intelligence: A Case Study in China. In Lin, C., Chew, F. P., Khan, I. A., & Popescu, C. (Eds.), *Proceedings of the 2024 9th International Conference on Modern Management, Education and Social Sciences (MMET 2024)* (Vol. 880, pp. 593–604). Atlantis Press SARL. DOI: 10.2991/978-2-38476-309-2_73

Westman, S., Kauttonen, J., Klemetti, A., Korhonen, N., Manninen, M., Mononen, A., Niittymäki, S., & Paananen, H. (2021). Artificial Intelligence for Career Guidance – Current Requirements and Prospects for the Future. *IAFOR Journal of Education, 9*(4), 43–62. DOI: 10.22492/ije.9.4.03

Chapter 13
Enhancing Learning Efficiency Using AI-Driven Adaptive Agents

Usharani Bhimavarapu
https://orcid.org/0000-0002-0246-1420
Koneru Lakshmaiah Education Foundation, India

ABSTRACT

Adaptive Learning Agents (ALAs) are intelligent computer software designed to provide tailored, adaptive, and data-driven learning experiences for higher education. Based on information on students obtained from in-school placements, self-learning reflections, and mentor feedback, ALAs are able to monitor learners' development and modify instruction content to address certain needs. Sophisticated feature selection methods such as Seagull Optimization recognize the most appropriate features, whereas hierarchical patterns are acquired by Bi-Stacked ResNet models for precise performance prediction. These functionalities facilitate real-time feedback, customized learning pathways, and constant surveillance, which empower effective skill acquisition and motivation. Inclusion of ALAs facilitates collaborative learning strategies, incorporation of theory and professional practice, and fine-tuning of scalability, sustainability, and education innovation.

INTRODUCTION

Adaptive Learning Agents, therefore, are set to engage learners in adaptive learning activities in the form of pedagogical content reorganization, dynamically, relative to a learner's capability and state of achievement. In contrast, ALAs tend to follow a strict study plan, which is inflexible toward the different learning needs

DOI: 10.4018/979-8-3373-4621-2.ch013

of individuals. Learning environments are therefore capable of learning in beat and harmony with the learner under the umbrella of ALAs. Personalization is more engaging; it reduces cognitive load and makes recall easy. ALAs are thereby capable of tracking student activities, establishing points of struggle, and intervening early enough. They do this through data-driven methods using a closed-loop system. This enables students to focus on mastering concepts instead of having to struggle in the one-size-fits-all approach. This flexibility hereby gives way to rendering learning challenging yet achievable. Generally, ALAs are designed with the purpose of optimizing the impact of learning, but they have the ability to adapt to dynamic learning profiles. ALAs have been designed so as to handle the dynamic needs of modern-day education systems. Among the major roles played by an Adaptive Learning Agent are maintaining the motivation of the learners.

Motivation is a very critical element in learning with success, and neither success nor repeated failure has the ability to eliminate motivation. ALAs detect such events and raise our challenge levels or offer alternative means for confidence-building among students. With timely personalized feedback these agents instill a feeling of accomplishment and progress. They detect the learning preference, visual, auditory, or kinesthetic, and modify instruction to it. Such tailored mentoring ensure engagement by students and dropouts are minimized. Furthermore, adaptive agents make learning game-like with challenges and reward proportional to the learner's ability. Adaptive agents also enable autonomous learning through the availability of scaffolding or prompts when needed. Through these applications, learners have a personalized learning cycle. This is because of improved long-term memory and knowledge acquisition. Adaptive Learning Agents play a significant role in facilitating heterogenous groups of learners. Students differ in the level of knowledge they have when they come to class, capacity to learn, and learning mode, and mass teaching thus becomes inefficient.

ALAs analyze the response of learners, trace the progress, and identify knowledge gaps. ALA manages the content delivery such that the gaps are filled so that no learner is left behind. Apart from this, adaptive aid in readable data display is provided to disabled students or disabled students. The text size may be variable or text-to-speech may be there to make them accessible. They may monitor the interest levels and detect frustration cues and signs of weariness. They facilitate equal learning opportunity through dynamic adaptation. Instructions may be set by teachers based on the feedback received through ALAs. The approach offers customized learning with batch curriculum objectives. ALAs are used to help to make the learning effective and efficient. During conventional learning, students waste time learning something which they already know or learning something which they never master without any intervention form. Adaptive agents avoid the wastage of efforts by revealing the material based on the knowledge of the learner.

They use learning goal prioritization and indicate the problem areas. The continuous monitoring of performance determines the best sequence of themes through ALAs. They also introduce spaced repetition and reinforcement possibilities to develop the best retrieval of memory. Mass practice is not always in the best interests of the students since individualized practice is ideal. Adaptive agents minimize the cognitive overload to a large degree because they segment difficult material into manageable procedures. Mastering takes place prior to the presentation of hard topics by the adaptive agents. Learning is effectively planned, efficient and targeted. It is also a must for testing and providing feedback in time for Adaptive Learning Agents. This is generally done on a periodic basis, at times after very elongated training sessions, and hence does not provide any scope for action in time. ALAs continually monitor the reaction and interaction of the students.

They detect misconceptions and give remedial feedback in real time. Right guidance provides for learning before error generation. Factors of progress measurement, such as accuracy and speed, are retained by adaptive agents. Teachers and managers get actionable insights in order to make adjustments in lesson planning or to provide assistance. Real-time feedback helps in providing an active learning culture in which the learners learn in time. Monitoring this way ensures long-term knowledge about the content. Learning comes across as an engaging and challenging process. Adaptive Learning Agents are built to bring lifelong learning into the picture. In this knowledge era, wherein the environment is changing at a very high pace on a continuous basis, capability development on a regular basis is very important. ALAs guide learners from school to corporate training at different stages of life.

They can create learning paths in accord with certain career goals or competency sets. Adaptive agents also provide appropriate resources and exercise problems for skill acquisition. Directions are provided to students depending on individual interest as well as organizational demands. ALAs drive self-directed, lifelong learning behaviors through customized paths. Second, they make knowledge creation needs consciousness and produce sufficient response in time during learning. This keeps students current and responsive. Adaptive systems therefore bridge the gap between professional training and continuing learning. ALAs also enable instruction in workload planning needs analysis and resource optimization. Personalized attention cannot be provided by teachers in large sections. Adaptive agents step in to help by monitoring students' performances and detecting students that need personalized attention. They do repetitive tasks such as grading, posting material, and tracking.

Now, instructors are free to focus on counseling, addressing intricate issues of students, and creating intricate activities. ALAs create feedback from data for planning lessons and renewing courses. Since human work is subcontracted, therefore, teachers can plan time more effectively. Adaptive systems do as much as possible to reach massive numbers of students without being individualized. It is mainly carried out in the scenario of e-learning and blended learning. Lastly, ALAs make pedagogy cost-effective and productive. Social learning and team learning are also helped by Adaptive Learning Agents. Learning is not a drill between two people but also a drill among peers and one teacher. ALAs are able to detect group dynamics and suggest group drills based on complementary sets of skills. ALAs enable peer learning by putting learners in between to assist each other.

Adaptive agents can be used to monitor workgroup activity or discussion boards and advise how best to maximize interaction. It makes the sharing of learning easy as the system presents the individual learners with the content that they must learn from. Adaptive interaction enhances problem-solving and critical thinking capabilities. The learners are provided with individual and social incentives. The system helps in community sense in distance learning too. Adaptive learning thus strikes a balance between individualization and sociality. ALAs help in tracking and predicting learning patterns. Closely monitoring student engagement figures, ALAs detect patterns of failure or success. Predictive analytics send early warnings and hence early intervention to students in danger of failing. Organizations and personnel can respond pro-actively.

ALAs also do pedagogic approach change recommendations in subsequent cohorts. Empirical inquiry into such data makes the curriculum design, material design, and assessment policy an evidence-based process. Besides, learning predisposition and interaction behavior involve even more individualization of learning. Calibration in real time enables accommodation in coordination with learner needs. Predictive ability also enables adaptive setting of goals and performance measurement. ALAs overall establish an intelligent, reactive, proactive learning environment. Last question: Adaptive Learning Agents enable educational technology and research innovation. ALAs provide room for which varied pedagogy and instructional models can be tried out. Effective pedagogies can be created by researchers from learning data analysis to large data analysis. ALAs enable content, learning process, and engagement styles to be more innovative too.

LITERATURE REVIEW

ALAs are scalable and hence can be applied in AI, machine learning, and natural language processing environments. This union of technology and education enables them to improve at their level round the clock. Adaptive agents can apply scalable data-driven personalized learning methods in schools and schools for teaching. Adaptive agents render the learning system effective, accessible, and inclusive. Adaptive agents help transition from old-fashioned learning to interactive and learner-centered learning. Finally, ALAs set the trend for creating the future of personalized and effective learning. Additionally, Manser Payne et al. (2021) experimented with the ability of artificial intelligence to create value in mobile banking applications. The experiment is limited by localization within the banking industry and hence applies across industries. The study was highly theory-dependent in the form of a model and weakly empirically rooted across a broad scope of user bases, hence limiting the extent it can apply to live environments. The situation and mood of the mobile banking users were not dichotomously matched, something that could affect the behavior of the AI-powered recommendations

The long-term and ethics of AI application were not even considered in the study. Therefore, although on paper it may be wonderful, in reality it is not all that practical for real general adaptive systems. Shuford and Islam (2024) give a sweeping overview of what is new about AI development. While the overview is sweeping in scope, as a review it is extremely descriptive with very little comparative effectiveness assessment of the reviewed AI approaches. Reference is given to potential legal, ethical and societal implications on AI usage without systematic review. The rapidity of state-of-the-art technological progress in AI creates the risk that the review is potentially subject to quick obsolescence.

In addition, utilitarian considerations that pertain to the deployment and actual performance measures of the deployment of the implicated technologies are not taken into enough account in the interest of limiting live action use by the systems implementers or instructors. Ai et al. (2011) present a low-cost path for synthesis of soluble reduced graphene oxide sheets. Though novel, the work remains in laboratory experiments and not scaled up to commercial or industrial scale. Long-term and environmental impacts of the reduction process were not explored in in-depth analyses. Variation in quality regarding the potential variation in conditions for sheet formation was not addressed.

It is highly content and technique-oriented, with relatively less know-how to justify generic AI or adaptive learning application use case scenarios. Kem (2022) writes on adaptive and personalized learning platforms for smart learning. The limitation of the study takes place on the conceptual phase of analysis with fewer empirical markers of real-world platform performance. Issues-related problems, i.e., teacher and student digital competence heterogeneity are not examined at a very high degree of depth. Scalability of chemistry and safety of MRI contrast media in other education systems is not defined. Other education technologies were also not explored, probably to impede practical application. (Hao et al. 2012) are concerned about MRI contrast media chemistry and safety. While extremely detailed in chemical examination, the article does not bring it to practical use differences in effectiveness or reaction on an individual patient level. The long-term toxicities and compatibilities with emergent medical technology are not attended to. The reviewing of basic chemistry takes away from the direct use within the AI adaptive systems or teaching. (Khanna et al. 2015) mention novel applications for AI in chatbot form. The research is tech-centric with no environmental awareness measure, measure of effective learning, or user experience. Neither general performance measures or longitudinal measures of chatbot proficiency are utilized and objectivity of AI decision-making or ethics aren't even touched on and can affect trust in real-world systems. (Sharma et al. 2019) propose a "grey-box" framework for AI-driven learning data pipelines. Technical implementation of the complex system is the only restriction on the research and has the potential to increase scalability and institutional uptake by technology-constrained institutions. The research does not build on an end-to-end assessment across multiple learning domains and restricts generalizability. When utilized secondly, multimodal data sources have the potential to increase pragmatic issues of acquiring quality data.

Jumpathong et al. (2024) built the summary corpus from the text of an economics textbook and reported results of the baseline models only. Limitations include modest size, the topic-specific nature of the data set may or may not be representative of other domains, baseline models are lacking, no evaluation involving more adaptive learning or AI approaches, and lack of actual real-world applications in education.

Seo (2024) also introduced a method that matched image search with semantics. Though creative, the method is computationally expensive, hence limiting scalability to enormous collections. Strong labelling extraction is used, capable of generating errors in a very short time. Application on an adaptive learning environment and personalization for the user was not explored; limiting its use to only learning.

An example of an exploratory-guided recommendation model for adaptive learning can be seen in the deep reinforcement learning model suggested by Han et al. (2020). On the other hand, this approach requires sufficient good-quality interaction data to learn from, which may not always be feasible. The second limitation is that this model is highly complex and may not be interpretable by instructors. Moreover, its approach was tested in simulated environments that may or may not perfectly reflect the actual classroom context.

This work tries to use an adaptive, fuzzy-logic-based system that may be personalized in English learning, as shown by Hsieh et al. (2012). This was still plagued with a fixed set of rules which cannot be adapted best into evolving learners' behavior. Furthermore, this system was tested on a small pilot with a small sample size and therefore had poor generalizability. Adaptation with other adaptive systems and scalability to other topics were also not experimented on.

Another application of ANFIS is in predictive modeling of biochemical oxygen demand in river systems by Ahmed and Shah (2017). The direct application in educational adaptive learning systems is not expected, but may be useful in environmental monitoring. This study is heavily dependent upon precise input data, with little apparent robustness for noisy or missing input conditions. Extrapolation to anything but environmental data sets is constrained by domain assumptions. Some of the drawbacks that existed in earlier work are overcome in this Adaptive Learning Agent architecture.

Compared to Chen et al. (2020), long-term measurement generalizes better in larger or heterogeneous groups of students than short-term exposure to social robots. The method uses multimodal learner data instead of browsing activities or classification by one model to reach across-subject and cross-environment generality from Zhang et al. (2020) and Lo and Shu (2005), for interventions such as Bang et al. (2023) and Kärki et al. (2022). Adaptive content personalization happens through shifting age brackets and shifting skills levels to make adaptive interventions scale the experimental needs of non-lab settings.

It uses, however, real-time analytics and AI-driven reward paradigms in an attempt to optimize scaffolding and gamified experience with heterogeneous or tainted data, and it is this that sets it apart from Faber et al. (2023) and Daghestani et al. (2020). Hybrid m-learning and e-learning designs are, according to Nedungadi and Raman (2012), best optimized through an optimal cloud-based context-aware system that has been fitted with technology limitations and accessibility minimized. (Mavroudi et al. 2018) and (Tseng et al. 2008) problems are overcome by enabling adaptive routes through variable and controllable levels of flexibility supported through continuous learner feedback. Improved cognitive diagnosis enhanced by Wu and Chang (2020) is improved by minimalist interfaces without loss of usability but with response capacity in testing fitted to the individual. User-generated content bias effects described by Nilashi et al. (2022) are reduced by cross-validation and multi-source fusion. Weaknesses of mentor-guided systems discussed in (Roach et al. 2001 and Zeng & Wang 2021) are reduced by automated scaffolding support, collaboration and feedback with guaranteed on-going support. Generally, the system described herein relies on AI, deep learning and adaptive algorithms for facilely scalable contextualized highly personalized gap-filling experience within current models. (Sermet & Demir 2021) had proposed a semantic web system for intelligent public health automatic assistants; the study is short of singularity to a single field, diminishes cross-applicability to others, and lacks empirical testing at a grand scale. (Zhang et al. 2022) conducted a scoping review of the application of AI for pain evaluation and management but suffers from the heterogeneity of studies included and low practicability recommendations.(Bandyopadhyay et al. 2018) have proposed an embedding-based information retrieval framework in disaster situations; practicability of their system is compromised by testing on history data and minimal testing in actual disaster situations. (Winkler & Söllner 2018) used chatbots as a learning tool; the article is very theoretical and does not include empirical learning evidence.

The study by (Fryer et al. 2017) used human versus chatbot task partners to acquire a second language, but small sample sizes and short measurement intervals can't guarantee generalizability of outcomes. (Gautam et al. 2022) used deep generative adversarial networks so that river images are realistic, although the study is marred with synthetic data quality and as-yet-un-confirmed-under-changing-environmental conditions. Demiray et al. (2021) used DEM super-resolution via EfficientNetV2, though marred with overfitting to training and computational intensity. (Li and Demir 2023) employed U-net-based semantic segmentation for the inundation extent mapping, while methodology is dependent upon high-resolution SAR images and fails in data availability scenarios. (Ewing et al. 2022) have developed client-side web applications with interactive hydrological modeling, but without extensive testing of user accessibility and flexibility to other learning environments. (Sit et al. 2021) showed a web-groundwater prediction platform with data analysis but limited by requirement of quality input data and inadequate coupling with heterogeneous data sources. (Ramirez et al. 2022) showed HydroLang, a web-computer programming interface to hydrology, but needs specific technical expertise and community support for the interface to be valuable. (Ramirez et al. 2023) added markup language ability to HydroLang, but use has been excluded by significant learning barriers and lack of testing over wide ranges of hydrologic conditions. (Huang et al. 2021) combined AI with learning, but the paper is extremely qualitative in content and does not seriously consider implementation issues or quantifiable improvements in learning. (Essel et al. 2022) pilot implemented a virtual teaching assistant within a Ghanaian tertiary education environment, but results constrained by single country study and small sample size. (Crompton and Song 2021) charted the possibility of AI changing higher education, but investigation was conceptual in nature with limited empirical basis, constraining practical recommendations. Adaptive Learning Agent system implemented is significantly more performance-effective than would be achieved in previous models with implementation of scalable, context-aware, and multi-modal AI capabilities. It is cross-discipline and not profession-specific, as provided by (Sermet and Demir 2021), hence implementable across a series of disciplines of learning and professions. It enhances heterogeneity and diversification of implementation through continuous learning and adaptive transformation based on suggestions independent of student diversity. Unlike intrinsic or composite data structures, as identified by (Bandyopadhyay et al. 2018 and Gautam et al. 2022), the system does not depend on pools of available dynamic data to ensure maximum reliability and generalization.

In the case of learning chatbots, according to Winkler and (Söllner 2018 and Fryer et al. 2017), the agent uses more adaptive scaffolding and intelligent feedback loops so as not to be limited by sample size and short-term testing. In Demiray et al. (2021), resource-intensive models are optimized with best network models as an attempt at resource conservation with the highest degree of precision. In the case of domain or domain-specific usage, as in (Ramirez et al. 2022, and Li and Demir

2023), error management and integration of heterogeneity data are put into the system so that it may execute safely even under noisy or incomplete data. Review or conceptual papers, as in (Huang et al. 2021 and Crompton and Song 2021), are complemented with empirical verifications and performance validations with field use in view. Indeed, integrated AI-driven personalization, individually oriented learning routes, and ongoing evaluation create a system that offers scalable, sustainable, and learner-focused learning processes which remove the usability and performance inefficiencies of the early systems. All in all, the proposed system is an all-rounded solution for improvement of interaction and learning performance, increasing domain flexibility without duplicating technical limitations, context, and appraisals.

MATERIALS AND METHODS

A large-scale learning dataset can be built up from Big Student Data gathered through in-school placement, self-study records, and mentor ratings. Preprocessing cleans the data in order to remove noisy data, normalize the data, and standardize the format of the data to be analyzed. Feature selection can be done to determine the most significant features with the aid of Seagull Optimization for selecting the most discriminative features to learn and predict on. The Bi-Stacked ResNet model in Adaptive Learning Agents may exploit hierarchical structure and predict the performance of students. This will ensure continuous monitoring, student-specific learning trajectories, and adaptive intervention based on knowledge estimates. Continuous monitoring and assessment could ensure that higher education learning enhancement is scalable, data-driven, and effective.

Material

This set of datasets will try to build on higher education through the encouragement of innovation and experimentation in the modes of learning based on cooperation within the intelligent technological environment. It has its main objective of constructing an efficient, scalable, and more sustainable system of education closer to professional settings for which the students are being trained. It supports knowledge construction through pedagogic innovation in teaching, education research, and technological change underpinning pedagogical innovation for evidence. It also makes it possible for coordination to be effected between non-university and university tutors who mentor and supervise practice experience students for consistency and continuity of mentoring. It allows for monitoring of students as individuals during their practice to allow for direct real-time student personal observation of progress, challenge, and competence development. This dataset gives the possibility to build an intelligent system that will support the future teachers in learning autonomously while being mentored by means of practice teaching in schools. Enhanced with the precious trace of all activities, reflections, and performances, the system provides actionable knowledge both to students and teachers. The system enables active learning, reflective practice, and continuous professional development. The dataset also allows adaptive intervention such that students receive support designed specifically, based on the needs of their development. Lastly, the set allows bridging theory and practice through innovative, data-driven, and collaborative learning.

Preprocessing

Preprocessing of the procured dataset would be imperative in order to make it uniform and accurate, so that afterwards these data can be analyzed on the smart technology and collaborative learning platform.

Cleaning removes duplicate, inconsistent, or missing records from raw teacher reports, raw data from self-study, and raw first-time student in-school placements. Missing values are treated either through imputation methods or by vigilant validation with mentors to reach integrity. Normalization of levels of student achievement, school activity, and teacher feedback as categorical variables has within them a normalized form. Mapping of text data such as comments or ideas is done by the employment of natural language techniques in trying to provide patterns and results that are informative. Temporal data such as student activity and the order of follow-up is structured in a way that they may be monitored for the long run and therefore longitudinally analyzed. Normalization or scaling is done on data to support actual comparison across students, schools, and overseer environments. Data encoding operations enable the handling of qualitative attributes presented in machine-encoded forms that are intelligent system-compatible. Feature extraction controls meaningful gain measures, capability measures, and teacher-student interpersonal relationships, each playing important roles toward adaptive learning processes. Finally, preprocessed data is saved and secured, eager to wait for real-time monitoring, astute recommendations, and decision-making, empowering instructors and students toward technology-enhanced, scalable, and secure learning platforms.

Feature Selection

SO feature selection is new in selecting the most important features of education data gathered so that it can make the smart learning system more scalable and efficient. The study will adopt coupling of the migratory free-flight and meat-seeking behavior of seagulls to enable the recursive search by the algorithm SO within the feature space for the selection of a subset of features for predictive accuracy optimization in an attempt to remove redundancy. In the independent study, school assignment and learning record, activity completion rate, reflective journal, mentor feedback ratings, and temporal progress will be assessed on how best they foster the advance of learning achievement. The movement of seagulls maintains the trade-offs between exploration and exploitation with the SO algorithm in constructing global and local optima identified within the feature space. The resultant model efficiency and omission of non-informative features or irrelevant features free the methodology from computational complexity. Features are investigated in such a way that the model is not sacrificed on its interpretability, and basic learning principles are not overlooked. Thus, optimization of the subset of features, therefore, enables the intelligent system to provide more accurate, customized, and adaptive interventions to each student. Besides, the SO-based selection allows scalability since the system will be able to accommodate a huge number of students across many schools and mentoring setups without degradation in performance. Algorithmic iterative nature means this system gets increasingly better with time since more inputs from the learners are received hence the system learns to adapt to the learning environment. Finally, it is Seagull Optimization feature selection where data intuition and facilitatory learning merge to deliver more intelligent, robust, and robust learning environments.

Bistacked Resnet

The Bi-Stacked ResNet architecture in adapting learning will hugely benefit the Adaptive Learning Agents, and performance of students is continuously monitored. Bi-Stacked ResNet consists of two residual networks arranged one behind the other back-to-back that extract both low-level features as well as high-level features from the combined education data set, i.e., student activity logs, self-learning comments, mentor comments, and in-school assignment logs. First ResNet layer detects underlying patterns, i.e., frequency of task accomplishment and underlying learning actions, and second detects latent interdependencies among learning activity, skill acquisition, and adaptive response. Synergistic hierarchical feature representations improve the capacity of the system to assess the performance of learners and forecast areas of need for intervention. Residual channels in Bi-Stacked ResNet prevent the vanishing gradient; hence, deeper network learning is enabled along with stable feature extraction. ALAs utilize features in order to dynamically detect learning paths, recommend personalized resources, and provide timely feedback to students. Students' motivation, interest, collaborative learning, and mentor engagement pattern detection is also enabled by the model. Further, the model accommodates huge, varied data in huge-scale heterogeneous learning environments; thus, the model is scalable and adaptive. Inclusion of the adaptive cleverness of ALAs along with the deep learning characteristic of Bi-Stacked ResNet helps the system create a better, individualized, and data-driven learning environment. Lastly, this approach brings the pedagogic practice school the practice-learning theory dynamic.

EXPERIMENTAL RESULTS

The empirical results demonstrate that the Adaptive Learning Agents, developed to maximize individual learning and performance tracking, are indeed effective. This was benchmarked against pre-processed school placement data, self-study tracking data, and mentor feedback data. Seagull Optimization was applied in the discovery of discriminative features, while hierarchical patterns were discovered using the Bi-Stacked ResNet model. Smart agent performance was monitored compared to prediction accuracy, learning effectiveness, participation rate, and responsiveness to learners' personalized learning needs. Baseline models were evaluated since they are compared in terms of optimization of personalized counseling and real-time feedback. Initial outcomes indicate that this system has a high learning achievement, does more accurate predictions on performance, and enables efficient adaptive interventions. This study, therefore, shows that the use of intelligent agents in conjunction with deep learning at tertiary institutions can be one means of enhancing quality teaching and learning.

Table 1 tabulates participation indicators of in-school placement and self-learning activities of the students Participation score, task-rate completion, and attendance rate describe the level at which the students have engaged themselves in the school activities. The reflection score measures the internal monitoring and recorded personal knowledge within the students. The collaboration index measures work and activities from peer to peer. Motivation Level - The motivation level measures students' intrinsic motivation toward task accomplishment. The table measures the variability of participation from the various students who were extremely active to those who were moderately active. Trends of participation and attendance drive individualized intervention. Scales with higher collaboration and reflection scores measure more intellectual and social interaction. Motivation level correlates with task completion and participation. Generally, this table gives a basic picture of how students interact with learning activity and students.

Table 1. Student engagement metrics

Attendance Rate (%)	Task Completion (%)	Participation Score	Reflection Score	Collaboration Index	Motivation Level
92	85	8	7	9	8
88	80	7	6	8	7
95	90	9	8	10	9
85	78	6	5	7	6
90	82	7	6	8	8
93	87	8	7	9	8
87	79	7	6	7	7
91	84	8	7	8	8
89	81	7	6	8	7
94	88	9	8	9	9

Table 2 represents student learning as performance and concept mastery vs. study activities. Percent concept mastery is a measure of mastering key topics. Study habits and effort are tracked over time on tasks and revision. Error rate is frequency of error measures and adaptive score measures sensitivity to suggestion from the system. Self-assessment tells us what students think that they are learning. The table illustrates it - trend since extensive revision shows better concept competence, greater error eliminating shows great reading and usage and adaptive score shows students' rate of adaptation to direction tailored for them. This table enables one to click on areas in need of more support. The information gets incorporated into the learning streams to student's own specification.

Table 2. Learning progress indicators

Concept Mastery (%)	Time on Tasks (hrs)	Revision Frequency	Error Rate (%)	Adaptive Score	Self-Assessment
85	12	3	10	8	7
78	10	2	15	7	6
92	14	4	8	9	8
80	11	2	12	7	7
88	13	3	9	8	8
90	12	4	7	9	8
83	10	2	11	7	7
86	11	3	10	8	7
79	10	2	14	7	6
91	13	4	8	9	8

Table 3 presents some qualitative measures of supervision and mentor guidance. Instructional skills and clarity are measures of communication skills. Mentor instruction style is a measure of teaching skills. Feedback rate is the frequency at which the mentors provide feedback to the students. Supportiveness includes the levels of advice and encouragement provided. Facilitation of participation includes the extent to which the mentor facilitates participation, and assessment consistency includes fairness and objectivity. The table has differences among mentors to identify best practice. The higher the scores for the same, the better the student performance. The table takes into consideration the effect of quality mentoring towards adaptive learning performance. The table justifies the basis for focused interventions to strengthen teacher-student relationships.

Table 3. Mentor feedback metrics

Communication Skill	Instruction Quality	Feedback Timeliness	Supportiveness	Engagement Encouragement	Evaluation Consistency
8	9	8	9	8	9
7	8	7	8	7	8
9	9	9	10	9	10
6	7	6	7	6	7
8	8	8	8	8	8
9	9	9	9	9	9
7	8	7	8	7	8
8	9	8	9	8	9
6	7	6	7	6	7
9	10	9	10	9	10

Table 4 attempts to quantify how effective smart systems are in isolation. Prediction accuracy adds to performance quality regarding how well it can predict student success. Model confidence: Confidence measurement at the time of prediction. Rate of intervention: A measure for the extent to which the system intervenes. Personalization score: A measure for how individualized recommendations are. Speed of adaptation: A measure for the rate at which the system adapts based on new information. Learning gain: Gain that comes from system guidance. It is observable from this table that with better accuracy and individualization, more outcomes are produced while adaptation properly prevents errors and speeds up mastering. These are metrics that describe one's ability to quantify system scalability and sustainability. In general, the table shows why Adaptive Learning Agents succeed in improving learning.

Table 4. Adaptive learning system performance

Prediction Accuracy (%)	Model Confidence	Intervention Rate (%)	Personalization Score	Adaptation Speed	Learning Gain
88	0.91	12	8	7	9
82	0.85	15	7	6	8
94	0.95	10	9	8	9
79	0.82	17	7	6	7
87	0.89	13	8	7	8
91	0.92	11	9	8	9
84	0.87	14	8	7	8
88	0.90	12	8	7	8
80	0.83	16	7	6	7
93	0.94	10	9	8	9

Table 5 captures independent student learning activity and resource use. Reflection quality defines reflection and critical thinking quality. Resource utilization is a log of resource utilization by learning resource. Peer monitoring cooperative action cooperative student performance. Problem-solving score captures cognitive capacity utilization. Autonomy in learning measures independence in task completion. Efficiency in task measures effort to completion ratio. Reflection and trend in the use of resources with improved problem-solving scores are shown. Peer interaction is a facilitator of learning and knowledge sharing. Table identifies autonomous learning student activity. Table identifies where adaptive support can aid greater ease of skills.

Table 5. Self-learning activity metrics

Reflection Quality	Resource Utilization (%)	Peer Collaboration	Problem-Solving Score	Learning Autonomy	Task Efficiency
8	85	7	8	8	9
7	80	6	7	7	8
9	90	8	9	9	9
6	75	5	6	6	7
8	83	7	8	8	8
9	88	8	9	9	9
7	80	6	7	7	8
8	84	7	8	8	8
6	78	5	6	6	7
9	89	8	9	9	9

Table 6 presents the performance of students in the assessment of group work and teamwork. Teamwork score measures overall team spirit, peer feedback quality measures the quality of peer constructive criticism. Group task achievement percentage is a measure of collective accomplishment. Communication effectiveness is a measure of communication effectiveness of interaction. Conflict resolution capacity is a measure of conflict resolution capacity and leadership capacity is a measure of leadership capacity to lead leading groups. The table shows categorization high and low achieving teamwork. Teamwork practice is associated with improved performance on the task. Effective communication and effective leadership enhance group performance. The table guides social and professional competence improvement intervention. The table enhances teamwork through adaptable learning strategies.

Table 6. Collaborative learning metrics

Teamwork Score	Peer Feedback Quality	Group Task Completion (%)	Communication Effectiveness	Conflict Resolution	Leadership Skill
8	7	85	8	7	8
7	6	80	7	6	7
9	8	90	9	8	9
6	5	75	6	5	6
8	7	83	8	7	8
9	8	88	9	8	9
7	6	79	7	6	7
8	7	84	8	7	8
6	5	76	6	5	6
9	8	90	9	8	9

Table 7 integrates assessment of time management in learning activity among students. Task time is hours spent on each task. Deadline completion denotes timeliness and reliability reached. Multitasking ability refers to the performance of the capability to accomplish several tasks at a time. Degree of attention is a measurement of attentional focus during task accomplishment. Procrastination degree is measurement of delay in task completion. Product value means an effort-and-time-based product value. Trends suggest that less procrastination and high concentration increase productivity. Improvement in multitasking ability ensures peak performance for compound tasks. The table is relevant to explaining temporal learning behavior. Results guide intervention for optimum learning behavior and enhancement of task design.

Table 7. Time management and efficiency

Task Duration (hrs)	Deadline Adherence (%)	Multitasking Ability	Focus Level	Procrastination Rate (%)	Productivity Score
12	95	8	9	5	9
14	90	7	8	8	8
11	97	9	9	4	9
15	85	6	7	10	7
13	92	8	8	6	8
12	96	9	9	5	9
14	88	7	8	7	8
13	91	8	8	6	8
15	84	6	7	10	7
11	97	9	9	4	9

Conceptual long-term memory as a measure of learning retention. Practical skill score as a measure of method transfer gained. Analytical reason power as a measure of critical thinking ability. Accuracy of task performance as a measure of problem-solving correctness. Creative solutions as measured by creativity score, technical skill by technical ability. Higher working skill and retention test scores mean higher problem-solving performance. Critical thinking and creativity maximize adaptive learning performance. The table explains individual strength and weakness in learning ability. The table directs improved training and adaptive improvement suggestions.

Table 8. Skill acquisition and competency

Knowledge Retention (%)	Practical Skill Score	Critical Thinking	Problem-Solving Accuracy (%)	Creativity Score	Technical Proficiency
88	85	8	90	7	8
82	80	7	85	6	7
92	90	9	95	8	9
79	78	6	80	6	7
87	83	8	88	7	8
91	88	9	93	8	9
84	81	7	86	6	7
86	82	8	87	7	8
80	78	6	82	6	7
93	90	9	96	8	9

Table 9 measures quality instructional interaction between the students and mentors. Instructional clarity measures performance. Response timeliness measures willingness to respond to questions. Support frequency measures interaction support frequency provided. Feedback during interaction measures motivation and encouragement. Level of positive reinforcement measures encouragement and conflict management measures resolution. Trends show high direct involvement that optimizes student performance. High learning performance is susceptible to collaborative effort and support. Table: Adaptive learning performance contribution of mentoring. It provides suggestions and training improvement to mentoring teachers.

Table 9. Mentor-student interaction quality

Guidance Clarity	Response Timeliness	Support Frequency	Engagement Feedback	Encouragement Level	Conflict Management
9	8	8	9	8	8
8	7	7	8	7	7
10	9	9	10	9	9
7	6	6	7	6	6
9	8	8	9	8	8
10	9	9	10	9	9
8	7	7	8	7	7
9	8	8	9	8	8
7	6	6	7	6	6
10	9	9	10	9	9

Table 10 shows system personalized suggestion influence and student improvement thereof. Suggestion accuracy estimation on the student level estimates adherence of student needs. Effectiveness of intervention at the system maintains that of the system. Percentage learning improvement measures improvement learned. Retention rate estimates storage of knowledge over time. Adaptation score approximates response of system, while student satisfaction rates perceived usefulness. Greater accuracy and efficacy of intervention correlate with greater learning. Retaining and adaptation scores gauge how well a system performs. Acceptance and usability of adaptive aid are student satisfaction. The table in general shows the positive impact of Adaptive Learning Agents on learning performance.

Table 10. Adaptive recommendations and learning outcomes

Personalized Suggestion Accuracy	Intervention Effectiveness	Learning Improvement (%)	Retention Rate (%)	Adaptation Score	Student Satisfaction
88	85	12	90	8	9
82	80	10	85	7	8
94	90	15	95	9	10
79	78	8	80	7	7
87	83	11	88	8	8
91	88	13	92	9	9
84	81	10	86	7	8
86	82	11	87	8	8
80	78	9	82	7	7
93	90	14	94	9	10

CONCLUSION

One of the Adaptive Learning technologies that have grown to integrate intelligent data analysis, feature extraction, and deep learning is ALAs. Inspired by the Bi-Stacked ResNet models, ALAs can perform predictions on student performance and adaptive guidance by fulfilling different needs. The system allows for continuous monitoring, immediate feedback, intervention, and guides students and teachers in higher education. In-school placement to learn functional skill competencies is added through interactive collaboration between university and non-university coaches. Besides, the scalability and flexibility of the framework are afforded for transferability in diverse education contexts; hence, effectiveness and sustainability are ensured. Lastly, the use of ALAs nurtures pedagogic innovation, enhances independent learning, and brings scholarship expertise into collaborative engagement with professional competence.

REFERENCES

Ahmed, A. M., & Shah, S. M. A. (2017). Application of adaptive neuro-fuzzy inference system (ANFIS) to estimate the biochemical oxygen demand (BOD) of Surma River. *Journal of King Saud University. Engineering Sciences*, *29*(3), 237–243. DOI: 10.1016/j.jksues.2015.02.001

Ai, K., Liu, Y., Lu, L., Cheng, X., & Huo, L. (2011). A novel strategy for making soluble reduced graphene oxide sheets cheaply by adopting an endogenous reducing agent. *Journal of Materials Chemistry*, *21*(10), 3365–3370. DOI: 10.1039/C0JM02865G

Bandyopadhyay, A., Ganguly, D., Mitra, M., Saha, S. K., & Jones, G. J. (2018). An embedding based IR model for disaster situations. *Information Systems Frontiers*, *20*(5), 925–932. DOI: 10.1007/s10796-018-9847-6

Bang, H. J., Li, L., & Flynn, K. (2023). Efficacy of an adaptive game-based math learning app to support personalized learning and improve early elementary school students' learning. *Early Childhood Education Journal*, *51*(1), 1–16. DOI: 10.1007/s10643-022-01332-3

Chen, H., Park, H. W., & Breazeal, C. (2020). Teaching and learning with children: Impact of reciprocal peer learning with a social robot on children's learning and emotive engagement. *Computers & Education*, *150*, 103836. Advance online publication. DOI: 10.1016/j.compedu.2020.103836

Crompton, H., & Song, D. (2021). The potential of artificial intelligence in higher education. *Revista Virtual Universidad Católica del Norte*, *62*(62), 1–4. DOI: 10.35575/rvucn.n62a1

Daghestani, L. F., Ibrahim, L. F., Al-Towirgi, R. S., & Salman, H. A. (2020). Adapting gamified learning systems using educational data mining techniques. *Computer Applications in Engineering Education*, *28*(3), 568–589. DOI: 10.1002/cae.22227

Demiray, B. Z., Sit, M., & Demir, İ. (2021). DEM super-resolution with EfficientNetV2. *arXiv*. https://arxiv.org/abs/2112.01277

Essel, H. B., Vlachopoulos, D., Tachie-Menson, A., Johnson, E. E., & Baah, P. K. (2022). The impact of a virtual teaching assistant (chatbot) on students' learning in Ghanaian higher education. *International Journal of Educational Technology in Higher Education*, *19*(1), 57. Advance online publication. DOI: 10.1186/s41239-022-00362-6

Ewing, G. J., Mantilla, R., Krajewski, W. F., & Demir, İ. (2022). Interactive hydrological modelling and simulation on client-side web systems: An educational case study. *Journal of Hydroinformatics, 24*(6), 1194–1206. DOI: 10.2166/hydro.2022.061

Faber, T. J., Dankbaar, M. E., Kickert, R., van den Broek, W. W., & van Merriënboer, J. J. (2023). Identifying indicators to guide adaptive scaffolding in games. *Learning and Instruction, 83*, 101666. Advance online publication. DOI: 10.1016/j.learninstruc.2022.101666

Fryer, L. K., Ainley, M., Thompson, A., Gibson, A., & Sherlock, Z. (2017). Stimulating and sustaining interest in a language course: An experimental comparison of chatbot and human task partners. *Computers in Human Behavior, 75*, 461–468. DOI: 10.1016/j.chb.2017.05.045

Gautam, A., Sit, M., & Demir, İ. (2022). Realistic river image synthesis using deep generative adversarial networks. *Frontiers in Water, 4*, 1037504. Advance online publication. DOI: 10.3389/frwa.2022.784441

Han, R., Chen, K., & Tan, C. (2020). Curiosity-driven recommendation strategy for adaptive learning via deep reinforcement learning. *British Journal of Mathematical & Statistical Psychology, 73*(3), 522–540. DOI: 10.1111/bmsp.12199

Hao, D., Ai, T., Goerner, F., Hu, X., Runge, V. M., & Tweedle, M. (2012). MRI contrast agents: Basic chemistry and safety. *Journal of Magnetic Resonance Imaging, 36*(5), 1060–1071. DOI: 10.1002/jmri.23725

Hsieh, T. C., Wang, T. I., Su, C. Y., & Lee, M. C. (2012). A fuzzy logic-based personalized learning system for supporting adaptive English learning. *Journal of Educational Technology & Society, 15*(1), 273–288.

Huang, J., Saleh, S., & Liu, Y. (2021). A review on artificial intelligence in education. *Academic Journal of Interdisciplinary Studies, 10*(3), 206–216. DOI: 10.36941/ajis-2021-0077

Jumpathong, S., Takhom, A., Boonkwan, P., Sutantayawalee, V., Porkaew, P., Phaholphinyo, S., Phrombut, C., Supnithi, T., Chokemanagmi, K., & Yamasathien, S.. (2024). Construction of text summarization corpus in economics domain and baseline models. *Journal of Information and Communication Convergence Engineering, 22*(1), 33–43. DOI: 10.56977/jicce.2024.22.1.33

Kärki, T., McMullen, J., & Lehtinen, E. (2022). Improving rational number knowledge using the NanoRoboMath digital game. *Educational Studies in Mathematics, 110*(1), 101–123. DOI: 10.1007/s10649-021-10120-6

Kem, D. (2022). Personalised and adaptive learning: Emerging learning platforms in the era of digital and smart learning. *International Journal of Social Science and Human Research*, *5*(2), 385–391. DOI: 10.47191/ijsshr/v5-i2-02

Khanna, A., Pandey, B., Vashishta, K., Kalia, K., Pradeepkumar, B., & Das, T. (2015). A study of today's AI through chatbots and rediscovery of machine intelligence. *International Journal of u- and e-Service. Science and Technology*, *8*(10), 277–284. DOI: 10.14257/ijunesst.2015.8.10.26

Li, Z., & Demir, İ. (2023). U-Net-based semantic classification for flood extent extraction using SAR imagery and GEE platform: A case study for 2019 central US flooding. *The Science of the Total Environment*, *869*, 161757. Advance online publication. DOI: 10.1016/j.scitotenv.2023.161757

Lo, J. J., & Shu, P. C. (2005). Identification of learning styles online by observing learners' browsing behaviour through a neural network. *British Journal of Educational Technology*, *36*(1), 43–55. DOI: 10.1111/j.1467-8535.2005.00437.x

Manser Payne, E. H., Peltier, J., & Barger, V. A. (2021). Enhancing the value co-creation process: Artificial intelligence and mobile banking service platforms. *Journal of Research in Interactive Marketing*, *15*(1), 68–85. DOI: 10.1108/JRIM-10-2020-0214

Mavroudi, A., Giannakos, M., & Krogstie, J. (2018). Supporting adaptive learning pathways through the use of learning analytics: Developments, challenges and future opportunities. *Interactive Learning Environments*, *26*(2), 206–220. DOI: 10.1080/10494820.2017.1292531

Nedungadi, P., & Raman, R. (2012). A new approach to personalization: Integrating e-learning and m-learning. *Educational Technology Research and Development*, *60*(4), 659–678. DOI: 10.1007/s11423-012-9250-9

Nilashi, M., Abumalloh, R. A., Zibarzani, M., Samad, S., Zogaan, W. A., Ismail, M. Y., & Akib, N. A. M. (2022). What factors influence students' satisfaction in massive open online courses? Findings from user-generated content using educational data mining. *Education and Information Technologies*, *27*(7), 9401–9435. DOI: 10.1007/s10639-022-10997-7

Ramirez, C. E., Sermet, Y., & Demir, İ. (2023). HydroLang Markup Language: Community-driven web components for hydrological analyses. *Journal of Hydroinformatics*, *25*(4), 1171–1187. DOI: 10.2166/hydro.2023.149

Ramirez, C. E., Sermet, Y., Molkenthin, F., & Demir, İ. (2022). HydroLang: An open-source web-based programming framework for hydrological sciences. *Environmental Modelling & Software*, *157*, 105525. Advance online publication. DOI: 10.1016/j.envsoft.2022.105525

Roach, M., Blackmore, P., & Dempster, J. A. (2001). Supporting high-level learning through research-based methods: A framework for course development. *Innovations in Education and Teaching International*, *38*(4), 369–382. DOI: 10.1080/14703290110074957

Seo, J. H. (2024). Similar image retrieval technique based on semantics through automatic labeling extraction of personalized images. *Journal of Information and Communication Convergence Engineering*, *22*(1), 64–69. DOI: 10.56977/jicce.2024.22.1.56

Sermet, Y., & Demir, İ. (2021). A semantic web framework for automated smart assistants: A case study for public health. *Big Data and Cognitive Computing*, *5*(4), 57. Advance online publication. DOI: 10.3390/bdcc5040057

Sharma, K., Papamitsiou, Z., & Giannakos, M. (2019). Building pipelines for educational data using AI and multimodal analytics: A "grey-box" approach. *British Journal of Educational Technology*, *50*(6), 3004–3031. DOI: 10.1111/bjet.12854

Shuford, J., & Islam, M. M. (2024). Exploring the latest trends in artificial intelligence technology: A comprehensive review. *Journal of Artificial Intelligence General Science*, *2*(1), 3006–4023. DOI: 10.60087/jaigs.v2i1.p13

Sit, M., Langel, R. J., Thompson, D. A., Cwiertny, D. M., & Demir, İ. (2021). Web-based data analytics framework for well forecasting and groundwater quality. *The Science of the Total Environment*, *761*, 144121. Advance online publication. DOI: 10.1016/j.scitotenv.2020.144121

Tseng, S. S., Su, J. M., Hwang, G. J., Hwang, G. H., Tsai, C. C., & Tsai, C. J. (2008). An object-oriented course framework for developing adaptive learning systems. *Journal of Educational Technology & Society*, *11*(2), 171–191.

Winkler, R., & Söllner, M. (2018). Unleashing the potential of chatbots in education: A state-of-the-art analysis. In *Proceedings of the Academy of Management Annual Meeting Proceedings, 2018*(1), Article 15903. https://doi.org/DOI: 10.5465/AMBPP.2018.15903abstract

Wu, L. J., & Chang, K. E. (2020). Effect of embedding a cognitive diagnosis into the adaptive dynamic assessment of spatial geometry learning. *Interactive Learning Environments*. Advance online publication. DOI: 10.1080/10494820.2020.1789673

Zeng, L., & Wang, Y. (2021). Independent and innovative learning of gymnastics teaching based on computer interaction. *International Journal of Electrical Engineering Education*. Advance online publication. DOI: 10.1177/0020720920984325

Zhang, H., Huang, T., Liu, S., Yin, H., Li, J., Yang, H., & Xia, Y. (2020). A learning style classification approach based on deep belief network for large-scale online education. *Journal of Cloud Computing (Heidelberg, Germany)*, *9*(1), 47. Advance online publication. DOI: 10.1186/s13677-020-00165-y

Zhang, M., Zhu, L., Lin, S.-Y., Herr, K., Chi, C.-L., Demir, I., Lopez, K. D., & Chi, N.-C. (2023). Using artificial intelligence to improve pain assessment and pain management: A scoping review. *Journal of the American Medical Informatics Association : JAMIA*, *30*(3), 570–587. DOI: 10.1093/jamia/ocac231

Compilation of References

Acharya, D. B., Kuppan, K., & Divya, B. (2025). Agentic AI: Autonomous Intelligence for Complex Goals - A Comprehensive Survey. *IEEE Access : Practical Innovations, Open Solutions*, *13*, 18912–18936. DOI: 10.1109/ACCESS.2025.3532853

Ahmed, A. M., & Shah, S. M. A. (2017). Application of adaptive neuro-fuzzy inference system (ANFIS) to estimate the biochemical oxygen demand (BOD) of Surma River. *Journal of King Saud University. Engineering Sciences*, *29*(3), 237–243. DOI: 10.1016/j.jksues.2015.02.001

Ai, K., Liu, Y., Lu, L., Cheng, X., & Huo, L. (2011). A novel strategy for making soluble reduced graphene oxide sheets cheaply by adopting an endogenous reducing agent. *Journal of Materials Chemistry*, *21*(10), 3365–3370. DOI: 10.1039/C0JM02865G

Akhil, B. (2025). *Agentic AI in Education: Revolutionizing Learning*. https://www.meratutor.ai/lms/blog/agentic-ai-in-education/

Akintayo, O. T., Eden, C. A., Ayeni, O. O., & Onyebuchi, N. C. (2024). Integrating AI with emotional and social learning in primary education: Developing a holistic adaptive learning ecosystem. *Computer Science & IT Research Journal*, *5*(5), 1076–1089. DOI: 10.51594/csitrj.v5i5.1116

Akinwalere, S. N., & Ivanov, V. (2022). Artificial Intelligence in Higher Education: Challenges and Opportunities. *BORDER CROSSING*, *12*(1), 1–15. DOI: 10.33182/bc.v12i1.2015

AKKA. (2025). *Agentic AI architecture 101: An enterprise guide*. https://akka.io/blog/agentic-ai-architecture?

Aldous, S. M., & Ismail, G. A. (2025). AI for Sustainable Emergency Preparedness and Response in Schools. In *Convergence of AI, Education, and Business for Sustainability* (pp. 51-74). IGI Global Scientific Publishing. DOI: 10.4018/979-8-3373-1917-9.ch003

Al-Mughairi, H., & Bhaskar, P. (2024). Exploring the factors affecting the adoption AI techniques in higher education: insights from teachers' perspectives on ChatGPT. *Journal of Research in Innovative Teaching & Learning*. DOI: 10.1108/JRIT-09-2023-0129

Aloisi, C. (2023). The future of standardised assessment: Validity and trust in algorithms for assessment and scoring. *European Journal of Education*, *58*(1), 98–110. DOI: 10.1111/ejed.12542

Alrakhawi, H., Jamiat, N., & Abu-Naser, S. (2023). Intelligent tutoring systems in education: A systematic review of usage, tools, effects and evaluation. *Journal of Theoretical and Applied Information Technology*, *101*, 1205–1226.

AlTwijri, L., & Alghizzi, T. M. (2024). Investigating the integration of artificial intelligence in English as foreign language classes for enhancing learners' affective factors: A systematic review [Review of Investigating the integration of artificial intelligence in English as foreign language classes for enhancing learners' affective factors: A systematic review]. Heliyon, 10(10). Elsevier BV. https://doi.org/DOI: 10.1016/j.heliyon.2024.e31053

Al-Zahrani, A. M. (2024). Unveiling the shadows: Beyond the hype of AI in education. *Heliyon*, *10*(9), e30696. Advance online publication. DOI: 10.1016/j.heliyon.2024.e30696

Anastasia, W., Murtisari, E., & Isharyanti, N. (2024). Less-proficient EFL students' use of Grammarly in writing : Behavior, cognition, and affect. *The JALT CALL Journal*, *20*(1), 1–25. DOI: 10.29140/jaltcall.v20n1.1089

Andreea, S., Vasileios, R., & Katerina, D. (2025). *Conformity Assessments under the EU AI Act: A step-by step guide.*

Artsn, M., & Bozkurt, A. (2025). Charting new horizons: What agentic artificial intelligence (AI) promises in the educational landscape. *EDULEARN25 Proceedings*, 2019–2023.

Ashtikar, S. P., & Manoharan, G. (2024). "Work-Load Management and Job Gratification: A Study on the Work-life Equilibrium of Higher Education Instructors," *2024 3rd International Conference on Computational Modelling, Simulation and Optimization (ICCMSO)*, Phuket, Thailand, pp. 193-197, doi: https://doi.org/DOI: 10.1109/ICCMSO61761.2024.00048

Ashwani, S. (2025). *Agentic AI in Education: Transforming Pedagogy and Personalized Learning*. 321–332. DOI: 10.1007/978-3-031-89424-4_21

Astuti, D., & Sumarni, S. (2023). Grammarly in students' self-directed learning for writing skills : Advantages and disadvantages. *INSANIA : Jurnal Pemikiran Alternatif Kependidikan*, *28*(1a), 36–50. DOI: 10.24090/insania.v28i1a.8899

Ayanwale, M. A., Sanusi, I. T., Adelana, O. P., Aruleba, K. D., & Oyelere, S. S. (2022). Teachers' readiness and intention to teach artificial intelligence in schools. *Computers and Education Artificial Intelligence*, *3*, 100099. DOI: 10.1016/j.caeai.2022.100099

Ayeni, A. O., Ovbiye, R. E., Onayemi, A. S., & Ojedele, K. E. (2024). Corresponding author: Ayobami O Ayeni AI-driven adaptive learning platforms: Enhancing educational outcomes for students with special needs through user-centric, tailored digital tools. *World Journal of Advanced Research and Reviews*, *2024*(03), 2253–2265. DOI: 10.30574/wjarr.2024.22.3.0843

Azennoud, A. (2024). Enhancing Writing Accuracy and Complexity through AI-Assisted Tools among Moroccan EFL University Learners. *International Journal of Linguistics and Translation Studies*, *5*(4), 211–226. DOI: 10.36892/ijlts.v5i4.529

Azzam, A., & Charles, T. (2024). A Review of Artificial Intelligence in K-12 Education [Review of A Review of Artificial Intelligence in K-12 Education]. Open Journal of Applied Sciences, 14(8), 2088. Scientific Research Publishing. https://doi.org/DOI: 10.4236/ojapps.2024.148137

Babar, P. A. (2025). Agentic AI for Personalized Education and Adaptive Learning Environments. *International Journal of Computing and Engineering*, *7*(12), 1–10. DOI: 10.47941/ijce.2973

Baker, R. S., Martin, T., & Rossi, L. M. (2016). Educational Data Mining and Learning Analytics. *The Handbook of Cognition and Assessment*, 379–396. DOI: 10.1002/9781118956588.ch16

Bandi, A., Kongari, B., Naguru, R., Pasnoor, S., & Vilipala, S. V. (2025). The Rise of Agentic AI: A Review of Definitions, Frameworks, Architectures, Applications, Evaluation Metrics, and Challenges. *Future Internet 2025, Vol. 17, Page 404, 17*(9), 404. DOI: 10.3390/fi17090404

Bandura, A., & Walters, R. H. (1977). *Social learning theory* (Vol. 1). Prentice hall Englewood Cliffs, NJ.

Bandyopadhyay, A., Ganguly, D., Mitra, M., Saha, S. K., & Jones, G. J. (2018). An embedding based IR model for disaster situations. *Information Systems Frontiers*, *20*(5), 925–932. DOI: 10.1007/s10796-018-9847-6

Bang, H. J., Li, L., & Flynn, K. (2023). Efficacy of an adaptive game-based math learning app to support personalized learning and improve early elementary school students' learning. *Early Childhood Education Journal*, *51*(1), 1–16. DOI: 10.1007/s10643-022-01332-3

Barrot, J. S. (2021). Using automated written corrective feedback in the writing classrooms : Effects on L2 writing accuracy. *Computer Assisted Language Learning*, *36*(4), 584–607. DOI: 10.1080/09588221.2021.1936071

Bećirović, S., Polz, E., & Tinkel, I. (2025). Exploring students' AI literacy and its effects on their AI output quality, self-efficacy, and academic performance. *Smart Learning Environments*, *12*(1), 29. DOI: 10.1186/s40561-025-00384-3

Benjamin, R. (2019). *Race after Technology: Abolitionist Tools for the New Jim Code*. Polity Press.

Bentley, S. V, Naughtin, C. K., Mcgrath, M. J., Irons, J. L., Patrick, ·, & Cooper, S. (2024). The digital divide in action: how experiences of digital technology shape future relationships with artificial intelligence. *AI and Ethics 2024 4:4*, *4*(4), 901–915. DOI: 10.1007/s43681-024-00452-3

Berisha Qehaja, A. (2025). Strategic integration of artificial intelligence solutions to transform teaching practices in higher education. *Foresight*, *27*(5), 970–991. DOI: 10.1108/FS-04-2024-0079

Bettayeb, A. M., Talib, M. A., Altayasinah, A. Z. S., & Dakalbab, F. (2024). Exploring the impact of ChatGPT: Conversational AI in education. *Frontiers in Education*, *9*, 1379796. Advance online publication. DOI: 10.3389/feduc.2024.1379796

Binns, R. (2018). Fairness in Machine Learning: Lessons from Political Philosophy. *Proceedings of Machine Learning Research*, •••, 81.

Bit, D., Biswas, S., & Nag, M. (2024). The Impact of Artificial Intelligence in Educational System. *International Journal of Scientific Research in Science and Technology*, *11*(4), 419–427. DOI: 10.32628/IJSRST2411424

Bogina, V., Hartman, A., Kuflik, T., & Shulner-Tal, A. (2022). Educating software and AI stakeholders about algorithmic fairness, accountability, transparency and ethics. *International Journal of Artificial Intelligence in Education*, *32*(3), 808–833. DOI: 10.1007/s40593-021-00248-0

Bonfield, C. A., Salter, M., Longmuir, A., Benson, M., & Adachi, C. (2020). Transformation or evolution?: Education 4.0, teaching and learning in the digital age. *Higher Education Pedagogies*, *5*(1), 223–246. DOI: 10.1080/23752696.2020.1816847

Božić, V. (2023). Artifical Intelligence as the Reason and the Solution of Digital Divide. *Language Education and Technology, 3*(2), 96–109. https://langedutech.com/letjournal/index.php/let/article/view/53

Bozkurt, A. (2025). Algorithmically manufactured minds: Generative and agentic AI in a time of post-truth, reconfiguration of student agency and death of critical pedagogy. In *Open Praxis* (Vol. 17, Issue 2, pp. 206–210). International Council for Open and Distance Education Oslo, Norway.

Brohi, S., Mastoi, Q. U. A., Jhanjhi, N. Z., & Pillai, T. R. (2025). A Research Landscape of Agentic AI and Large Language Models: Applications, Challenges and Future Directions. *Algorithms 2025, Vol. 18, Page 499, 18*(8), 499. DOI: 10.3390/a18080499

Brusilovsky, P., & Peylo, C. (2003). Adaptive and intelligent web-based educational systems. *International Journal of Artificial Intelligence in Education, 13*(2-4), 159–172. DOI: 10.3233/IRG-2003-13(2-4)02

Buiten, M. C. (2024). Product liability for defective AI. *European Journal of Law and Economics, 57*(1), 239–273. DOI: 10.1007/s10657-024-09794-z

Bulathwela, S., Pérez-Ortiz, M., Holloway, C., & Shawe-Taylor, J. (2021). Could AI Democratise Education? Socio-Technical Imaginaries of an EdTech Revolution. arXiv (Cornell University). https://doi.org//arxiv.2112.02034DOI: 10.48550

Bulathwela, S., Pérez-Ortiz, M., Holloway, C., Cukurova, M., & Shawe-Taylor, J. (2024). Artificial Intelligence Alone Will Not Democratise Education: On Educational Inequality, Techno-Solutionism, and Inclusive Tools. *Sustainability (Basel), 16*(2), 781. DOI: 10.3390/su16020781

Buolamwini, J. (2018). Gender Shades: Intersectional Accuracy Disparities in Commercial Gender Classification *. In *Proceedings of Machine Learning Research* (Vol. 81).

Cachat-Rosset, G., & Klarsfeld, A. (2023). Diversity, Equity, and Inclusion in Artificial Intelligence: An Evaluation of Guidelines. *Applied Artificial Intelligence, 37*(1), 2176618. Advance online publication. DOI: 10.1080/08839514.2023.2176618

Calma, A., Cotronei-Baird, V., & Chia, A. (2022). Grammarly : An instructional intervention for writing enhancement in management education. *International Journal of Management Education, 20*(3), 100704. DOI: 10.1016/j.ijme.2022.100704

Cambria, E. (2016). Affective Computing and Sentiment Analysis. *IEEE Intelligent Systems, 31*(2), 102–107. Advance online publication. DOI: 10.1109/MIS.2016.31

Camilleri, M. A. (2024). Artificial intelligence governance: Ethical considerations and implications for social responsibility. *Expert Systems: International Journal of Knowledge Engineering and Neural Networks*, *41*(7), e13406. DOI: 10.1111/exsy.13406

Carbonell, J. R. (1970). AI in CAI: An artificial-intelligence approach to computer-assisted instruction. *IEEE Transactions on Man-Machine Systems*, *11*(4), 190–202. DOI: 10.1109/TMMS.1970.299942

Cavaleri, M., & Dianati, S. (2016). *You want me to check your grammar again ? The usefulness of an online grammar checker as perceived by students*.

Celik, I. (2022). Towards Intelligent-TPACK: An empirical study on teachers' professional knowledge to ethically integrate artificial intelligence (AI)-based tools into education. *Computers in Human Behavior*, *138*, 107468. DOI: 10.1016/j.chb.2022.107468

Celik, I., Dindar, M., Muukkonen, H., & Järvelä, S. (2022). The Promises and Challenges of Artificial Intelligence for Teachers: A Systematic Review of Research. *TechTrends*, *66*(4), 616–630. DOI: 10.1007/s11528-022-00715-y

Champaneria, H. K. (2025). From Insight to Impact: Architecting AI-Driven Learning Ecosystems for Personalized, Predictive and Proactive Education. *Journal Of Engineering And Computer Sciences*, *4*(7), 791–801.

Chan, C. K. Y. (2023). A comprehensive AI policy education framework for university teaching and learning. *International Journal of Educational Technology in Higher Education*, *20*(1), 38. DOI: 10.1186/s41239-023-00408-3

Chaudhry, M. A., & Kazim, E. (2021). Artificial Intelligence in Education (AIEd): A high-level academic and industry note 2021. *AI and Ethics*, *2*(1), 157–165. DOI: 10.1007/s43681-021-00074-z

Cheng, F.-F., Wu, J., Huang, Y.-W., & Yen, D. (2006). *An Empirical Investigation of User Acceptance of Wireless Technology at Work*.

Chen, H., Park, H. W., & Breazeal, C. (2020). Teaching and learning with children: Impact of reciprocal peer learning with a social robot on children's learning and emotive engagement. *Computers & Education*, *150*, 103836. Advance online publication. DOI: 10.1016/j.compedu.2020.103836

Chen, S., Xie, J., Wang, G., Wang, H., Cheng, H., & Huang, Y. (2025). From Scores to Careers: Understanding AI's Role in Supporting Collaborative Family Decision-Making in Chinese College Applications. *Proceedings of the 2025 CHI Conference on Human Factors in Computing Systems*, 1–20. DOI: 10.1145/3706598.3713341

Chen, Z., Zhang, J., Jiang, X., Hu, Z., Han, X., & Xu, M., Savitha, & Vivekananda, G. N. (2020). Education 4.0 using artificial intelligence for students performance analysis. *Intelligent Automation & Soft Computing*, *23*, 124–137.

China Aerospace Studies Institute. (2023). *Interim Measures for the Management of Generative Artificial Intelligence Services*. https://www.cac.gov.cn/2023-07/13/c_1690898327029107.htm

Chiu, W.-K. (2021). Pedagogy of emerging technologies in chemical education during the era of digitalization and artificial intelligence: A systematic review. *Education Sciences*, *11*(11), 709. DOI: 10.3390/educsci11110709

Ciolacu, M. I., Tehrani, A. F., Binder, L., & Svasta, P. (2018, October 25–28). Education 4.0—Artificial intelligence assisted higher education: Early recognition system with machine learning to support students' success. In *Proceedings of the IEEE 24th International Symposium for Design and Technology in Electronic Packaging (SIITME)* (pp. 23–30). Ia i, Romania. DOI: 10.1109/SIITME.2018.8599203

Cónego, L., Pinto, R., & Gonçalves, G. (2021). Education 4.0 and the smart manufacturing paradigm: A conceptual gateway for learning factories. In Camarinha-Matos, L. M., Boucher, X., & Afsarmanesh, H. (Eds.), *Smart and sustainable collaborative networks 4.0*. PRO-VE. DOI: 10.1007/978-3-030-85969-5_68

Cordero, J., Torres-Zambrano, J., & Cordero-Castillo, A. (2024). Integration of Generative Artificial Intelligence in Higher Education: Best Practices. *Education Sciences*, *15*(1), 32. DOI: 10.3390/educsci15010032

Costan, E., Gonzales, G., Gonzales, R., Enriquez, L., Costan, F., Suladay, D., Atibing, N. M., Aro, J. L., Evangelista, S. S., Maturan, F., Selerio, E.Jr, & Ocampo, L. (2021). Education 4.0 in developing economies: A systematic literature review of implementation barriers and future research agenda. *Sustainability (Basel)*, *13*(22), 12763. DOI: 10.3390/su132212763

Creely, E., & Carabott, K. (2025). Teaching and learning with AI: An Integrated AI-Oriented Pedagogical Model. *Australian Educational Researcher*, *52*(6), 1–22. DOI: 10.1007/s13384-025-00913-6

Crescenzi-Lanna, L. (2023). Literature review of the reciprocal value of artificial and human intelligence in early childhood education. *Journal of Research on Technology in Education*, *55*(1), 21–33. DOI: 10.1080/15391523.2022.2128480

Crompton, H., & Song, D. (2021). The potential of artificial intelligence in higher education. *Revista Virtual Universidad Católica del Norte*, *62*(62), 1–4. DOI: 10.35575/rvucn.n62a1

Cukurova, M., Kent, C., & Luckin, R. (2019). Artificial intelligence and multimodal data in the service of human decision-making: A case study in debate tutoring. *British Journal of Educational Technology*, *50*(6), 3032–3046. DOI: 10.1111/bjet.12829

D'mello, S., & Graesser, A.DMello. (2012). AutoTutor and affective autotutor: Learning by talking with cognitively and emotionally intelligent computers that talk back. *ACM Transactions on Interactive Intelligent Systems*, *2*(4), 1–39. Advance online publication. DOI: 10.1145/2395123.2395128

Daghestani, L. F., Ibrahim, L. F., Al-Towirgi, R. S., & Salman, H. A. (2020). Adapting gamified learning systems using educational data mining techniques. *Computer Applications in Engineering Education*, *28*(3), 568–589. DOI: 10.1002/cae.22227

Daher, R. (2025). Integrating AI literacy into teacher education: A critical perspective paper. *Discover Artificial Intelligence*, *5*(1), 1–20. DOI: 10.1007/s44163-025-00475-7

Dai, L., Jiang, Y.-H., Chen, Y., Guo, Z., Liu, T.-Y., & Shao, X. (2024). Agent4EDU: Advancing AI for Education with Agentic Workflows. *Proceedings of the 2024 3rd International Conference on Artificial Intelligence and Education*, 180–185. DOI: 10.1145/3722237.3722268

Daniel, R. M., De Stavola, B. L., Cousens, S. N., & Vansteelandt, S. (2015). Causal mediation analysis with multiple mediators. *Biometrics*, *71*(1), 1–14. DOI: 10.1111/biom.12248 PMID: 25351114

Danisa, A. (2025). *The Ethics of Using AI in Education*. https://www.brainzmagazine.com/post/the-ethics-of-using-ai-in-education?

Davar, N. F., Dewan, M. A. A., & Zhang, X. (2025). AI Chatbots in Education: Challenges and Opportunities. *Information (Basel)*, *16*(3), 235. DOI: 10.3390/info16030235

Davis, F. D. (1989). Perceived Usefulness, Perceived Ease of Use, and User Acceptance of Information Technology. *Management Information Systems Quarterly*, *13*(3), 319–340. DOI: 10.2307/249008

Davis, F., & Granić, A. (2024). *Revolution of TAM*., DOI: 10.1007/978-3-030-45274-2_3

Deci, E. L., & Ryan, R. M. (2012). Self-determination theory. *Handbook of Theories of Social Psychology, 1*(20), 416–436.

Delello, J. A., Sung, W., Mokhtari, K., Hebert, J., Bronson, A., & Giuseppe, T. D. (2025). AI in the Classroom: Insights from Educators on Usage, Challenges, and Mental Health. *Education Sciences*, *15*(2), 113. DOI: 10.3390/educsci15020113

Demiray, B. Z., Sit, M., & Demir, İ. (2021). DEM super-resolution with Efficient-NetV2. *arXiv*. https://arxiv.org/abs/2112.01277

Dey, D. (2025). Enhancing Educational Tools Through Artificial Intelligence in Perspective of Need of AI. https://doi.org/DOI: 10.2139/ssrn.5031275

Diebel, C., Goutier, M., Adam, M., & Benlian, A. (2025). When AI-Based Agents Are Proactive: Implications for Competence and System Satisfaction in Human–AI Collaboration. *Business & Information Systems Engineering*, •••, 1–20. DOI: 10.1007/s12599-024-00918-y

Diliberti, M. K., Schwartz, H. L., Doan, S. Y., Shapiro, A., Rainey, L. R., & Lake, R. J. (n.d.). *Using Artificial Intelligence Tools in K-12 Classrooms*. Retrieved October 16, 2025, from www.getbento.info/about

Ding, L. J., Li, J. M., & Hui, B. H. (2025). Will Teacher-AI Collaboration Enhance Teaching Engagement? *Behavioral Sciences 2025, Vol. 15, Page 866, 15*(7), 866. DOI: 10.3390/bs15070866

du Plooy, E., Casteleijn, D., & Franzsen, D. (2024). Personalized adaptive learning in higher education: A scoping review of key characteristics and impact on academic performance and engagement. *Heliyon*, *10*(21), e39630. DOI: 10.1016/j.heliyon.2024.e39630 PMID: 39524879

Dwivedi, Y. K., Helal, M. Y. I., Elgendy, I. A., Albashrawi, M. A., Hughes, L., Shawosh, M., Dutot, V., & Jeon, I. (2025). Artificial intelligence agents and agentic systems in hospitality and tourism: Challenges, opportunities and research agenda. *International Journal of Contemporary Hospitality Management*. Advance online publication. DOI: 10.1108/IJCHM-02-2025-0287

Edwards, J., Nguyen, A., Lämsä, J., Sobocinski, M., Whitehead, R., Dang, B., Roberts, A. S., & Järvelä, S. (2025). Human-AI collaboration: Designing artificial agents to facilitate socially shared regulation among learners. *British Journal of Educational Technology*, *56*(2), 712–733. DOI: 10.1111/bjet.13534

Ejjami, R. (2024). *Revolutionizing Moroccan Education with AI: A Path to Customized Learning. 6*(3).

El Missi, M., Jarmouni, R., & Chibi, M. (2024). Exploring Students' Perceptions of Using Grammarly in Academic Writing : Master Students of the English Department as a Case Study. *International Journal of Innovative Research and Development*. Advance online publication. DOI: 10.24940/ijird/2024/v13/i6/JUN24003

Elazab, M. (2024). Artificial Intelligence and Future of Teaching and Learning. *International Journal of Internet Education, 23*(2), 1–16. Advance online publication. DOI: 10.21608/ijie.2024.414601

Emergentmind. (2025). *Agentic LLMs Overview*. https://www.emergentmind.com/topics/agentic-llms

Essel, H. B., Vlachopoulos, D., Tachie-Menson, A., Johnson, E. E., & Baah, P. K. (2022). The impact of a virtual teaching assistant (chatbot) on students' learning in Ghanaian higher education. *International Journal of Educational Technology in Higher Education, 19*(1), 57. Advance online publication. DOI: 10.1186/s41239-022-00362-6

Ewing, G. J., Mantilla, R., Krajewski, W. F., & Demir, İ. (2022). Interactive hydrological modelling and simulation on client-side web systems: An educational case study. *Journal of Hydroinformatics, 24*(6), 1194–1206. DOI: 10.2166/hydro.2022.061

Faber, T. J., Dankbaar, M. E., Kickert, R., van den Broek, W. W., & van Merriënboer, J. J. (2023). Identifying indicators to guide adaptive scaffolding in games. *Learning and Instruction, 83*, 101666. Advance online publication. DOI: 10.1016/j.learninstruc.2022.101666

Fahimirad, M., & Kotamjani, S. S. (2018). A Review on Application of AI in Teaching and Learning in Educational Contexts. *International Journal of Learning and Development, 8*(4), 106. DOI: 10.5296/ijld.v8i4.14057

Fakour, H., & Imani, M. (2025). Socratic wisdom in the age of AI: A comparative study of ChatGPT and human tutors in enhancing critical thinking skills. *Frontiers in Education, 10*, 1528603. Advance online publication. DOI: 10.3389/feduc.2025.1528603

Fan, N. (2023). Exploring the Effects of Automated Written Corrective Feedback on EFL Students' Writing Quality : A Mixed-Methods Study. *SAGE Open, 13*(2), 21582440231181296. DOI: 10.1177/21582440231181296

Federal Register. (2023). *Safe, Secure, and Trustworthy Development and Use of Artificial Intelligence*. https://www.federalregister.gov/documents/2023/11/01/2023-24283/safe-secure-and-trustworthy-development-and-use-of-artificial-intelligence

Fernoaga, P. V., Sandu, F., Stelea, G. A., & Gavrila, C. (2018, April 19–20). Intelligent education assistant powered by chatbots. In *Proceedings of the 14th International Scientific Conference of eLearning and Software for Education (eLSE)* (pp. 376–383). Bucharest, Romania.

Filgueiras, F. (2024). Artificial intelligence and education governance. *Education, Citizenship and Social Justice*, *19*(3), 349–361. DOI: 10.1177/17461979231160674

Filiz, O., Kaya, M. H., & Adiguzel, T. (2025). Teachers and AI: Understanding the factors influencing AI integration in K-12 education. *Education and Information Technologies*, *30*(13), 17931–17967. Advance online publication. DOI: 10.1007/s10639-025-13463-2

Fitria, R. A., Sabarun, S., & Miftah, M. Z. (2022). STUDENTS' PERCEPTION OF THE USE OF GRAMMARLY IN UNDERGRADUATE THESIS WRITING. *PROJECT (Professional Journal of English Education)*, *5*(2), 366. DOI: 10.22460/project.v5i2.p366-371

Fitriana, K., & Nurazni, L. (2022). Exploring Students' Perception of Using Grammarly to Check Grammar in Their Writing. [Journal of English Teaching]. *JET*, *8*(1), 15–25. DOI: 10.33541/jet.v8i1.3044

Flavell, J. H. (1979). Metacognition and cognitive monitoring: A new area of cognitive-developmental inquiry. *The American Psychologist*, *34*(10), 906–911. Advance online publication. DOI: 10.1037/0003-066X.34.10.906

FLI. (2025). *Annex III: High-Risk AI Systems Referred to in Article 6(2) | EU Artificial Intelligence Act*. https://artificialintelligenceact.eu/annex/3

Fotea, S., Fotea, I., & undrea, E. (2019). *Artificial intelligence in education - romanian students' attitudes toward artificial intelligence and its impact on their career development*. 9330–9338. DOI: 10.21125/iceri.2019.2259

Fryer, L. K., Ainley, M., Thompson, A., Gibson, A., & Sherlock, Z. (2017). Stimulating and sustaining interest in a language course: An experimental comparison of chatbot and human task partners. *Computers in Human Behavior*, *75*, 461–468. DOI: 10.1016/j.chb.2017.05.045

FTC. (1998). *Children's Online Privacy Protection Rule ("COPPA")*. https://www.ftc.gov/legal-library/browse/rules/childrens-online-privacy-protection-rule-coppa

García-López, I. M., & Trujillo-Liñán, L. (2025). Generative Artificial Intelligence in Education: Ethical Challenges, Regulatory Frameworks and Educational Quality in a Systematic Review of the Literature. [). Frontiers.]. *Frontiers in Education*, *10*, 1565938. DOI: 10.3389/feduc.2025.1565938

Gautam, A., Sit, M., & Demir, İ. (2022). Realistic river image synthesis using deep generative adversarial networks. *Frontiers in Water*, *4*, 1037504. Advance online publication. DOI: 10.3389/frwa.2022.784441

Ghimire, A., & Edwards, J. (2024, July). From guidelines to governance: A study of ai policies in education. In *International Conference on Artificial Intelligence in Education* (pp. 299-307). Cham: Springer Nature Switzerland. DOI: 10.1007/978-3-031-64312-5_36

Goel, R., Jaiswal, U. K., Singh, P., Yadav, S. P., & Upadhyay, P. (2025). Deep Learning for Early Brain Tumor Detection: A Keras-Based Approach Using MRI and CT Imaging. In Mishra, A., Yadav, S. P., Kumar, M., Biju, S. M., & Deka, G. C. (Eds.), *Demystifying the Role of Natural Language Processing (NLP) in Mental Health* (pp. 145–180). IGI Global., DOI: 10.4018/979-8-3693-4203-9.ch009

Goldin, T., Rauch, E., Pacher, C., & Woschank, M. (2022). Reference architecture for an integrated and synergetic use of digital tools in Education 4.0. *Procedia Computer Science*, *200*, 407–417. DOI: 10.1016/j.procs.2022.01.239

González-Pérez, L. I., & Ramírez-Montoya, M. S. (2022). Components of Education 4.0 in 21st century skills frameworks: Systematic review. *Sustainability (Basel)*, *14*(3), 1493. DOI: 10.3390/su14031493

Grammarly. (2025). *About Us | Grammarly*. https://www.grammarly.com/about

Grimes, D., & Warschauer, M. (2010). *Utility in a Fallible Tool : A Multi-Site Case Study of Automated Writing Evaluation*.

Grünberg, N. F. (2024). El uso de la inteligencia artificial en la evaluación educativa y sus desafíos (The use of artificial intelligence in educational evaluation and its challenges.). https://doi.org/DOI: 10.2139/ssrn.4920158

Guerin, F. (2008). Constructivism in AI: Prospects, progress and challenges. *AISB 2008 Convention: Communication, Interaction and Social Intelligence - Proceedings of the AISB 2008 Symposium on Computing and Philosophy*.

Gulson, K. N., & Witzenberger, K. (2022). Repackaging authority: Artificial intelligence, automated governance and education trade shows. *Journal of Education Policy*, *37*(1), 145–160. DOI: 10.1080/02680939.2020.1785552

Guo, Q., Feng, R., & Hua, Y. (2021). How effectively can EFL students use automated written corrective feedback (AWCF) in research writing? *Computer Assisted Language Learning*, •••, 1–20. DOI: 10.1080/09588221.2021.1879161

Guo, Y. J., Chen, L., Guo, Y., & Chen, L. (2020, December 13–17). An investigation on online learning for K12 in rural areas in China during COVID-19 pandemic. In *Proceedings of the Ninth International Conference of Educational Innovation through Technology (EITT)* (pp. 13–18). Porto, Portugal. DOI: 10.1109/EITT50754.2020.00009

Gutiérrez, J. C. G., Chiappe, A., Rodríguez, D. F. B., & González-Pérez, L. I. (2025). The Transformative Journey of Artificial Intelligence Toward Personalized Learning. *New Educator, 1*(3), 257–275. Advance online publication. DOI: 10.1080/1547688X.2025.2475811

Halkiopoulos, C., & Gkintoni, E. (2024). Leveraging AI in E-Learning: Personalized Learning and Adaptive Assessment through Cognitive Neuropsychology—A Systematic Analysis. *Electronics 2024, Vol. 13, Page 3762, 13*(18), 3762. DOI: 10.3390/electronics13183762

Hamam, D. (2021). The new teacher assistant: A review of chatbots' use in higher education. In Stephanidis, C., Antona, M., & Ntoa, S. (Eds.), *HCI International 2021—Posters. HCII 2021. Communications in Computer and Information Science* (Vol. 1421). Springer. DOI: 10.1007/978-3-030-78645-8_8

Han, R., Chen, K., & Tan, C. (2020). Curiosity-driven recommendation strategy for adaptive learning via deep reinforcement learning. *British Journal of Mathematical & Statistical Psychology, 73*(3), 522–540. DOI: 10.1111/bmsp.12199

Hao, K. (2019). AI is sending people to jail—and getting it wrong. In *MIT Technology Review.*

Hao, D., Ai, T., Goerner, F., Hu, X., Runge, V. M., & Tweedle, M. (2012). MRI contrast agents: Basic chemistry and safety. *Journal of Magnetic Resonance Imaging, 36*(5), 1060–1071. DOI: 10.1002/jmri.23725

Harry, A., & Sayudin, S. (2023). Role of AI in Education. [INJURITY]. *Interdiciplinary Journal and Hummanity, 2*(3), 260–268. DOI: 10.58631/injurity.v2i3.52

Hartley, J. S., Jolevski, F., Melo, V., & Moore, B. (n.d.). *The Labor Market Effects of Generative Artificial Intelligence.*

He, Z., Huang, C., He, T., & Bo, K. (2021). Applying an Intelligent Learning Partner in Teacher Education for Improving CT-Related TPACK. *Lecture Notes in Computer Science (Including Subseries Lecture Notes in Artificial Intelligence and Lecture Notes in Bioinformatics), 12830 LNCS*, 152–163. DOI: 10.1007/978-3-030-80504-3_13

Heffernan, N. T., & Heffernan, C. L. (2014). The ASSISTments ecosystem: Building a platform that brings scientists and teachers together for minimally invasive research on human learning and teaching. *International Journal of Artificial Intelligence in Education, 24*(4), 470–497. Advance online publication. DOI: 10.1007/s40593-014-0024-x

Hein, G. E. (1991). Constructivist learning theory. *Institute for Inquiry, 14.*

Holmes, W., Persson, J., Chounta, I. A., Wasson, B., & Dimitrova, V. (2022). *Artificial intelligence and education: A critical view through the lens of human rights, democracy and the rule of law*. Council of Europe. Burton, R., Brown, J. S., & Sleeman, D. (1982). Intelligent tutoring systems.

Holmes, W., Bialik, M., & Fadel, C. (2019). *Artificial Intelligence in Education*. Promise and Implications for Teaching and Learning.

Holstein, K., & Aleven, V. (2022). Designing for human–AI complementarity in K-12 education. *AI Magazine*, *43*(2), 239–248. DOI: 10.1002/aaai.12058

Holstein, K., McLaren, B. M., & Aleven, V. (2018, June). Student learning benefits of a mixed-reality teacher awareness tool in AI-enhanced classrooms. In *International conference on artificial intelligence in education* (pp. 154-168). Cham: Springer International Publishing. DOI: 10.1007/978-3-319-93843-1_12

Hooda, M., Rana, C., Dahiya, O., Rizwan, A., & Hossain, M. S. (2022). Artificial Intelligence for Assessment and Feedback to Enhance Student Success in Higher Education. *Mathematical Problems in Engineering*, *2022*, 1–19. Advance online publication. DOI: 10.1155/2022/5215722

Hosseini, S., & Seilani, H. (2025). The role of agentic AI in shaping a smart future: A systematic review. *Array (New York, N.Y.)*, *26*, 100399. DOI: 10.1016/j.array.2025.100399

Hsieh, T. C., Wang, T. I., Su, C. Y., & Lee, M. C. (2012). A fuzzy logic-based personalized learning system for supporting adaptive English learning. *Journal of Educational Technology & Society*, *15*(1), 273–288.

Huang, K., & Hughes, C. (2025a). *Agentic AI Capability and Security Benchmark*. 145–167. DOI: 10.1007/978-3-032-02130-4_6

Huang, K., & Hughes, C. (2025b). *Agentic AI Communication Protocols and Security*. 81–110. DOI: 10.1007/978-3-032-02130-4_4

Huang, A. Y. Q., Lu, O. H. T., & Yang, S. J. H. (2022). Effects of artificial Intelligence–Enabled personalized recommendations on learners' learning engagement, motivation, and outcomes in a flipped classroom. *Computers & Education*, *194*, 104684. DOI: 10.1016/j.compedu.2022.104684

Huang, J., Saleh, S., & Liu, Y. (2021). A review on artificial intelligence in education. *Academic Journal of Interdisciplinary Studies*, *10*(3), 206–216. DOI: 10.36941/ajis-2021-0077

Huang, K. (2025). *Agentic AI*. Springer. DOI: 10.1007/978-3-031-90026-6

Hughes, L., Dwivedi, Y. K., Li, K., Appanderanda, M., Al-Bashrawi, M. A., & Chae, I. (2025). AI Agents and Agentic Systems: Redefining Global it Management. *Journal of Global Information Technology Management*, *28*(3), 175–185. DOI: 10.1080/1097198X.2025.2524286

Hughes, L., Dwivedi, Y. K., Malik, T., Shawosh, M., Albashrawi, M. A., Jeon, I., Dutot, V., Appanderanda, M., Crick, T., De', R., Fenwick, M., Gunaratnege, S. M., Jurcys, P., Kar, A. K., Kshetri, N., Li, K., Mutasa, S., Samothrakis, S., Wade, M., & Walton, P. (2025). AI Agents and Agentic Systems: A Multi-Expert Analysis. *Journal of Computer Information Systems*, *65*(4), 489–517. DOI: 10.1080/08874417.2025.2483832

ICO. (2024). *Introduction to the Children's code*. https://ico.org.uk/for-organisations/uk-gdpr-guidance-and-resources/childrens-information/childrens-code-guidance-and-resources/introduction-to-the-childrens-code/

Ihichr, A., Oustous, O., El Bouzekri, Y., Idrissi, E., & Lahcen, A. A. (n.d.). A Systematic Review on Assessment in Adaptive Learning: Theories, Algorithms and Techniques. *IJACSA) International Journal of Advanced Computer Science and Applications, 15*(7), 2024. Retrieved October 26, 2025, from www.ijacsa.thesai.org

Infocomm Media Development Authority. (2024). *Model Al Governance Framework for Generative Al Fostering a Trusted Ecosystem*. https://aiverifyfoundation.sg/wp-content/uploads/2024/05/Model-AI-Governance-Framework-for-Generative-AI-May-2024-1-1.pdf

Ishaq, S. M., Bangulzai, A. R., & Asif, M. (2025). Artificial Intelligence as a Co-Teacher: Enhancing Educator Efficiency through Intelligent Systems. *The Critical Review of Social Sciences Studies*, *3*(3), 1324–1342. DOI: 10.59075/gy5b5f42

Järvelä, S., Nguyen, A., & Hadwin, A. (2023). Human and artificial intelligence collaboration for socially shared regulation in learning. *British Journal of Educational Technology*, *54*(5), 1057–1076. DOI: 10.1111/bjet.13325

Jian, M. J. K. O. (2023). Personalized learning through AI. *Advances in Engineering Innovation*, *5*(1), 16–19. DOI: 10.54254/2977-3903/5/2023039

Jose, B., Cherian, J., Verghis, A. M., Varghise, S. M., Mumthas, S., & Joseph, S. (2025). The cognitive paradox of AI in education: Between enhancement and erosion. *Frontiers in Psychology*, *16*, 1550621. Advance online publication. DOI: 10.3389/fpsyg.2025.1550621

Jumpathong, S., Takhom, A., Boonkwan, P., Sutantayawalee, V., Porkaew, P., Phaholphinyo, S., Phrombut, C., Supnithi, T., Chokemanagmi, K., & Yamasathien, S.. (2024). Construction of text summarization corpus in economics domain and baseline models. *Journal of Information and Communication Convergence Engineering*, *22*(1), 33–43. DOI: 10.56977/jicce.2024.22.1.33

Kaledio, P., Robert, A., & Frank, L. A. (2024). The Impact of Artificial Intelligence on Students' Learning Experience. SSRN Electronic Journal. https://doi.org/DOI: 10.2139/ssrn.4716747

Kalniņa, D., Nīmante, D., & Baranova, S. (2024). Artificial intelligence for higher education: Benefits and challenges for pre-service teachers. *Frontiers in Education*, *9*, 1501819. Advance online publication. DOI: 10.3389/feduc.2024.1501819

Kamalov, F., Calonge, D. S., Smail, L., Azizov, D., Thadani, D. R., Kwong, T., & Atif, A. (2025). Evolution of ai in education: Agentic workflows. *ArXiv Preprint ArXiv:2504.20082*.

Kang, S. H. K. (2016). Spaced Repetition Promotes Efficient and Effective Learning: Policy Implications for Instruction. *Policy Insights from the Behavioral and Brain Sciences*, *3*(1), 12–19. Advance online publication. DOI: 10.1177/2372732215624708

Kärki, T., McMullen, J., & Lehtinen, E. (2022). Improving rational number knowledge using the NanoRoboMath digital game. *Educational Studies in Mathematics*, *110*(1), 101–123. DOI: 10.1007/s10649-021-10120-6

Karpouzis, K. (2024). Artificial Intelligence in Education. *Ethical Considerations and Insights from Ancient Greek Philosophy.*, *1*, 1–7. Advance online publication. DOI: 10.1145/3688671.3688772

Kaswan, K. S., Dhatterwal, J. S., & Ojha, R. P. (2024). AI in personalized learning. *Advances in Technological Innovations in Higher Education: Theory and Practices*, 103–117. /DOI: 10.1201/9781003376699-9

Katsenou, R., Kotsidis, K., Papadopoulou, A., Anastasiadis, P., & Deliyannis, I. (2025). Beyond Assistance: Embracing AI as a Collaborative Co-Agent in Education. *Education Sciences 2025, Vol. 15, Page 1006, 15*(8), 1006. DOI: 10.3390/educsci15081006

Kayal, A. (2024). *Transformative Pedagogy: A Comprehensive Framework for AI Integration in Education*. 247–270. DOI: 10.1007/978-3-031-72410-7_14

Kem, D. (2022). Personalised and adaptive learning: Emerging learning platforms in the era of digital and smart learning. *International Journal of Social Science and Human Research*, *5*(2), 385–391. DOI: 10.47191/ijsshr/v5-i2-02

Khanna, A., Pandey, B., Vashishta, K., Kalia, K., Pradeepkumar, B., & Das, T. (2015). A study of today's AI through chatbots and rediscovery of machine intelligence. *International Journal of u- and e-Service. Science and Technology*, *8*(10), 277–284. DOI: 10.14257/ijunesst.2015.8.10.26

Kim, J. (2024a). Leading teachers' perspective on teacher-AI collaboration in education. *Education and Information Technologies*, *29*(7), 8693–8724. DOI: 10.1007/s10639-023-12109-5

Kim, J. (2024b). Types of teacher-AI collaboration in K-12 classroom instruction: Chinese teachers' perspective. *Education and Information Technologies*, *29*(13), 17433–17465. DOI: 10.1007/s10639-024-12523-3

Kim, J., Lee, H., & Cho, Y. H. (2022). Learning design to support student-AI collaboration: Perspectives of leading teachers for AI in education. *Education and Information Technologies*, *27*(5), 6069–6104. DOI: 10.1007/s10639-021-10831-6

Kim, T., & Biocca, F. (1997). Telepresence via television: Two dimensions of telepresence may have different connections to memory and persuasion. *Journal of Computer-Mediated Communication*, *3*(2), 0. Advance online publication. DOI: 10.1111/j.1083-6101.1997.tb00073.x

Koh, J., Cowling, M., Jha, M., & Sim, K. N. (2023). The human teacher, the AI teacher and the AIed-Teacher relationship. *Journal of Higher Education Theory and Practice*, *23*(17), 199–202. DOI: 10.33423/jhetp.v23i17.6543

Kolchenko, V. (2018). Can Modern AI replace teachers? Not so fast! AI and Adaptive Learning: Personalized Education in the AI age. *HAPS Educator*, *22*(3), 249–252. DOI: 10.21692/haps.2018.032

Koltovskaia, S. (2020). Student engagement with automated written corrective feedback (AWCF) provided by Grammarly : A multiple case study. *Assessing Writing*, *44*, 100450. DOI: 10.1016/j.asw.2020.100450

Koltovskaia, S. (2023). Postsecondary L2 writing teachers' use and perceptions of Grammarly as a complement to their feedback. *ReCALL*, *35*(3), 290–304. DOI: 10.1017/S0958344022000179

Kooli, C., & Chakraoui, R. (2025). AI-driven assistive technologies in inclusive education: Benefits, challenges, and policy recommendations. *Sustainable Futures : An Applied Journal of Technology, Environment and Society*, *10*, 101042. DOI: 10.1016/j.sftr.2025.101042

Kostopoulos, G., Gkamas, V., Rigou, M., & Kotsiantis, S. (2025). Agentic AI in Education: State of the Art and Future Directions. *IEEE Access : Practical Innovations, Open Solutions*, *13*, 177467–177491. DOI: 10.1109/ACCESS.2025.3620473

Kotsis, K. T. (n.d.). *Integrating Artificial Intelligence into Higher Education Curricula: Challenges and Opportunities for Science-Based Programs*. DOI: 10.54660/IJAIET.2025.6.1.04-12

Krishna, A., Shinde, A., Ardham, S., & Malhotra, C. (2025). *A Collaborative Multi-Agent LLM Approach for Knowledge Graph Curation and Query from Multi-Modal Data Sources*. DOI: 10.36227/techrxiv.173886317.71891930/v1

Kulugh, V. E., Aondover, K. P., & Faki, A. S. (n.d.). Artificial Intelligence-Powered Personalised Career Guidance System. *Artificial Intelligence*.

Lai, T., Xie, C., Ruan, M., Wang, Z., Lu, H., & Fu, S. (2023). Influence of artificial intelligence in education on adolescents' social adaptability: The mediatory role of social support. *PLoS One*, *18*(3), e0283170. Advance online publication. DOI: 10.1371/journal.pone.0283170

Lameras, P., & Arnab, S. (2022). Power to the Teachers: An Exploratory review on AI in education. In Kerres, M., & Agre, G. (Eds.), *Information* (Vol. 13–14)., DOI: 10.3390/info13010014

Lampou, R. (2023). The Integration of Artificial Intelligence in Education: Opportunities and Challenges. *Review of Artificial Intelligence in Education*, *4*(00), e015. Advance online publication. DOI: 10.37497/rev.artif.intell.educ.v4i00.15

Lee, I., & Perret, B., & Education Development Center, Inc. (2022). Preparing High School Teachers to Integrate AI Methods into STEM Classrooms. In *The Thirty-Sixth AAAI Conference on AI (AAAI-22)*. DOI: 10.1609/aaai.v36i11.21557

Lee, Y. J., Davis, R. O., & Ryu, J. (2024). Korean In-Service Teachers' perceptions of implementing artificial intelligence (AI) education for teaching in schools and their AI teacher training programs. *International Journal of Information and Education Technology (IJIET)*, *14*(2), 214–219. DOI: 10.18178/ijiet.2024.14.2.2042

Lens, (2025). *Teacher AI collaboration*. https://www.lens.org/lens/search/scholar/list?q=Teacher-AI%20collaboration

Li, L., Yu, F., & Zhang, E. (2024). A systematic review of learning task design for K-12 AI education: Trends, challenges, and opportunities. *Computers and Education: Artificial Intelligence*, *6*, 100217. DOI: 10.1016/j.caeai.2024.100217

Lim, W. M., Gunasekara, A., Pallant, J. L., Pallant, J. I., & Pechenkina, E. (2023). Generative AI and the future of education: Ragnarök or reformation? A paradoxical perspective from management educators. *International Journal of Management Education*, *21*(2), 100790. DOI: 10.1016/j.ijme.2023.100790

Lin, C.-C., Huang, A. Y. Q., & Lu, O. H. T. (2023). Artificial intelligence in intelligent tutoring systems toward sustainable education: a systematic review [Review of Artificial intelligence in intelligent tutoring systems toward sustainable education: a systematic review]. Smart Learning Environments, 10(1). Springer Nature. https://doi.org/DOI: 10.1186/s40561-023-00260-y

Lindner, A., & Romeike, R. (2019). Teachers' perspectives on AI. ISSEP 2019: 12th International conference on informatics in schools. Situation, evaluation and perspectives. Cyprus

Lin, X., Chen, L., Chan, K. K., Peng, S., Chen, X., Xie, S., Liu, J., & Hu, Q. (2022). Teachers' perceptions of teaching Sustainable AI: A Design frame perspective. *Sustainability*, *14*(13), 7811. DOI: 10.3390/su14137811

Liu, G. L., Lee, J. S., & Zhao, X. (2025). Critical digital literacies, agentic practices, and AI-mediated informal digital learning of English. *System*, *134*, 103797. DOI: 10.1016/j.system.2025.103797

Liu, J., Chu, C., Zhao, Y., Aoki, G., & Xiao, Z. (2025). Agentic AI for Sustainable Development: Leveraging Large Language Model-Enhanced Agent-Based Modeling for Complex Policy Strategies. *Emerging Media*, *3*(3), 401–413. DOI: 10.1177/27523543251365678

Liu, Y. (2025). Psychological Adaptation and Affective Feedback in AI-Enhanced Education: A Systematic Review. *Simen Owen Academic Proceedings Series*, *1*, 17–27.

Li, Z., & Demir, İ. (2023). U-Net-based semantic classification for flood extent extraction using SAR imagery and GEE platform: A case study for 2019 central US flooding. *The Science of the Total Environment*, *869*, 161757. Advance online publication. DOI: 10.1016/j.scitotenv.2023.161757

Lizano-Sánchez, F., Idoyaga, I., Orduña, P., Rodríguez-Gil, L., & Arguedas-Matarrita, C. (2025). Teachers' perspective on the use of artificial intelligence on remote experimentation. *Frontiers in Education*, *10*, 1518896. Advance online publication. DOI: 10.3389/feduc.2025.1518896

Llausas, S. M., Ruiz, E., Ayucan, S. M., & Evardo, O. J.Jr. (2024). A Systematic Literature Review on the Use of Grammarly in Improving the Writing Skills of ESL/EFL Students. *International Journal of Multidisciplinary: Applied Business and Education Research*, *5*(9), 3507–3516. DOI: 10.11594/ijmaber.05.09.10

Lo, J. J., & Shu, P. C. (2005). Identification of learning styles online by observing learners' browsing behaviour through a neural network. *British Journal of Educational Technology*, *36*(1), 43–55. DOI: 10.1111/j.1467-8535.2005.00437.x

Luckin, R., & Holmes, W. (2016). Intelligence Unleashed: An argument for AI in Education. In *UCL Knowledge Lab: London, UK.*

Luckin, R., Holmes, W., Griffiths, M., & Forcier, L. B. (2018). *Artificial intelligence and the future of learning*. The Brookings Institution.

Luo, H. E. H., Chen, G., Lin, Q., Guo, Y., Xu, F., Kuang, Z., Song, M., Wu, X., Zhu, Y., & Tuan, L. A. (2025). *Graph-R1: Towards Agentic GraphRAG Framework via End-to-end Reinforcement Learning*. https://arxiv.org/pdf/2507.21892

Madelaine, H. (2025). *The European Commission opens public consultation on high-risk AI systems*. https://www.insideglobaltech.com/2025/06/24/the-european-commission-opens-public-consultation-on-high-risk-ai-systems/

Maghsudi, S., Lan, A., Xu, J., & van der Schaar, M. (2021). Personalized Education in the Artificial Intelligence Era: What to Expect Next. *IEEE Signal Processing Magazine*, *38*(3), 37–50. DOI: 10.1109/MSP.2021.3055032

Mahmoud, C. F., & Sørensen, J. T. (2024). Artificial Intelligence in Personalized Learning with a Focus on Current Developments and Future Prospects. *Research and Advances in Education*, *3*(8), 25–31. DOI: 10.56397/RAE.2024.08.04

Maiti, P., & Goel, A. (2025). Can an AI Partner Empower Learners to Ask Critical Questions? *International Conference on Intelligent User Interfaces, Proceedings IUI*, 314–324. DOI: 10.1145/3708359.3712134

Ma, K., Zhang, Y., & Hui, B.-H. (2024). How Does AI Affect College? The Impact of AI Usage in College Teaching on Students' Innovative Behavior and Well-Being. *Behavioral Sciences (Basel, Switzerland)*, *14*(12), 1223. DOI: 10.3390/bs14121223

Malik, G., Tayal, D. K., & Vij, S. (2018). An Analysis of the Role of Artificial Intelligence in Education and Teaching. In *Advances in intelligent systems and computing* (p. 407). Springer Nature., DOI: 10.1007/978-981-10-8639-7_42

Malik, M. A., & Shah, R. (2025). AI teachers (AI-based robots as teachers): History, potential, concerns and recommendations. *Frontiers in Education*, *10*, 1–5. DOI: 10.3389/feduc.2025.1541543

Mallik, S., & Gangopadhyay, A. (2023). Proactive and reactive engagement of artificial intelligence methods for education: A review. *Frontiers in Artificial Intelligence*, *6*, 1151391. DOI: 10.3389/frai.2023.1151391 PMID: 37215064

Manoharan, G. (2026). Academic Research in the Age of Artificial Intelligence: A Revolutionary Look. In Tariq, M. (Ed.), *Improving Doctoral Education and Research Development for Sustainability* (pp. 363–388). IGI Global Scientific Publishing., DOI: 10.4018/979-8-3373-0225-6.ch012

Manoharan, G., Ashtikar, S. P., & Dudhagara, C. R. (2025). Ethics of AI in the Educational Sector - Navigating the Moral Landscape. In Rajagopal, S., Popat, K., Meva, D., Bajeja, S., & Mudholkar, P. (Eds.), *Artificial Intelligence Based Smart and Secured Applications. ASCIS 2024. Communications in Computer and Information Science* (Vol. 2427). Springer., DOI: 10.1007/978-3-031-86299-1_19

Manser Payne, E. H., Peltier, J., & Barger, V. A. (2021). Enhancing the value co-creation process: Artificial intelligence and mobile banking service platforms. *Journal of Research in Interactive Marketing*, *15*(1), 68–85. DOI: 10.1108/JRIM-10-2020-0214

Manzoor, A., Hameed, A., & Sultan, F. (2025). AI as a Teaching Partner: Redefining Educator Roles in the Digital Age. `, *3*(02), 2262–2276. https://assajournal.com/index.php/36/article/view/544

Maphalala, M. C., & Ajani, O. A. (2025). Leveraging artificial intelligence as a learning tool in higher education. *Interdisciplinary Journal of Education Research*, *7*(1), a01. Advance online publication. DOI: 10.38140/ijer-2025.vol7.1.01

Martínez-Carrasco, R., & Chabert, A. (2023). Writing on steroids? Accuracy of automatic corrective feedback in L2 competence development. *Bellaterra Journal of Teaching & Learning Language & Literature*, *16*(3), e1142. DOI: 10.5565/rev/jtl3.1142

Mavroudi, A., Giannakos, M., & Krogstie, J. (2018). Supporting adaptive learning pathways through the use of learning analytics: Developments, challenges and future opportunities. *Interactive Learning Environments*, *26*(2), 206–220. DOI: 10.1080/10494820.2017.1292531

Maypida, A., & Damanik, E. S. D. (2024). *Exploring Grammarly's Effectiveness in EFL Writing through a Student Perception Study.*

McKay, A. K., Stellingwerff, T., Smith, E. S., Martin, D. T., Mujika, I., Goosey-Tolfrey, V. L., Sheppard, J., & Burke, L. M. (2021). Defining training and performance caliber: A participant classification framework. *International Journal of Sports Physiology and Performance*, *17*(2), 317–331. DOI: 10.1123/ijspp.2021-0451 PMID: 34965513

Mehraj, T., & Baba, A. M. (2019). *Scrutinising Artificial Intelligence based Career Guidance and Counselling Systems: An Appraisal. 7*(1).

Memarian, B., & Doleck, T. (2023). Fairness, Accountability, Transparency, and Ethics (FATE) in Artificial Intelligence (AI) and higher education: A systematic review. *Computers and Education: Artificial Intelligence*, *5*, 100152. DOI: 10.1016/j.caeai.2023.100152

Mendoza Zaragoza, N. E., Téllez Tula, Á., & Herrera Corona, L. (2024). Artificial Intelligence in Thesis Writing : Exploring the Role of Advanced Grammar Checkers (Grammarly). *Estudios y Perspectivas Revista Científica y Académica, 4*(2), 649-683. DOI: 10.61384/r.c.a.v4i2.248

Merino-Campos, C. (2025). The Impact of Artificial Intelligence on Personalized Learning in Higher Education: A Systematic Review [Review of The Impact of Artificial Intelligence on Personalized Learning in Higher Education: A Systematic Review]. Trends in Higher Education, 4(2), 17. Multidisciplinary Digital Publishing Institute. https://doi.org/DOI: 10.3390/higheredu4020017

Mhlanga, D., & Moloi, T. (2020). COVID-19 and the digital transformation of education: What are we learning on 4IR in South Africa? *Education Sciences*, *10*(7), 180. DOI: 10.3390/educsci10070180

Miao, F., Holmes, W., Huang, R., & Zhang, H. (2021). *AI and education guidance for policy-makers*. UNESCO Publishing.

Michelson, R., DeWitt, A., Nagar, R., Hiniker, A., Yip, J., Munson, S. A., & Kientz, J. A. (2021). Parenting in a Pandemic: Juggling Multiple Roles and Managing Technology Use in Family Life During COVID-19 in the United States. *Proceedings of the ACM on Human-Computer Interaction, 5*(CSCW2), 1–39. DOI: 10.1145/3479546

Minn, S. (2022). AI-assisted knowledge assessment techniques for adaptive learning environments. *Computers and Education: Artificial Intelligence*, *3*, 100050. Advance online publication. DOI: 10.1016/j.caeai.2022.100050

Miranda, J., Navarrete, C., Noguez, J., Molina-Espinosa, J. M., Ramírez-Montoya, M. S., Navarro-Tuch, S. A., Bustamante-Bello, M. R., Rosas-Fernández, J. B., & Molina, A. (2021). The core components of education 4.0 in higher education: Three case studies in engineering education. *Computers & Electrical Engineering*, *93*, 107278. DOI: 10.1016/j.compeleceng.2021.107278

Mogos, R., Bodea, C. N., Dascalu, M., Lazarou, E., Trifan, L., Safonkina, O., & Nemoianu, I. (2018). Technology enhanced learning for Industry 4.0 engineering education. *Revue Roumaine des Sciences Techniques—Électrotechnique et Énergétique, 63*, 429–435.

Molenaar, I. (2022). The concept of hybrid human-AI regulation: Exemplifying how to support young learners' self-regulated learning. *Computers and Education: Artificial Intelligence*, *3*, 100070. DOI: 10.1016/j.caeai.2022.100070

Moraes, E. B., Kipper, L. M., Hackenhaar Kellermann, A. C., Austria, L., Leivas, P., Moraes, J. A. R., & Witczak, M. (2022). Integration of Industry 4.0 technologies with Education 4.0: Advantages for improvements in learning. *Interactive Technology and Smart Education*, *20*(2), 271–287. DOI: 10.1108/ITSE-11-2021-0201

Morsy, R. M. A. (2024). *The Impact of Expert Systems and Big Data Analytics Capabilities on Decision-Making in Private Higher Educational Sector in Egypt.*

Mousavinasab, E., Zarifsanaiey, N., Kalhori, S. R. N., Rakhshan, M., Keikha, L., & Saeedi, M. G. (2021). Intelligent tutoring systems: A systematic review of characteristics, applications, and evaluation methods. *Interactive Learning Environments*, *29*, 142–163. DOI: 10.1080/10494820.2018.1558257

Mouta, A., Pinto-Llorente, A. M., & Torrecilla-Sánchez, E. M. (2025). "Where is Agency Moving to?": Exploring the Interplay between AI Technologies in Education and Human Agency. *Digital Society : Ethics, Socio-Legal and Governance of Digital Technology*, *4*(2), 49. DOI: 10.1007/s44206-025-00203-9

Mudzar, N. M. B. M., & Chew, K. W. (2022). Change in labour force skillset for the fourth industrial revolution: A literature review. *International Journal of Technology*, *13*(5), 969–978. DOI: 10.14716/ijtech.v13i5.5875

Murugesan, S. (2025). The Rise of Agentic AI: Implications, Concerns, and the Path Forward. *IEEE Intelligent Systems*, *40*(2), 8–14. DOI: 10.1109/MIS.2025.3544940

Nath, S., Peridis, C., Benjamin, E., Liu, X., Kolouri, S., Kinnell, P., Li, Z., Liu, C., Dora, S., & Soltoggio, A. (2025). *Policy Search, Retrieval, and Composition via Task Similarity in Collaborative Agentic Systems.* https://arxiv.org/pdf/2506.05577

Nazaretsky, T., Ariely, M., Cukurova, M., & Alexandron, G. (2022). Teachers' trust in AI -powered educational technology and a professional development program to improve it. *British Journal of Educational Technology*, *53*(4), 914–931. DOI: 10.1111/bjet.13232

Nedungadi, P., & Raman, R. (2012). A new approach to personalization: Integrating e-learning and m-learning. *Educational Technology Research and Development*, *60*(4), 659–678. DOI: 10.1007/s11423-012-9250-9

Neelu, A., Pramod, J. P., & Lahari, A. (2025). *Optimizing Networks Using AI and Machine Learning: The Role of Agentic AI in Transforming Network Management*. 229–254. DOI: 10.1007/978-3-031-89424-4_16

Ng, D. T. K., Chan, E. K. C., & Lo, C. K. (2025). Opportunities, challenges and school strategies for integrating generative AI in education. *Computers and Education: Artificial Intelligence*, 100373.

Ng, D. T. K., Chan, E. K. C., & Lo, C. K. (2025). Opportunities, challenges and school strategies for integrating generative AI in education. *Computers and Education: Artificial Intelligence*, *8*, 100373. DOI: 10.1016/j.caeai.2025.100373

Nguyen, A., Ngo, H. N., Hong, Y., Dang, B., & Nguyen, B.-P. T. (2022). Ethical principles for artificial intelligence in education. *Education and Information Technologies*, *28*(4), 4221–4241. DOI: 10.1007/s10639-022-11316-w

Nguyen, N. N., & Barbieri, W. (2025). Mentorship in the Age of Generative AI: ChatGPT to Support Self-Regulated Learning of Pre-Service Teachers Before and During Placements. *Education Sciences*, *15*(6), 642. DOI: 10.3390/educsci15060642

Nguyen, V. (2025). The Use of Generative AI Tools in Higher Education: Ethical and Pedagogical Principles. *Journal of Academic Ethics*, *23*(3), 1435–1455. Advance online publication. DOI: 10.1007/s10805-025-09607-1

Nilashi, M., Abumalloh, R. A., Zibarzani, M., Samad, S., Zogaan, W. A., Ismail, M. Y., & Akib, N. A. M. (2022). What factors influence students' satisfaction in massive open online courses? Findings from user-generated content using educational data mining. *Education and Information Technologies*, *27*(7), 9401–9435. DOI: 10.1007/s10639-022-10997-7

O'Neill, R., & Russell, A. M. T. (2019). Grammarly : Help or hindrance ? Academic Learning Advisors' perceptions of an online grammar checker. *R. O.*

OECD. (2024). *AI Principles Overview*. https://oecd.ai/en/ai-principles

Ofrita, H., Darmis, A., & Rosmanizar, R. (2023). The Effect of Automated Written Corrective Feedback (AWCF) on Students' Writing at SMP 47 Pekanbaru. *Jurnal Pendidikan Tuntas, 1*(4), 352–361. DOI: 10.37985/jpt.v1i4.282

Onesi-Ozigagun, O., Ololade, Y. J., Eyo-Udo, N. L., & Ogundipe, D. O. (2024). Revolutionizing education through AI: A comprehensive review of enhancing learning experiences. *International Journal of Applied Research in Social Sciences, 6*(4), 589. https://doi.org/DOI: 10.51594/ijarss.v6i4.1011

Ong, X. Q., & Lim, K. H. (2023). *SkillRec: A Data-Driven Approach to Job Skill Recommendation for Career Insights* (No. arXiv:2302.09938). arXiv. /arXiv.2302.09938DOI: 10.1109/ICCAE56788.2023.10111438

Opesemowo, O. A. G., & Adewuyi, H. O. (2024). A systematic review of artificial intelligence in mathematics education: The emergence of 4IR [Review of A systematic review of artificial intelligence in mathematics education: The emergence of 4IR]. Eurasia Journal of Mathematics Science and Technology Education, 20(7). Modestum Limited. https://doi.org/DOI: 10.29333/ejmste/14762

Or, C. (2024). Watch That Attitude! Examining the Role of Attitude in the Technology Acceptance Model through Meta-Analytic Structural Equation Modelling. *International Journal of Technology in Education and Science, 8*(4), 558–582. DOI: 10.46328/ijtes.575

Origin, (2025). https://www.originlab.com/

Ouhnine, I. (2026). The Future of Human Autonomy: Will Agentic Artificial Intelligence Augment or Replace Human Decision-Making. In *Transparency in AI-Assisted Management Decisions* (pp. 79–108). IGI Global Scientific Publishing.

Ouwehand, K., Lespiau, F., Tricot, A., & Paas, F. (2025). Cognitive Load Theory: Emerging Trends and Innovations. *Education Sciences 2025, Vol. 15, Page 458, 15*(4), 458. DOI: 10.3390/educsci15040458

Pancham, S., Updesh, K. J., Eshank, J., Nikhil, K., & Vimlesh, M. (2025). A Novel Methodology Utilizing Modern CCTV Cameras and Software as a Service Model for Crime Detection and Prediction. *International Journal of Performability Engineering, 21*(2), 112. DOI: 10.23940/ijpe.25.02.p6.112121

Panjwani-Charania, S., & Zhai, X. (2024). AI for Students with Learning Disabilities: A Systematic Review. *Uses of Artificial Intelligence in STEM Education*, 469–493. DOI: 10.1093/oso/9780198882077.003.0021

Pati, A. K. (2025). Agentic AI: A Comprehensive Survey of Technologies, Applications, and Societal Implications. *IEEE Access : Practical Innovations, Open Solutions*, *13*, 151824–151837. DOI: 10.1109/ACCESS.2025.3585609

Patki, M., Sanadi, S., Jadhav, S., Musale, A., & Kadam, K. (2023). Ethical Implications of Utilizing Artificial Intelligence in Education for Assessment. *International Conference on Computers in Education, 2*, 600–608. DOI: 10.58459/icce.2023.1439

Peddi, S., & Manoharan, G. (2025). Innovative Approaches to Staff Development in Education Using AI. In Morris, G., & Ye, J. (Eds.), *Training and Development in Transnational Higher Education* (pp. 347–368). IGI Global Scientific Publishing., DOI: 10.4018/979-8-3373-1897-4.ch017

Peddi, S., & Manoharan, G. (2025). Research Issues and Challenges in Higher Education. In Mdikana, A. (Ed.), *Social Implications of Research in Higher Education* (pp. 297–326). IGI Global Scientific Publishing., DOI: 10.4018/979-8-3373-0654-4.ch011

Perkins Coie. (2023). *FTC's COPPA Enforcement Action Provides Lessons for Edtech Providers*. https://perkinscoie.com/insights/update/ftcs-coppa-enforcement-action-provides-lessons-edtech-providers

Perry, N., Sun, C., Munro, M., Boulton, K. A., & Guastella, A. J. (2024). AI technology to support adaptive functioning in neurodevelopmental conditions in everyday environments: A systematic review. *NPJ Digital Medicine*, *7*(1), 370. DOI: 10.1038/s41746-024-01355-7 PMID: 39702672

Peterson, L., Scharber, C., Thuesen, A., & Baskin, K. (2020). A rapid response to COVID-19: One district's pivot from technology integration to distance learning. *Information and Learning Science*, *121*(5/6), 461–469. DOI: 10.1108/ILS-04-2020-0131

Phua, J. T. K., Neo, H. F., & Teo, C.-C. (2025). Evaluating the Impact of Artificial Intelligence Tools on Enhancing Student Academic Performance: Efficacy Amidst Security and Privacy Concerns. *Big Data and Cognitive Computing*, *9*(5), 131. DOI: 10.3390/bdcc9050131

Piper, D. L. A. (2024). *Data protection laws in Brazil - Data Protection Laws of the World*. https://www.dlapiperdataprotection.com/index.html

Piramuthu, S. (2005). Knowledge-based web-enabled agents and intelligent tutoring systems. *IEEE Transactions on Education*, *48*(4), 750–756. DOI: 10.1109/TE.2005.854574

Poornesh, M. (2024). Through a Teacher's Lens: Combating Bias in AI-Powered Education for a Just Future. *The Clearing House: A Journal of Educational Strategies, Issues and Ideas*, *97*(4), 119–124. DOI: 10.1080/00098655.2024.2393153

Popenici, S. A. D., & Kerr, S. (2017). Exploring the impact of AI on teaching and learning in higher education. *Research and Practice in Technology Enhanced Learning*, *12*(1), 1–13. DOI: 10.1186/s41039-017-0062-8 PMID: 30613250

Prinsloo, P. (2020). Big data in education. The digital future of learning, policy and practice. *International Studies in Sociology of Education*, *29*(1–2), 183–186. Advance online publication. DOI: 10.1080/09620214.2019.1690546

Projectpro. (2025). *AI Agent Architectures: Modular, Multi-Agent, and Evolving*. https://www.projectpro.io/article/ai-agent-architectures/1135?

Psotka, J., Massey, L. D., & Mutter, S. A. (Eds.). (1988). *Intelligent tutoring systems: Lessons learned*. Lawrence Erlbaum Associates.

Purushottamashtikar, S., & Manoharan, G. (2024, June 5). Emotional intelligence on higher education educators: A systematic literature review. *AIP Conference Proceedings*, *2971*(1), 030004. DOI: 10.1063/5.0195788

Radhika, K., Sai Vamsee, B., Sushruth Samson Kumar, K., & Rayalu, G. V. R. (2025). The Co-teacher—A Tool for Learning Using ChatGPT. *Cognitive Science and Technology*, *2025*, 325–339. DOI: 10.1007/978-981-97-9266-5_33

Raheem, T., & Hossain, G. (2025). Agentic AI Systems: Opportunities, Challenges, and Trustworthiness. *2025 IEEE International Conference on Electro Information Technology (EIT)*, 618–624. DOI: 10.1109/eIT64391.2025.11103638

Ramirez, C. E., Sermet, Y., & Demir, İ. (2023). HydroLang Markup Language: Community-driven web components for hydrological analyses. *Journal of Hydroinformatics*, *25*(4), 1171–1187. DOI: 10.2166/hydro.2023.149

Ramirez, C. E., Sermet, Y., Molkenthin, F., & Demir, İ. (2022). HydroLang: An open-source web-based programming framework for hydrological sciences. *Environmental Modelling & Software*, *157*, 105525. Advance online publication. DOI: 10.1016/j.envsoft.2022.105525

Ranalli, J. (2018). Automated written corrective feedback : How well can students make use of it? *Computer Assisted Language Learning*, *31*(7), 653–674. DOI: 10.1080/09588221.2018.1428994

Rao, M. (2019). *Usage of Grammarly – Online Grammar and Spelling Checker Tool at the Health Sciences Library, Manipal Academy of Higher Education, Manipal : A Study*.

Rao, A. S., Kamath, B. S., & Kundar, R. K. (2020). Use of Artificial Neural Network in Developing a Personality Prediction Model for Career Guidance: A Boon for Career Counselors. *International Journal of Control and Automation, 13*(4).

Reddy, C. K. K., Joseph, S., Joshi, H., Doss, S., & Ouaissa, M. (Eds.). (2025). *The Power of Agentic AI: Redefining Human Life and Decision-Making*. DOI: 10.1007/978-3-031-89424-4

Resnick, M. (2024). *Generative AI and Creative Learning: Concerns*. Opportunities, and Choices., DOI: 10.21428/e4baedd9.cf3e35e5

Roach, M., Blackmore, P., & Dempster, J. A. (2001). Supporting high-level learning through research-based methods: A framework for course development. *Innovations in Education and Teaching International, 38*(4), 369–382. DOI: 10.1080/14703290110074957

Roe, J., & Perkins, M. (2024). *Generative AI and Agency in Education: A Critical Scoping Review and Thematic Analysis*. https://arxiv.org/pdf/2411.00631

Roll, I., & Wylie, R. (2016). Evolution and Revolution in Artificial Intelligence in Education. *International Journal of Artificial Intelligence in Education, 26*(2), 582–599. Advance online publication. DOI: 10.1007/s40593-016-0110-3

Roscoe, R. D., Salehi, S., Nixon, N., Worsley, M., Piech, C., & Luckin, R. (2022). Inclusion and equity as a paradigm shift for artificial intelligence in education. In *Artificial Intelligence in STEM Education* (pp. 359–374). CRC Press. DOI: 10.1201/9781003181187-28

Roshanaei, M. (2024). Towards best practices for mitigating artificial intelligence implicit bias in shaping diversity, inclusion and equity in higher education. *Education and Information Technologies, 29*(14), 18959–18984. DOI: 10.1007/s10639-024-12605-2

Roshanaei, M., Olivares, H., & Lopez, R. R. (2023). Harnessing AI to Foster Equity in Education: Opportunities, Challenges, and Emerging Strategies. *Journal of Intelligent Learning Systems and Applications, 15*(4), 123–143. DOI: 10.4236/jilsa.2023.154009

Saini, A. (2024). IMPACT OF ARTIFICIAL INTELLIGENCE ON STUDENTS' SUSTAINABLE EDUCATION AND CAREER DEVELOPMENT USING EXTENDED TOE FRAMEWORK. *International Research Journal of Education and Technology*, *6*(11), 224–243. DOI: 10.70127/irjedt.vol.7.issue02.243

Sajja, R., Sermet, Y., & Demir, I. (2025). End-to-End Deployment of the Educational AI Hub for Personalized Learning and Engagement: A Case Study on Environmental Science Education. *IEEE Access : Practical Innovations, Open Solutions*, *13*, 55169–55186. DOI: 10.1109/ACCESS.2025.3554222

Sandema-Sombe, C. N. (2019). *Relationship between perceived usefulness, ease of use, and acceptance of business intelligence systems*. Walden University.

Santos, F. M. D. A., Pereira, A., Shanches, A., Crespo, D., & Pala, H. (2025). The impacts of AI and automation on human resource management – systematic review. *Brazilian Journal of Development*, *11*(2), e78003. DOI: 10.34117/bjdv11n2-079

Saputra, I., Astuti, M., Sayuti, M., & Kusumastuti, D. (2023). Integration of Artificial Intelligence in Education: Opportunities, Challenges, Threats and Obstacles. A Literature Review. *Indonesian Journal of Computer Science*, *12*(4). Advance online publication. DOI: 10.33022/ijcs.v12i4.3266

Satu, M. S., Parvez, M. H., & Al-Mamun, S. (2015, November 26–27). Review of integrated applications with AIML based chatbot. In *Proceedings of the International Conference on Computer and Information Engineering (ICCIE)* (pp. 87–90). Rajshahi, Bangladesh. DOI: 10.1109/CCIE.2015.7399324

Schiff, D. (2022). Education for AI, not AI for education: The role of education and ethics in national AI policy strategies. *International Journal of Artificial Intelligence in Education*, *32*(3), 527–563. DOI: 10.1007/s40593-021-00270-2

Selwyn, N. (2019). *Should Robots Replace Teachers? AI and the Future of Education*. John Wiley & Sons, Inc.

Seo, J. H. (2024). Similar image retrieval technique based on semantics through automatic labeling extraction of personalized images. *Journal of Information and Communication Convergence Engineering*, *22*(1), 64–69. DOI: 10.56977/jicce.2024.22.1.56

Sermet, Y., & Demir, İ. (2021). A semantic web framework for automated smart assistants: A case study for public health. *Big Data and Cognitive Computing*, *5*(4), 57. Advance online publication. DOI: 10.3390/bdcc5040057

Sharma, A., Rao, S., Brockett, C., Malhotra, A., Jojic, N., & Dolan, B. (2023). *Investigating Agency of LLMs in Human-AI Collaboration Tasks*. https://www.microsoft.com/en-us/research/publication/investigating-agency-of-llms-in-human-ai-collaboration-tasks/

Sharma, K., Papamitsiou, Z., & Giannakos, M. (2019). Building pipelines for educational data using AI and multimodal analytics: A "grey-box" approach. *British Journal of Educational Technology*, *50*(6), 3004–3031. DOI: 10.1111/bjet.12854

Shkurko, S. Y. (2025). Human-AI Interaction from an Evolutionary Neurosociological Perspective. In *Handbook of Neurosociology* (pp. 387–409). Springer.

Shuford, J., & Islam, M. M. (2024). Exploring the latest trends in artificial intelligence technology: A comprehensive review. *Journal of Artificial Intelligence General Science*, *2*(1), 3006–4023. DOI: 10.60087/jaigs.v2i1.p13

Shute, V. J., & Psotka, J. (1994). Intelligent tutoring systems: Past, present, and future. Human Resources Directorate Manpower and Personnel Research Division, 2–52.

Singh, P., Kansal, M., Singh, A. P., Verma, A., Tyagi, S., & Singh, A. V. (2024). Real-Time Symptomatic Disease Predictor Using Multi-Layer Perceptron. In Sharma, A. K., Chanderwal, N., Tyagi, S., & Upadhyay, P. (Eds.), (pp. 155–167). Advances in Medical Technologies and Clinical Practice. IGI Global., DOI: 10.4018/979-8-3693-2359-5.ch010

Sit, M., Langel, R. J., Thompson, D. A., Cwiertny, D. M., & Demir, İ. (2021). Web-based data analytics framework for well forecasting and groundwater quality. *The Science of the Total Environment*, *761*, 144121. Advance online publication. DOI: 10.1016/j.scitotenv.2020.144121

Smuha, N. A. (2021). From a 'race to AI'to a 'race to AI regulation': Regulatory competition for artificial intelligence. *Law, Innovation and Technology*, *13*(1), 57–84. DOI: 10.1080/17579961.2021.1898300

Song, J., Wang, S., Shun, J., & Zhu, Y. (2025). *Efficient and Transferable Agentic Knowledge Graph RAG via Reinforcement Learning*. https://arxiv.org/pdf/2509.26383

Song, D., Oh, E. Y., & Rice, M. (2017, July 17–19). Interacting with a conversational agent system for educational purposes in online courses. In *Proceedings of the 10th International Conference on Human System Interactions (HSI)* (pp. 78–82). Ulsan, Republic of Korea. DOI: 10.1109/HSI.2017.8005002

Strielkowski, W., Grebennikova, V., Lisovskiy, A., Rakhimova, G., & Vasileva, T. (2025). AI-driven adaptive learning for sustainable educational transformation. *Sustainable Development (Bradford)*, *33*(2), 1921–1947. DOI: 10.1002/sd.3221

Sweller, J. (1988). Cognitive load during problem solving: Effects on learning. *Cognitive Science*, *12*(2), 257–285. Advance online publication. DOI: 10.1207/s15516709cog1202_4

Sweller, J. (2023). The Development of Cognitive Load Theory: Replication Crises and Incorporation of Other Theories Can Lead to Theory Expansion. *Educational Psychology Review*, *35*(4), 1–20. DOI: 10.1007/s10648-023-09817-2

Sweller, J., & Chandler, P. (1991). Evidence for Cognitive Load Theory. *Cognition and Instruction*, *8*(4), 351–362. Advance online publication. DOI: 10.1207/s1532690xci0804_5

Tahiru, F. (2021). AI in education: A systematic literature review. *Journal of Cases on Information Technology*, *23*(1), 1–20. DOI: 10.4018/JCIT.2021010101

Thakare, Y. A., Satote, R. R., Kenkar, S. A., Nathile, S. R., Watane, S. A., & Hade, S. C. (2025). AI-based career counsellor: An AI driven career advisor. *International Journal of Science and Research Archive*, *15*(1), 1013–1023. DOI: 10.30574/ijsra.2025.15.1.1088

Thomas Metzinger. (2019). Ethics washing made in Europe. *Der Tagesspiegel, 20*(2).

Thomas, D. R., Lin, J., Gatz, E., Gurung, A., Gupta, S., Norberg, K., Fancsali, S., Aleven, V., Branstetter, L., Brunskill, E., & Koedinger, K. R. (2024). Improving Student Learning with Hybrid Human-AI Tutoring: A Three-Study Quasi-Experimental Investigation. https://doi.org/DOI: 10.1145/3636555.3636896

Thomas, S. (2024). Agentic AI: The Power of Genai and LLMs in Autonomous Systems. *International Journal of Core Engineering & Management*, *12*(7).

Tripathi, T., Sharma, S. R., Singh, V., Bhargava, P., & Raj, C. (2025). Teaching and learning with AI: A qualitative study on K-12 teachers' use and engagement with artificial intelligence. *Frontiers in Education*, *10*, 1651217. DOI: 10.3389/feduc.2025.1651217

Trujillo, F., Pozo, M., & Suntaxi, G. (2025). Artificial intelligence in education: A systematic literature review of machine learning approaches in student career prediction. *Journal of Technology and Science Education*, *15*(1), 162. DOI: 10.3926/jotse.3124

Tsai, S. T., Lu, M. K., San, S., & Tsai, C. H. (2020). The neurologic manifestations of coronavirus disease 2019 pandemic: A systemic review. *Frontiers in Neurology*, *11*, 498. DOI: 10.3389/fneur.2020.00498 PMID: 32574246

Tsania, N. A., & Puspitasari, D. (n. d.). *STUDENTS' EXPERIENCES IN USING GRAMMARLY APPLICATION : A CASE STUDY.*

Tseng, S. S., Su, J. M., Hwang, G. J., Hwang, G. H., Tsai, C. C., & Tsai, C. J. (2008). An object-oriented course framework for developing adaptive learning systems. *Journal of Educational Technology & Society, 11*(2), 171–191.

Tyng, C. M., Amin, H. U., Saad, M. N. M., & Malik, A. S. (2017). The influences of emotion on learning and memory. In *Frontiers in Psychology* (Vol. 8). Issue AUG., DOI: 10.3389/fpsyg.2017.01454

Ullrich, A., Vladova, G., Eigelshoven, F., & Renz, A. (2022). Data mining of scientific research on artificial intelligence in teaching and administration in higher education institutions: A bibliometrics analysis and recommendation for future research. *Discover Artificial Intelligence, 2*(1), 16. Advance online publication. DOI: 10.1007/s44163-022-00031-7

Ummah, L. K., & Bisriyah, M. (2022). EFL students' perception of Grammarly's feedback and how they deal with the inaccuracy. [Journal of English Educators Society]. *JEES, 7*(2). Advance online publication. DOI: 10.21070/jees.v7i2.1687

Umoke, C. C., Nwangbo, S. O., & Onwe, O. A. (n.d.). *AI-Driven Educational Policy Design: Enhancing Equity and Access through Intelligent Data Analytics. International Journal of Computer Science and Mathematical Theory*. IJCSMT International Journal of Computer Science and Mathematical Theory., DOI: 10.56201/ijcsmt.v11.no3.2025.pg1.19

UNESCO. (2023). *Guidance for generative AI in education and research*. https://www.unesco.org/en/open-access/cc-sa

Van Merriënboer, J. J. G., & Sweller, J. (2005). Cognitive load theory and complex learning: Recent developments and future directions. In *Educational Psychology Review* (Vol. 17, Issue 2). DOI: 10.1007/s10648-005-3951-0

VanLehn, K. (2011). The relative effectiveness of human tutoring, intelligent tutoring systems, and other tutoring systems. *Educational Psychologist, 46*(4), 197–221. DOI: 10.1080/00461520.2011.611369

Venugopal, R., & Mamatha, V. (2023). Impact of artificial intelligence (AI) on teaching and learning in India's higher education sector. *IOSR Journal of Research & Method in Education (IOSRJRME)*, 1–6. https://doi.org/.DOI: 10.9790/7388-1305020106

Viberg, O., Kizilcec, R. F., Wise, A. F., Jivet, I., & Nixon, N. (2024). Advancing equity and inclusion in educational practices with AI-powered educational decision support systems (AI-EDSS). *British Journal of Educational Technology*, *55*(5), 1974–1981. DOI: 10.1111/bjet.13507

Vieriu, A. M., & Petrea, G. (2025). The Impact of Artificial Intelligence (AI) on Students' Academic Development. *Education Sciences*, *15*(3), 343. DOI: 10.3390/educsci15030343

Vo, N. H. K. V., & Nguyen, Q. T. (2021). *Applying Grammarly as an Online Grammar Checker Tool to Enhance Writing Skills for English-Major Students.*

Volin, J., van Assen, M., Bala, W., Safdar, N., & Balthazar, P. (2025). Artificial Intelligence and Its Effect on Radiology Residency Education: Current Challenges, Opportunities, and Future Directions. *Journal of the American College of Radiology*, *22*(11), 1264–1270. Advance online publication. DOI: 10.1016/j.jacr.2025.07.004 PMID: 40659237

VOSViewer. (2025). Retrieved October 2025. https://www.vosviewer.com/

Vygotsky, L. S. (2020). Mind in society: The development of higher psychological processes. In *Accounting in Australia*. RLE Accounting.

Walter, S. (2024). Harmonising humans and technology: Exploring the dynamics of cognitive production, artificial intelligence and social communication in cybernetic systems. *Open Research Europe*, *4*(201), 201. DOI: 10.12688/openreseurope.18418.1

Walter, Y. (2024). Embracing the future of Artificial Intelligence in the classroom: The relevance of AI literacy, prompt engineering, and critical thinking in modern education. *International Journal of Educational Technology in Higher Education*, *21*(1), 15. Advance online publication. DOI: 10.1186/s41239-024-00448-3

Wang, H., Wang, C., Chen, Z., Liu, F., Bao, C., & Xu, X. (2025). Impact of AI-agent-supported collaborative learning on the learning outcomes of University programming courses. *Education and Information Technologies*, *30*(12), 17717–17749. DOI: 10.1007/s10639-025-13487-8

Wang, V. (2025). Ethics and Equity in AI-Driven Education. In *AI Integration Into Andragogical Education* (pp. 231–254). IGI Global Scientific Publishing. DOI: 10.4018/979-8-3373-0502-8.ch010

Wang, W. (2024). Exploring the Attitudes of Higher Vocational College Students toward Artificial Intelligence: A Case Study in China. In Lin, C., Chew, F. P., Khan, I. A., & Popescu, C. (Eds.), *Proceedings of the 2024 9th International Conference on Modern Management, Education and Social Sciences (MMET 2024)* (Vol. 880, pp. 593–604). Atlantis Press SARL. DOI: 10.2991/978-2-38476-309-2_73

Ward, B., Bhati, D., Neha, F., & Guercio, A. (2025). Analyzing the Impact of AI Tools on Student Study Habits and Academic Performance. 2022 IEEE 12th Annual Computing and Communication Workshop and Conference (CCWC), 434. https://doi.org/DOI: 10.1109/CCWC62904.2025.10903692

Wei, H., Qiu, J., Yu, H., & Yuan, W. (2024). MEDCO: Medical Education Copilots Based on A Multi-Agent Framework. *Lecture Notes in Computer Science, 15630 LNCS*, 119–135. DOI: 10.1007/978-3-031-91813-1_8

Westman, S., Kauttonen, J., Klemetti, A., Korhonen, N., Manninen, M., Mononen, A., Niittymäki, S., & Paananen, H. (2021). Artificial Intelligence for Career Guidance – Current Requirements and Prospects for the Future. *IAFOR Journal of Education*, *9*(4), 43–62. DOI: 10.22492/ije.9.4.03

White Board Advisors. (2024). *Proposed Changes to Federal Privacy Rules May Impact Edtech.* https://whiteboardadvisors.com/proposed-changes-to-federal-privacy-rules-coppa-edtech-impact/

Williamson, B., & Eynon, R. (2020). Historical threads, missing links, and future directions in AI in education. In *Learning, Media and Technology* (Vol. 45, Issue 3). DOI: 10.1080/17439884.2020.1798995

Williams, P. (2025). *Human-AI Learning: Architecture of a Human-agenticAI Learning System*. DOI: 10.20944/preprints202508.1351.v1

Williom Fry. (2024). *Is your Annex III AI System High-Risk? Definitely Maybe.* https://www.williamfry.com/knowledge/is-your-annex-iii-ai-system-high-risk-definitely-maybe

Wilmerhale. (2024). *What Are High-Risk AI Systems Within the Meaning of the EU's AI Act, and What Requirements Apply to Them?* https://www.wilmerhale.com/en/insights/blogs/wilmerhale-privacy-and-cybersecurity-law/20240717-what-are-highrisk-ai-systems-within-the-meaning-of-the-eus-ai-act-and-what-requirements-apply-to-them

Winkler, R., & Söllner, M. (2018). Unleashing the potential of chatbots in education: A state-of-the-art analysis. In *Proceedings of the Academy of Management Annual Meeting Proceedings, 2018*(1), Article 15903. https://doi.org/DOI: 10.5465/AMBPP.2018.15903abstract

Wu, L. J., & Chang, K. E. (2020). Effect of embedding a cognitive diagnosis into the adaptive dynamic assessment of spatial geometry learning. *Interactive Learning Environments*. Advance online publication. DOI: 10.1080/10494820.2020.1789673

Xiao, K., & He, Y. (2025).. . *Adaptive AI Agent Systems for Personalized Learning: Frameworks, Algorithms, and Practical Applications in Education, 108–112*, 108–112. Advance online publication. DOI: 10.1109/ICAIE64856.2025.11158641

Yan, L. (2025). From Passive Tool to Socio-cognitive Teammate: A Conceptual Framework for Agentic AI in Human-AI Collaborative Learning. *ArXiv Preprint ArXiv:2508.14825.*

Yang, H. (2023, février 24). *Grammarly Free vs Premium : What's the Difference?* https://prowritingaid.com/grammarly-free-vs-premium

Yang, Y., & Tian, Y. (2024). Exploring the Chinese AWCF Platform's value in improving CSL learners' writing performance in a ChatGPT context. *NaN, NaN*, NaN-NaN. DOI: 10.1075/csl.24008.yan

Yao, Y., & González-Vélez, H. (2025). AI-Powered System to Facilitate Personalized Adaptive Learning in Digital Transformation. *Applied Sciences 2025, Vol. 15, Page 4989, 15*(9), 4989. DOI: 10.3390/app15094989

Yaseen, H., Mohammad, A. S., Ashal, N., Abusaimeh, H., Ali, A., & Sharabati, A. A. A. (2025). The Impact of Adaptive Learning Technologies, Personalized Feedback, and Interactive AI Tools on Student Engagement: The Moderating Role of Digital Literacy. *Sustainability 2025, Vol. 17, Page 1133, 17*(3), 1133. DOI: 10.3390/su17031133

Yuhan, G. (2025). *Agentic AI in Higher Education.* https://ascode.osu.edu/news/agentic-ai-higher-education?

Yu, L., & Yu, Z. (2023). Qualitative and quantitative analyses of artificial intelligence ethics in education using VOSviewer and CitNetExplorer. *Frontiers in Psychology, 14*, 1061778. Advance online publication. DOI: 10.3389/fpsyg.2023.1061778

Zawacki-Richter, O., Marín, V. I., Bond, M., & Gouverneur, F. (2019). Systematic review of research on artificial intelligence applications in higher education – where are the educators? In *International Journal of Educational Technology in Higher Education* (Vol. 16, Issue 1). DOI: 10.1186/s41239-019-0171-0

Zeng, L., & Wang, Y. (2021). Independent and innovative learning of gymnastics teaching based on computer interaction. *International Journal of Electrical Engineering Education*. Advance online publication. DOI: 10.1177/0020720920984325

Zhai, X., Chu, X., Chai, C. S., Jong, M. S. Y., Istenic, A., Spector, M., & Li, Y. (2021). A Review of Artificial Intelligence (AI) in Education from 2010 to 2020. *Complexity*, *2021*(1), 8812542. DOI: 10.1155/2021/8812542

Zhang, H., Huang, T., Liu, S., Yin, H., Li, J., Yang, H., & Xia, Y. (2020). A learning style classification approach based on deep belief network for large-scale online education. *Journal of Cloud Computing (Heidelberg, Germany)*, *9*(1), 47. Advance online publication. DOI: 10.1186/s13677-020-00165-y

Zhang, J. (2025). Ethics of Artificial Intelligence in Education: Balancing Automation and Human-Centered Learning. *Applied Mathematics and Nonlinear Sciences*, *10*(1), 20250843. Advance online publication. DOI: 10.2478/amns-2025-0843

Zhang, K., & Aslan, A. B. (2021). AI technologies for education: Recent research & future directions. *Computers and education. Artificial Intelligence*, *2*, 100025.

Zhang, M., Zhu, L., Lin, S.-Y., Herr, K., Chi, C.-L., Demir, I., Lopez, K. D., & Chi, N.-C. (2023). Using artificial intelligence to improve pain assessment and pain management: A scoping review. *Journal of the American Medical Informatics Association : JAMIA*, *30*(3), 570–587. DOI: 10.1093/jamia/ocac231

Zou, Y. L., Kuek, F., Feng, W., & Cheng, X. (2025). Digital learning in the 21st century: Trends, challenges, and innovations in technology integration. *Frontiers in Education*, *10*, 1562391. Advance online publication. DOI: 10.3389/feduc.2025.1562391

About the Contributors

Munir Ahmad is a dedicated expert in Spatial Data Infrastructure (SDI), Geo-Information Production, Information Systems, and Information Governance, with over 25 years of experience driving innovation across the geospatial domain. Holding a PhD in Computer Science, he specializes in the production, management, analysis, visualization, and quality control of spatial data, and has led major SDI development and deployment initiatives, particularly in Pakistan. His work spans spatial database design, Web/Mobile/Desktop GIS development, and Geo Web Services architecture, complemented by significant contributions to Volunteered Geographic Information (VGI), Open Source Geoportals, and Metadata Portals. He is also at the forefront of integrating emerging technologies such as blockchain for trusted geospatial data exchange, artificial intelligence and machine learning for automated analytics, prediction, and quality assurance, and metaverse environments for immersive geospatial visualization and planning into next-generation SDI ecosystems. Beyond geospatial applications, he advances the use of AI, ML, blockchain, and metaverse technologies across sectors, including education, health, business, tourism, disaster management, environment, governance, and marketing, enabling data-driven decision-making and digital transformation. As a researcher, trainer, and mentor with more than 100 publications, he also serves as a reviewer for several reputed international journals published by Frontiers, IGI Global, Wiley, Springer, and others. He continues to expand knowledge in geo-technology, data governance, and information infrastructure while supporting R&D and guiding the next generation of geo-information professionals.

***

Syed Ali Reza is an experienced engineer and operations professional with specific interest in applying technology, strategic management, and data-driven intelligence to organizational performance. His academic background in Bangladesh witnessed him graduating in a Bachelor of Science in Electrical & Electronics Engineering (EEE) in the Ahsanullah University of Science and Technology. Driven by a need for lifelong learning and professional development, he is studying for a Master of Science degree in the University of the Potomac in the United States, with a specific interest in further developing leadership and analytical knowledge. Syed was a well-experienced industrial and manufacturing professional for 13 years in Bangladesh, with exceptional operating and leadership abilities. He began his professional journey with Doreen Power, continued as Maintenance In-Charge with Kapita Holdings Ltd., and eventually scaled the corporate ladder to Senior Manager, Operations in the renowned PRAN-RFL Group — the largest food and plastic manufacturing conglomerate in the country. The specialty of Syed is in the combination of engineering, operations, and strategy management. It is also apparent that Syed is well qualified to streamline production functions, introduce ideal maintenance systems, and drive cross-functional teams in the direction of achieving efficiency and innovation. To top it all, Syed is also a CPD Certification holder in Project Management from Edupro-UK, further boosting his ability to plan, execute, and deliver projects with tangible results. Now settled in the U.S., Syed is committed to further extending his experience in automation, business analytics, and technology-oriented operations with a mission of combining engineering innovation with cutting-edge business intelligence.

Kashvi Chaturvedi, is studying B.Tech, specialisation in Artificial Intelligence and Data Science at Ajeenkya DY Patil University. She started solidifying her programming skills by completing various certification courses like Data Structures in C, Tableau functions and Operating Systems along with doing few projects using languages like Python, C, C++ and creating Web Page using HTML, CSS and Java Script. She had also attended an Arduino-Based Automation course at Dolphin Labs to enhance her software knowledge. There, she learned how to work with sensors, microcontrollers, and circuit design. She has also written multiple review papers on topics such as Geographic Information Systems, Comparative Analysis of BJT Configurations, Swiss Bank vs. European Central Bank: Data Analysis. She is also researching on and learning many topics such as Small Modular Reactors, Bibliometric Analysis, UNSDGs etc. Because of her interest in latest technologies, she also participated in Global Hyperloop Competition hosted by IIT Madras representing her college as team Vac-Vectoor where she learnt more about various subtopics from the mentors.

Arihant Prashant Chobharkar is a B-Tech student in Computer Science and Engineering at Ajeenkya D Y Patil University, where he has cultivated a robust foundation in programming, data structures, algorithms, and software engineering.

With a keen passion for technological innovation, Arihant demonstrates proficiency in Python, C++, and database management systems (DBMS), leveraging Linux environments to develop efficient and scalable solutions. He is actively involved in the university's Hyperloop project, which has sharpened his skills in interdisciplinary collaboration, systems thinking, innovation mechanical engineering, and innovative problem-solving. His active engagement in hackathons, coding competitions, and technical symposia has further refined his technical insight and raised essential skills in leadership, teamwork, and strategic communication. Arihant's technical range extends to advanced tools such as Fusion 360 and AutoCAD, complemented by an emerging proficiency in web development and robotics. His academic curiosity drives him to explore transformative fields such as healthcare management and Robotic Automation Research Committed to addressing global challenges, Arihant aspires to develop solutions that harmonize technological advancement with environmental stewardship.

Susanta Das is a seasoned educator with a proven record of teaching and mentoring diverse students, working at multiple institutions, and providing service to the various initiatives of organizations. He received his Ph.D. and M.A. degrees from Western Michigan University (WMU), USA, and M.Sc. degree from Banaras Hindu University (BHU), India all in Physics. He continued his research as a Marie-Curie post-doctoral fellow at Stockholm University, Stockholm, Sweden on beam diagnostics for the DESIREE (Double ElectroStatic Ion Ring ExpEriment) in the project DITANET (Diagnostic Techniques for particle Accelerators – a Marie-Curie initial training NETwork), at the Indian Institute of Science Education and Research-Kolkata, India on high-pressure physics as a Project Scientist-B, and at the University of Electro-Communications, Tokyo, Japan on ion-surface interactions as a Post-doctoral fellow. Throughout his career, Dr. Das worked and collaborated with many researchers, Ph.D., master, and visiting students from different countries. He further visited many countries to discuss research and an international conference participant (UK, Italy, Germany, Greece, Belgium, Bulgaria, Romania, Brazil etc.). He worked at several institutions before assuming his current role at Ajeenkya D Y Patil University. He received the Marie-Curie post-doctoral fellowship in Sweden, Science Academies' Summer Research Fellowship in India, Gowen Frostic Doctoral Fellowship, Department Graduate Research and Creative Scholar Award by WMU, and Leo R. Parpart Doctoral Fellowship by Dept. of Physics, WMU, among many others, throughout his academic journey. He co-authored several research articles in WoS/Scopus indexed international journals, conference proceedings, and scholarly book chapters and co-edited several books published by renowned international publishing houses (IGI-Global, Springer Nature, Nova Science Publishers, Wiley, Scrivener-Wiley, Notion Press). At present, Dr. Das continues to delve into cutting-edge fields, with a keen interest in nanotechnology, UN SDGs, and data science. His multifaceted contributions, spanning teaching, research, and administrative leadership, showcase a dedicated professional who is instrumental in advancing the vision and mission of the institutions he serves.

S. Ida Evangeline, presently working as an Assistant Professor in the Department of Electrical and Electronics Engineering at the Government College of Engineering, Tirunelveli, Tamilnadu, India. She obtained her Bachelor's in Electrical and Electronics Engineering from Manonmaniam Sundaranar University in 2003, and Master's in Power Systems Engineering from Anna University, Chennai, Tamilnadu, India in 2005. She completed her PhD degree in 2023 at Anna University, Chennai, Tamilnadu, India. She has published six research papers in international journals. Her current research interests include optimal power flow, renewable energy, soft computing, machine learning, and deep learning.

GeethaManoharan is currently working in Telangana as an assistant professor at SR University. She is the university-level PhD program coordinator and has also been given the additional responsibility of In Charge Director of Publications and Patents under the Research Division at SR University.

Maida Maqsood did MS in English from Government College Women University, Sialkot. Throughout her academic journey, she has achieved notable successes that have strengthened her foundation in literature, education and linguistics. Her Master's research reflects her dedication to exploring critical themes in literature with the use of linguistics style. Additionally, her active participation in different conferences and seminars, such as The International Conference on Modern Trends in Applied Linguistics, and 7th ASNeT International Multidisciplinary Academic Conference 2024 (AIMAC 2024) highlight her commitment to staying updated with current trends in her field.

Sunehra Khan Sajin is currently pursuing her Master of Education in Educational Evaluation and Research at the Institute of Education and Research, University of Dhaka. She works in early childhood development and education and is presently involved with BRAC-IED, where she supports child-centered learning programs. She has also served as a research fellow and intern teacher, gaining experience in classroom teaching, research, and curriculum-based projects. Her interests include early childhood education, educational equity, and research that creates practical impact on learning and communities. She is passionate about building inclusive learning environments and actively engages in educational and social development initiatives.

Sunil Sankathala is pursuing B. Tech Computer Science and Engineering at Ajeenkya DY Patil University, with a diverse range of interests that bridge technology, sustainability, and innovation. His academic focus lies in computer science fundamentals like programming, data structures, algorithms, and software development. He actively supplements this with hands-on experience in web development and robotics. Beyond the core curriculum, He has a strong research inclination in emerging and impactful fields. His current research interests include Artificial Intelligence in Healthcare, bioplastics, nano bioplastics, e-waste management, and solid waste management—areas where he believes technology can make a meaningful difference in solving real-world problems. He has been publishing research articles and book chapters in reputed national and international journals and books. He is also part of an ambitious Hyperloop project, which involves interdisciplinary collaboration and cutting-edge engineering aimed at revolutionizing transportation. Working on this project has enhanced his skills in teamwork, innovation, and systems thinking. In the tech domain, he has developed proficiency in web development using technologies such as HTML, CSS, JavaScript, and React. His interests in robotics further reflect building smart, responsive systems that interact with the physical world. Throughout his course, he has helped strengthen problem-solving and collaborative skills. He is proficient in languages such as Python, C, C++, MySQL, Ubuntu, Machine Learning and familiar with frameworks and tools like React, Git. He actively participates in hackathons, coding competitions, and tech events to challenge himself and learn from peers. He is also a quick learner and highly adaptable, with an eagerness to stay updated with the latest trends in the tech world. He aspires to become a skilled software engineer and contribute to building innovative solutions that have a positive impact on society. The long-term goal is to work in a dynamic environment where knowledge, grow professionally, and make meaningful contributions to the field of technology. Driven by a spirit of exploration and sustainability, he aims to contribute to technological solutions that address both human and environmental needs. The long-term goal is to become a versatile engineer and researcher, working at the intersection of computer science, environmental innovation, and human well-being.

Aiman Shehzadi has always had a passion for learning. She completed her master's degree in Mathematics from Virtual University and holds a certificate in basic IT from the Government of Punjab. Aiman has extensive knowledge of MS Office and a deep interest in graphic design. Beyond her technical skills, she has a keen interest in research, always eager to explore new ideas and concepts. Known for her warm personality, Aiman enjoys helping others and actively participates in community activities.

Irim Shehzadi is a dedicated and passionate individual with a strong educational background, holding a Master's degree in Environmental Sciences from PMAS Arid Agricultural University in Rawalpindi.

Aditya Shrivastav is an aspiring technologist currently pursuing a Bachelor of Technology (B. Tech.) in Computer Science and Engineering at Ajeenkya D. Y. Patil University. He holds solid programming expertise in C, C++, and Python, alongside strong command over data and business tools such as Microsoft Excel and Tally software. Aditya is a member of Team Vac-Vectoor Hyperloop and participated with the team in the Global Hyperloop Competition organized by IIT Madras, contributing to cutting-edge transportation solutions. He actively engages in hackathons and various technical events to expand his skills and contribute to innovative problem-solving. He has authored and co-authored book chapters in the domains of solid waste management, bioplastics, nanotechnology applications, and artificial intelligence, showcasing his multidisciplinary approach and research acumen. Aditya is also working on an innovative project on predictive e-waste management. The project is targeted toward IT departments, schools, and colleges, aiming to support sustainable practices and resource optimization. In parallel with his academic journey, Aditya is serving as a faculty intern at Disha Computer Institute, where he teaches C, C++, basic Python, basic Java, Excel formulas, and Tally software. His dedication and teaching proficiency earned him a Letter of Appreciation and the opportunity to conduct a workshop on Advanced Excel at G. H. Raisoni College of Arts, Commerce and Science. With a strong foundation in technology, a passion for sustainability, and hands-on experience in both teaching and project development, Aditya Shrivastav is committed to driving impact through research, education, and innovation.

Pancham Singh is working as an Assistant Professor in the Information Technology Department at AKGEC, Ghaziabad since 2007. He has over 17 years of teaching experience and one year of industry experience. He completed his B.Tech. in Computer Science & Engineering from Dr. A.P.J. Abdul Kalam Technical University (formerly UPTU), Lucknow, in 2005. He earned a Master's Degree in Information Technology from RTU, Kota, in 2013. Currently, he is pursuing a Ph.D. at Netaji Subhas University of Technology (NSUT), New Delhi, since January 2023. He has written and edited four books in Computer Science and Engineering. He has presented and published more than 45 papers in reputed Conferences and Journals. He has also reviewed more than 100 research papers in IEEE, Springer conferences and Journals. Mr. Singh has published 35 National and International Patents, 5 design grants and 1 Utility Grant. He was a session chair at the International Conference ICDT 2024. At AKGEC, he worked as a timetable in-charge for over 13 years (2010-

2023) and a media in-charge for over 8 years (2015-2023). He has performed Flying Squad Duty for AKTU as an in-charge and team member four times. He has attended

Nishanova Zamira is working in Applied Psychology Department, Tashkent State Pedagogical University named after Nizami, Uzbekistan

Jan Vrba is an academic and innovation leader, born in September 1990, with citizenship in the European Union and the Czech Republic. Based in both the Czech Republic and Vietnam, he is available for global hybrid and remote work. Prof. Jan Vrba holds the title of Senior Full Professor ("Profesor Titular C") at Universidad Azteca (Mexico), a D.B.A. in Human Resource Management, a PhDr. in Political Science, and several Master's Degrees in administration, economics & management, big data, and business analysis. His career includes roles such as Vice-Dean and University Lecturer in the Czech Republic & Poland, Academic Expert in India, and Chief Innovation Officer in Malaysia. He excels in international partnership development, global research management, and academic support in multicultural settings. Prof. Jan Vrba is active in academic publishing, serving as Deputy Editor-in-Chief and reviewer for peer-reviewed journals, and regularly speaks at international conferences. Fluent in Czech, Slovak, English, and Japanese, he holds multiple teaching and language certificates. Recognized with awards as "Distinguished Professor" and the Rector's Award, his recent research emphasizes AI, public administration, and sustainability.

Index

A

B

C

D

E

G

H

I

L

M

P

R

S

T

www.ingramcontent.com/pod-product-compliance
Lightning Source LLC
LaVergne TN
LVHW080903300926
849162LV00003B/538